WOMEN READERS IN THE M

Throughout the Middle Ages, the number of female readers was far greater than is commonly assumed. D. H. Green shows that, after clerics and monks, religious women were the main bearers of written culture and its expansion. Moreover, laywomen played a vital part in the process whereby the expansion of literacy brought reading from religious institutions into homes, and increasingly from Latin into vernacular languages. This study assesses the various ways in which reading was practised between c.700 and 1500 and how these differed from what we mean by reading today. Focusing on Germany, France and England, it considers the different categories of women for whom reading is attested (laywomen, nuns, recluses, semi-religious women, heretics), as well as women's general engagement with literature as scribes, dedicatees, sponsors, and authors. This fascinating study opens up the world of the medieval woman reader to new generations of scholars and students.

D. H. GREEN is Professor Emeritus in the University of Cambridge and a Fellow of Trinity College.

CAMBRIDGE STUDIES IN MEDIEVAL LITERATURE

General editor
Alastair Minnis, *Ohio State University*

Editorial board
Zygmunt G. Barański, *University of Cambridge*
Christopher C. Baswell, *University of California, Los Angeles*
John Burrow, *University of Bristol*
Mary Carruthers, *New York University*
Rita Copeland, *University of Pennsylvania*
Simon Gaunt, *King's College, London*
Steven Kruger, *City University of New York*
Nigel Palmer, *University of Oxford*
Winthrop Wetherbee, *Cornell University*
Jocelyn Wogan-Browne, *University of York*

This series of critical books seeks to cover the whole area of literature written in the major medieval languages – the main European vernaculars, and medieval Latin and Greek – during the period c. 1100–1500. Its chief aim is to publish and stimulate fresh scholarship and criticism on medieval literature, special emphasis being placed on understanding major works of poetry, prose, and drama in relation to the contemporary culture and learning which fostered them.

Recent titles in the series
Simon Gilson *Dante and Renaissance Florence*
Ralph Hanna *London Literature, 1300–1380*
Maura Nolan *John Lydgate and the Making of Public Culture*
Nicolette Zeeman *Piers Plowman and the Medieval Discourse of Desire*
Anthony Bale *The Jew in the Medieval Book: English Antisemitisms 1300–1500*
Robert J. Meyer-Lee *Poets and Power from Chaucer to Wyatt*
Isabel Davis *Writing Masculinity in the Later Middle Ages*
John M. Fyler *Language and the Declining World in Chaucer, Dante and Jean de Meun*
Matthew Giancarlo *Parliament and Literature in Late Medieval England*
D. H. Green *Women Readers in the Middle Ages*

A complete list of titles in the series can be found at the end of the volume.

Contents

Illustrations

Preface

In preparing this book I find myself indebted to many individuals. I must thank the staff of many libraries (above all the Cambridge University Library) for their unfailing patience and helpfulness. My College has supported my research visits to Germany and helped towards the expense of the illustrations included in this book. Aware, too, of the irony that, dealing with medieval literacy, I am myself computer-illiterate, I am grateful to Laura Pieters Cordy (with help from Hansa Chauhan) for her skill and forbearance in preparing this book.

For their critical comments and willingness to discuss my problems at all stages in the genesis of this book I am especially indebted to Michael Clanchy and Nigel Palmer. I also thank Jürgen Wolf for sending me an advance version of his *Buch und Text*.

Only my wife Sarah knows how great is my gratitude to her for encouragement in this project and so much else. To her this book is dedicated.

Abbreviations

AASS	*Acta Sanctorum*, Antwerp 1643ff.
AfK	*Archiv für Kulturgeschichte*
AGB	*Archiv für Geschichte des Buchwesens*
AH	*Art History*
AHR	*American Historical Review*
ASE	*Anglo-Saxon England*
ASNSL	*Archiv für das Studium der neueren Sprachen und Literatur*
BMZ	G. F. Benecke, W. Müller and F. Zarncke, *Mittelhochdeutsches Wörterbuch*, Leipzig 1854–61
CCM	*Cahiers de Civilisation Médiévale*
CH	*Church History*
CJ	*Classical Journal*
CN	*Cultura Neolatina*
DVjs	*Deutsche Vierteljahrsschrift*
EME	*Early Medieval Europe*
Ep.	Epistola
FMS	*Frühmittelalterliche Studien*
FS	Festschrift
GRBS	*Greek, Roman and Byzantine Studies*
GRM	*Germanisch-Romanische Monatsschrift*
HLF	*Histoire Littéraire de la France*
HZ	*Historische Zeitschrift*
IASL	*Internationales Archiv für Sozialgeschichte der Literatur*
JMEMS	*Journal of Medieval and Early Modern Studies*
JML	*Journal of Medieval Latin*
JMRS	*Journal of Medieval and Renaissance Studies*
LDO	Hildegard von Bingen, *Liber divinorum operum*
LiLi	*Zeitschrift für Literaturwissenschaft und Linguistik*
MÆ	*Medium Ævum*

MGH	*Monumenta Germaniae Historica*
AA	*Auctores Antiquissimi*
SRM	*Scriptores rerum Merovingicarum*
SS	*Scriptores*
MHG	Middle High German
MIÖG	*Mitteilungen des Instituts für Österreichische Geschichtsforschung*
MlJb	*Mittellateinisches Jahrbuch*
MLQ	*Modern Language Quarterly*
MM	*Miscellanea Mediaevalia*
MS	*Mediaeval Studies*
NML	*New Medieval Literature*
OGE	*Ons Geestelijk Erf*
PBB	*Paul und Braunes Beiträge*
PL	J. P. Migne, *Patrologia Latina*
RB	*Revue Bénédictine*
RMS	*Reading Medieval Studies*
SMV	*Studi Mediolatini e Volgari*
StPh	*Studies in Philology*
VfL	K. Ruh (ed.), *Die deutsche Literatur des Mittelalters. Verfasserlexikon*, Berlin 1978ff.
WI	*Word and Image*
WJbK	*Wiener Jahrbuch für Kunstgeschichte*
ZfdA	*Zeitschrift für deutsches Altertum*
ZfdPh	*Zeitschrift für deutsche Philologie*
ZHF	*Zeitschrift für Historische Forschung*

Introduction

In considering three countries and four languages from the early to the late Middle Ages this book has perforce to be highly selective, omitting what others might have included. It has been written by a Germanist, and the picture would look different (but supplementary?) from another discipline. The main purpose behind this wide span is to suggest comparisons between what may otherwise be seen in isolation, in the conviction that medieval studies cannot be monoglot and that questions raised and work done in one literature may illuminate the position in others. This span and the selectivity it imposes mean that a consecutive historical development cannot be traced here or any differentiation between periods and regions attempted. My argument rests largely on textual evidence, although I also make use of recent palaeographical and codicological work on texts written by or for women.

In 1935 Grundmann published an essay on the role of women in medieval literature. Since then much work has been done on this theme, including a post-war article by him on medieval literacy. Combining these two themes, the title of this book refers to women and to readers. Accordingly, it falls into two parts, the first dealing with how reading was understood and practised in the Middle Ages and how it differed from modern reading, and the second with the various categories of women who read and were engaged in literature. The first part aims to give as wide a coverage as possible to the nature of reading (whether women are specifically mentioned or not), because only on this basis can any assessment of their reading be made. To discuss their activity without previously considering what was then meant by reading risks unthinkingly importing modern ideas into a quite different situation. Women may therefore not always be apparent in the first part of this book, but they come into their own in the second only because of this preparatory evaluation.

What this book attempts is a factual survey of the many different classes of women in three countries (Germany, France, England) who were active as readers or otherwise engaged in literature, but also of what kinds of text they read and to some extent how they read. In a companion volume under active preparation, *Gendered reading around 1200*, I focus on three of the earliest romances in Germany, together with their French antecedents, asking how their male authors made a special appeal to women and their interests.

PART I

Reading in the Middle Ages

A book like this one which treats of women readers in the Middle Ages cannot avoid considering the nature of literacy and reading in that period, what differences there are from modern views and how things may have changed even in the Middle Ages.

A thorough discussion of medieval literacy was presented by the historian Grundmann, for whom it covered three features: it was the monopoly of clerics, who were able to read and write, and did this in the medium of Latin.[1] In conducting his survey from classical to medieval practice largely in Latin, his equation of literacy with Latinity reflects and does not question the medieval cleric's view that literacy was restricted to his own Latin world. Moreover, as the ample evidence adduced makes clear, there is much to support this view. In the first place, literacy or *litteratus* was often explicitly equated with Latinity. To speak *literaliter* or *literate* meant to speak Latin. In French, Latin was seen as the prerogative of a *lettrez* (*litteratus* or cleric) as distinct from a layman, so that a work was translated from Latin into French for those who did not understand 'la lettre'. In German *buochisch* meant the language of books or Latin. In England Ælfric equated the acquisition of Latin with literacy.[2] Secondly, literacy or the ability to read was seen as the hallmark of the cleric, as when, in French, Latin literature ('lettre en Latyn') is equated with *clergie* or elsewhere letters (*lettreure*) likewise with *clergie*.[3] Thirdly, the converse is also frequently attested: the layman was one who had no Latin and therefore could not read. A drastic illustration comes from England when, for lack of instruction in *grammatica*, the canons of

---

[1] Grundmann, *AfK* 40 (1958), 1–65; Green, *Listening*, pp. 8–10. By stressing that 'generally' *litterati* were clerics and monks, men of the Church and monastery (p. 14), Grundmann appears to suggest that a woman could not be *litterata* and thereby to question the theme of this book. Our task will be to question what precisely is implied by Grundmann's use of 'generally' (twice).

[2] *Literaliter*: Grundmann, *AfK* 40 (1958), 4; Ohly, *ZfdA* 87 (1956/7), 16f; *Lettrez*: Legge, *Literature*, p. 95; *Lettre*: Vitz, *Orality*, p. 55; *Buochisch*: BMZ I 280; Ælfric: Hill, 'Learning', p. 7.

[3] Legge, *Literature*, p. 288; Bell, *Nuns*, p. 69.

Newnham neglected their books and were regarded virtually as laymen ('quasi . . . laici').[4]

Underlining these three features is the greatest merit of Grundmann's argument, his demonstration of how different medieval literacy was from modern: in being restricted to Latin and to the clergy, and its exclusion of laymen and women. Included in this, however, is a point where he fails to make a distinction. In referring to the clerics' ability to read and write he is importing a modern view of literacy into the Middle Ages, when the ability to read did not imply the skill of writing, and reading was regarded as an intellectual faculty, but writing as a quite separate technical skill.[5] From this criticism of a detail we may turn to more fundamental shortcomings in Grundmann's thesis.

Judging medieval literacy by the criterion of understanding Latin has been rightly termed narrow, especially since, by definition, it excludes vernacular literacy and thereby continues the polarity between literate clergy and illiterate laity which it was in the clerics' interest to maintain.[6] Such a restrictive view hampers our assessment of the most important development in this period, the rise of written literature in the vernacular for laymen. Doubts have been voiced whether the two sets of opposites with which Grundmann worked (clerical and lay, literate and illiterate) do justice to the complexity of the case.[7] We need to spread our net wider and take account of the position in at least four contexts: social status (layman and cleric), educational status (illiterate and literate), language (vernacular and Latin) and means of communication (oral and written).

If we apply a more complex grid like this some of Grundmann's opposites no longer appear watertight as theory succumbs to reality. In the first place, not every cleric was literate or Latinate. An important example, disturbing of Grundmann's thesis because it breaks down his distinction between literate cleric and illiterate layman, comes from Philip of Harvengt.[8] Speaking of some clerics, he applies to them terms conventionally used of illiterate laymen (*simplices, idiotae, illitterati*) because of their deplorable Latin. Later, Philip goes much further by bringing a literate layman, a knight, into play. He says of this knight, able to read with understanding and to speak Latin correctly, that he is a better cleric than many a priest. Even though Philip realises that he is using terminology incorrectly ('improprii sermonis usus'), the situation he describes is closer to reality than the theory that laymen were by definition illiterate. That this was no isolated usage is

---

[4] Bell, *Nuns*, p. 85, n. 46.   [5] Schreiner, *ZHF* 11 (1984), 328, n. 254; Clanchy, *Memory*, p. 47.
[6] Clanchy, *Memory*, p. 9; Green, *Listening*, p. 8.   [7] Bruckner, *Shaping*, p. 194.
[8] PL 203, 701 and 816. Cf. Vàrvaro, *SMV* 10 (1962), 305.

confirmed by the German prose *Lancelot* saying of its knightly hero that he could read ('Er kund wol lesen'), just as Heinrich von dem Türlin says of him in the *Crône* that he was both a knight and, because of his ability to read, a cleric ('der zweier ampte pflac/Daz er ritter unde pfaffe was').[9] Medievalist scholarship reflects this position by talking of a *miles clericus* or *miles litteratus*.[10]

These last two failures of medieval reality to conform to clerical theory (unlearned clerics, educated laymen) could occur as exceptions to the rule at any time in the Middle Ages (although the educated laymen begins to be more noticeable only from the twelfth century). By contrast, a third feature (the layman's literacy is confined to the vernacular, which involves an increasing vernacularisation of written literature) is characteristic of the late Middle Ages, with earliest traces in the twelfth century. An early example is the heretic Valdes who asks two clerics to translate the gospels for him to read for use in his sermons: he could therefore read, but not in Latin. By Grundmann's thesis Valdes must be judged *illitteratus* (which is how Walter Map saw him), but that is to judge him by the categories of clerics with a vested interest in denying the possibility of vernacular literacy.[11]

Although Grundmann's definition has the merit of showing where medieval literacy differed from modern, its terms have the disadvantage of concealing changes within the Middle Ages, especially with regard to the turning-point of the twelfth century and the historically decisive emergence of vernacular literacy for laymen. Riché's studies of medieval education have stressed the importance of this century, indicating the first beginnings of a vernacular culture which, however much it owed to Latin, slowly made itself independent and encouraged a literature for laymen, some of whom were literate in a new sense, vernacular rather than Latin.[12]

This change in the nature of literacy also affected reading, involving what has been called a 'prise de conscience de l'acte de lire', which encouraged reflection on the nature of reading.[13] John of Salisbury was on the brink of distinguishing three meanings for the verb *legere*, but then leaves it at two. He says that the word 'to read' is equivocal, indicating either the activity of a teacher reading out and a listening learner ('docentis et discentis') or that of studying what is written for oneself ('per se scrutantis scripturam').[14]

---

[9] *Crône* 2075–7. Cf. Steinhoff, *Prosalancelot* IV 830f.
[10] Vàrvaro, *SMV* 10 (1962), 313–21; Turner, *AHR* 83 (1978), 928–45; Fleckenstein, 'Miles', pp. 319f.
[11] Grundmann, *Bewegungen*, pp. 29f. and *AfK* 40 (1958), 56f.; Green, *Listening*, p. 10.
[12] Riché, 'L'instruction', pp. 212–17; *CCM* 5 (1962), 175–82; 'L'éducation', pp. 37–49.
[13] Hamesse, 'Modèle', p. 125.   [14] *Metalogicon* I 24. Quoted in Green, *Listening*, p. 337, n. 155.

John therefore refers to three different persons (teacher, learner, individual reader), but lumps the first two together by seeing them under *prelectio*, the communication between teacher and pupil, as distinct from *lectio*, individual reading. By thus squeezing out the learner-listener (*discens*) from the usage of *legere*, John has confined himself to a double function of this verb. He therefore remains content with the suggested distinction between *prelegere* (to read aloud to others) and *legere* (to read for oneself).

Hugh of St Victor (paralleled by Abelard) is not content with this, but rescues the threefold distinction latent in John's words.[15] Unlike John, Hugh explicitly refers to three kinds of reading ('Trimodum est lectionis genus') and grants an independent role to the pupil alongside the teacher and the individual reader (*docentis, discentis, vel per se inspicientis*). Accordingly, Hugh establishes three functions of the verb *legere*: for the teacher who reads aloud to his pupil ('lego librum illi'), for the pupil who is read to and therefore reads through the teacher ('lego librum ab illo') and for the individual reader ('lego librum'). Hugh is concerned with the theme of teaching, but his classification is also applicable more widely: the teacher can be replaced by someone reading out a text on occasions outside the classroom, and the pupil by any listener.

Such a threefold distinction, made already in the twelfth century, should alert us to the need for a broader spectrum than Grundmann provided, allowing for a number of variables taken into account in what follows (in reading itself, but also in writing; in the level of Latin involved, but also in the position of the vernacular). Just as there were different degrees of literacy, so were there different ways of reading. Following Hugh of St Victor, we too need to interpret 'reading' in its broadest sense, including listening to a text being read aloud to others.

This broad interpretation underlies the division of Part I into two chapters on reading in the literal and figurative senses. 'Literal reading' consists in visual reading of written letters that make up words and constitute meaning. This has to be distinguished, on the other hand, from 'figurative reading', involving a process of reading with one's mind's eye, in the imagination, not of actually written letters.

---

[15] *Didascalicon* III 8 (PL 176, 772); Green, *Listening*, p. 347, n. 179. Abelard: Coleman, *Reading*, pp. 90f.

CHAPTER I

Literal reading

READING TO ONESELF

In this section we deal with the individual reader, termed by John of Salisbury 'per se scrutans scripturam' and by Hugh of St Victor 'per se inspiciens' (scrutinising, inspecting a text by oneself), whose activity is described by 'lectio' and 'lego librum' respectively. In what follows I give examples for women reading, but not confined to them, since our concern here is with the nature of medieval reading as such. Only after establishing on a wide basis what was meant by reading in the Middle Ages can we turn to consider explicitly women engaged in this. If *legere* (like its vernacular equivalents) is as equivocal as these two writers make it out to be, we need to look for pointers suggesting what meaning is present.

A first indicator is the use of the verb with a reflexive dative, the situation of reading to oneself, engaged in communion with a written text.[1] The Benedictine Rule prescribed individual reading by the monk for himself ('sibi legere'), a construction which is followed in vernacular versions. Similarly, Otfrid conceived reception of his work by an individual reader ('lis thir selbo'), as did Notker with another verb for 'reading' ('sih dir selbo lector' see for yourself reader). Although they are not explicitly mentioned, women can be included here as readers (as nuns for whom *lectio divina* was also prescribed or as possible recipients of Otfrid's or Notker's works).[2] This grammatical construction can also be used expressly of them, however, as in the reading programme laid down for anchoresses by Aelred of Rievaulx ('sibi secretius legat'), where the adverb stresses solitary withdrawal for the act of individual reading.[3]

A second pointer is the reinforcement of a reflexive sense such as Latin *ipse* or German *selbo* (the latter already illustrated by Otfrid and Notker in their construction).[4] As reinforcements such words make it clear that the

---

[1] Green, *Listening*, pp. 136f.   [2] Women recipients: *ibid.*, pp. 180, 184.
[3] *De institutione*, p. 645.   [4] Green, *Listening*, pp. 137–9, with these examples.

person addressed could independently read the text and did not rely on
having it read out (a possibility also envisaged by Otfrid and Notker). This
can be made explicitly clear by a double formula expressing two modes
of reception, by reading oneself or by hearing someone read. In Latin
William of Malmesbury addresses Robert of Gloucester in this way ('aut
ipsi legere, aut legentes possitis audire'), and in German Wetzel von Bernau
highlights the reader by contrast with the listener (' . . . höret lesen/oder
selber liset'). So common is this twofold reception that it can be implicit
even without a double formula. Chrétien's Lancelot is able to read the
names on a tombstone himself ('il meïsmes . . . /comença lors les nons
a lire'), independently of the monk who accompanies him, just as in the
Rolandslied Marsilie is able to read a letter himself from Karl ('selbe er
den brief las'), since he is expressly described as educated (literate) and
therefore can dispense with a scribe reading for him, as was frequently
done in the Middle Ages.[5] How a woman reader may be signalled in this
way is shown by Ulrich von Etzenbach, even though he uses a visual verb
other than *lesen*. When Candacis receives a messenger with a letter she
retires into a private room ('an ir heimelîche') and reads it ('die schrift selbe si
besach').[6] Secluded in this way, not in full view of the messenger, who would
normally also convey his message orally, the queen is shown to be reading to
herself.

This last example, where seeing stands for reading, leads us to a third
pointer, where a visual verb conveys the idea of reading.[7] This is made clear
where writing is also mentioned ('to see something in writing'), where no
amount of merely seeing a text can convey its contents if actual reading
is not meant. Veldeke therefore refers to reading his source in two ways:
either 'alse ich't geschreven sach' or 'alse ich et las', with no difference of
meaning, while Wolfram presupposes women readers with his equivalent
of the first construction ('diu diz maere geschriben siht'). The same usage
occurs in French, as when Béroul refers to what he had read in his source:
'(L)a ou Berox le vit escrit'.[8]

Much more common, however, is the use of a verb of seeing by itself.
Hugh of St Victor used *inspicere* of the individual reader, and the same
verb refers to a nun being permitted, if sufficiently educated, to read more
than the Psalter ('in aliquem alium librum inspicere').[9] In German the
most common equivalent is *sehen*, sometimes with a further preposition or

[5] *Lancelot* 1863f. *Rolandslied* 2113. Cf. Köhn, 'Latein', pp. 340–56.
[6] *Alexandreis* 20271–5.   [7] Green, *Listening*, pp. 139–41.
[8] Veldeke, *Servatius* 1560, 4808. Wolfram, *Parzival* 337, 1–3. Béroul, *Tristran* 1790.
[9] Beach, *Women*, p. 115.

prefix. The meaning is clear in what Veldeke says of the Sibyl holding a book in her hand: 'dar ane sah si unde las', but also when Gottfried depicts Isold reading names carved on chips of wood for an assignation ('und sach sie an,/si las'), since looking is an integral part of her reading.[10] Another German verb used in this way is *schouwen* implying, like *ansehen*, rather closer scrutiny than *sehen*. In the epilogue to Veldeke's *Eneasroman* it is said that he gave the still incomplete work to the Countess of Cleves to read ('her liez ez einer frouwen/ze lesene und ze schouwen'), where the two verbs reinforce the idea of reading and are not to be distinguished as implying reading and looking at the pictures of an illustrated manuscript. One reason for rejecting this suggestion is the fact that *schouwen* can denote reading as conventionally as *sehen*. Before Veldeke a parallel between *lesen* and *schouwen* had been drawn by Priester Wernher with regard to his work's reception, expressly including women alongside clerics, so that they cannot be regarded as second-class recipients, confined to merely looking rather than reading. Similarly, when in the fifteenth-century *Münchner Oswald* the protagonist breaks open a sealed letter and 'begund den prief schauen eben', we are not to picture him gazing at it uncomprehendingly, but reading it.[11]

Corresponding to these German examples, we find *veoir* employed in French (Lancelot's reading of the names on the tombstones is commented on by the monk: 'Vos avez les lettres veües') and equivalent verbs later still in Middle English. With Gower Socrates' wife is annoyed to find her husband reading ('Was sette and loked on a book') while she worked. Whereas it may be uncertain in *Troilus and Criseyde* whether Pandarus is actually reading or pretending ('As for to looke upon an old romaunce'), even the appearance is meant to suggest reading. Hoccleve uses *ouersy* ('oversee') in the sense 'to read'.[12]

The search for the individual reader in the Middle Ages cannot neglect the term to designate him or her, the *lector*.[13] This confronts us with the difficulty of which John of Salisbury was well aware: if contemporary usage (even his own sometimes) failed to distinguish *legere* from *prelegere*, how can we be certain when the noun *lector* denotes the individual reader rather than one reading to others? Here too we need indicators. Although Otfrid uses *legentes* to refer to those who deliver his work orally, he also employs

---

[10] Veldeke, *Eneasroman* 2715 (following B and FS, although Kartschoke prefers the reading *saz*). Gottfried, *Tristan* 14677–8.

[11] Veldeke, *Eneasroman* 13445–6. Priester Wernher, *Maria* A 138–41. *Münchner Oswald* 1418.

[12] Chrétien, *Lancelot* 1877. Gower, *Confessio* 3, 659. Chaucer, *Troilus* III 980. Hoccleve: Coleman, *Reading*, pp. 193f.

[13] Green, *Listening*, pp. 142–7, for these and other examples.

the same word to denote the individual reader to whom he wishes to make his meaning perfectly clear. When Notker, who also reckoned with oral delivery, recommends the individual reader of his *Psalter* to consult Augustine he calls him a *lector*, just as Williram uses 'studiosus lector' in his prologue, whom he refers to an earlier point in his work by the visual sign X. Women play a part as individual readers with a woman author who with rare explicitness not merely refers to her audience as readers and listeners, but also divides the former into male and female ('leser und leserinne')[14]. A variant of the term 'reader' is 'whoever may read this book', which occurs at the conclusion of the *Tristan* of Ulrich von Türheim: 'swelhe vrouwen an disem buoche lesen'. Ulrich von Lichtenstein is even more pointblank in likewise recommending his book to women readers ('die vrouwen suln ez gerne lesen'), whilst Der Pleier includes them with men in the same role.[15] Whether distinguished by their sex or not, individual readers can also be addressed in French (*lecteur* and *lisiere*) and in English as the *redere*, whom Chaucer addresses only once in his *Troilus and Criseyde*.[16]

Although these cases all pertain to one individual reader, there are also occasions where two persons, with close emotional ties, are shown reading together, although we have no means of telling how their reading was conducted: did one read throughout to the other, did they take it in turns to do so, or did they literally both read together? The classic example is Dante's Paolo and Francesca reading the romance of *Lancelot* together, with its close pictorial counterpart in the Manesse manuscript where, in the illustration for Alram von Gresten, two lovers are shown reading a book together, the opening words of which are those of the *Lanzelet* of Ulrich von Zatzikhoven.[17] Another example is the story of *Floire et Blancheflor* in which the two lovers, brought up together as children, read classical literature together ('Ensamle lisent et aprendent'), in particular a work which Konrad Fleck in his German version calls the 'buoch von minnen', presumably Ovid's *Ars amatoria*. Likewise, Chaucer's Deiphebus, the brother of Troilus, joins Helen in studying and reading a text between them.[18]

Another pointer to the individual reader is a phrasing on which we have already touched in passing: the double formula referring to an author's anticipation of his work's reception in two ways: by readers or by listeners.[19]

---

[14] *Secretum*, 4, 34.
[15] Ulrich von Türheim, *Tristan* 3658. Ulrich von Lichtenstein, *Frauenbuch* 2130. Der Pleier: Scholz, *Hören*, p. 50.
[16] French: Scholz, *Hören*, p. 46. *Troilus* V 270.
[17] Green, *Listening*, p. 306, and Walther, *Codex*, pl. 103.
[18] *Floire* 239. Fleck, *Flore* 712–7. Chaucer, *Troilus* II 1702–8.
[19] Green, *Listening*, pp. 93f., 141f., 225–30.

This formula was at home in classical antiquity, continued in Latin through-out the Middle Ages and began to occur in vernacular form ('lesen oder hoeren') in the twelfth century with the onset of written literature destined for laymen. It is possible to isolate two usages in advance. First, the two dimensions, visual and acoustic, could belong together as complementary features of the same activity (someone reads aloud to himself), in which case the formula denotes an individual reader. Secondly, the formula could refer to two simultaneous aspects of a collective occasion (someone reads out and others listen), in which case we have no individual reader as a recipient. If we leave these possibilities on one side, the formula can also be used to denote two alternative modes of reception at different times: an audience listens to a reading, but some may also be in a position to read the text for themselves. This was the position envisaged by William of Malmesbury with Robert of Gloucester. Even though there may be flattery in this, the individual reader is still admitted as a real possibility.

From what will emerge as the far-reaching engagement of women with medieval literature there is every reason why they should be included in this formula, as listeners and as readers. Some examples are quite explicit. We are told how Empress Kunigunde passed her leisure time in these two ways, both in her Latin *vita* ('legere aut legentem audire') and in the vernacular work of Ebernand von Erfurt ('man las ir oder sie las'). In the *Geistlicher Herzen Bavngart* the nun is viewed as a listener or reader ('swaz du gehoret oder gelesen hast'), and the sister-book of Kirchberg anticipates the same situation in its prologue ('die es lesen oder horen lesen').[20] Nor is the situation different in the secular context of the aristocratic court. In his *Weltchronik* Rudolf von Ems foresaw a double reception of his work at the royal court ('die/dú mere lesin und horent hie'), but twice expressly mentioned noble-women among his audience. In the same way, Caxton addressed his first edition of Malory to a twofold audience ('that desyre to rede or here redde') made up of lords and ladies, gentlemen and gentlewomen.[21] It is quite improbable, in view of what we shall see of noblewomen's literacy and reading habits, especially by contrast with their menfolk, that in these two secular examples the men are envisaged as literate readers and the women as no more than listeners. Precisely the opposite is more likely. In view of this, although women may not be mentioned, it is conceivable that Chaucer's use of the double formula ('herkne . . . or rede') may also include them.[22]

---

[20] *Vita S. Cunegundis*, p. 823. Ebernand, *Heinrich* 3468. *Bavngart* 25, 17. *Kirchberger Schwesternbuch*, p. 104.
[21] Rudolf, *Weltchronik*: Green, *Listening*, p. 173. Caxton: Coleman, *Reading*, p. 214.
[22] Coleman, *Reading*, pp. 37, 152.

To read for oneself, as distinct from listening to a collective reading, implies a degree of withdrawal, spatial and/or mental, the possibility of some degree of privacy.[23] For the nun, as for the monk, reading took place not merely in the refectory and chapter, but also in niches of solitude built into her daily cycle. Even in the feudal castle, despite the noisy hurly-burly of which Walther and Wolfram complained, the *kemenâte* or women's chamber provided a place of withdrawal for them. It may have been meant patriarchally to seclude women and keep them safely under observation, but it could be turned by them to positive ends. If they could here devote themselves to women's affairs, these are often associated with literacy, so that the *kemenâte* may be regarded as a distant forerunner (for reading) of the room of one's own whose absence Virginia Woolf lamented for modern women (as writers).

Ulrich von Lichtenstein describes how his lady withdrew into a private chamber (*heinlîch*) to read a letter he sent her, just as for Johann von Würzburg the lady reads for herself, but only after seeking seclusion in a small chamber. The Candacis of Ulrich von Etzenbach also reads her letter in privacy ('an ir heimelîche').[24] Chaucer's Criseyde is in the same situation when she receives a letter from Troilus, for she takes it into her chamber 'Ful pryvely this lettre for to rede', a seclusion captured in an illustration in the *Roman de Troilus*, a source for Chaucer.[25] Whether we can talk of the 'oddness' of this situation, as does Coleman, instead of a recurrent possibility for medieval women is, however, another matter. In all such cases, withdrawal into isolation means that the woman reads by and for herself, there is no one who reads to her or to whom she reads.

The same is true of another reading context for women when they are shown at their private devotions. A model for them in this was Mary at the Annunciation. Already with Otfrid she has a Psalter in her hands, so that the privacy of this scene, interrupted by Gabriel, means that she was reading to herself, not to others.[26] In the *Klage* Uote kneels at prayer and also uses her Psalter for private devotions, just as does Guinevere in her chapel in Wolfram's *Parzival*.[27] Although we cannot always tell whether these women reading their prayers are spatially alone in their chapel (or, in the case of Der Pleier's Flordibel, in their church)[28] we can assume that their inwardness withdraws them from their surroundings.

[23] Green, *Listening*, pp. 303–9.
[24] Ulrich: *Frauendienst* 165, 4–6 and 320, 1–4. Johann: *Wilhelm* 9976–84. *Alexandreis* 20274.
[25] *Troilus* II 1273–6. See also Coleman, *Reading*, p. 158 and Fig. 2 in her book.
[26] *Evangelienbuch* I 5, 20.   [27] *Klage* 3682–6. *Parzival* 644, 23f.   [28] *Tandareis* 8065–7.

Any doubts about spatial isolation are laid to rest, however, in the case of reading by women recluses. Wolfram's Sigune, alone in her cell, uses a Psalter for her devotions, resembling a recluse in the prose *Lancelot*, also reading her Psalter in seclusion. Criseyde, still regarding herself a widow, conjures up the idea of an anchoress, dwelling in a cave, whose duty it is to 'bidde and rede on holy seyntes lyves'. Veldeke's Sibyl we have seen reading in her book, but she has been medievalised, secluded in her oratory ('betehûs').[29]

Reading in such isolation, even with inwardness, has led some to equate private reading with silent reading.[30] That could be true in some cases, but the example of Agly in *Wilhelm von Österreich* shows that this is not always so. She wished to read a letter for herself and not reveal its contents to others, whom she therefore dismissed from her room, so that her reading, even by herself, must have been aloud.[31] Nor is it any more convincing when the words 'per se', used of the individual reader by John of Salisbury and Hugh of St Victor, are taken to indicate silent reading, even to the point that the latter is claimed as the first express witness for silent reading.[32] The most we can say of 'per se' is that it designates reading by or for oneself, which may be silent or may not.

So far, we have been considering a distinction between reading for oneself as opposed to reading aloud to others. Now we come to a distinction within the act of reading for oneself which has come to the fore only in the last paragraph: was this reading aloud or silent? That expresses the two extreme poles, but in between distinct oral voicing and pure eye-reading there come such intermediate possibilities as indistinct murmuring, lip movements and unconscious movement of the tongue without our being able to plot from our evidence where we stand on this line.[33]

The practice of reading aloud in antiquity, in part occasioned by the use of *scriptura continua*, was passed on to the early Middle Ages.[34] One pointer to this way of reading (the complement to writing 'with one's tongue and hand')[35] is to say that one reads with one's mouth, as with the nun in the *Geistlicher Herzen Bavngart*, with Bruder Philipp's *Marienleben*, with Der Pleier's *Garel*, or with a fourteenth-century letter to a woman quoted by Scholz. In France Froissart describes a woman reading a romance to herself, but she must be reading aloud, for when interrupted she places her hand

---

[29] Wolfram, *Parzival* 438, 1. Prose *Lancelot* I 550, 13–15. Chaucer, *Troilus*, II 113–19. Veldeke, *Eneasroman* 2705.
[30] Hindman, *Parchment*, p. 44 ('read privately in silence').   [31] Green, *Listening*, p. 308f.
[32] Illich, *Vineyard*, p. 87; Offergeld, *Didascalicon*, pp. 88, fn. 166, and 242, fn. 52.
[33] Hendrickson, *CJ* 25 (1929/30), 193.   [34] Saenger, *Space*.   [35] Green, *Listening*, p. 148.

on the book and closes her mouth.[36] The example of Agly in *Wilhelm von Österreich* we have already mentioned. All these examples concern women reading aloud, but male readers keep them company. In the *Väterbuch* a hermit reads aloud ('Dar uz sprach er waz er las') without others present whom he could be addressing; in *Wolfdietrich* A the protagonist reads a letter aloud and is overheard by a mermaid who thus learns its contents; in her handbook written for her son Dhuoda recommends him to read with his mouth and hold in his heart.[37] Reading with his mouth ('ore lege') corresponds to the vernacular 'mit dem munde lesen'. In England the author of *The Book of Privy Counselling* talks revealingly of hearing while reading,[38] which reminds us that one interpretation of the double formula (when the link is 'and' rather than 'or') could be with reference to someone reading aloud.

Alongside reading aloud antiquity also knew of silent reading, perhaps seldom and for special reasons, but still more of a possibility than has been thought.[39] Accordingly, there is also evidence for this in the Middle Ages, but still tied to particular contexts. One of these is letter writing, as depicted in literature, especially letters with a politically tricky message or with a highly personal one (love letters). The normal practice was for a letter to be read out in public (anything confidential being conveyed by the messenger's word of mouth),[40] but in cases where the letter itself contained something embarrassing we find whoever was charged with reading it out hesitating or refusing to do so, which implies that he had first read it silently to himself. Both political and erotic considerations are present in the one case from antiquity (Caesar receives a letter in the senate from Cato's sister) where Balogh was ready to concede silent reading, but his critics have widened the field and there are medieval examples enough.[41]

Two other features making for silent reading concern the growing supply of books, in setting up monastic and university libraries and reading-rooms, as well as for the use of students in classrooms.[42] The use of a library as a place for reading in common, rather than in separation, imposed a need for a greater degree of silence to avoid distraction, while the growing availability

---

[36] *Bavngart* 25, 31. *Marienleben* 766f. *Garel* 17483; Scholz, *Hören*, p. 106. Froissart, *L'Espinette* 702f.

[37] *Väterbuch* 8515. *Wolfdietrich* A 477, 3f. Dhuoda IV 8 (title).   [38] *Counselling*, p. 85, 1 and 11.

[39] Hendrickson, *CJ* 25 (1929/30), 182–96; Knox, *GRBS* 9 (1968), 421–35, as against Balogh, *Philologus* 82 (1927), 84–109, 202–40.

[40] Köhn, 'Latein', pp. 340–56.

[41] Ernst, *FMS* 31 (1997), 323, 324–42 ('Private Briefe'), especially 326, 327f.; Reuvekamp-Felber, *Volkssprache*, pp. 246, fn. 359, 253, 268f.

[42] Carruthers, *Book*, p. 170; Saenger, *Space*, pp. 258–64; Hamesse, 'Vocabulaire', p. 177; Miethke, *Universitäten*, p. 19, fn. 38.

of books for students at universities (to the extent that it could be statutorily demanded that they have them with them in the classroom) meant that students no longer read only indirectly through the lecturer ('lego ab illo'), but also for themselves in following what he expounded, but had to do this in silence.

Saenger has dealt with the historical and palaeographic conditions which underlie reading aloud and silently, and also with the slow process by which the first yielded ground to the other in the Middle Ages. We are more concerned with the characteristic features of each and how they affected the individual reader. The move plotted by Saenger can be seen as leading to greater internalisation (from public recital to two people reading together, to one person reading alone, to reading silently), but this internalisation can be seen in intellectual as well as devotional terms.[43] Already for Isidore of Seville it was clear that silent reading served better understanding: when the voice is quiet and the tongue moves only in silence the body is not tired and the mind is better informed.[44] When reading involved hearing (no matter whether the words were vocalised or merely muttered) the speed of comprehension was slower than when, employing eyes alone, the reader did not have to articulate every syllable.[45] The Cistercian Richalm stressed the advantages of silent reading in his account of devils forcing him to read aloud, for he complained that this robbed him of inward understanding. This internalised reading is in accord with the Cistercian view that silent reading was the precondition of *meditatio*.[46]

The position of women within this increasing spread of silent reading in the late Middle Ages is ambiguous. They were barred from higher education, especially from the cathedral schools and universities, and were therefore unaffected by the silent reading practised in the classroom or the reading-room. (As regards the latter, however, we should recall that for the sisters of Syon Abbey in the fifteenth century one of the places where silence was to be observed was the library[47].) On the other hand, silent reading as a means to meditational inwardness was not merely available to women, it was one of the major fields in which they were active from 1200 onwards.

READING TO OTHERS

We now come to the other aspect of the verb *legere* whose ambiguity struck John of Salisbury, the reading aloud of a text to a listener. Both reader and

---

[43] Green, *Listening*, p. 309; Stock, *Augustine*, pp. 14f., 61f., 97.
[44] *Sententiae*, PL 83, 689.   [45] Aston, *Lollards*, p. 117; di Capua, 'Osservazioni', pp. 65f.
[46] Saenger, *Space*, p. 248; 'Lire', p. 151.   [47] Hutchison, 'Reading', p. 217.

listener are present in the concise examples given by Hugh of St Victor: the former is the subject and the latter the indirect object in 'lego illi', but the reverse is so with 'lego ab illo'.

The last section dealt with one person only, the individual reader (*lector*), but this section now deals with two readers: one who reads out loud (*lector*) and one who listens (*auditor*). The former agrees with the individual reader in the act of reading, but differs in how he reads (to others in front of him), whilst the listener, as a second entity, is a novelty (if he could be imagined with the individual reader he was identical with him, reading aloud to himself). These two participants can therefore be explicitly mentioned. As for the *auditor*, the vernacular Zwiefalten version of the Benedictine Rule mentions the *collatio*, where the reader edifies his listeners ('hoeraere'), but these can also be women, as with the same practice with reading in the refectory in nunneries. Thus the *St. Trudperter Hoheslied*, meant for reading to nuns probably at the double monastery Admont, refers to them as 'hôrâre', while listeners are also presupposed for the reading of nuns' *vitae* at the convent Kirchberg ('diss büchlein . . . offenlich . . . in dem convent gelesen').[48] The *lector*, implicit in these cases, can also be expressly mentioned. A literate nun charged with this task in the convent is the 'lesarinne' and this feminine form also occurs in the *Breviarien von Sankt Lambrecht*, whilst in a totally different context the entertainments given by Gottfried's Isold at the Irish court include her reading to them.[49]

The numbers involved in these reading sessions vary considerably, but women play a noticeable part, either amongst themselves or in mixed company. The closest degree of intimate privacy, often involving two lovers, is one person reading to another (in Veldeke's *Servatius* Charles the Great has the saint's *vita* read to him and, although they are hardly lovers, in Chaucer's *Wife of Bath's Prologue* Jankyn reads aloud to his wife).[50] We come to family intimacy with two listeners in Chrétien's *Yvain* and its German adaptation, when the daughter reads aloud to her parents in a secluded garden, but further to three listeners in *Troilus and Criseyde*, where Criseyde and two other ladies listen to a girl reading them the story of Thebes.[51] After that point we are dealing with what is best called group literacy (smallish or much larger). It has been suggested that, as in antiquity, the comedies of Terence were read aloud in a group to train and test Latin fluency, but

---

[48] *Zwiefaltener Benediktinerregel* 34, 4. *St. Trudperter Hoheslied* 55, 16 (p. 154). *Kirchberger Schwesternbuch*, p. 147.
[49] Küsters, *Garten*, p. 303; Green, *Listening*, p. 347, n. 175.
[50] *Servatius* 4240–2. *Wife of Bath's Prologue* 721–87.
[51] *Yvain* 5362–70. *Iwein* 6455–62. *Troilus* II 81–4.

also that Hrotsvitha's drama adaptations may point to reading aloud with parts allocated.[52] An obvious occasion for group literacy was mealtime, in the monastic refectory or at the nobleman's table. The Constitutions for Dominican sisters laid down that there should always be reading in the refectory, to which the sisters should listen in silence, on the general principle that the mind should be nourished with reading while the body was fattened with food.[53] For reasons of self-presentation and group solidarity, as well as entertainment, public readings took place at the nobleman's table. In all these cases public reading does not necessarily imply an inability to read on the part of listeners. Already in antiquity public reading occurred alongside and could even be preferred to private reading, while in the Middle Ages Latin works, destined for the Latinate who could read, were also read out publicly.[54]

Given the ambiguity of *legere*, it is as necessary in this section as in the last to look for indicators to its meaning, in this case reading to others rather than to oneself. There are several that point in this direction.

Whereas the use of a verb of reading with the reflexive dative suggested individual reading, an indirect object implying a different person (Hugh of St Victor: *illi*) describes Charles the Great having a book read to him ('dede he sich lesen'), Ulrich von Lichtenstein has to request the same with a letter ('den brief ich mir . . . lesen bat') and when Rudolf von Ems anticipates the reception of his *Weltchronik* at court he sees Konrad ordering it to be read to him ('swenner im lesin hieze').[55] In these cases the reader may be too unimportant to be mentioned, but even without verbs of 'ordering' or 'requesting' the use of the dative for someone else is sufficient evidence. In French the construction *lire* + *à* replaces the dative when Guinevere reads from a romance to knights and maidens, whilst with a pronoun the dative can be used (John of Howden, writing for Eleanor of Provence, wishes his story to be read to her: 'Li soiez leue'). In English the dative pronoun serves the same purpose: in the singular when the Wife of Bath is read to by Jankyn ('Tho redde he me') and in the plural when Criseyde and her companions listen to the tale of Thebes ('Herden a mayden reden hem the geste').[56]

[52] Parkes, *ASE* 26 (1997), 8f.; Dronke, *Women*, p. 55; Bodarwé, *Sanctimoniales*, p. 308, fn. 43.

[53] Lewis, *Women*, p. 269; Carruthers, *Book*, pp. 166f. See also the illustration in Klapisch-Zuber, *History*, p. 416.

[54] Green, *Listening*, pp. 30–2.

[55] Charles: *Servatius* 4240–2. Ulrich, *Frauendienst* 604, 5f. *Weltchronik* 21700–7.

[56] *Chevaliers as deus espees* 4952f.; Howden, *Rossignos*: Legge, *Literature*, pp. 233f. *Wife of Bath's Prologue* 721, 724. *Troilus* II 83.

A second pointer is to the spatial relationship between reader and listener, expressed by John of Salisbury's choice of prefix in *prelegere* and captured pictorially in a French manuscript, where Machaut stands with the scroll from which he reads to his lady and others before him.[57] In Hartmann's *Iwein* the maiden reading to her parents sits in front of them ('vor in beiden'), a similar situation is sketched in *Wigalois* ('ein schoeniu maget vor ir las/an einem buoche') and by Ebernand von Erfurt describing a maiden reading to her mistress by her bedside ('sô saz ein juncvrou unde las/vor ir bette schône lesen').[58] In these cases we are not to imagine someone reading to himself in the same setting as another, but engaged in reading to and for that person. The same is true in other languages. In Latin Hrabanus Maurus hopes that Ludwig the German will have his work read aloud in his presence ('coram vobis relegi illud faciatis') and Baldwin of Guines has translations frequently read to him ('sepius ante se legere fecit'). In French Chrétien uses a construction in *Yvain* imitated by Hartmann ('et lisoit/une pucele devant lui/En un romanz') and other authors use the phrase *devant lui* in combination with a causative expressing the feudal lord's wish for a public reading. The same is true in English, as with the instruction for Edward IV's son that at meals there 'be reade before him, such noble storyes'.[59]

Sometimes, but not often, the situation can be captured by using a verb of reading with an adverb such as MHG *offenlîche* ('publicly'), as in the *vitae* of the nuns of Kirchberg, read out to them collectively ('Da diss büchlein . . . offenlich in dem convent gelesen wart'). This is the conventual equivalent of what is often referred to in court literature without any explicit adverb, but in the public context of a court festival. At the start of the *Roman de Rou* Wace envisages his commemoration of Norman ancestors being read out ('les estoires lire as festes').[60] Strengthening group identity in this way is common both to Norman court and south German convent.

A further pointer is the use of a verb for reading in a causative construction, implying an order or request not for a text to be read by any number of individuals, but for it to be read to an assembled audience. What Hrabanus Maurus hoped for in the case of Ludwig the German has its counterpart in a similar construction applied to the same ruler by Otfrid ('thaz er sa lésan heizit'). That such a royal command implies public reading is clear from the prose *Lancelot*, where the causative ('disen brieff thunt lesen') is

[57] Huot, *Song*, Fig. 25, p. 267.
[58] *Iwein* 6453. Wirnt von Grafenberg, *Wigalois* 2713f. Ebernand, *Heinrich* 3504f.
[59] Hrabanus, *De universo*, PL 111, 9. Baldwin: in Lambert of Ardres, *Historia*, MGH SS 24, 598. *Yvain* 5364–6; Coleman, *Reading*, pp. 117f., 120, 123. Edward IV: Coleman, *Reading*, p. 129.
[60] *Offenlîche*: Green, *Listening*, p. 88. Kirchberg: see fn. 48. *Roman de Rou* 1–10.

reinforced by references to assembled listeners ('vor allen') and to reading aloud ('aller lutest').[61] Similar explicitness can occur with the corresponding French construction. In Chrétien's *Lancelot* a messenger is instructed to read out his letter ('les fist li rois, oiant toz, lire') and Denis Piramus specifies how the works of Marie de France were read at court ('lire le font') by adding that the ladies heard them with pleasure ('De joie les oient e de gré').[62]

Finally, a verb of reading can be used without further support to suggest reading to others, just as it could also designate reading to oneself. It is this twofold usage which necessitates John of Salisbury's distinction between *legere* and *prelegere*. In Gottfried's scene of Tristan courting Isold of the White Hands ('er sanc, er schreib ir unde las') the verb 'to read' stands alone, but has to be understood together with the dative used only with *schreib*, so that the whole implies that he sang before her, wrote for her and read to her. When in *Le Chevalier à l'épée* the entertainment at court is described in different ways ('Cil list romanz et cist dist fables') we can be sure that *lire* implies, like *dire*, vocalisation before listeners.[63]

Reading of this kind involves two entities: one who reads aloud and one who listens. In what sense can these listeners be seen as reading, if only indirectly and with the help of another? That this view of the position was possible in the Middle Ages is again clear from John of Salisbury and Hugh of St Victor, both of whom include the listener as well as the public reader and individual reader under the heading *legere*, while Hugh even applies this verb to the listener ('lego ab illo'). There is other evidence to support this equation. Already with Augustine one can be said to have 'read' what one has heard ('Legistis quod audistis'), just as John of Salisbury, referring to the Old Testament prophets, argued that the mind of the prince could read in the tongue of the priest when he listens to him.[64] The author of the *Cloud of Unknowing* suggests that, in a way, reading and listening are the same, for the learned read books, but the uneducated 'read' the learned when they listen to them preaching. A similar telescoping of the act of indirect reading occurs when Chaucer describes Criseyde with two other ladies in her parlour listening to a young woman reading the story of Thebes to them. Pandarus's excuse for interrupting their listening makes the acoustic dimension doubly clear, but the crucial point is that this group

[61] Otfrid, *Evangelienbuch*, Lud. 87f. Prose *Lancelot*: II 34, 18, 28–30.
[62] *Lancelot* 5255. Piramus, *Vie* 44f., 47.
[63] *Tristan* 19193 (cf. Green, *Listening*, p. 91). *Chevalier à l'épée* 803.
[64] Augustine: Stock, *Augustine*, pp. 6, 288, n. 77. John of Salisbury: Clanchy, *Memory*, p. 272 ('not altogether destitute of reading').

by hearing together reads together ('This romaunce is of Thebes that we rede').[65] Strictly speaking, in this scene only the young woman actually reads, whilst the others 'read' indirectly by listening to her. When Criseyde is able to point to the red rubric where the reading has stopped she reveals herself to be a reader, but not on this occasion.

This equation of listening with reading belongs to a much wider context. Frequently phrases like 'we read' or 'one reads' recur in clerical works addressed to a congregation to whom the text was read out, so that strictly reading refers to the priest addressing his flock, not to members of his congregation as individual readers.[66] This is all the more obvious when an allusion is made at the same time to the illiteracy of that flock or when the phrase is combined with a dative implying reading to them. However different the context, the congregation listening to the priest are 'readers' in the same sense as Criseyde and her companions listening to the story of Thebes (even the congregation could theoretically include someone able to read, like Criseyde). This clerical use of 'we read' found its way into secular literature in the prologue to Gottfried's *Tristan*, where the liturgical use of 'wir lesen' occurs ('wir lesen ir leben, wir lesen ir tôt') in a reference to the commemorative celebration of the eucharist. The author may well have anticipated individual readers for this work, but we cannot argue for them on the strength of this formula.[67] Telescoping the action of having a text read out to the act of reading for oneself is the counterpart to equating the action of having a text written with the act of writing for oneself. This latter possibility recurs with Margery Kempe, who can vary between these two constructions repeatedly. It is no coincidence that she likewise 'reads' by listening to a priest read to her.[68]

Those who 'read' with their ears rather than with their eyes may be divided into two categories, although admittedly the evidence is not always sufficient to permit classification. Although both these categories read with their ears, I reserve the term 'aural reader' (as distinct from 'oral reader', someone reading aloud for himself, or from 'ocular reader') for those of whom we know no more than an isolated act of listening to someone reading to them, whereas the term 'quasi-literate' is best applied to those whose knowledge was acquired over time by a number of such acts. 'Aural reader' is preferable to other suggestions such as 'recitational literacy' (which more readily suggests the reciter, not the audience) or the linguistic barbarism 'audiate literacy'.[69] Isolated acts of reading by one person to another without

---

[65] *Cloud*, p. 39. Chaucer, *Troilus* II 100, 103.   [66] Green, *Listening*, pp. 116f.
[67] *Tristan* 235f.   [68] *Book* 76–87 (pp. 46f.), 158–63 (p. 51), 7273–88 (p. 379).
[69] 'Aural': Schibanoff, 'Taking', p. 88; Coleman, *Reading*, p. 228. 'Recitational': Wogan-Browne, *Saints*, p. 157. 'Audiate': Coleman, *Reading*, p. 228; Wogan-Browne, *Saints*, p. 162.

any suggestion of continuity on other occasions amounting to accumulated knowledge count therefore as aural reading involving women: in *Mai und Beaflor* ('welt ir lenger hinne wesen,/ich lâze iu mîne tohter lesen' if you care to stay here I shall have my daughter read to you), in *Wigalois* ('ein schoeniu maget vor ir las/ . . . wie Troye zevuort waere' a fair maiden read before her how Troy was destroyed) or in Wolfram's *Titurel* with regard to Sigune reading the words on the spaniel's leash (to Schionatulander?).[70]

Something much more ambitious is involved when an *illitteratus* is presented as *quasi litteratus*. It is wrong to assume that *illitteratus* meant simply 'uneducated', since there existed an oral culture for the layman alongside a written culture for the cleric. In addition to his oral culture the layman could have access to written culture, transmitted to him by clerics at court or in a religious context.[71] It is with this continuous indirect access, making of the *illitteratus* a *quasi litteratus*, that we are now concerned. What this could amount to is suggested of Servulus by Gregory the Great: he was quite illiterate, but bought copies of scripture and had them read to him regularly by religious persons so that he acquired a knowledge of the whole of scripture.[72]

Comparable examples occur throughout the Middle Ages. Cassiodorus reports that Theoderic had the works of the sages of antiquity read to him so that, equipped with learning in this way, he appeared as a philosopher wearing the purple. At a time when King Alfred could not yet read he called upon priests to read to him so that, as a result, he possessed a knowledge of almost all books. The Emperor Henry V, like his father, had clerics and *litterati* constantly around him and discussed their knowledge with them, asking them questions about the scriptures and the liberal arts. Baldwin II of Guines, a layman and illiterate, collected books on learned subjects, theological or otherwise, had them read to him, learned much by heart and discussed them so eagerly with clerics and *magistri* that his chronicler dubs him *quasi litteratus*. In similar terms Henry the Lion's interest in history was such that he had the ancient written chronicles collected and recited in his presence, spending many a sleepless night doing this.[73]

The examples given all concern men, but women, historical and literary, are also shown acquiring knowledge in this way. Margery Kempe (born *c.*1373) could neither read nor write, yet gained access to a wide variety of

---

[70] *Mai und Beaflor* 230, 29f. *Wigalois*: see fn. 58. *Titurel*, stanzas 148–51.

[71] Grundmann, *AfK* 40 (1958), 8, 13; Schreiner, *ZHF* 11 (1984), 328, fn. 254.

[72] Everett, *Literacy*, p. 8.

[73] Theoderic: Riché, *Ecoles*, p. 14. Alfred: Asser, *Life*, chs. 77, 87; Crosby, *Speculum* 11 (1936), 90; O'Brien O'Keeffe, 'Listening', pp. 21, 22. Henry V: Grundmann, *AfK* 40 (1958), 47. Baldwin II: Bezzola, *Origines* III 2, 433; Duby, *Moyen Age*, pp. 201f. and *Women* II 111f.; Fleckenstein, 'Miles', pp. 320f. Henry the Lion: *Annales Stederburgenses*, p. 230; Reuvekamp-Felber, *Volkssprache*, p. 157.

spiritual books not merely by talking with clerics but by having devotional works and biblical commentaries read to her. Her range of indirect reading included such English classics in this field as Walter Hilton's *Scale of Perfection*, the *Stimulus Amoris*, and the *Incendium Amoris* of Richard Rolle, but also extended to the continent (Bridget of Sweden, but also works from what Margery calls 'Dewchland', Germany as well as the Low Countries).[74] Although she may not be explicitly termed illiterate, a very different character, Chaucer's Wife of Bath, could belong here, too. Her detailed knowledge moves further back in time, for in her arguments against the traditional authorities of medieval misogyny she shows acquaintance with the Bible but also patristic and classical authors on whom this tradition fed. Where she acquired this knowledge is clear: not from individual reading, but from her fifth husband, a former clerk of Oxford who constantly read these antifeminine *exempla* to her. In one way, the husband's reading resembles that of the clerics to Margery Kempe, for he reads his book to her 'with ful good devocioun', when he has no other worldly occupation, and knows of more such 'legendes'.[75] The obsessive frequency of such reading in both cases makes a *quasi litterata* of the woman in question, raising her above pure illiteracy.

To conclude this section we may mention one specialised meaning of the verb 'to read' in application to teacher and pupil, a usage known to John of Salisbury and Hugh of St Victor (*docens* and *discens*). Accordingly, the MHG verb *lesen* occurs in both these senses, examples of which I have discussed elsewhere which there is no need to rehearse here.[76] More important are the implications which these meanings had for women.

With regard to women learning, their marginalisation in the Middle Ages derived mainly from Paul's injunction that all they needed to know they should learn from their husbands at home,[77] but even this position was worsened later with the rise of universities, since women's exclusion from them (my own included, effectively until the twentieth century!) debarred them from higher education, even though a few exceptional women acquired this by other means.

It was the disturbing possibility that women might gain the right to teach or preach that was more controversial, calling forth the dangerous possibilities of vernacular Bible study and heretical preaching. (If women

---

[74] Kempe, *Book* 4790–831 (pp. 279f.); Duffy, *Stripping*, pp. 62f; Uhlman, *StPh* 91 (1994), 66–8; Bartlett, *Authors*, p. 22; Watson, *JMEMS* 27/2 (1997), 153.

[75] Winny, *Wife*, pp. 18f.; Martin, *Women*, p. 9. Krug, *Families*, p. 2, talks of the Wife's 'exclusion from written culture', but more correctly it is her lack of direct access to it.

[76] Green, *Listening*, pp. 317f.   [77] I Cor. 14, 35.

could teach at all it was only in the restricted domestic context.) Again, Paul was in the lead in prohibiting teaching or preaching by women, since that could imply a form of authority over men. Humbert of Romans quotes reasons for Paul's veto, including woman's lack of understanding, her naturally inferior status and the foolishness of Eve. As *illitterati*, laymen may not preach, but especially not women, no matter how learned or saintly. Robert of Basevorn adds explicitly that it will not do to claim without proof a command from God, for that is what heretics claim.[78] As we shall see, this is precisely what many women mystics and visionaries claimed for themselves (in the case of Hildegard von Bingen with spectacular success). However, in order to avoid this accusation excuses were also made. When confronted with the Pauline text Margery Kempe argued that she did not preach since she did not go into any pulpit, while Julian of Norwich denied that she taught (because of her feeble condition as a woman), but argued the authority of her 'showings' as stemming from God.[79]

Involved in the continuing controversy over women teaching or preaching are a number of separate issues: women's educational status (illiterate, non-Latinate), the development of religious literature in the vernacular, the suspicious proximity of women to heretical tendencies, and their claim of divine inspiration (especially by contrast with the book-learning of clerics). These are all features that will recur in the following pages.

READING INVOLVED IN WRITING

Although Grundmann saw both reading and writing as integral to medieval literacy, we have learned to see them as different categories: reading as an intellectual attainment, writing as a manual skill. Despite this, there were connections between the two in each direction: writing could be involved in reading,[80] but reading could also be at issue in writing. It is the latter that concerns us now with regard to two meanings of the act of writing. Bonaventura identified four ways of making a book: the scribe (*scriptor*) merely copied someone else's material; the compiler (*compilator*) adds to this material, but not of his own; the *commentator* subordinates his own material to that of others; the author (*auctor*) writes mainly his own material, but also that of others.[81] Applying this differentiation between the two extremes

---

[78] Paul: Tim. 2, 12. Humbert: Blamires, *Viator* 26 (1995), 141. Robert: Blamires and Marx, *JML* 3 (1993), 45.

[79] Kempe, *Book* 4213 (p. 253); Blamires, *Viator* 26 (1995), 150. Julian, *Book*, ST 6; Johnson, *Speculum* 66 (1991), 830.

[80] For example, the MS of Kempe's *Book* was annotated by interested readers at Mount Grace Priory.

[81] Minnis, *Theory*, pp. 94f.

of *scriptor* and *auctor*, we may ask how far reading could be involved in the process of writing.

If we take writing in the sense of composing a work (as an *auctor*), reading can play a part as a preliminary act (consulting a written source, collating several sources, compiling from other works), but also as a subsequent act (revision, expansion, contraction). In between these two acts the *scriptor* has a role to play, whether he is the author or someone else. Reading obviously comes into question when we are dealing with a copyist or translator, transposing the words of one text into another. But even when we are dealing with an *auctor* who composes his own text as he writes it, the physical act of putting words into written shape leads the writer to read each letter or word as he writes it, so that eye and hand work together in one process, reading and writing go together. Whereas Hugh of St Victor used the words 'lego librum' of someone reading an already existing text, I propose 'lego scriptum' for the writer reading the letters of his text as he writes each word.

By seeing both the *scriptor* and the *auctor* engaged in reading in two different senses of writing the relevance of what follows to women in the Middle Ages should become clear. Although they may not be often mentioned expressly in this section, we shall later see that they could be active as scribes or copyists, but also as authors. It is therefore fitting to illustrate the interplay between reading and writing in the case of a woman author.

In the *Book of Margery Kempe* we are given a detailed description how this work of an illiterate came into being as a written text.[82] She had had one written version made, but this was almost illegible or incomprehensible, so that she asked a priest to read it and then write it afresh. The various steps in which reading, in one way or another, is part of the process of writing can be distinguished in sequence. First, the priest reads the earlier version, with whatever difficulty (what we may call 'lego librum'). Then he re-writes the work in his own hand, reading each word as he writes it ('lego scriptum'). Thirdly, we are told that the priest reads through his version, finding it easier ('lego librum'). As a next step he reads what he has written to Margery, so that to his reading aloud in her presence ('lego illi') there corresponds her indirect reading by listening to him ('lego ab illo'). Even ignoring the earlier unsuccessful version, we have here a sequence of five different cases of reading in the genesis of Margery's final written text. As for the process of writing, this is done by the priest himself, but Margery is involved in it by requesting him to do it ('dede . . . wryten'), an activity which is

---

[82] Kempe, *Book*, 123–39 (p. 49).

expressed more directly by verbal variations between Margery 'having the book written' and 'writing' it.[83] Thanks to this exceptionally informative passage we are shown how close and detailed was the interaction between reading and writing. In the light of this we may now turn to more cases, considering them with regard first to the *scriptor*, then to the *auctor*.

Our first case concerns the scribe taking down in writing what the author dictates to him. Where we are uninformed whether the author had a written draft before him, literacy explicitly concerns only the scribe, who writes, but also reads as he writes ('lego scriptum'). How common this method was is illustrated by the frequent combination 'reading and dictating' instead of 'reading and writing'.[84] Of the authors depicted in the Manesse manuscript three are shown dictating to scribes (Bligger von Steinach, Reinmar von Zweter, Konrad von Würzburg).[85] Reinmar, for example, has his eyes closed in contemplation, while his words are taken down first by a scribe onto a wax tablet, then by a woman scribe in the more permanent form of parchment.

The scope of reading in the act of writing is expanded when the scribe writes not to dictation, but copies a first draft, as presumably with the woman scribe with Reinmar von Zweter. Here two acts of reading are involved ('lego librum' and 'lego scriptum'). Baudri de Bourgueil does not speak of composing his poems by dictation, but does refer to tablets and stylus (for later transfer to parchment by a scribe). An Admont *vita* shows an abbess observing the Benedictine Rule's requirement for nocturnal silence by composing in writing by night, then dictating to a scribe next day ('nocte litteras composuit et scribenti praedixit'). In an author portrait Hildegard von Bingen is shown recording her visions onto wax tablets, whilst separately, as the next stage, the monk Volmar transposes her text into book form.[86]

So much was the scribe involved in reading as he wrote that he has also been termed Chaucer's first reader or critic when, too frequently for the author, he edited, rather than merely copied the text.[87] However much we may sympathise with the author's annoyance, this presupposes a thinking scribe, not simply a mechanical copyist, a *scriptor* who read with understanding, even if his understanding differed from the author's. Although writing in the Middle Ages may have been judged a skill, this does not

[83] *Ibid.*, 76–87 (pp. 46f.), 158–63 (p. 51). These variations correspond to what we have seen between reading for oneself and having a text read out.
[84] Clanchy, *Memory*, pp. 125f.   [85] Walther, *Codex*, plates 58, 112, 124.
[86] Baudri: Bond, *Subject*, p. 54. Admont: Ohly, *ZfdA* 87 (1956/7), 15f. Hildegard: Fig. 1.
[87] Johnson, *Speculum* 66 (1991), 826f.

mean that the scribe always read without understanding. How closely he read what he copied has been shown by Malcom Parkes in his unpublished Lyell lectures (1999). When a scribe copied a text he had to divide his attention between exemplar and copy, between reading and writing, between 'lego librum' and 'lego scriptum'. The transition is often detectable from slight discrepancies in the spacing or alignment of his copy as his eyes move hither and thither.[88]

Inevitably, complaints about the scribe's errors, misreadings or miswritings, loom larger than praise for his skill. For those dissatisfied he was not even a thinking being, but one confined to the subordinate task of copying. But if the annoyed customer insisted that the scribe should copy and not read, this implies that he did in fact read (if wrongly).[89] Even a reviser's corrections of an earlier scribe's errors were not always proof against a later scribe's misunderstanding. A copyist of Béroul copied his exemplar's mistakes, but also the reviser's corrections one after the other, failing to see that the latter cancelled the former. In view of such possibilities it is no wonder that Chaucer gives voice in *Troilus and Criseyde* to the fear that the dialectal diversity of English may lead to his text being miswritten and 'mismetred'. Even more radically, Chaucer speaks out against the errors of his scribe ('Adam scriveyn'), causing the author to 'rub and scrape' away the results of his negligence. In Germany Seuse has a similar complaint in the prologue to his *Exemplar* about incompetent scribes of both sexes who have mangled his text ('von mengerley unkunnenden schribern und schriberin ungantzlich abgeschriben'). That this was a recurrent danger in a manuscript culture was already clear to Jerome, complaining of copyists who, like a modern proofreader, write not what they find, but what they think should be there ('qui scribunt non quod inveniunt, sed quod intelligunt').[90] Mistaken they may be, but these copyists still read and understand in their own way.

To redress the balance, there are also cases where the scribe (or his scriptorium) took active steps to revise and correct, incorporating a further stage of reading in the production of a written text. The scribe of a gospel lectionary of Queen Margaret of Scotland worked carefully and himself erased and corrected most of his own mistakes. Marginal corrections can even be inserted by what is taken to be the author (as in the Vienna MS of Otfrid's *Evangelienbuch*), suggesting in the monastic context a close connection between author and scriptorium. Where monastic houses, especially

---

[88] Personal letter, 25 May 2004.   [89] Carruthers, *Book*, p. 214.
[90] Béroul: Legge, *Literature*, p. 368. *Troilus* V 1793–8. Chaucer's scribe: *Works*, p. 534, and Scattergood, 'Jongleur', pp. 500f. Seuse, *Exemplar*, p. 4. Jerome: Scattergood, 'Jongleur', pp. 503f.

convents, were engaged in book production for themselves and others the scriptorium included correctors as well as copyists. That a similar concern for accuracy could be found in a secular context is suggested by Otte's *Eraclius* where care is taken that the Emperor's letter should be written and corrected ('Geschriben und gerihtet').[91]

We reach a last stage, at which the *scriptor* passes over to the *auctor*, whenever the author acts as his own scribe (much like Otfrid correcting his manuscript). The medieval image of the author writing his own book is an old one, going back in the Christian context to illuminations of the four evangelists writing their gospels at their desks. This pictorial tradition finds literary expression in Germany as early as the *Heliand*'s opening description of the evangelists writing their books with their own hands ('endi mid iro handon scrîban/berehtlîco an buok').[92] Authorship (the human writer) and authority (divine inspiration) are seen here as one, but when the image is applied to a non-religious context the authority derives instead from the trustworthiness of written tradition itself. In a poetic letter to Constantia Baudri de Bourgueil assures her that the friend's hand that wrote it was the hand that composed it ('scripsit amica manus et idem dictavit amicus'), and Thomasin von Zerclaere implies the same combination of roles for himself when in the process of composition he refers to his stylus ('mîn griffel'). Although they are depicted at what must be the preliminary stage of drafting their work in written form, two authors (Der von Gliers and Gottfried von Strassburg) are shown equipped with their tablets in the Manesse manuscript. In the illuminations of a number of her MSS Christine de Pizan is shown seated in her room in the process of writing, just as, to return to the religious context from which this medieval image descended, the Dominican nun Elsbeth Stagel is depicted writing at her desk.[93]

The last paragraph has prepared us for the involvement of the *auctor* in reading, at the very least in his dictation to a scribe who takes it down in writing before a fair copy is made from the draft and then revised and corrected by the author. But we must also go back one stage, for medieval dependence on authority points to the need for sources. The authority of the source can be shown pictorially when the evangelists are sometimes shown copying from an exemplar held by angels or when Elsbeth Stagel, based on

[91] Queen Margaret: Gameson, *Gospels*, p. 152. Otfrid: Haubrichs, *Anfänge*, p. 296. Monastic correctors: Leclercq, *Love*, p. 127, and McKitterick, *Francia* 19/1 (1992), 10. *Eraclius* 1862–79.
[92] *Heliand* 7f.
[93] Baudri: Bond, *Subject*, p. 170, n. 5. Thomasin, *Welscher Gast* 2527f. Der von Gliers and Gottfried: Walther, *Codex*, plates 28, 121. Christine de Pizan: Saenger, 'Lire', p. 169, and Smith, '*Scriba*', pp. 26f. Elsbeth Stagel: Hamburger, *Visual*, pp. 465f. and Ehrenschwendtner, 'Library', p. 129.

her reading, composes by making excerpts from the works of Meister Eck-hart.[94] In literary terms the authority sought in a written source informs the manner in which Hartmann von Aue pointedly refers to his reading at the opening of his work, but also, more emphatically and in greater detail, the search for reliable sources which both Gottfried von Strassburg and Thomas claim lies behind their respective versions, undertaken because there are others who have not 'read the tale aright' ('die von im rehte habe gelesen'). Presenting a satisfactory version of the story depends on read-ing the correct source and collating it with other possible sources. For all Wolfram's disclaimer of literacy and bookishness, he pushes the argument back one stage by claiming a similar procedure for his fictitious source Kyot.[95]

As we saw with the *scriptor*, the first stage of writing was normally the draft version on tablets. Two twelfth-century MSS of Boethius' *Consolatio Philosophiae* depict him holding writing tablets on his lap; the intermediate stage between the vision of Hildegard of Bingen and Volmar's book is rep-resented by her writing her vision onto tablets, just as they also represent the first step towards writing on parchment with Reinmar von Zweter in the Manesse portrait.[96] Textual evidence is not lacking. A *vita* of Boniface was written first on tablets for approval before transcription into perma-nent form on parchment ('primitus in ceratis tabulis ad probationem'), so that reading the draft, but also reading in the act of writing (twice) are all involved here. Although Guibert of Nogent boasts that he can com-pose mentally, he acknowledges that the alternative is using tablets ('nullis impressa tabulis'). Bernard of Clairvaux is also known to have written first drafts in his own hand.[97]

A fair copy on parchment was the next stage. In writing to Baudri Con-stantia may refer to her wax tablet (*cera*), but this was only for the first stage, since later terms make it clear that it led to a more permanent writ-ing material, parchment: *carta*, *volumen* and *scheda*. As we saw with the *auctor* acting as his own *scriptor*, these two senses of 'writing' can be con-flated when the author presents himself as writing (whether physically or figuratively). In the Arsenal MS of Marie de France's *Fables* she is shown at the beginning writing in a large codex and equipped with pen and knife (just as Thomasin presented himself with his 'griffel'). In the same manner,

---

[94] Evangelists: Saenger, *Space*, pp. 252f. Elsbeth Stagel: Schiewer, 'Möglichkeiten', pp. 185f.
[95] Hartmann, *Armer Heinrich* 1–15 and *Iwein* 21f. Gottfried, *Tristan* 155–66. Thomas, *Tristan* Douce 845–51 and Gottfried, *Tristan* 149–54. Wolfram, *Parzival* 455, 2–22.
[96] Boethius: Clanchy, *Memory*, pp. 118f. Hildegard: Fig. 1. Reinmar: Walther, *Codex*, plate 112.
[97] Boniface and Guibert: Rouse, 'Vocabulary', pp. 220, 227. Bernard: Saenger, *Space*, p. 250.

when Chaucer reaches one stage in his 'tragedye' of *Troilus and Criseyde* it is his pen that trembles at the prospect of what he must write.[98] Whether the author actually wrote his text in all such cases is immaterial, for what they suggest is that one stage in the transition to permanent form, after stylus and tablet, was pen and parchment. In either case, however, reading in a technical sense was involved in the act of writing.

Even after a fair copy was produced, the task of reading was not completed, for it had to be checked and corrected, not just by scribe or scriptorium, but ideally by the author himself, as we have seen in Otfrid's case. Reading is obviously involved in correcting when actual readers are invited to correct any error,[99] but apart from that the responsibility falls, after the scribe, on the author himself. Sometimes he may still need assistance, as when Hildegard, after Volmar's death, wishes to show a new work to an abbot for correction, and sometimes the correction takes the form of reading back to the author, who therefore 'reads' only indirectly. Bernard can correct in this way, hearing how his text sounds, but he also, more rarely, corrects his own text and the 'reportationes' of his oral sermons. Chaucer, too, must have been his own aggravated corrector if he complained of the excessive rubbing and scraping to which this led.[100]

Correction can even amount to revision. Bernard not merely corrected his texts, he also revised his sermons on the *Song of Songs* and saw to a second redaction. A passage in Wolfram's *Parzival* dealing with Kyot (451–5) bears every sign of a later revision in order to accommodate the novelty of this figure. Precisely the knowledge that bowdlerised copies of his text were in circulation may have prompted Seuse to work on his *Exemplar* to give it the shape he intended.[101] How careful revision by an author can issue in a sense of completion is best shown in the MS of Marie de France's *Fables* mentioned above. It begins with a miniature showing her at work as an author writing her own book, but concludes with another in which she holds up the book to her gaze (critical or satisfied?). By its placing this second miniature suggests completion of the task taken in hand in the first, but together they suggest that her writing of the work runs parallel to the reader's reception.[102]

---

[98] Baudri: Schaller, *MlJb* 3 (1966), 26. Marie de France: Fig. 2 and Smith, 'Scriba', p. 31. Chaucer, *Troilus* IV 13f.

[99] Clanchy, *Memory*, pp. 130f.

[100] Hildegard: Dronke, *Women*, pp. 193f. Reading back: Saenger, *Viator* 13 (1982), 382. Bernard: Illich, *Vineyard*, p. 90 and Carruthers, *Book*, p. 196. Chaucer, *Works*, p. 534.

[101] Bernard: Leclercq, *RB* 64 (1954), 208–23; Talbot, 'Entstehung', pp. 202–14. Wolfram: Mohr, 'Kyot', pp. 152–69. Seuse: Ruh, *Geschichte* III 426.

[102] Fig. 3. Hindman, 'Authorship', p. 49; Ward, 'Fables', pp. 195f.

In both senses of writing (scribal copying and authorial composition) reading was also involved in various ways and at different stages. In many of these cases women play a part and the following pages will exemplify this still further.

READING IN LATIN AND THE VERNACULAR

Before the end of the twelfth century the title of this section would have made no sense, since reading in the vernacular would have seemed a contradiction in terms. If for Grundmann, following clerical views of this period, a non-Latin literature was inconceivable (since *littera(tura)* meant 'writing in Latin'), it follows that reading anything but Latin was out of the question.[103] To accept that view, however, is to be captive to the medieval clergy's vested interest in retaining a monopoly of literacy for itself and to ignore one of the major changes of the twelfth century, the first beginnings of a vernacular literacy (with the precocious exception of Anglo-Saxon England). This is one of the key questions to be looked at in this section, in which the attempt is not made to discuss examples of women who could read (Latin or the vernacular), but instead the problems arising from such reading activities and what they tell us about medieval literacy, especially, but not exclusively as affecting women. Women's literacy and Latinity will be discussed later.

A first question, much discussed with regard to religious literature, concerns the linguistic adequacy of Latin and the vernacular, together with the intellectual adequacy of those reading these languages. The claims made for Latin by the clergy as an interested party were time-honoured (it was the language of the Vulgate and liturgy, of classical and theological literature, with which medieval vernaculars had traditionally gone to school in developing a vocabulary and syntax of any precision). It was therefore the institutionalised language of orthodoxy, the richly conceptualised tool of an intellectual élite for centuries.[104] By comparison, the vernaculars were held to offer much less in these early centuries, which made it easy for the clergy to defend its prerogative, arguing that the lack of conceptual precision in the vernacular could only cause confusion and that, in the case of translations from Latin, the result could only be a loss of intellectual substance. In addition, those whose lack of education confined them to the vernacular could not be considered capable of correctly understanding a text already imperfectly rendered in their tongue and were thereby exposed

---

[103] *AfK* 40 (1958), 4.   [104] Köbele, *Bilder*, pp. 10, 11, 45f.

to the errors of heresy. This fear, it has been speculated, perhaps explains the Latin translation of the vernacular work of Mechthild von Magdeburg, safely removing it from the hands of those who could be endangered.[105]

There was, however, another side to this question. At a time when vernacular literatures flourished it became possible to question the linguistic monopoly of Latin and to argue that the miracle of Whitsun had sanctified the vernaculars in which the apostles preached and that Jerome, as a Latin-speaker, had translated the Bible into his mother-tongue (even if nobody hit upon the historical irony that Greek fathers of the Church had in their day questioned the adequacy of Latin for a translation of the Bible).[106] Even more tellingly, it has been suggested that when the vernaculars flourished in court literature, but above all in the richly innovative vocabulary of mysticism, Latin had so far become a onesidedly intellectual tool of scholasticism that it was less well equipped for the new demands of mystical experience than it had still been in the hands of Bernard of Clairvaux.[107]

Our second question concerns different levels of Latinity in the Middle Ages. A preliminary observation is called for here. It is sometimes said that medieval reading was taught by the medium of Latin and we shall later see this confirmed with the use of Psalters and Books of Hours for this purpose. From this it does not follow, however, that whoever could read could also read Latin, since Latin was the medium, but not always the result. The first stage (often the only stage) in learning to read was to identify the letters in an elementary Latin text and to pronounce the sounds they stood for, without necessarily understanding them. Learning this with Latin could be applied to a vernacular text, with the difference that vocalisation now conveyed understanding. If reading was taught by means of a Latin text it need not lead to a knowledge of Latin, but could instead bypass this and assist understanding a vernacular text.[108]

This preliminary point opens the door to the first of four levels of medieval Latinity, to what has been called phonetic literacy or the ability to read, but without understanding.[109] This was the case with the earliest stage in reading Latin, but could be accompanied by memorisation of frequently used texts (prayers, liturgy), so that what appeared to be reading may have involved a general idea of what was written, but no precise or detailed understanding. This is often made explicitly clear. The author of

---

[105] Schreiner, *ZHF* 11 (1984), 292, 305; Ruh, *Geschichte* II 252f.
[106] Schreiner, *ZHF* 11 (1984), 295, fn. 132, and 299, fn. 145.
[107] Ruh, *Geschichte* I 18f., III 235, fn. 58, 261; *Eckhart*, pp. 44f.
[108] Grundmann, *AfK* 40 (1958), 4; Clanchy, 'Learning', p. 33; Woods, 'Books', pp. 186f.
[109] Four levels: Bell, *Nuns*, pp. 59f.; Robertson, 'Hand', pp. 12f.

The Mirror of our Lady states in his preface why he has composed it in English for nuns at Syon Abbey with no Latin: 'many of you, though ye can synge and rede, yet ye can not se what the meanynge thereof ys', and Richard Whytford makes the same point of those who 'rede the same martiloge in latyn, not vnderstandynge what they redde'. Eberlin von Günzburg criticises the waste of time when nuns with no Latin spend hours on Latin prayers they cannot understand and replies to the defence that God and the angels understand the prayers by saying that their undoubted linguistic competence is irrelevant, for what counts is the understanding of those who pray.[110]

A second level of Latin competence, embracing a slightly higher degree of comprehension literacy, is shown by those who read, but by dint of practice in dealing with common liturgical texts have some understanding of them. In a late thirteenth-century *Memoriale* an intermediate position is allotted to those who know the Psalter ('scientes psalterium'), although what is meant by 'knowing' is left undefined. At any rate, they are distinguished on the one hand from *clerici* (presumably literate) and on the other from *illitterati*.[111] If those who are not clerics know how to read ('sciunt legere') and can recite the office they must have passed beyond the stage of merely phonetic literacy. A third stage is reached, however, with the ability to read Latin with understanding, but not confined to liturgical texts or common ones where familiarity would assist comprehension. This presupposes an ability to decode a written Latin text word for word independently of context and to grasp its meaning. The Latin books known to have been housed in some numbers in English and south German nunneries were presumably meant for readers to be found there (not only for clerics attached for the *cura monialium*) and did not serve a merely decorative purpose.[112] A last and highest stage in Latin competence is the ability to write and compose in the language.[113] Even if fewer women may have been engaged in this than men, their numbers are not so few as has sometimes been assumed, and in any case their relative paucity may be due to women's greater inclination for vernacular literacy, in other words for literacy of another kind.

These comments on differences in Latinity have already touched upon literacy, where again different ideas of what is meant by *litteratus* can be traced. On the one hand, concessions for a simpler Latin can be made for

---

[110] Saenger, 'Books', p. 142; Bell, *Nuns*, p. 60; Schreiner, *ZHF* 11 (1984), 309, but also Ehrenschwendtner, *Bildung*, p. 140, on Geiler von Kaysersberg; Orme, *Childhood*, pp. 160f. On reading, hearing, and praying in Latin without understanding cf. Zieman, 'Reading', pp. 97–120.

[111] Bell, *Nuns*, pp. 60f.; Millett, 'Ancrene', pp. 29f.

[112] Saenger, 'Books', p. 142; Bell, *Nuns*, p. 61.   [113] Bell, *Nuns*, pp. 66f.

those in need of such consideration. Thus, the Scotsman David adapted his Latin style, simplifying it for laymen who were less instructed ('minus docti'), just like Giraldus Cambrensis in dealing with laymen and princes who were similarly less literate ('parum literati').[114] On the other hand, we have the extreme case of John of Salisbury, whose ambitious conception of literacy (embracing a knowledge of the poets, historians, orators and even mathematicians) meant that those falling short could not be termed literate, even if they could read ('etsi litteras noverint').[115] Such an elevated view of what is meant by literacy, denying the ability to those who do not measure up, combined with the long-lasting failure to acknowledge vernacular literacy, raises an important question. What precisely does it mean when someone, in our case a woman, calls herself illiterate? Could it not imply a simpler level of literacy or even vernacular literacy, neither of which could qualify in rigorist clerics' eyes as literacy proper?

To illustrate this problem we may look briefly at the case of Hildegard von Bingen.[116] She makes it clear that she can read Latin, even though she may not have been taught it formally, since she cannot analyse a text grammatically. Although not taught by external instruction, she is learned within her soul ('indoctus de ulla magistratione . . . sed intus in anima mea sum docta').[117] Moreover, even if her Latin may be unpolished (more oral than learned), this is because God addresses her in her visions in a simple, not literary Latin, which is how she dictates them. With this source of inspiration she can bypass the complex language of philosophers and rhetoricians, speaking simply because God speaks to her in the Latin of the Bible. Although she calls herself uneducated and a writer of unpolished Latin, she also concedes that she can read and write in Latin, even though she needed someone to correct her grammar. This did not stop her, however, from insisting that corrections were to be confined to grammar and that nothing was to be added or subtracted. There is much more to Hildegard's literacy than this, but this paragraph must suffice to show that, even apart from the novelty of vernacular literacy (in which she did not participate), the twelfth century witnessed unsettling changes in literacy and reading.

The example of Hildegard leads us to a fourth question, the way in which frequently a double equation was made: of men with an education in Latin and women with a restriction to the vernacular, although we need to be extremely cautious in interpreting such evidence. In the first place,

---

[114] Grundmann, *AfK* 40 (1958), 46f.; Vàrvaro, *SMV* 10 (1962), 321.
[115] Grundmann, *AfK* 40 (1958), 52; Green, *Listening*, p. 10.
[116] Newman, *Sister*, pp. 5, 7, 22f.; Ferrante, *Glory*, p. 156; 'Scribe', pp. 102f., 106f., 126.
[117] Hildegard: see below, p. 225, and *Epistolarium* 1 24f.

ignorance of Latin was by no means confined to women and could be
continually voiced as a criticism of clerics from whom Latinity should have
been expected (for example, Guibert de Nogent describes one cleric as
'mediocriter litteratus').[118] Secondly, to argue from the opposite point of
view, there are cases, as we saw with Hildegard, where a woman's Latin
literacy, however imperfect grammatically, produced undeniably visionary
writing of a high order, accepted and admired by men in authority, clerical
and lay, and immensely influential. But there is also no shortage of evidence
for women acquiring a high degree of Latinity. The early Anglo-Norman
dynasty included a notable number of royal women (Queen Mathilda,
Countess Adela of Blois, and Empress Mathilda) all of whom commissioned
histories in Latin, a linguistic slant which is significantly different from the
vernacular historiography of the Anglo-Normans a little later, itself again
encouraged by women, albeit with a different linguistic interest.[119] Thirdly
and much more important, we have to reckon with the possibility of an
antifeminine circular argument: if women lack the rational ability of men
they cannot ascend from the vernacular to Latin, but if conversely they are
commonly associated with vernacular reading that can be advanced as a
token of their lack of reason. The argument of female incapacity can be
used to debar women from access to religious writing, Latin or vernacular:
from the former because their education has closed this door to them, from
the latter because their lack of reason would render it too dangerous to
make vernacular versions available to them.[120]

In view of this we have to be careful (while recognising that some women's
reading ability, like men's, may have been deficient) in accepting some
comments at face value. Hugh of Digne echoes the late medieval proverb
about reading the Psalter like a nun in speaking of reading a Psalter like
a woman ('sicut una mulier'), meaning by that reading without any real
understanding. Jean Gerson justified writing a mystical text in French rather
than Latin because he intended it primarily for women. In his *Vita Nuova*
Dante defended vernacular poetry by saying that it arose from the need
to make it intelligible to a lady (whether this is historically correct or not
is irrelevant to the fact that Dante wished to make this point). In a more
scurrilous tone Chaunticleer in Chaucer's *Nun's Priest's Tale* quotes the Latin
tag 'Mulier est hominis confusio' to his wife, but relies on her ignorance of
Latin in translating it by its opposite: 'Woman is man's joy and all his bliss'.
We are left uncertain whether the cynicism is Chaunticleer's or whether

---

[118] Guibert, *Vita* II 6.   [119] Ferrante, *Glory*, p. 96; Damian-Grint, *Historians, passim.*
[120] Cf. the antifeminine remarks by Henricus a Gandavo and by Berthold, Archbishop of Mainz,
  quoted by Schreiner, 'Marienverehrung', pp. 339, 343.

the learned men in the audience are meant to feel strengthened in their sense of superiority.[121] The uncertainties of such cases fade away, however, before the more pragmatic facts that both in Vadstena, the Swedish double monastery founded by Bridget, and in the likewise double Syon Abbey in England there is a striking discrepancy between the number of Latin book holdings (almost entirely for the brethren) and vernacular ones (for the sisters).[122]

Several points in this last problem have prepared us for the fifth question we face, the fact of vernacular literacy, with which we return to the point made at the opening of this section. From the late Middle Ages we have a number of explicit references to laymen who read in their mother tongue (e.g. 'die das latin nit verstanden grüntlich und doch lesen können teutsch' who do not thoroughly understand Latin, but can read German).[123] Not all such passages go as far as this in claiming ignorance of Latin; nor need they for our purposes, for the fact of vernacular literacy is what concerns us here, reflected in the need to offer a translation from Latin. With such passages we have reached a position radically different from the medieval cleric's view of literacy and Grundmann's discussion. In place of the dichotomy between literate cleric and illiterate layman, we now have to find room for laymen who may not be literate in the traditional clerical sense (they have no Latin), but who are literate in a novel sense as readers in the vernacular. The novel division of laymen between those who are literate in the new sense and those who are illiterate in any sense finds linguistic expression in German in the distinction between those laymen who are termed *verstanden, klug* or *vernonftig* (intelligent) and those who are *einfaltig* (simple).[124]

Work done on this phenomenon has mainly concentrated on the later Middle Ages, where the evidence is richer, but examples can be found much earlier, reaching back to the late twelfth century as the turning-point in medieval literacy, even though this earlier testimony may be scattered and less frequent. (Quite isolated and for long without parallel is the case of King Alfred in England, of whom Asser reports that he learned to read the vernacular long before he mastered the same in Latin.) A German example from the thirteenth century contrasts incapability in Latin with ability in German when the author says that he does not understand Latin, but has

---

[121] Hugh of Digne: Grundmann, *AfK* 26 (1936), 135, fn. 13 (cf. Ehrenschwendtner, *Bildung*, p. 165, fn. 506). Gerson: Rubin, *Corpus*, p. 98, fn. 97. Dante: Balfour, 'Francesca', pp. 79, 81. Chaucer: Martin, *Women*, pp. 2, 3.

[122] Woods, 'Books', pp. 177f.; Bell, *Nuns*, pp. 75, 78.

[123] Schreiner, *ZHF* 11 (1984), 330; Green, *Listening*, p. 328, n. 93.

[124] Steer, 'Laie', p. 360; Green, *Listening*, p. 328, n. 95.

read a point in German.[125] This contrast is only implicit in the earliest example known to me (from the twelfth century) in what is reported of the heretical preacher Valdes. Converted to the apostolic ideal, he asked two clerics to translate the gospels and other texts for him to read and use in his preaching, so that Valdes was able to read, but only in the vernacular. How shocking this unheard of literacy was to a Latinate *litteratus* may be gauged from the reaction of Walter Map, who calls the followers of Valdes *ydiotas, illiteratos*.[126] For the rest, however, we have to do without a contrast, implicit or not, especially in an important twelfth-century supplement to the isolated case of Valdes, the beginnings of the court romance in the vernacular. Of the Latinity (or lack of it) of the audience to whom this genre was addressed we are singularly uninformed. We do know, however, that two kinds of reception were envisaged for most of these works, by listeners to a public reading and by individual readers, however much in the minority these latter may have been.[127] These readers, like Valdes, do not fit into Grundmann's definition, whose embarrassment is shown by his calling them illiterates who could read (but had no Latin).[128] They can only be called illiterates by the terms of a definition from which they represent the first significant break away, and we do better to acknowledge them as literate, but in this new sense.

Prominent among those literate in the vernacular are women, not merely in the secular sphere (court authors are notably concerned with women readers), but above all in religious life. In his work on religious movements Grundmann was aware of the importance of these semi-religious women, hungry for spiritual texts to read, but needing translations because of their lack of Latin. In their case, at least, he came close to breaking free from his own definition: he admitted that this new readership can hardly still be called illiterate, but that it was not literate in the old sense, so that the old distinction is no longer valid.[129] This loss of validity is precisely the point made by Steer with regard to the fourteenth century, so that the vernacular literacy for which he argues in that century had its first beginnings in the twelfth and thirteenth centuries, with women closely involved from the start.[130]

---

[125] King Alfred: Asser, *Life*, chs. 23, 77, 87–9, together with the commentary of Keynes and Lapidge, *Alfred*, pp. 28, 53, 239. Cf. also O'Brien O'Keeffe, 'Listening', pp. 19–24. German example (*Von dem übeln wîbe* 92f.): Green, *Listening*, p. 10.

[126] Grundmann, *AfK* 40 (1958), 56f.; Green, *Listening*, p. 10. Grundmann (p. 10, fn. 30) also refers to the follower of Baldwin II of Guines who had books translated from Latin into French which he then read and understood.

[127] Green, *Listening, passim*.   [128] Grundmann, *AfK* 40 (1958), 57.

[129] *Ibid.*, p. 59.   [130] Steer, 'Laie', p. 356.

Vernacular literacy, whether with translations or not, was felt by the ecclesiastical establishment to open the doors to heresy. That was clearly the case with Valdes, but was also a threat which dogged the beguines, including Mechthild von Magdeburg, and underlies the Church's reservations about the ability of the vernacular to capture the nuances of theological Latin without the danger of misunderstanding. Schreiner has written at length on the Church's view of the illegitimacy of vernacular translations of the Bible, meant by their language for the use of laymen who 'by definition' were uneducated in theological abstractions and therefore prone to misunderstand what they read.[131] Alarmed by its experiences with heretical movements in the high Middle Ages, the Church viewed with suspicion later developments such as religious communities of laypeople, Bible-reading by them and lay preaching. The danger it saw was two-pronged: the inadequacy of the vernacular, but also the uneducated status of laypeople who, heretics or not, were keen to gain access to religious literature for themselves, without the intermediacy or supervisory control of the clergy, who rightly saw in this bypassing a threat to their authoritative status. However, to dismiss the competence of laypeople in theological matters by stressing their lack of education and illiteracy was a double-edged weapon, as was soon pointed out, for in choosing his disciples Christ had selected simple, uneducated fishermen. Heretics and those suspiciously close to heresy could therefore fall back on a New Testament authority for their simplicity.

To those upholding the authority of Latin the use of the vernacular in religious matters, especially in the case of women mystics, represented a scandal on several scores at once. It was regarded as a challenge to clerical authority by laypeople, and by women at that; it presented a provocation in its use of the vernacular; and it offered a form of experiential instruction by the uneducated alongside that of Latin theology ('das der ungelerte munt die gelerte zunge . . . leret' that the unlearned teaches the learned).[132] Clerical suspicions about the vernacular therefore involved a number of different issues: the conceptual imperfections of the vernacular by contrast with Latin, the objection to laymen meddling in theological matters of which they had no understanding, and the scorn for women in particular dabbling in such things. There is no need to single out this last, antifeminine point alone, for all three play a part together.

The nature of this orthodox reaction to the dangers of vernacular religious texts for laypeople has been illustrated for England in the case of Nicholas Love's *Mirror of the Blessed Life of Jesus Christ*, written as a reply to

---

[131] Schreiner, *ZHF* 11 (1984), 257–354.   [132] See below, fn. 140.

Wycliffe's English translation of the Bible and as part of a controversy over vernacular translations. Love is concerned with the lay recipients of such translations, ignorant ('lewde') men and women, 'symple soules of symple vndirstondyng'. In Love's eyes such an uneducated layperson can only think in physical terms ('kan not thenke bot bodyes or bodily thinges'), a phrasing reminiscent of the charge made by those opposed to vernacular Bible translations that both the uneducated and the vernacular to which they were restricted were unable to pass beyond the literal sense of scripture and were therefore subject to misreading and error.[133]

The practical results of such clerical doubts could be drastic, especially in England after Wycliffe and the rise of the Lollard heresy. It was here, above all with the Constitutions of Archbishop Arundel (1409) that censorship of theological thinking and writing in the vernacular was of a severity far exceeding what was to be found on the continent. It was forbidden to make or possess a written translation of a biblical text or for vernacular writers to include a (translated) biblical quotation in their own texts. The point was reached where to voice an opinion gathered from a written English text deriving from Latin could be taken *ipso facto* as evidence of heresy. Amongst the victims of this censorship were well-known devotional works like *The Prick of Conscience* and *The Mirror of Sinners*, but also Chaucer's *Canterbury Tales*.[134]

To such criticisms of the use of the vernacular in religious writing two responses were possible. The first concerns the late medieval theological implications of the style of writing known as *sermo humilis*, already used in the Vulgate and analysed in its implications by Auerbach.[135] This stylistic level was particularly suited to Christian ends since the qualities embraced by *humilis* (lowly, submissive, meek, even uneducated)[136] were those favoured by Christ in choosing not philosophers or rhetoricians to convey his message, but simple fishermen. Not only that, for the incarnation itself was proof of Christ's own *humilitas*, of what is known theologically as kenosis, the self-emptying and self-limitation of divine power by the Second Person in the incarnation. Both the *sermo humilis* and the concept kenosis were central to Christianity from the beginning, but acquired renewed importance in the late Middle Ages in what is termed incarnational theology, with its greater emphasis on the humanity of Christ (involving his weakness and suffering) than on awe-inspiring power and majesty.

---

[133] Watson, *NML* 1 (1997), 93–5.　　[134] Watson, *Speculum* 70 (1995), 822–64, especially 828f., 831.
[135] Auerbach, 'Sermo', pp. 25–53.　　[136] *Ibid.*, pp. 34f., 42f.

The vernacular was part of this in a very particular way. If the Christian message was to be conveyed to everyone, to the simple and low-born as well as to the wise and powerful, it had to be couched in a language accessible to all. In classical antiquity, with Latin common to all, *sermo humilis* meant speech stripped of the polished complexities of rhetoric available only to the educated. However, in the early Middle Ages with the growing divergence between written Latin and spoken Romance, and even more in the non-Romance speaking parts of western Europe, the requirements of *sermo humilis* as intrinsic to Christian *humilitas* granted a positive value to the vernacular. The wish to include all, especially the lowest and most neglected, specifically the uneducated, brought with it a revaluation of the mother tongue, whose qualities, previously seen as inadequacies, could now be seen more positively.

This conjunction of incarnational theology with the vernacular in the late Middle Ages has been discussed with reference to English literature by Watson, with a revealing subtitle to one of his essays: 'The mother tongue and the incarnation of God'.[137] He stresses not merely the contemporaneity of the two phenomena, but also the justification of the vernacular which was achieved. He argues that with Julian of Norwich, for example, the Church had to 'learn to be instructed (in the vernacular and by a woman)' and to humble itself by accepting the ancillary role she gave it.[138] The shock to established thought was a double one: instruction was conveyed in what had been regarded as the deficient speech of laypeople and moreover by the sex debarred from theological education and largely non-Latinate. What had been looked down upon as inferior is now proposed as the channel through which God's message reached all and sundry. Where woman's restriction to the vernacular could be regarded by clerics as an indication of her intellectual incapacity, the combination of *sermo humilis* with kenosis turned things upside down, making her, like the unlearned at large, more accessible to God, not merely linguistically, but also, if we recall that the qualities associated with *humilis* (lowly, submissive, meek, uneducated) are those patriarchally associated with woman, by virtue of her inborn nature.

Watson also draws a parallel with Mechthild von Magdeburg on this point. She wonders why God has vouchsafed these visions to her (doubly disqualified by sex and lack of education) rather than to a learned cleric ('ein geleret geistlich man') and is told by God that grace flows downwards to the lowest, least regarded and most hidden places and not the highest

---

[137] Watson, *NML* I (1997), 85–124; *JMEMS* 27, 2 (1997), 145–87.   [138] Watson, *NML* I (1997), 121.

mountains, incapable of receiving the revelation of grace ('da sûchte ich
ie zû die nidersten, minsten, heimlichosten stat; die irdenschen hohsten
berge môgent nit empfan die offenbarunge miner gnaden').[139] As with
Julian of Norwich, this is a clear statement of the scandal of Christian
values: precisely her lack of a theological Latin education predestines this
woman for closeness to God. It also qualifies her, uneducated, to teach
the learned ('. . . das der ungelerte munt die gelerte zungen von minem
heligen geiste leret').[140] Again as with Julian, this is a radical challenge to
the Church hierarchy and illustrates how easily the latter could see this in
terms of heresy.

This last point, with its polemical contrast between the unlearned and the
educated, the *idiota* and the *philosophus*, brings us to a second response to
suspicions about the vernacular: the suggestion that the illiterate layperson,
confined to the vernacular by the clerics' own definition of literacy, may
have visionary access to a divine inspiration that bypassed the learned clergy
(the highest mountains with Mechthild or the learned cleric with whom
she contrasts herself). Again, this is a view early sanctioned by Christianity.
Paul said that the letter kills, but the spirit gives life; the apostles Peter
and John are termed *idiotae* in the Vulgate for their lack of education;
Augustine argued that the apostles, monoglot 'homines idiotae', received
the gift of (vernacular!) tongues by inspiration from the Holy Ghost at
Whitsun.[141] There is also the long-standing Christian tradition of holy
simplicity ('sancta simplicitas') and knowing ignorance ('docta ignorantia')
which tellingly ties up with humility in the case of Francis of Assisi who
said of his followers that they were ignorant and subject to all ('ydiote et
subditi omnibus').[142]

By this argument holy simplicity not merely enjoys direct access to inspiration and divine wisdom, it can also claim to be superior to the theological
learning of scholasticism, from which women were directly excluded but
which by this means they could transcend. Once more it is Mechthild von
Magdeburg who, when discussing the three gifts of wisdom, distinguishes
explicitly between the wisdom of priests ('pfeffelichú wîsheit') and another
kind of wisdom, informed throughout by grace and humility, but sees
the first as inferior to the latter.[143] She makes the contrast more pointedly
polemical by contrasting her own unlearned discourse (of a woman in the

[139] *Ibid.*, pp. 122f.; Mechthild, *Licht* II 26 (pp. 136, 138).   [140] Mechthild, *Licht* II 26 (p. 138).
[141] Paul: II Cor. 3, 6. Peter and John: Acts 4, 13 (also 'sine litteris'). Augustine: Grundmann, *AfK* 40 (1958), 6.
[142] 'Docta ignorantia': Schreiner *ZHF* 11 (1984), 264, fn. 20. Francis: Grundmann, *AfK* 40 (1958), 55.
[143] Mechthild, *Licht* IV 3 (pp. 240, 244).

vernacular) with the scholastic learning of university-trained clerics. She directs her words expressly against the latter ('Dis ist vil sere wider die lúte' This speaks clearly against those people), who speak outwardly with many fine (Latin!) words to convey no more than the impression that they are informed by the Holy Ghost.[144] What in their case appears to be wisdom in the eyes of the world is in fact foolishness before God ('Man vindet manigen wisen meister an der schrift, der an im selber vor minen ögen ein tore ist' There are many masters learned in letters who in themselves are fools in my eyes).[145] Occasionally religious women were able to convince even clerics that they must be divinely inspired. The spiritual directors of women mystics and visionaries could view their own clerical authority and learning (*auctoritas, scientia*) as inferior to the spiritual experience (*experientia, sapientia*) of these women. The vicar of Norwich to whom Margery Kempe spoke could automatically assume that she was intellectually inferior and therefore incapable of theological speculation, but others, aware that she can have received little formal education, were persuaded of her divine inspiration.[146] Margery was of course herself convinced of this, as were also trained lawyers at Lincoln (for all their education unable to answer as she did) or the clerics over whom she was able to score.[147]

This justification of the wisdom of the uneducated, of the vernacular they used and of their right to teach spiritual truths to the learned derives from the *docta ignorantia* implicit in Christianity from its beginnings, but it was also informed by a rivalry which came to a head in the high Middle Ages. Langer has stressed the importance for medieval mysticism of the contrast between monastic and scholastic theology (which will occupy us later as a background to two different ways of reading). He sees the monastic view, engaged in controversy with scholasticism, as incorporated in thinkers such as Peter Damian, John of Fécamp, Rupert von Deutz and Bernard of Clairvaux.[148] For them, too, the contrast was between experiential *sapientia* and rational *scientia*: the former inspired and humble, the latter too persuaded of the ability of unaided human reason to penetrate to truths beyond its grasp. By drawing on these two traditions religious women who had little choice but to use the vernacular were enabled to make superior claims for their position. The fact, however, that such an ambitious defence could be conducted in response to criticisms that the use of the vernacular opened the doors to heresy shows how vital a topic of discussion was the vernacular

---

[144] *Ibid.* V 11 (p. 342). For suggestions of a similar contrast amongst Dominican nuns cf. Ehrenschwendtner, *Bildung*, p. 29 and fn. 189.

[145] *Ibid.* II 26 (p. 138).   [146] Watson, *NML* 1 (1997), 102; Watt, *Secretaries*, p. 38.

[147] Watt, *Secretaries*, p. 39.   [148] Langer, *Mystik*, pp. 151–208.

in the late Middle Ages. It has even been claimed, in a study of the books
and libraries in English nunneries, that because of their restricted access to
Latin English nuns in the late Middle Ages kept up more thoroughly than
did monks with the latest developments in an increasingly vernacular spirituality.[149] In this period, exclusion from Latin no longer meant exclusion
from spiritual reading. To confine one's definition of literacy to Latin alone
is to ignore the revolutionary change in medieval reading from the twelfth
century on.

[149] Bell, *Nuns*, pp. 76f.

CHAPTER 2

Figurative reading

With this chapter we pass beyond literal reading in the sense of visual reading of letters that exist tangibly in written form and approach reading with one's mind's eye where, even if reference may be made to letters, these are not present in written form. This implies that reading is not simply a matter of the literacy that has so far concerned us, of visually decoding written signs, and that much more is involved than this first step. That this was well known in the Middle Ages is clear from the frequent double formula 'to read and understand' (*legere et intelligere*), confirming that the opposite could also happen, that a Latin text could be read without understanding. Even where Latin was not involved, understanding a text could aim at its deeper meaning, passing beyond the merely literal, as with Thomasin von Zerclaere's view that the reader is not simply one who reads, but one who reads correctly (who reads what is correct and with understanding).[1] How far understanding belongs to reading is made clear by Mechthild von Magdeburg, whose work begins with the firm recommendation that whoever wishes to understand it should read it nine times ('Alle, die dis bůch wellen vernemen, die sőllent es ze nún malen lesen'), an injunction repeated in the Latin version, the *Revelationes* ('Legenda est autem hec scriptura pie, et religiose intelligenda').[2] With this we leave the physical aspect of reading for the intellectual or inwardly meditational.

MENTAL READING

With this title I imply a parallel to 'mental arithmetic', in this case reading with the mind's eye in the absence of any material written text. What this involves can be illustrated with two examples, one secular and the

---

[1] Curschmann, *PBB* 106 (1984), 246, 248.
[2] *Licht*, p. 18, 6f. (I prefer to read 'vernemen' as 'understand' instead of the nondescript 'aufnehmen' suggested by Ortmann 'Buch', p. 176); *Revelationes* 436, 12–18.

other religious, but showing women practising or recommended to practise this kind of reading. The secular example concerns episodes from two versions of *Tristan* where the protagonist in dangerous circumstances has to conceal his identity and adopt a pseudonym.[3] With Heinrich von Freiberg Tristan returns to Marke's court despite his banishment, calling himself *Peilnetosi* and muttering the word *Tosi* to himself.[4] It is of course Isold who decodes both these words, but what interests us is the way in which she does this, described in detail. Both words she reads backwards ('den namen widersinnes las' and 'sie greif aber an daz ort/des wortes unde las hin wider') and discovers that the pseudonym means *Isotenliep* 'dear to Isold' and the muttered word her own name. Isold's ability in decoding is twice explicitly attributed to her reading, hence to her educated status (she is described as 'kluoc', gifted with 'wîsheit', and Gottfried, whose version Heinrich continues, had amply described Isold's literate education). What is also clear is that there is no physical text for her to read, she reads with her mind's eye ('in irem herzen') and her reading is completely internalised. But Tristan's pseudonym is not as foolproof as he would like, since it is also decoded by an enemy of the lovers at court (it takes either love or hatred to unlock the door to interpretation).[5] Described more briefly, Pfelerin goes to work in the same way, reading the pseudonym backwards ('den namen er widersinnes las') and reading the truth out of it ('er gelas Isotenliep'). Although we are not told, he must have done this mentally like Isold, without any actual writing before him, and is enabled to do this because like her he is educated ('Pfelerîn gelêret was'). In both cases this mental reading is based on a literate person's awareness of individual letters behind a voiced sound and the possibility of arranging them anew to produce another sense.

This last point is confirmed by Gottfried's comparable scene when Tristan, in danger of his identity being discovered at the Irish court, disguises himself, albeit more simply, with the pseudonym *Tantris*.[6] Again it is Isold, inwardly attracted by and preoccupied with him, who muses on his name. She knows that her uncle had been killed by a certain Tristan and is struck by the similarity of the two names ('si lûtent nâhe ein ander bî'). She follows this up in a way possible only for the literate we already know her to be by mentally juggling with the letters ('buochstabe') and syllables ('sillaben') that make up these names, reading them now one way to produce one name ('vür sich sô las si Tristan'), now another way to

[3] Green, *Listening*, p. 133.   [4] Heinrich, *Tristan* 5326–40, 5360–70.
[5] *Ibid.* 5539–43.   [6] Gottfried, *Tristan* 10100–26.

give the other ('her wider sô las si Tantris').[7] In all this Isold is speaking
to herself ('sprach si wider sich'), we follow the thought processes of her
mental reading, made possible only by her literate education, but rising
here above any dependence on a written text. Common to these examples
from the Tristan story is their threefold stress on the fact of literacy, the act
of reading, and the inwardness of that process.

My second example, different by theme and implications, but likewise
involving reading without an actual written text, comes from devotional
literature in the late Middle Ages, in which meditation takes the form of
imagining Christ's body at the Passion as a book to be read by the devout
beholder, even if uneducated and unable to read in the literal sense.[8] In this
devotional and mystical literature, especially popular with women, Christ's
crucified body is seen as a book to be read by those who have acquired
the grammar and syntax not of school-based literacy, but of this type of
meditation. This is where mental, imagined reading of this devotional
kind differs from the *Tristan* examples: it suggests that 'reading' Christ's
body in this way can replace the reading of actual books. Huot talks of
'pious meditation as a process of reading books accessed within the self'. In
Prickynge of Love book-knowledge is dispensed with in favour of affective
wisdom ('This is my boke and my clergie my studie'), which opens the door
for illiterate believers, including religious women of little or no Latinity.
This re-ordering of priorities is made explicit in the Carthusian *Speculum
Devotorum*: 'The ofte thynkynge of my passyon makyth an vnlernyde man
a ful lernyd man; and vnwyse men and ydyotys hyt makyth to profyte
into mastyrs not of the sciens that bloweth a man wythinne but of charyte
that edifyeth'.[9] How far this reading of the image of Christ's Passion by
the unlearned corresponds to the view of Gregory the Great that pictures
could serve as books for the *illitterati* we shall see in the next section, on
reading pictures.

We do not lack for details of the way in which this meditational reading
of Christ's body was practised. For Johannes Milicius Christ is the 'liber
mandatorum dei', while for Petrus de Palude the cross itself is, as it were,
a book in which we are to read our salvation ('tamquam in libro'). In his
Meditations Richard Rolle is rather more informative about reading in this
way: 'þy body is lyke a boke written al with rede ynke . . . Now, swete
Jhesu, graunt me to rede upon þy boke, and somewhat to undrestond þe

---

[7] This detail undermines the categorical statement of Illich, *Vineyard*, p. 67, that in the Middle Ages
there was no way of analysing the vernacular in syllables or words.
[8] Gillespie, 'Images', p. 111. Cf. Huot, 'Reading', pp. 207–9 (and Fig. 1).
[9] Huot, 'Reading', p. 206; Gillespie, 'Images', pp. 111f.

swetnes of þat writynge, and to have likynge in studious abydynge of þat redynge'.[10] Elsewhere, the nailing of Christ is seen as a writing, his skin a piece of vellum, while the wounds of Christ are likened to the vowels and consonants of the book. In less detailed terms William Melton sees the Passion at large as 'a bok of scripture and wrytyng'. Julian of Norwich can even describe her growing ability to read the book in this way in terms of a child learning his ABC, so that actual literacy is the point of comparison for her mental, devotional literacy. In *Book to a Mother*, the believer's love of Christ can even dispense with reading altogether, while still claiming 'literacy' for itself: 'for who loveþ best God, can best Holi Writ . . . but Crist, Godis Sone, he is uerreiliche Holi Writ, and who þat louiþ him best is best clerk'.[11]

One adaptation of reading Christ's body is known in late-medieval England as the Charter of Christ. It is based on the metaphor of a legal document in which the promise of salvation held out by Christ's suffering body is seen to be written on the parchment of that body. Comparisons are made of Christ's skin with parchment, the wounds with letters, the blood with sealing-wax. It is the task of the devout to read the letters of this book ('How mony lettres þeron beon,/Red, and þou miht wite and seon').[12]

The metaphorical reading possible with Christ's body was also applied by Philip of Clairvaux to Elisabeth of Spalbeck, a beguine with miraculous stigmata, the five wounds of Christ. Philip argues that such stigmata were not confined to the male sex (Francis of Assisi), but were also granted to women. The divine purpose behind this was that the illiterate and simple, denied access to books, could instead read in the limbs and body of Elisabeth as though they were reading parchments or documents, as though they were literate.[13] Here again, actual literacy is replaced by metaphorical reading.

The two types of example we have been considering (reading Tristan's pseudonym and reading Christ's body) have this much in common: in each we face reading with the mind's eye, without a written text. But they also differ essentially: in the *Tristan* examples we are still dealing with letters and syllables (even if not written), the mental readers are in fact literate, whereas the religious examples pass beyond this dependence on writing in using textual imagery (they address those who read *as if* they were literate). In other words, these latter cases stand at a greater distance from actual

[10] Milicius and Palude: Schreiner, *AGB* 11 (1970), 1450, 1448. Rolle: Gillespie, 'Lectio', p. 11.
[11] Nailing: Gillespie, 'Images', p. 126. Melton and Julian: *ibid.*, pp. 141f. *Book to a Mother*: Gillespie, 'Lectio', p. 11.
[12] Rubin, *Corpus*, pp. 306–8.   [13] Simons, 'Reading', pp. 11–13; *Cities*, p. 130.

writing and suggest an even greater degree of internalisation. With that we pass now to other ways in which inwardness of reading could be suggested.

Metaphorical reading of this kind is attested already with Paul, who compares the Christian community in Corinth with an epistle of Christ written not with ink, but in the heart and to be known and read by all men.[14] Such a comparison belongs to the widespread symbolism of the book,[15] in particular to the argument that there are two kinds of book, a literal one available to *litterati*, but also a symbolic one which illiterate laymen can read metaphorically. Berthold von Regensburg parallels the clerics' two books (Old and New Testament) with two books for laymen, heaven and earth ('Wan ir leien niht lesen kunnet als wir pfaffen, sô hât iu got ouch zwei grôziu buoch geben ... Daz eine ist der himel, daz ander diu erde' You laymen cannot read like us clerics, so that God has given you two great books: one is heaven, the other earth). Nikolaus von Cues draws the same conventional parallel in the fifteenth century, but with an edge to it similar to what we have already seen, namely that the laymen, uncluttered by scholastic bookishness, may even draw nearer to wisdom.[16]

This contrast between two kinds of book finds expression in the frequent references to inner eyes (or eyes of the soul, of the heart) as distinct from outer eyes, although it must be stressed that those who read books with their outer eyes were also expected, ideally, to read 'inwardly'. Augustine knew of the inner eyes ('oculi interiores'), the eyes of the soul ('oculi animae') and the eyes of the heart ('oculi cordis').[17] The two kinds of seeing which these terms presuppose are well-known in the twelfth century,[18] as for example with Rupert von Deutz who saw the Son of God not with his physical sight, for he closed these eyes of the body in order to see more clearly with his inner eyes.[19] This internalised vision is best at home in women's visionary or mystical literature, whether or not the further implication is made that literal reading can actually be dispensed with or put into second place. Hildegard von Bingen, for example, maintains that she was commanded by God to write what she saw in a vision with her inner eyes and that she did not receive her visions through any of her five physical senses.[20] Mechthild von Magdeburg may refer to two of these senses, sight and hearing, but takes care to internalise them: 'Ich enkan noch mag nit schriben, ich sehe es mit den ôgen miner sele und hôre es mit den oren mines ewigen geistes' (I cannot and know not how to write unless I see it with the eyes of my soul

---

[14] II Cor. 3, 2f.   [15] Curtius, *Literatur*, pp. 304–51.
[16] Berthold II 233. Nikolaus: Schreiner, *ZHF* II (1984), 268.
[17] Bumke, *Blutstropfen*, p. 16.   [18] *Ibid.*, pp. 40f.   [19] Langer, *Mystik*, p. 178.
[20] In her first letter to Guibert of Gembloux: Dronke, *Women*, p. 252.

and hear it with the ears of my eternal spirit). She stresses this elsewhere, saying that she beheld the heavenly vision with the eyes of her soul ('Do sach ich mit miner selen ŏgen') and that the loving soul has an eye that is illumined by God, who enables it to see ('Die minnende sele . . . hat ein ŏge, das hat got erlúhtet. Da mit sihet si in die ewige gotheit').[21]

That this inward vision was by no means confined to religious literature, even though it may have derived from it, but could also occur in secular court literature, especially with regard to the imaginative, at times even trance-like, longing of a lover for his absent beloved has been shown by Bumke. He reminds us of Heinrich von Morungen's vision of his lady through his inner eyes ('swen ich eine bin, si schînt mir vor den ougen' whenever I am alone she appears to me before my eyes), but more particularly he deals with Parzival's vision of his wife Condwiramurs in the scene of the three drops of blood in the snow. Of this vision he says that Parzival sees these drops of blood with his physical eyes, but that what he beholds can only be seen with his inner eyes in what amounts to a secular love vision.[22]

This internalisation of vision confirms what we touched upon earlier, namely the suggestion that reading in the external sense of decoding written signs had ideally to be supplemented by the mental process of understanding. *Legere* had to be accompanied by *intelligere*. This finds expression when Calogrenant addresses his audience in *Yvain*, thereby standing in for Chrétien before his audience (including readers), and recommends them to register what he says not just with their ears but also with their heart. Hartmann does the same.[23] So much was this double process to be aimed at that William Wykeham, following Cato's *Monostichs*, could claim that to read without understanding is to neglect or not to read at all ('legere et non intellegere necgligere est'). For Bonaventura the two aspects, visual and mental, belong intrinsically together ('Lege ergo me . . . et lectum intellige'), as they did much earlier for Dhuoda in writing her manual for her son ('Haec verba a me tibi directa lege, intellige'). At a later point Dhuoda goes even further in internalising her son's reading. He is first to read ('ore lege'), so far externally that he reads aloud, with his lips, but then he is to hold what he reads forever in his heart ('et corde retine semper').[24]

With these examples we have passed from inner vision to inner reading, to a reading that goes beyond the decoding of letters. How close these

---

[21] Mechthild, *Licht* IV 13 (p. 266), IV 2 (p. 230), VI 31 (p. 492).
[22] Bumke, *Blutstropfen*, pp. 29–34. On Parzival: pp. 3, 50.   [23] *Yvain* 150–70, *Iwein* 251–6.
[24] Wykeham: Zieman, 'Reading', p. 103. Bonaventura: Gillespie, '*Lectio*', p. 11. Dhuoda, *Liber*, pp. 70, 148.

are to each other has been suggested by Bumke's remark that the drops of blood in the snow are a sign which Parzival correctly reads, moreover a sign that the audience, as we shall see, are also intended to read correctly.[25] The reading of signs, where no actual writing may be involved and where the reader is to pass from an external indicator to the concealed meaning, is no stranger to medieval literature, from which only a few examples can be given. In Herbort von Fritzlar's *Liet von Troye* a ring is correctly read as a token of kinship ('Daz er sin naher mag was /An sime vinger er do las/Vnd zalte vil rechte/Ir beider geslechte' He then read from his ring that he was his close relative and reckoned correctly their kinship). In Wolfram's *Parzival* the heathen Flegetanis reads the name of the Grail in the stars ('Flegetânis der heiden sach,/dâ von er blûweclîchen sprach,/ime gestirne mit sînen ougen/ . . . des namen las er sunder twâl/inme gestirne, wie der hiez' Flegetanis saw with his own eyes things in the stars he was shy to talk about . . . whose name he read in the constellation). The heathen may read with his physical eyes, but what (and how) he reads is cloaked in mystery and there is no express mention that he reads letters in the sky, rather than the stars themselves.[26] (If literacy in the external sense comes into play at all in this description of sources it is rather with Kyot, who has to learn the ABC to decipher the Arabic text he found in Toledo.) Dreams, too, can be read in this transferred sense, as when Chaucer in *The Book of the Duchess* maintains that not even Macrobius, the editor of the *Somnium Scipionis*, would be able to read his dream correctly ('Ne nat skarsly Macrobeus,/ . . . I trowe, arede my dremes even'). The idea that a human face can be read occurs with Alanus ab Insulis in the form that a person's features are like a book from which his thoughts can be read, with Henricus Septimellensis, for whom the face is a book and a page conveying the inner state of mind ('Internique status liber est et pagina vultus') or with Guibert of Nogent's suggestion that one can read in oneself as if in a book ('intra se ipsum quasi in libro scriptum attendat'), where 'quasi' captures the figurative usage here.[27] In court literature Chaucer's Troilus, for the first time in bed with Criseyde, hesitantly seeks to sustain himself by reading her expression ('Though ther be mercy writen in youre cheere,/God woot the text ful hard is, sooth, to fynde'). The same image also occurs in Chaucer's *Parliament of Fowls* ('It stondeth writen in thy face').[28]

[25] Bumke, *Blutstropfen*, pp. 54, 59.
[26] Herbort, *Liet* 5937–40. *Parzival* 454, 17–23 (here I differ from Draesner, *Wege*, p. 396).
[27] Chaucer, *Book* 284–9. Alanus, Henricus and Guibert: Curtius, *Literatur*, pp. 318 and 320.
[28] *Troilus* III 1342f. (as a parallel to Chaucer's use of 'fynde' for reading, cf. 'vinden' in German: Scholz, *Hören*, pp. 115f. and Green, *Listening*, pp. 119f.). *Parliament* 155.

From this usage, particularly from an example like that of Guibert of Nogent, it is but a short step to the idea of reading one's own conscience as if it were a book, an image owing much to the biblical Book of Life in which men's offences are divinely recorded. With the book of conscience it is the individual himself who, even if illiterate, has 'written' his offences into it and is to be confronted with them by 'reading' them. Two English devotional texts stress the figurative sense of writing and reading in this way by saying that the text is accessible even to the illiterate, the 'lewd'. *The Treatise of Ghostly Battle* sees this book opened at the Day of Judgment ('Then shullen all wicked men se þe iust cause of hir dampnacioun written with her owene hands in þe boke of her owen conscience which boke boþe lettered and lewd shullen rede'). The author of *The Three Arrows of Doomsday* argues similarly, adding: 'And yef þou seie þat lewede men kunne not reede, i. seye þat þeer is noon so lewede þat he ne kan reede þe lettre of hyr owene writynge'.[29] The book of conscience can also be seen as a book of the heart ('liber conscientie scriptus in corde'). A florilegium makes this clear ('In libro cordis lege quicquid habes ibi sordis;/Non legis hoc alibi tam bene sicut ibi') and for Herbert of Bosham one reads and knows from one's heart more than from a book ('jam primus in te legis quod nosti in tuo corde quam in codice').[30] In cases like these reading is both figurative and entirely inward, thereby cutting across the difference between *litterati* and *illitterati*.

From this section three conclusions may be drawn. The first is that our examples all point to an unmistakable internalisation of reading (in mind, heart, conscience). If this was already true to some extent with our first example, with Heinrich von Freiberg's Isold who read internally ('in irem herzen'), this has to be qualified to the extent that Gottfried's figure, although she too addresses only herself, still voices orally the names she compares ('Nu sî die namen begunde/ze trîbenne in dem munde' As she began to try out the names on her tongue).[31] Only with the following figurative examples, largely meditational (as with reading Christ's body), could reading be entirely silent, because there were no words to be read out loud. Secondly, the mental process of understanding emerges as essential to the act of reading, but to this must be added the fact that internalised reading can often be seen as more important or more enriching than reading focused on book learning. This is a an order of priorities of particular interest for

[29] *Treatise* and *Arrows*: Gillespie, 'Lectio', p. 8.
[30] *Liber conscientie*: Bumke, *Blutstropfen*, p. 138, fn. 87. Florilegium: Curtius, *Literatur*, p. 321. Herbert: Bumke, *Blutstropfen*, pp. 137f.
[31] 10113f.

us, since it reinforces what we saw in respect of religious women's reading by comparison with learned clerics. Finally, internalised reading, conceived figuratively as dispensing with letters and the education that grants access to them, opened an opportunity for *illitterati* in religious matters, for laymen at large and, in our specific case, for educationally disadvantaged women in particular.

READING PICTURES

In this section women will be mentioned only occasionally, but will appear as much more relevant when we later consider aspects of their devotional reading, combining text and image in the act of meditation, in illustrated Psalters and Books of Hours.

Camille, an art historian who has worked on the visual implications of medieval literacy,[32] speaks of a visual literacy, which raises for us the question how far 'reading pictures' belongs to this chapter and differs from literal reading. We shall see that reading pictures was to some extent metaphorical, that it did not cover reading alone, but reading combined with beholding, and that the visual activity involved was of another order, passing beyond the written text alone. Literal reading may not always even come into play, but where it does it may not be by the viewer, but by someone else, so that we have to ask who reads and who views.

The authority to whose dictum on reading pictures most frequent references were made throughout the Middle Ages and who has dominated modern scholarly discussion is Gregory the Great. He addressed two letters to Serenus, the iconoclastic bishop of Marseilles, telling him not to strip the walls of churches of their paintings and arguing that there is a difference between worshipping a picture and learning from a picture what is to be worshipped. More specifically Gregory adds that what writing presents to readers is conveyed to the uneducated (*idiote*) when they look at a picture, so that the ignorant (*ignorantes*) see in a picture what they ought to follow. In it those who do not know letters read ('in ipsa legunt qui litteras nesciunt'), so that the picture acts in place of reading matter ('pro lectione pictura est').[33] In Gregory's eyes looking at a picture is for the layman what reading is for the cleric, looking is a form of reading. Behind this view, however, there stands the clerical bipolarity regarding literacy: only clerics were

---

[32] Camille, *AH* 8 (1985), 34.
[33] Duggan, *WI* 3 (1989), 227–51; Chazelle, *WI* 6 (1990), 138–53; Curschmann, '*Pictura*', pp. 211–29. Letters to Serenus: Gregory, *Registrum* IX 209 and XI 10 (quotations from the latter).

literate, so that laymen, by definition illiterate, were restricted to 'reading' pictures.

Just as the traditional clerical view confined the layman to illiteracy, so too did the Gregorian view of the layman as a reader of pictures become the standard clerical view, constantly repeated and even incorporated into canon law.[34] This view was repeated, for example, by authors such as Bede (who takes care to insert the qualification 'as it were') and Walahfrid Strabo (for whom a picture is no more than a certain kind of writing: 'quaedam litteratura inlitterato'). Thomasin von Zerclaere is as apodictic as Gregory, distinguishing the cleric who reads from the layman who looks at pictures because he cannot read, but using the same verb 'sehen' for both activities. Matthew Paris translates a legend into French for those who are illiterate in the clerical sense (non-Latinate), but also equips it with pictures for laymen.[35] Further examples of this tradition include Hugh of Folieto and such leading thinkers as Bonaventura, Thomas Aquinas and Jean Gerson.[36] These make it clear that we are dealing not simply with a clerical view, but an authoritative one, as is confirmed not merely by canon law, but also by a ruling to the same effect by a synod of Arras.[37] Although these cases imply a similarity in reading, they also reveal a condescension towards the layman. His visual activity is, 'as it were', 'a certain kind of writing'; his reading is, at the most, metaphorical, not literate, and does not approach the level of reading by a *litteratus*. The Church presented its position to *illitterati* by means of pictures, whilst its myteries remained locked in writing inaccessible to them.[38] The layman's confinement to pictures echoed his exclusion from literacy; in both respects he was ultimately dependent on the clergy whose interpretative monopoly was meant to remain unchallenged.

We must ask, however, whether the Gregorian view can be regarded as adequate (not merely because two recent articles dealing with it phrase their titles as questions).[39] Curschmann seems somewhat impatient with those who focus their attention on whether Gregory was correct, and from his point of view that may be justified, but our question (how far did 'reading' pictures come into play and what kind of reading was involved?)

---

[34] Gillespie, 'Lectio', p. 10, fn. 32; Curschmann, 'Pictura', p. 214; Rushing, *Images*, p. 9.

[35] Bede (*Vita sanctorum abbatum*): Duggan, *WI* 3 (1989), 229f. Walahfrid (*De exordiis*): *ibid.*, p. 230. Thomasin (*Welscher Gast* 1103–6): Curschmann, 'Pictura', pp. 216f. Matthew Paris (*Estoire de Seint Aedward*): Camille, *AH* 8 (1985), 41f.; Curschmann, 'Pictura', p. 212.

[36] Hugh of Folieto (PL 177, 15f.): Carruthers, *Book*, pp. 241f. Bonaventura, Aquinas, Gerson: Duggan, *WI* 3 (1989), 232, 234.

[37] Fischer, *History*, p. 167.   [38] Hamburger, *Canticles*, p. 245, n. 54 (quoting Kessler).

[39] Duggan, *WI* 3 (1989), 227; Curschmann, 'Pictura', p. 211.

requires this focus. Here we are supported by Hamburger's observation that Gregory's view on reading pictures, predicated on a distinction between *litterati* and *illitterati*, as little applied to the later Middle Ages as did that distinction itself in this later period.[40]

If we are to consider what reading may be involved in laymen looking at pictures we do better to go back to Paulinus of Nola, who discusses a comparable situation, but more informatively for us. In describing a basilica Paulinus refers not to pictures (*picta*) alone, but also to *tituli* that indicate in writing what the pictures are about (implying that this might be difficult without such a text).[41] In the context of such writing Paulinus then adds that understanding the meaning of pictures could be a group activity which includes pointing out and reading out to each other ('ostendunt releguntque sibi'), the latter presumably for the benefit of the illiterate rustics imagined present.[42] This description undoes the bipolar simplicity of Gregory's remark, since it introduces two kinds of literal reading ('lego illi' and 'lego ab illo'), but places them in the context of a picture looked at by the *illitterati* as well as a text read by the *litteratus*. Against this background, word and picture belong together and work together for the rustics, however, only through the intermediacy of one who can read.

Although he wrote earlier than Gregory, Paulinus stands closer to medieval practice, where pictures of whatever kind are frequently equipped with explanatory *tituli*. These written additions can take various forms. They may simply provide the identifying name above the depiction of an otherwise not always identifiable person, as with Arthur in the Otranto mosaic or Iwein and other characters at Rodenegg. Sometimes the *tituli* go a little further and provide an abbreviated explanation of what is depicted, as in the Bayeux Tapestry. On occasions a figure can be provided with a banderole equipped with informative wording, as with the Berlin manuscript of Veldeke's *Eneasroman*. Finally, a picture can be accompanied by whole lines of explanatory text, as with the Wienhausen Tristan tapestry or the illumination of the French prose *Lancelot* (Paris BN fr. 112, III 193ᵛ).[43] In different ways and to a different extent these written additions make clear what would not otherwise be so readily intelligible.

[40] Hamburger, *Visual*, pp. 112f.
[41] On Paulinus see Arnulf, *Versus*, pp. 47–66, who writes on *tituli* from an art-historical standpoint.
[42] Paulinus (Carmen 27, 583–6): Duggan, *WI* 3 (1989), 229; Curschmann, '*Pictura*', pp. 214f.; Ott, 'Texte', p. 119.
[43] Otranto: Haug, 'Artussage', pp. 409–46. Rodenegg: Rushing, *Images*, pp. 30–90, and Schupp and Szklenar, *Ywain*. Bayeux Tapestry: Brilliant, *WI* 7 (1991), 98–126. *Eneasroman*: Henkel, 'Bildtexte', pp. 1–47. Wienhausen: Fouquet, *Wort*, pp. 125–38. French prose *Lancelot*: reproduced in Wenzel, *Hören*, plate IX (facing p. 145).

The desirability of such *tituli* was quite clear at the time. In the Wien-hausen tapestry scene I, 1 depicts Marke standing in front of Tristan, but the accompanying text tells us what Tristan says and Marke's reply, details that could only be conveyed by words. In Bertold von Holle's *Demantin* a guest asks about the subject of a painting and who is depicted, but is referred to what is written, identifying the persons shown ('daz moit ir lesin/iz is al gebrîvêret' you can read that, it is all given in writing). Manuscripts of Seuse's *Exemplar* contain drawings integral to the text, one depicting the mystical way of the soul, made up of fourteen miniatures accompanied by short explanatory texts without which they would be only partly or uncer-tainly intelligible. In *Floire et Blancheflor* the theme of paintings is accessible by means of writing ('Moult a apris de l'escripture/Qui puet savoir de la painture').[44]

More interesting than these isolated examples, because it explains why *tituli* are required, is what is said in the *Libri Carolini* by Theodulf of Orléans, convinced equally of the importance of religious paintings and of the need to clarify their meaning by words. He argues by quoting as an example a picture of a woman with a child on her lap and suggesting that without a *titulus* this could just as well be regarded as, say, Venus with Aeneas or Mary with Christ.[45] For him, therefore, the picture stands in need of writing which has to be read if the painting as to be 'read' or understood correctly. Two different senses of reading are therefore involved if misunderstanding is to be avoided. How necessary this is for modern scholarship, too, can be seen from a bronze mirror from Bussen depicting a couple in bed together, but with no inscription, and accordingly regarded as showing Tristan and Isold, or Aeneas and Dido, or even the Song of Songs.[46]

If for Theodulf the need to avoid idolatry made a *titulus* desirable, medieval examples, by contrast with the best-known classical one, also prefer explanatory words. With Virgil, when Aeneas on arrival at Carthage sees pictures on the walls of a temple he immediately recognises the past events at Troy as well as himself, even without any inscription to guide him. (This is not undermined by his later inability to understand the pic-tures on Vulcan's shield, for these illustrate what lies in a future unknown to him.)[47] Virgil's example is in marked contrast with the prose *Lancelot* where

---

[44] Wienhausen: Fouquet, *Wort*, pp. 129, 132. *Demantin* 7129–39 (I am grateful to Horst Wenzel for drawing my attention to this). Seuse: Ruh, *Geschichte* III 465 and Hamburger, *Visual*, pp. 200f. *Floire* 1657–60: Wenzel, *Hören*, p. 304.

[45] PL 98, 1230. Cf. Bäuml, 'Autorität', pp. 155f.   [46] Rushing, *Images*, p. 107.

[47] *Aeneid* I 456–8, VIII 729–31; Wandhoff, *Poetica* 28 (1996), 66, 85.

the protagonist from his prison window sees a painter decorating the outer walls with scenes which he is able to recognise as Aeneas fleeing from Troy. Lancelot can do this because each scene includes writing ('off eim yglichen bild ein buchstaben') and because he himself is presented as literate.[48] Seeing these paintings outside prompts Lancelot to while away his captive hours and to recall his time with Guinevere. He obtains material from the painter and himself covers the inside walls of his room with scenes from the lovers' past to which verbal captions are likewise added ('die buchstaben . . . die da bezeichent die gescheffniß von den bilden'). This conjunction of text with pictures has disastrous consequences when Arthur later gains entry into the prison, sees the paintings and, as literate as Lancelot, understands what they mean from their captions ('ist diß bedútniß war von dißer schrifft, so hatt mich Lanczlot geschant mit der konigin' If what this writing says is true, Lancelot has dishonoured me with the queen).[49] At each stage in this prolonged sequence (outside painting – Lancelot reads it – Lancelot's painting – Arthur reads it) writing is expressly involved (by contrast with Virgil) and makes understanding the paintings at all possible.

Nor does the prose *Lancelot* stand alone in this conjunction of word with picture. In his *Crône* Heinrich von dem Türlin describes a golden bowl, carved and inscribed, whose writing Gawein at first fails to understand, but he manages to read his own name on one figure and thereby recognise himself ('Daz er sînen namen las'). Der Stricker's *Daniel* includes an exotic land with works of similarly fashioned workmanship (' . . . daran ergraben,/getiutet mit den buochstaben' carved on it, with the meaning made clear by letters).[50] To these may be added two examples from Chaucer. In the *House of Fame* the dreamer, like Aeneas at Carthage, comes across a temple whose wall depicts a narrative account, variously described as carved and painted, of Aeneas's flight after the fall of Troy. Unlike the Roman hero, however, the medieval dreamer, placed in a comparable position, is able to decipher what he sees because of the presence of an inscription ('I fond that on a wall ther was/Thus writen on a table of bras') which even bears the opening words of Virgil's epic. Throughout the following lengthy description we are told what the dreamer saw ('saugh'), but this verb refers both to the pictures and to the text, since in the Middle Ages the verb 'to see' could also denote the act of reading. In the *Book of the Duchess* the story of Troy is again depicted, this time in stained glass windows, but what concerns us

[48] IV 46, 14. Lancelot's literacy: see above, p. 5.
[49] III 465, 10 and 466, 2–4 (Kluge edition).
[50] *Crône* 8936–49: Wandhoff, *Poetica* 28 (1996), 81f.; Reuvekamp-Felber, *Volkssprache*, p. 276. *Daniel* 631f.

is rather the depiction of the *Romance of the Rose* in paintings on the wall, for they are combined with an explanatory text ('And alle the walles with colours fyne/Were peynted, bothe text and glose,/Of al the Romaunce of the Rose').[51]

The conjunction of images with *tituli* in such examples illustrates that the reading mentioned by Paulinus (*relegere*) can be taken in the literal sense. Gregory, however, was probably less concerned with how reading actually took place than with drawing a firm line between laymen and clerics, so that with him it cannot be said whether he meant reading pictures metaphorically or like Paulinus literally, but without making this clear.

For us Paulinus is more informative in that his description implies both a viewer (of the *picta*) and a reader (of the *tituli*). In the case of a *litteratus* these two can be one and the same person, for the viewer can also read. This has been worked out in detail for the women recipients of the *Rothschild Canticles*, specifically in the way in which text and image are tied to each other by preventing the text from spilling over into what follows. From this Hamburger has concluded that the 'texts and the miniatures form complementary series of verbal and visual *materia meditandi*' and that we cannot therefore speak of either a reader or a viewer, but only of a conflation of the two. He therefore speaks of a 'reader/viewer', a composite entity which recurs in German scholarship when, again with regard to the prose *Lancelot*, von Merveldt speaks not simply of a reader and viewer, but more tellingly of a viewing reader and a reading beholder ('den schauenden Leser and lesenden Betrachter').[52]

In the case of an *illitteratus*, however, the viewer is not also a reader, so that if he is to understand what he sees he is dependent on a literate intermediary to explain the *tituli*, and therefore the picture, to him, a situation already adumbrated by Paulinus. It may also be implicit in Gregory's statement if we follow Chazelle's interpretation of the *illitterati* gathering knowledge from the paintings ('scientiam historiae colligere') as possibly suggesting someone explaining to them basic points about the pictures while they viewed them.[53] In the light of this Camille has drawn attention to the careful alignment between text and picture, similar to that in the *Rothschild Canticles*, in the *Life of St Edward* for Henry III's queen Eleanor, suggesting that the owner might have wanted to look at the drawings while the text was read aloud to her.[54] That presupposes, however, that Eleanor, unlike the

---

[51] *House of Fame* 141–44; *Book of the Duchess* 332f. On verbs of seeing meaning 'to read' see above, pp. 8f.
[52] Hamburger, *Canticles*, pp. 9, 25, 42, 162; von Merveldt, *Translatio*, pp. 337, 340.
[53] *WI* 6 (1990), 141.　　　[54] *AH* 8 (1985), 42.

women for whom the *Canticles* were meant, was unable or unwilling to read herself. Less doubt attaches to the *tituli* accompanying the various scenes of the Bayeux Tapestry. Although some of the themes depicted may have been comprehensible by themselves, others were less accessible, requiring explanation of what was written for the benefit of those who could not read.[55]

From this brief survey of a complex problem three conclusions are to be drawn. The first concerns the concept of visual literacy used by Camille with which we began this section. It is necessary to distinguish between the *litteratus* and the *illitteratus* in its application. The former could behold a picture, read a *titulus* and thus acquire full understanding. The latter, however, could only look at the picture, sometimes possibly understanding or 'reading' it, but sometimes failing to do so. For the *illitteratus* to 'read' the picture he needed the help of a literate interlocutor, explaining the written words and enabling him to read indirectly. With that we return to Hugh of St Victor's invaluable distinction between 'lego ab illo' and 'lego illi', but now no longer restricted to written words alone.

The second conclusion, the correspondence between recourse to pictures and the use of the vernacular for the benefit of the uneducated layman, follows from this. The Gregorian view that the layman was restricted to reading pictures reinforces the traditional clerical monopoly of literacy and learning and hence the authority which this conferred.[56] It is significant that Thomasin von Zerclaere's view of the function of pictures (for rustics, children, the uneducated) as opposed to writing (for clerics) is placed in the same context as his concession that vernacular literature (he has the romance in mind) has a certain educational value for the young.[57] The two positions in which, from the cleric's point of view, the illiterate layman was felt to be disadvantaged are seen as closely connected. The same has been suggested for the St Albans Psalter in which text and image are brought together for the recluse Christina of Markyate and which also contains the Gregorian passage in defence of images, but in this context possibly as a justification of the vernacular Alexis poem which the Psalter also contains.[58]

Mention of Christina brings us to a third conclusion, concerning the position of women in this reading of pictures. It is an accidental fact of no central importance that Arthur's reading of Lancelot's picture-cycle is assisted by his sister Morgane acting as a witness to the fact that Lancelot was indeed the painter. However, women come more to the fore when we

[55] Brilliant, *WI* 7 (1991), 102, 108f.
[56] Rushing, *Images*, pp. 10f.   [57] *Welscher Gast* 1026–96 and 1097–1106.
[58] Clanchy, *Memory*, p. 191; Camille, 'Iconoclasm', pp. 372f., 390; Rushing, *Images*, p. 11.

later consider their activity in nunneries as both scribes and illuminators or in embroidery with *tituli* as well as pictures, as in the Bayeux Tapestry or the Tristan tapestry from the convent Wienhausen. (In this context it pays to consider Wenzel's observation that MHG 'schrîben' (to write) could also be used for the act of painting, 'mâlen'.)[59] Of greater relevance, even if it may reflect the medieval clergy's misogynous view of women's lack of education or intelligence, is Matthew Paris's combination of vernacular and illustrations in adapting Latin hagiography for a circle of aristocratic women. If the clergy looked down condescendingly on the intellectual shortcomings of the laity (illiterate, confined to the vernacular, dependent on pictures) their attitude towards women would doubly disqualify them. Finally, women as readers and as viewers are even more important when we consider them specifically as religious women. Mention has been made only of Christina of Markyate's Psalter with its combination of text and images, but the field is much wider than this isolated example. Hamburger has studied the *Rothschild Canticles*, meant for women reader/viewers, in depth from this point of view and has written another work on devotional texts, again largely, if not exclusively meant for women, with an interplay between reading, the visual and the visionary.[60] In the late Middle Ages it was above all Books of Hours, to a large extent the spiritual reading of women, in which looking meditatively at images was seen as a form of spiritual reading which, like the literal reading it could accompany, led the way to prayer. In all these respects women had a prominent part to play.

READING AND MEMORY

In this section, too, women are expressly referred to only rarely but, to the extent that reading in general is presented as both 'memorised' and 'memorial', they are involved as readers just as much as men.

The Middle Ages have been described as an oral culture, but also as a memorial culture,[61] and in view of the obvious dependence of an oral, non-literate society on memory, these two descriptions might seem easily reconcilable. However, the matter is not quite so simple. On the one hand, the Middle Ages had a strong written tradition (Latin, then vernacular) so that we do better to regard it as a bimedial society characterised by a shifting relationship between oral and written.[62] On the other hand, from the value

---

[59] Wienhausen: Fouquet, *Wort*, p. 133; Wenzel, *Hören*, pp. 292–6.   [60] Hamburger, *Visual*.
[61] Oral: Vollrath, *HZ* 233 (1981), 571–94. Memorial: Oexle, 'Memoria', pp. 297–323.
[62] Green, 'Mittelalter', pp. 333–37.

placed on memory by an oral society the converse does not necessarily follow, namely that a literate society could find no home for memory and would allow it to fall into disuse. If this is so, then the Middle Ages should be seen as displaying a memorial alongside a bookish culture, sometimes in conjunction in the same person or work.

That memory also had a role to play in writing (and hence in reading) can be seen from a linguistic construction like 'commit something to memory'. In our literate society that would imply memorisation, learning by heart, as it could in the Middle Ages. Alongside that, however, committing to memory also meant preserving for the future by writing. Einhard uses the phrase in this sense of a written collection ordered by Charles the Great for posterity ('scripsit memoriaeque mandavit'); Notker translates Boethius's 'mandavi stilo memorieque' (where 'stilus' is revealing) more pointedly as writing ('ih habo . . . gescriben'); Marie de France writes her *Espurgatoire* in the vernacular for the benefit of laypeople and sees her writing as committing to memory ('Jo, Marie, ai mis en memoire').[63]

From these examples it is clear that *memoria* had two meanings: first, the faculty of memory (we shall not be concerned with the *art* of memory studied by Yates)[64] and, secondly, the tangible form in which memory was preserved, such as a record, document or writing. Accordingly, in what follows we shall consider briefly memory in connection with orality and then with writing before turning to the relationship between memory and reading.

We have learnt to distrust the universalist claims of the oral-formulaic school and to recognise that, in addition to its thesis of composition-in-performance, oral delivery could rest on prior (oral) composition, memorised and recalled in subsequent performance. For these two types Coleman proposes the terms 'oral-formulaic' and 'oral-memorial'.[65] Both depend on memory, but in different ways. The oral-formulaic performer does not memorise his text, but instead retains a stock of conventional formulas in his memory on which he can call immediately, adjusting them slightly to the particular context. On the other hand, the oral-memorial performer delivers by heart what he has already composed mentally. However, in both cases memory is involved in a much wider sense, as is seen in the opening lines of heroic poems. The *Hildebrandslied* may start in the poet's first person ('Ik gihôrta ðat seggen' I heard that recounted), who sees himself as the latest exponent in a long line of memorial tradition before him. With

---

[63] Einhard, *Vita* 29 (pp. 33f.). Notker, *De consolatione* 34, 21. *Espurgatoire* 2297.
[64] Yates, *Art.*   [65] Finnegan, *Poetry*, pp. 52–87; Coleman, *Reading*, p. 35.

the *Annolied* ('Wir horten ie dikke singen' We have often heard sung) and
the *Nibelungenlied* ('Uns ist in alten maeren wunders vil geseit' Wondrous
deeds are told us in old stories) the first person plural brings the listeners
into play, they too belong to this memorial tradition and its values are
reaffirmed for them by recital. The conventional nature of oral tradition,
maintaining collective memory, means that the listeners' memory is acti-
vated, however differently, as well as the performer's, since it is their past
and their memory of it which are being celebrated. The themes treated are
already present in their memory (hence the opening use of the first person
plural) and the listener's memory can even go as far as King Alfred, by
dint of hearing them frequently recited, remembering vernacular poems by
heart.[66] At issue here is not simply the individual memory of the performer,
but also the collective memory of the tradition to which his listeners belong
as well.

There were, however, limits to what oral tradition could effectively
achieve. An obvious one was the fallibility of human memory, especially
resulting from its overloading, as was expressed in Augustine's comment
that memory was a faithless custodian ('infida custos') and rendered even
more of a danger by the explosion of writing (Latin and vernacular) in the
twelfth century.[67] But the deficiencies of oral tradition, even in its central
function of preserving historical memory for *illitterati*, were more readily
visible when viewed from a rival vantage point, the written Latin historiography of clerics. The point at which heroic oral tradition was frequently,
and most easily, subjected to criticism was its conflation of historical figures
living at different times into a single heroic age, so that Theoderic, Erma-
naric and Attila were all presented as contemporaries. The chronicler Frutolf
von Michelsberg, aware of Jordanes's history of the Goths, knows that this
is false and that heroic tradition presents unreliable history. In this criticism Frutolf was followed by the clerical author of the *Kaiserchronik* and by
another chronicler, Jacob Twinger von Königshofen.[68] Yet faulty chronology was only the occasion for criticism, the reason lies deeper, namely the
unreliability of oral transmission as opposed to the fixity of written record.
Frutolf makes a clear distinction between popular, but mistaken tradition
('vulgaris fabulatio') and his own written source (Jordanes is a 'grammati-
cus'). The author of the *Kaiserchronik* knows that he is on safe ground in
challenging those from whom he differs to produce written evidence, whilst
Jacob Twinger also distinguishes between what 'geburen' (in the sense of

[66] Asser, *Life*, ch. 22.
[67] Augustine: Stock, *Augustine*, pp. 131, 355, n. 87. Explosion: Hamesse, 'Modèle', pp. 131f.
[68] Green, *Listening*, pp. 243f.

illiterate *rustici*) recount and his own literate informant ('meister').[69] Literacy in various forms (clerical historiography, growth in literacy, explosion of written texts) exerts pressure towards conveying *memoria* (historical or not) in writing.

With that we reach the second stage in our argument. Writing provided another means of information storage with many advantages over fallible memory, but for long it was regarded as little more than a memory-aid, an adjunct to the needs of memory. This view of a still non-autonomous function of writing is voiced by Isidore of Seville saying that writing was invented as a storage of memory ('Vsus litterarum repertus propter memoriam'), thereby implying a distrust of the reliability of memory alone, even though it may be granted a primacy over writing.[70] For Wace in the twelfth century writing still performs this memorial function: at the start of his *Roman de Rou* he argues that writing and books, recited at feasts, preserve the memory of ancestors ('Pur remembrer des ancesurs . . .') and rescue them from oblivion. Marie de France puts her vernacular *Espurgatoire* into writing as a means of safeguarding memory ('Vueil en Romanz metre/ . . . en remembrance e en memoire').[71] This secondary role of writing can even reach the point where it functions as no more than a prompt to recall what is already stored in the memory and known by heart, as was often the case with written prayer texts.[72] Devotions based on books could therefore involve not reading proper, but memorised reading where headings or opening words triggered the memory of what was already known.

Seen in this light, memory could be as good as books, especially for illiterate laymen with no direct access to writing. This comparison is made directly in the case of Baldwin VIII of Flanders, who is said to have known the *Consolatio* of Boethius (and several other authors) almost by heart ('quasi corde tenus sciebat'), presumably by having heard frequent readings. For this *illitteratus* memory took the place of books: 'ut memoria pro codicibus sepius videbatur'.[73] A similar act of memorising, instead of reading, is reported by Asser of King Alfred who, at a time when he could not yet read, learned the content of a book by hearing his teacher read it to him, so that he was himself able to recite it. The verb used of Alfred here, *legere*, would be used in the sense 'to learn', but another reading would mean that the teacher read aloud to him ('lego illi'), so that Alfred read only indirectly. In either case, memorising replaces direct or literal reading by Alfred.[74]

[69] Frutolf, *Chronica*, p. 130. *Kaiserchronik* 14176–8. Jacob Twinger, *Chronik*, pp. 376f.
[70] *Etymologiae* I 3. [71] Wace, *Rou* 1–10. Marie, *Espurgatoire* 3–5.
[72] Cf. Boffey, 'Lyrics', p. 148. [73] Krüger, 'Krieger', p. 334 and fn. 48.
[74] Asser, *Life*, ch. 23; Keynes and Lapidge, *Alfred*, p. 239, n. 48.

Learning by rote has a bad name with us nowadays, implying a mechanical activity without true understanding, but that was not always the view of memorising what is written in the Middle Ages. Rote-learning could even be seen as the opposite of something external or superficial, it could be regarded as an absorption or assimilation into one's own self. To know something by heart is to incorporate it into one's inner being, so that, like a cow chewing the cud ('ruminare'), what is absorbed has to be inwardly digested. Accordingly, Hugh of St Victor can speak of the stomach of memory ('venter memoriae'), from which items are recalled to the tongue ('palatum') if they are not to perish. Learning by heart allowed such constant recall or 'ruminatio' and was seen as a means to devotional meditation.[75]

In turning now to memory and reading we have to recognise that the slow transition from orality to writing in the Middle Ages means that the full advantages of the latter were not always recognised, that reading was not readily seen as autonomous and that, like its counterpart writing, it could serve as no more than a possible alternative to memory. As in antiquity, reading and memorising were taught together as if they were one activity, which is perhaps one reason why remembering can be seen as an act of reading and the memory as a wax tablet or book.[76] Of the admittedly exceptional case of Thomas Aquinas's memory it is said that knowledge increased in his soul as if page were added to page in the making of a book, and Thomas himself uses this image (what is held in the memory is metaphorically written on the mind). This image derives from Cicero and the *Rhetorica ad Herennium*: with both, memorising is compared with writing (letters, wax tablets, papyrus), but from this it follows that remembering can be equated with reading, as if turning over the pages of a book. As late as the fifteenth century Petrus Ravenna could claim that he read his lectures on canon law without a book. Even if he should at times have a book before him, this acted only as a cue to his memory, on which he relied more than on any written text.[77]

This suggestion that memory could continue to play a greater role than reading is confirmed by the frequency with which what was read was meant to be memorised. For long, before the explosion of written material, reading was for the 'memorization and oral performance of prayer in a familiar

---

[75] Hamburger, *Canticles*, p. 21a; Carruthers, *Book*, pp. 164f.; Hamesse, 'Modèle', p. 126. Hugh of St Victor, *Didascalicon* III 12 (PL 176, 773).

[76] Teaching: Carruthers, *Book*, p. 101. Wax-tablet: *ibid.*, pp. 3, 28f., 72, and Fischer, *History*, pp. 89, 188.

[77] Carruthers, *Book*, pp. 3, 28, 72, 109.

and intensively read corpus inherited from antiquity'.[78] In agreement with this it is frequently reported, especially in the case of individual women, that what was read by them was committed to memory (e.g. Rusticula of Arles, Gertrude of Nivelles, the Anglo-Saxon missionary abbess Leoba).[79] Although hagiographic exaggeration may be suspected (did Rusticula learn *all* the scriptures?) these reports must reflect something of contemporary practice, and if this memorising is sometimes said to rest on what was heard as well as read, it is the latter that concerns us here. That this combination of reading and memory had a long prehistory is clear from the case of Augustine who had read many things from the philosophers and committed them to memory, so that he was ready to compare them with what dualist heretics said.[80] Most frequently memorised from reading were the Psalms, especially since the Psalter was used for instruction in elementary reading, combined with learning by heart. Ida of Nivelles, escaping from an arranged marriage, took with her a Psalter which she had just started to memorise, and Thomas of Cantimpré reports of a girl sent to a *magistra* who taught the Psalter to daughters of rich people, so that she came to know the Psalter by heart. In a thirteenth-century *vita rhythmica* an equation is made between 'psalmos ruminare' (to recite by heart) and 'legere psalmum'.[81] In many such cases 'literacy' in Latin may have meant simply the ability to read the Psalter by memorising it, amounting neither to reading proper nor to an understanding of Latin.

The mention of Augustine and dualists brings us to a last respect in which memorised reading[82] served a very practical purpose, namely amongst heretics. Of Valdes it is reported that, knowing no Latin, he had books of the Bible translated for him into the vernacular, which he then frequently read and learned by heart ('sepe legerat et cordetenus firmaret'). It was these memorised gospels that he used as the basis of his preaching ('ea que corde retinuerat . . . predicando'). Amongst the Lollards in England the evidence for such heretics as 'walking books' is particularly informative, but also the practical utility of memorisation. Heretical books may well have been hidden, but memorised books were undetectable in an age of persecution. For reasons of safety the physical book was not just superfluous, but best avoided altogether.[83]

---

[78] Saenger, *Space*, p. 120.
[79] Schulenburg, *Forgetful*, pp. 97–100.   [80] Stock, *Augustine*, p. 54.
[81] Ida and Thomas: Simons, *Cities*, pp. 40, 84f. *Vita rhythmica*: Schreiner, *FMS* 24 (1990), 321.
[82] I distinguish between 'memorised reading' in the present sense and 'memorial reading', as discussed below with Gottfried and Wolfram.
[83] Valdes: Grundmann, *Bewegungen*, pp. 443, 446 and fns. 14, 15. Lollards: Aston, *Lollards*, p. 201; McSheffrey, 'Literacy', pp. 164f.; Krug, *Families*, p. 147.

In these last cases reading cannot be said to be entirely autonomous or free from serving memory. There are, however, surprisingly early cases where this position is reached, where memory is indeed subservient to an act of reading inwardly. However gradual the transition from orality to writing may have been, some of its effects were more immediate, especially with the romances, with their authors, but also potentially with readers whom it was hoped to introduce to these new possibilities of literacy. In a recent work von Merveldt has fruitfully discussed the role of *memoria* in the prose *Lancelot* in this light.[84] In this work demands are made on the reader's memory by a seemingly infinite regress of *entrelacements* which have to be linked with one another over long stretches of narrative. In what follows, however, I focus on Gottfried's *Tristan* and Wolfram's *Parzival*. In these works memory still has a part to play, but its functioning is now dependent on the written text and the role of the reader. Memorial work has to be done by the author, by characters in his work, but also by the reader.

The first word in Gottfried's work is the verb 'gedenken' 'to remember', introducing a *sententia* with which the author wards off 'oblivium' ('Gedaehte man ir ze guote niht,/von den der werlde guot geschiht . . .' If one failed to recall and think well of those who benefit the world).[85] Two possibilities are covered by this need to remember. Above all, those who have benefited the world and who therefore deserve to be remembered are the lovers Tristan and Isold by virtue of the model love they represent, a reading confirmed by the close of the prologue in which their life and death are commemorated in eucharistic terms.[86] Secondly, the memory of Gottfried himself, the transmitter of this story, could be implied here: the initial letter of 'Gedaehte' introduces the acrostic 'Gotefrid', who is also present, if only implicitly as 'man', in the quasi-priestly function of celebrating the eucharist at the close of the prologue. But the eucharist figure involves the readers, too, for they are invited to commemorate, together with the author, the life and death of the lovers as they would in the case of Christ. *Memoria* in this prologue therefore involves author, characters and readers, but by virtue of the eucharist association passes beyond a purely literal sense of reading or the historical sense present in Wace's prologue to the *Roman de Rou*.

In presenting himself as a reader Gottfried puts forward a model of reading for his recipients. When reading he cogitates, meditating on the story of the lovers with the inward eyes of memory and repeatedly turning it over within his heart ('ich hân von in zwein vil gedâht/und gedenke

[84] Von Merveldt, *Translatio*.   [85] Chinca, *History*, p. 54.   [86] 233–8.

hiute und alle tage;/swenne ich liebe und senede klage/vür mîniu ougen breite/und ir gelegenheite/in mînem herzen ahte' I have thought much about them both and still do today and henceforth. Whenever I unfold love and yearning before my inner eyes and ponder their nature in my heart). This kind of inward reading is what he urges upon his own readers ('ein senelîchez maere/daz trîbe ein senedaere/mit herzen und mit munde' let a lover occupy himself with a tale of love with his heart and his mouth), where the words 'mit munde', far from implying the external act of reading aloud, suggest devotional rumination with the mouth of his heart, as Augustine reported of Ambrose ('in corde eius . . . ruminaret').[87] To read Gottfried's commemorative story in the right way (which is where Thomas and he differ, as he claims, from other versions) is to memorise it in the sense of taking it to heart, to meditate upon it. Such memorial reading, adapting devotional practice to the ends of secular literature, is completely internalised.

Memory and reading enter upon a quite different, but equally ambitious partnership in Wolfram's *Parzival*, once more embracing memorial work by the author, characters in his work, and readers (to whom Wolfram refers only once explicitly, but significantly as women).[88] Memorial work of a complex order is done by the author in devising detailed parallels, correspondences as well as variations, over varying spans of time. This structural patterning has its predecessors in Chrétien's *conjointure* and Hartmann's adaptation, but with Wolfram this memorial achievement of the Arthurian romance[89] reaches a complexity which makes considerable demands on the author's memory in the process of composition. With what virtuosity Wolfram worked can be seen in his handling of narrative time over long stretches of a twofold narrative with numerous sidelines, changing what he found in Chrétien to produce his own time-schemes with indications of the lapse of time at widely separated points. One detail (the summer snowfall, contradicting the conventional association of King Arthur with Maytime or Whitsun) is particularly telling since Wolfram, having made fun of this convention, arranges much later, but only by scattered time-references, to place Arthur's last appearance in the work in what implicitly works out as this same time of the year.[90] Only these spaced time-references make this possible, but they presuppose an author whose memory is in control of such details.

---

[87] 12204–9. Cf. 97–9. Ambrose: Stevens, 'Memory', p. 324 (on this article this paragraph largely rests).
[88] 337, 1–3; Green, *Listening*, p. 191.
[89] On Chrétien's achievement in this see Stierle, 'Unverfügbarkeit', pp. 117–59.
[90] Time-scheme: Weigand, *Parzival*, pp. 42–74. Arthur's Maytime: pp. 55, 60–2.

Memory is also a task which falls to characters in Wolfram's work, not least to Parzival himself whose path to knowledge of himself proceeds through episodes which hark back to the past and demand the same of him. (That his recall of his past has to be matched by the readers' memory of earlier episodes strengthens the import of memory in the work.) Parzival thus changes, and we grow aware of these changes, through acts of memory on his part (and on ours).[91] A central illustration of Parzival's memory of his wife is the episode of summer snow, where three drops of blood in the snow conjure up the memory of Condwiramurs.[92] On seeing Parzival lost in his trance two members of the Round Table camped nearby, Segramors and Keie, are headstrong and obtuse enough to attack him and are easily dispatched, but Gawan approaches more tactfully and peacefully, catches sight of the blood, as the others had not, and 'reads' the signs correctly as occasioning the hero's love trance. Gawan is able to do this, however, only by recalling a similar experience of his own ('waz op diu minne disen man/twinget als si mich dô twanc' what if love oppresses this man as it once did me).[93] The contrast between those who read the signs in this episode correctly (Parzival, Gawan) and those who fail to (Segramors, Keie) is not confined to them, it also has a possible bearing on the work's recipients.[94] Whereas Gottfried presented himself as a model reader, Wolfram projects this task onto characters in his work. Gawan reads the signs in the snow correctly by imaginatively using his memory, just as Wolfram's readers are meant to understand his work by likewise using their memory, by recalling earlier signals, however insignificant they seemed at the time, and seeing them in the light of information released to them only later. At countless points they are expected to look back and establish a meaningful connection between past and present details.[95] To illustrate how much was expected from them I take two examples which, because I have discussed them at greater length elsewhere, can be presented here more briefly.

The first example concerns Parzival's place in the Grail dynasty, which we learn gradually and piecemeal, not just as a series of facts released as information, but as details that have to be recalled from the distant narrative past and pieced together to reveal the pattern they constitute.[96] In the account of Parzival's birth (end of Book II) we are given no hint of the decisive nature of his maternal descent, but only towards the end of Book VI are we given a significant, but still indecisive one-word suggestion that he is related to the Grail world ('ganerbe' co-heir). Finally, Book IX gives us

---

[91] Ridder, *Lili* 114 (1999), 21–41.   [92] 282, 24–305, 6; Bumke, *Blutstropfen*.
[93] 301, 22f.   [94] Bumke, *Blutstropfen*, pp. 54, 59.   [95] *Ibid.*, p. 59.
[96] For details of what follows see Green, *Art*, pp. 214–23.

in succession recognition that Parzival's mother is related to the Grail-king Anfortas, knowledge of the Grail dynasty, and his place in the male line of succession, qualifying him for kingship. Parzival therefore slowly learns about his genealogical self and we learn with him, sometimes in advance of him, but only if we remember what was said earlier. How great the reader's memory span must be is shown by the distance between the first and last of the references that have to be borne in mind and correlated, amounting to nearly 11,000 lines.

Our second example is the instruction or advice given the young Parzival first by his mother and then by Gurnemanz, where the folk tale pattern of subsequent episodes illustrating each piece of advice in action stretches almost as far into the future (over about 9,000 lines).[97] The pattern is complicated, and makes demands on the reader, by having a double application. Herzeloyde gives her son advice on various matters in Book III which, true to the conventional pattern, is then tested in the following Book, so that little demand is made on the reader's memory. However, unexpected in terms of the folk tale, one piece of her advice is also realised in practice much later in Book IX, first with the pilgrim-knight Kahenis and then with the hermit Trevrizent.[98] The position is similar with Gurnemanz's advice. He gives it in Book III and it is followed in practice by Parzival in Book IV, again with little demand on our memory. However, details in what Gurnemanz says also have an application to the events of Book V (when Parzival comes to the Grail-castle and Anfortas), events which are finally clarified only in Book IX.[99] With both Herzeloyde and Gurnemanz Wolfram goes against convention in working with a double application, he catches his audience unawares, demanding from them greater insight, attention to verbal details, and a longer memory span.

By any account, this is reading of a very high order. So high that Stierle, discussing the similar case of Chrétien, suggests that the French author's demands were too great for his readers and that he envisaged a readership not yet existent when he wrote.[100] However, Stierle qualifies his own remark, which we can accept if we see his future enlightened readers not self-centredly in ourselves, but in readers of his own day whom Chrétien hoped to train in this kind of memorial reading. He certainly found them in Germany, with Hartmann and Wolfram. In this they were assisted by precedents in which a reader was recommended to refer to an earlier passage: this made no demand on his memory, but encouraged the idea of correlating

---

[97] Details in Green, 'Advice', pp. 33–81.   [98] *Ibid.*, p. 65.
[99] *Ibid.*, pp. 67–71.   [100] Stierle, 'Unverfügbarkeit', p. 158.

present with past.[101] Gottfried gives a similar authorial reminder once, prompting his readers to turn to a previous passage (but over an unimportant detail).[102] Wolfram makes no such suggestion, leaving the rest to the readers' imaginative memory. The ideal reader postulated by Wolfram (whom he praises 2, 13f.) is engaged in a process of twofold reading. She reads the text in front of her, but is also expected to remember earlier passages or details which she has once read, but which are present now only in her memory. She therefore reads a text literally, but also memorially. It is fitting to conclude this section with Wolfram's encouragement of memorial reading, for he refers to readers of his work as women. This suggests that it was from them that he may have expected both literal and memorial reading.

WAYS OF READING

We conclude this chapter with a section dealing with both kinds of reading that have preoccupied us so far: with figurative or inward reading and, more briefly, with techniques of literal reading. Again, the figurative reading discussed is not gender specific, it concerns women readers as much as men. Only in the context of literal, scholastic reading, from which women were excluded, do they not play a part.

With figurative reading we revert to the association of *legere* with *intelligere*, asking how the reader may have been meant to understand what he read or how a writer, dealing with a subject already treated by others, may have read or understood that theme.

Nowadays we talk of reading or understanding a book or passage in a certain way ('My reading of this passage differs from yours'), and this was also possible with medieval verbs for reading. Alanus ab Insulis recognised two ways of understanding a text, wrong and right, and hence two kinds of recipient, one who remained content with the outer shell of what was said and one who pierced to its inner meaning. Although the latter is termed a listener (*auditor, audiens*), we do not need to see him as an indirect reader, for Alanus later refers to him as a reader (*lector*).[103] His way of interpreting the text is therefore the correct way of reading it. The integumental theory which Alanus applies here to poetry (he expressly refers to *poete*) derives from biblical exegesis with its multiple ways of interpreting the text, which can also be seen as ways of reading. Thus Hugh of St Victor stresses that

---

[101] Green, *Listening*, pp. 123, 155, but also 132 (instructions on reading an earlier acrostic).
[102] 874 1f.   [103] Alanus, *De planctu* 837, 128–36; Minnis, *Magister*, p. 84.

these ways of interpreting the text (historical, allegorical, tropological) must be practised in the correct order of reading (*ordo legendi*).[104] For him, too, the *modus intelligendi* follows from the *modus legendi*. (To what disparities this could lead is best seen in the Song of Songs, interpreted over time with reference to God's relationship with the Church, with Mary and with the individual soul.) Although Alanus, when referring to secular poets, almost certainly had only Latin poets in mind, their vernacular colleagues who had had a clerical education would know of this equation of *legere* with *intelligere*, as is made programmatically clear in the prologue to Gottfried's *Tristan*. Claiming to follow the version of Thomas and distancing himself critically from other authors of the story Gottfried says of the latter that they have not read correctly ('daz si niht rehte haben gelesen'), by contrast with Thomas ('sine sprâchen in der rihte niht,/als Thômas von Britanje giht' they did not speak correctly, as Thomas of Britain does).[105] Although Gottfried, like Thomas, attaches importance to source reading, he is concerned here with what follows from that, namely a convincing interpretation of the story itself. A correct reading of the story implies the possibility of an incorrect reading, therefore more than one way of reading.

If an oral culture constantly 'rereads' its 'texts' in the light of changing conditions, this is also true of a bimedial culture like the Middle Ages with a still strong oral tradition. Medieval literature is characterised by a repeated refashioning of old stories, not merely those from antiquity (Troy, Alexander), but also medieval themes (Tristan, Parzival). These new versions not merely demand to be accepted on their own terms as valid readings, they also invite comparison (intertextually) with earlier versions to establish their own validity.

An example of such rereading from Latin literature which found an echo in medieval literature concerns Virgil's depiction of the love affair between Aeneas and Dido (with the man's duty to abandon her for the sake of his mission to found Rome) and the different reading of these events in Ovid's *Heroides*, seen from the woman's point of view and with scant sympathy for the political dimension. In doing this for other women, too, in his *Heroides* Ovid 'gives a voice to those minor characters in the stories of the heroes'.[106] Ovid himself, however, could be reread in the Middle Ages in ways that would have surprised him, according to one commentator as showing how the results of living chastely may benefit us.[107] The intertextuality which informs Ovid's *Heroides* also gave ample

---

[104] *Didascalicon* VI 4 (PL 176, 802); Bumke, *Blutstropfen*, p. 152.
[105] *Tristan* 147, 149f.; Schröder, *ZfdA* 104 (1975), 308, 312.
[106] Percival, *Women*, p. 174.   [107] Minnis, *Magister*, p. 69.

scope for rereadings of medieval works. In his *Parzival* Wolfram mentions
a defeat of Erec by Orilus at Karnant which has no basis in Hartmann's
work and which must have occurred, so it is implied, after the conclusion
of events narrated in *Erec*, so that Wolfram thereby questions and rereads
the optimistically successful conclusion of the earlier work. He similarly
suggests that Brandigan remained a hotbed of violence after Hartmann's
ending.[108] Without making use of intertextuality Wolfram can also call
into question the apparently harmonising conclusion of his own *Parzival*,
leaving it open whether the disturbing signals built in at this point are to
be ignored by the 'tumben' in his audience or whether more perceptive
readers will interpret them correctly.[109] Different readings of the Tristan
story, positive or negative, come into play if we accept the suggestion that,
contrary to Gottfried's idealising view of love, Thomas's intention was to
tell the story of adulterous love as a negative exemplum, although this leaves
unexplained what Gottfried had in mind in praising the correctness ('rihte')
of his predecessor's version.[110] Nonetheless, this does not undermine the
fact that Gottfried makes it clear in his prologue that he reckons with two
kinds of recipient, on the one hand the 'edelen herzen' (noble hearts) who
accept the pains as well as the joys of love and on the other hand the many
who relish only the latter and thereby fall short of the author's idea of
the good reader ('die pflegent niht, si widerpflegent' they act not rightly,
but wrongly).[111] If, however, we were to accept radically different readings
of the Tristan story suggested by Thomas and Gottfried, then the latter's
recasting of the story in his positive sense could be compared with what has
been said of Chaucer's *Troilus* and the *Legend of Good Women*. The English
poet's ability to produce his own meaning out of resistant source material
(a sympathetic appreciation of Criseyde's position and her sisters) demands
a similar response from his readers, a willingness to join him in rereading
traditional material.[112]

Different readings are involved in the use of irony in the romance, and
therewith different readers, even if they may be the same reader at different
stages in his understanding. Irony operates with a discrepancy between what
is said and what is meant, using signals to suggest this, normally without
expressly indicating it. Some readers may therefore perceive what is afoot,
others may not; some may read correctly (figuratively), others superficially
(literally). An example of ironic speech not understood by a character is
Gottfried's Marke who arranges a hunting-party from which Tristan excuses

[108] Green, *Beginnings*, pp. 62, 64f.   [109] Bumke, *DVjs* 65 (1991), 236–64.
[110] Hunt, *RMS* 7 (1981), 41–61; Keck, *Liebeskonzeption*, pp. 129–71.
[111] *Tristan* 32.   [112] Percival, *Women*, pp. 135f.

himself on trumped-up grounds of sickness. But we are told more than is conveyed in the message to Marke: 'der sieche weidenaere/wolt' ouch an sîne weide' (the sick huntsman, too, longed to go on his hunt). Tristan, too, wished to go on a hunt (an erotic hunt for a different quarry, Isold) and his sickness was that of love.[113] The contrast between Marke's failure to recognise ironic speech (he remains a prisoner of the literal) and what the reader is privileged to see underlines the necessity for the reader, too, to avoid being a prisoner of literal understanding. Marke acts here as much as a warning as do Segramors and Keie in their failure to 'read' the drops of blood in the snow in Wolfram's *Parzival*.

A text can also be read in different ways by different readers or on different occasions. The choice between a more ambitious verse-form and simpler prose could play a part here, as when Alcuin commented on the different uses to which his three versions of the life of St Willibrord could be put: the prose version was to be read out to the assembled monks in church, the verse-form was intended for private reading, and the homily for preaching to the people.[114] The dual nature of the prose *Lancelot* (knightly, courtly adventures and a metaphysical quest for the Grail) means that it could be read in either way in different contexts, so that by the fifteenth century its reception suggests a clear distinction according to these differing readings.[115] It has been proposed that the *Livre de Leesce* of Jean Lefèvre was meant to invite a playful response to what only pretended to be a defence of women. As such it could rely misogynously on the men's ability to decode the irony and read between the lines, whilst assuming that the ladies addressed would read that their defence was meant seriously.[116] What is presupposed here (and need not in any way correspond to the actual reception conditions) is the assumption that only men would be perceptive or educated enough to understand the author's unvoiced intention, which means in turn that *illitterati* and *litterati* would understand a work in quite different ways. Whether or not literacy or educational status is meant to play a part, authors can employ a similar distinction in claiming that their version of a tale, amongst many in circulation, is the correct reading. Just as Gottfried affirms that he follows the correct version of Thomas, so that his own must also be correct, so does Thomas, amongst the many different accounts of Tristan, criticise those who do not accord with Breri, as his poem does. Beroul likewise dismisses rival tellers of the tale of Tristan on the grounds that they do not know the truth, of which he has a better

---

[113] *Tristan* 14376–81; Green, *Irony*, pp. 210f.; *Erkennen*, pp. 49–51.
[114] Schulenburg, *Forgetful*, pp. 34, 430, n. 73.
[115] Blank, 'Schwierigkeiten', p. 129; von Merveldt, *Translatio*, p. 281.   [116] Pratt, 'Strains', pp. 114f.

record.[117] If Gottfried, Thomas and Beroul all read or interpret the same tale differently (which for them means better) from others, this means that their recipients also read differently or better.

Repeatedly, different ways of reading turn on reading correctly or not. The most famous example of incorrect reading in medieval literature is Dante's description of Paolo and Francesca reading the Lancelot romance together.[118] The sin for which they are condemned lies not in their choice of the wrong book to read (in the vernacular), but rather in their partial and therefore reductive reading, in not reading far enough to finish the sentence to see in Lancelot and Guinevere instructive examples for themselves. In Chaucer's *Legend of Good Women*, however, when Cupid reproaches the poet for having spoken ill of lovers (as in *Troilus*) the god is presented as guilty of a shallow misreading, of reducing the poet's complex art to a simplistic exemplary function.[119] However much Dante and Chaucer may differ over this point, they agree in recognising a wrong way of reading and therefore also, by implication, a right way. There are also cases where the misreading may follow from a cause outside the reader himself. Like other medieval authors, Chaucer had his difficulties with errors committed by his scribe (and also with the dialectal variety of English in his day). He refers to these at the close of *Troilus* when sending his book forth, hoping that it will not be miswritten, mismetred, and therefore misread and misunderstood.[120]

Given the frequency of allegorical reading in the Middle Ages, in religious but also, as Alanus made clear, in non-religious texts, one of the most frequently discussed forms of misreading was to interpret a text literally, rather than figuratively, a fault against which Gottfried had warned in Marke's failure to understand Tristan. Occasionally, it is true, a case can be made for the literal reading, quite apart from the fact that it was the indispensable foundation of any allegorical reading, as is made quite clear by Hugh of St Victor in *Didascalicon*.[121] A well-known example of defending a literal reading is Christine de Pizan's criticism of Pierre Col, one of her opponents in the debate on the *Roman de la Rose*, for his misreading of a text which is for her literally clear ('Tu . . . mervilleusement interpretes ce qui est dit clerement et a la lectre'). In this she had support in Jean de Meun's own text and in Chaucer's version (with his preference for the 'naked text' as opposed to the 'glose'), but also in Lydgate's castigation

---

[117] Thomas, *Tristan*, Douce 835–51. Béroul, *Tristran* 1265–8.
[118] *Inferno* V 127–38; Balfour, 'Francesca', pp. 71–83.
[119] Meale, *ASNSL* 144 (1992), 58; Blamires, *Case*, p. 213.   [120] *Troilus* V 1793–8.
[121] *Didascalicon* VI 3 (PL 176, 799).

of obscurantist interpreters of scripture.[122] More common, however, is the criticism not of a literal reading itself, but of a reading that remains, like Marke, a prisoner of the literal and does not penetrate beyond it. For Bernard of Clairvaux reading had to probe beyond the literal sense and failure to do so amounted to blindness.[123] The erotic imagery of the Song of Songs was an obvious case for not reading the text literally and being deceived by its naked meaning (Chaucer's naked text!): 'Lector quisque uide ne te sententia nuda/Titillante fide fallat uel littera cruda'. For this reason it is to be kept out of the hands of children or the immature who would fall victim to a literal understanding.[124] In accord with his mysticism of the *via negativa* the author of *The Cloud of Unknowing* has no time for literal-minded contemplatives and demonstrates that even prepositions cannot apply literally to God.[125] Even more belittling is the equation of literal reading of the Bible with heretics, and their use of the vernacular. In clerical eyes laymen's untutored reading of a vernacular Bible could only unlock the literal sense. In the case of the Waldensians this was for Walter Map casting pearls before swine; for a fourteenth-century Dominican, Passavanti, the vernacular was tied to an unrelenting literalism. To cling to the Bible as the basis of religious truth, rejecting centuries of clerical exegesis as irrelevant, as did the Lollards in England, was to expose oneself to a literal interpretation.[126]

Contrary to Jean Lefèvre's assumption that women readers would be unable to read his ironic text in any way but literally, Christine de Pizan describes at the start of her *Livre de la Cité des Dames* how she was instructed to read a misogynous book which had distressed her, using *antiphrasis* to convert what appeared to be criticism into praise of women.[127] Christine may here be going against her literal reading of the *Roman de la Rose*, but avails herself, as one educated in the art of rhetoric, of the right to read an objectionable text as a woman in self-defence. Marie de France also shows that women may read a text differently from men, offering varying titles for two of her lais, dependent on the perspective from which they are viewed. *Chaitivel* is either 'the four sorrows' or 'the unfortunate one' according to whether it is seen from the woman's or the man's point of view, while *Eliduc* was later given the new title *Guildelüec ha Gualadun* because it befell the women ('kar des dames est avenu').[128]

---

[122] Minnis, *Magister*, pp. v, 136f. See also Copeland, *Pedagogy*, pp. 55–98.
[123] Hamburger, *Visual*, p. 147.   [124] Ohly, *Hohelied-Studien*, pp. 156, 284f.
[125] Windeatt, *Book*, p. 16.
[126] Map and Passavanti: Copeland, 'Women', pp. 163–5. Lollards: Krug, *Families*, p. 149, fn. 78.
[127] *Cité* I 2 (p. 8).   [128] *Chaitival* 6–8, 203–37. *Eliduc* 17–25.

Elsewhere, women are shown reading literally, as we have seen with Christine. It does not surprise us that Christine's adversary, Pierre Col, regards her as a misguided reader, because her literal reading was no more than superficial, as it had to be in the light of allegorical reading.[129] The argument against women's misreading goes further in Nicholas Love's *Myrrour*, whose female audience is reminded of the distinction between literal and figurative reading. As part of this they are told to abandon the attempt to perceive the spiritual with their physical senses, to give up pursuing the matter further and simply to believe what the Church teaches.[130] Whether we call this anti-intellectual or anti-feminine, it ties up with the medieval topos that, in contrast to man, woman was bound up with the flesh and the physical, but also with the literal sense of reading. This topos had a long prehistory reaching back to Aristotelian physiology, passing through Paul (II Cor. 3, 6: 'The letter kills but the spirit gives life'), Augustine's commentary linking the letter with the flesh, and Ambrose's view that the progress from the carnal to the spiritual is one from womanhood to manhood.[131] In short, to read like a woman is to read carnally or literally, so that if an individual woman learns to read spiritually it is only because she has abandoned her feminine nature and assumed a masculine one. This is what, in the eyes of her opponents, Christine failed to achieve, so that for Jean de Montreuil she was reading like a woman.[132]

We come finally to another pair of contrasting ways of reading, based on Leclercq's work on monastic and scholastic learning, including two different ways of reading.[133] As presented by Leclercq, monastic theology and the reading it inculcated were meditational, helping the individual monk or reader to internalise scripture until it was part of himself, whereas scholastic learning and the pragmatic reading it demanded sought to extend and systematise Christian knowledge by rational argument and disputation.[134] These contrasting approaches form part of a much wider development traced further back by Langer. He places them in the context of a rivalry between monastic contemplative and affective *sapientia* on the one hand and a ratiocinative *scientia* at home in cathedral schools and universities, and confident in the accessibility of religious truths to human reason, on the other hand.[135] Leclercq's concern was monastic theology itself and he used scholasticism as a contrast helping him to define the former more accurately. He was therefore justified in talking of a specifically monastic

[129] Pratt, 'Strains', pp. 117f.   [130] Bartlett, *Authors*, pp. 25–7.
[131] Copeland, 'Women', pp. 255–7.   [132] Schibanoff, 'Taking', pp. 94f.
[133] Leclercq, *Love*.   [134] Cf. Newman, *Goddesses*, pp. 294f.
[135] Langer, *Mystik*, pp. 151–208. See also Köhn, *MM* 10 (1976), 1–37.

theology, but we should guard against two possible misunderstandings. In the first place, the rise of scholastic learning in the eleventh/twelfth centuries as a new phenomenon did not simply oust the old learning, which indeed continued vigorously long after the new challenge was made, not only in the setting of monasteries, but also in the affective piety of new religious movements amongst laypeople, particularly women.[136] Secondly, for that reason it is no longer always apposite to talk of monastic reading in this context. Other suggestions are devotional, contemplative and meditational reading.

Monastic reading has been defined by Parkes as a 'spiritual exercise which involved steady reading to oneself, interspersed by prayer, and pausing for rumination on the text as a basis for *meditatio*'.[137] *Lectio* was directed less towards obtaining new information by reading than towards savouring divine wisdom within a book, so much so that rumination could dispense with reading a text and be picture-based in contemplation of Christ's body at the Passion.[138] Rumination of this kind could replace literate learning for the author of the *Prickynge of Love* ('This is my boke and my clergie my studie and my meditacioun'), so that the contrast between wisdom and learning emancipated those whose literacy was limited ('The ofte thynkynge of my passyon makyth an vnlernyde man a ful lernyd man'). Meditative reading required rumination and an affective response to the text, in such a way that Gregory the Great maintained that the Bible was to be read for its power to restore, not studied in order to raise questions, a telling rejoinder, centuries *avant la lettre*, to the scholastic method of reading.[139] How affective such reading was meant to be is shown by Anselm of Canterbury's remark that his *Orationes* are to be read meditatively, in peace and quiet, not speedily but slowly and frequently in order to excite the mind of the reader to love and fear of God.[140] What counts in monastic reading is not its quantity, but its quality. Anselm recommended slow and frequent reading, just as it was the practice of the Benedictines and other orders for the monk in charge of the library to issue a book at Lent for each monk to read and inwardly digest over the coming year.[141] Without falling victim to medieval stereotypes of what was natural to a woman, we may see such emphasis on affective reading, together with the conviction that it could replace the learning from which women were largely debarred educationally, as

[136] Hamburger, *Canticles*, p. 160; Newman, *Goddesses*, p. 294; Lutz, 'Überlegungen', p. 300.
[137] Parkes, 'Influence', p. 115.   [138] Clanchy, *Memory*, p. 269; Gillespie, 'Images', pp. 111f.
[139] See above, p. 45; Parkes, *ASE* 26 (1997), 15.
[140] Anselm, *Orationes*, prologue ll. 2–5; Olson, 'Women', pp. 89f. and fn. 80.
[141] Fichtenau, 'Lesen', p. 323.

meaning that this kind of reading was available especially to women, even in the vernacular.

We enter a different world, characterised by a different manner of reading, pragmatic and utilitarian, and from which women were excluded, when we turn to scholastic learning. With it we also leave figurative reading and return to the literal reading of Chapter I. Here, too, we may begin with a definition given by Parkes, for whom scholastic reading 'was a process of study which involved a more ratiocinative scrutiny of the text and consultation for reference purposes'.[142] That this represents a different world from the monastery was clear to Peter Comestor, who saw two types of men: those who dedicate themselves more to prayer than to reading (they are at home in monasteries) and those who are concerned with reading and less often with prayer (they are at home in the schools).[143] In this new context reading is not dominated by meditation and prayer, but by reasoning and cognition, by rational *scientia* instead of spiritual *sapientia*. The rational inquiry, ratiocinative speculation and disputation which informed such reading are worlds removed from the rejection of inquiry which underlay Gregory the Great's view of monastic reading. In place of the prolonged incorporation of a book by repeated ingestion, typified by the issue of a book for a year at a time in a monastery, we find two new departures. First, a move towards swifter reading, even amounting to skimming through a book, dictated in part by the sheer volume of texts now available and in part by the limited length of time spent in the schools in contrast with a lifetime spent in a monastery.[144] Secondly, reading was dominated more by reference-reading, consulting a volume such as a collection of *sententiae* for a particular point rather than reading through from beginning to end.[145] This necessitated a new type of layout in which the text was subdivided into chapters, paragraphs and subparagraphs to facilitate consultation. Vincent of Beauvais explains that this arrangement was made so that 'operis partes singule lectori facilius elucescant', and Peter Lombard uses various expressions to indicate the same procedure, such as *statim invenire*, *presto habere* and *facilius occurrere*.[146] This permitted rapid and selective reading for purposes of consultation. Where devotional monastic reading had been deliberately slow Anselm's warning against reading too rapidly would have had little point, just as he is also one of the first to point out that his division of the text into paragraphs allowed the reader to begin his selective reading

---

[142] Parkes, 'Influence', p. 115.   [143] Fichtenau, 'Lesen', p. 331.
[144] Parkes, 'Influence', *passim*; Rouse, '*Statim*', *passim*. See also Rouse, 'Naissance', p. 78; Hamesse, 'Modèle', p. 129.
[145] Hamesse, 'Modèle', pp. 125f.; Fichtenau, 'Lesen', p. 335.   [146] Rouse, '*Statim*', pp. 206f.

at any desired point,[147] it allowed him multiple points of entry. The use of folios for cross-referencing is another codicological symptom of a different reading habit[148] which has its counterpart in vernacular romances: in the prose *Lancelot*, in Gottfried's explicit reference to looking back, and in Wolfram's expectation that some of his readers might remember earlier passages, consulting them either memorially or in actual fact.

If we seek, in conclusion, to find a place for women in the two ways of reading we have been considering it will be to say that although men's reading (or more precisely clerics' reading) changed during the Middle Ages, especially as a result of scholasticism, women were excluded from this, so that their devotional reading remained largely what it had been before.[149] However, as we shall see, women managed to give a new turn to the argument by their (educationally enforced) distance from what monastic thinkers like Peter Damian criticised as the hubris of scholastic theology, claiming to unravel divine mysteries by means of fallible human reason assuming autonomy for itself.[150] If women were largely deprived of the education enjoyed by future clerics they could at least cling to what monastic theology valued as the simplicity of belief as against the negatively assessed subtleties of reason. Their exclusion from the new way of reading placed them close to Bernard's attitude to Abelard, maintaining the primacy of belief over dialectic ('Fides piorum credit, non discutit').[151] Lacking access to higher education, women could claim, like monks, to belong to the *schola Christi* where, in accord with Peter of Celle, they learned without the formal instruction available to men ('sine studio et lectione').[152] What in the eyes not just of the world but of educated male clerics placed these women in a disadvantageous position could be turned into one of spiritual strength, as late medieval religious movements were to show.

---

[147] Saenger, *Space*, pp. 203f.   [148] *Ibid.*, pp. 230f.
[149] Bartlett, *Authors*, p. 18.   [150] Langer, *Mystik*, p. 159.
[151] *Ibid.*, p. 189; PL 182, 543 (ep. 338).   [152] Langer, *Mystik*, p. 175.

PART II

Women and reading in the Middle Ages

For some the title of this Part, and indeed of this book itself, could be as much a contradiction in terms as was the case with reading in the vernacular, and for much the same reason. Grundmann's three-point definition of medieval literacy (a cleric who read in Latin), which he constructed from medieval sources, theoretically excluded laymen, but more particularly women (lay or religious) from the act of reading. To this can be added a practical consideration, affecting readers of either sex, namely the view that the collective life and din of the medieval castle (criticised by Walther von der Vogelweide) provided little chance of solitude for private reading for a noblewoman. About this, as about Grundmann's definition, doubts may be entertained,[1] although the conventional view that women readers were rare can still be encountered. Brooke has argued that the history of medieval women is difficult to write in that most records were kept by men since few women were literate and wrote.[2] The idea that the engagement with books was a man's affair might seem to be supported by Christine de Pizan and Chaucer's Wife of Bath, both of whom complain that the traditional view of women conveyed in written texts would look very different if they had been composed by women instead of men.[3] Both examples call for qualification: Christine because she is herself a woman author and depicts herself also as a reader, and the Wife because, as we have seen, she is at the least an indirect reader, read to by her husband and thereby granted access to a whole range of literature, making of her a *quasi litterata*.[4] Against the view expressed by Brooke we may set Clanchy's suggestion that women had a decisive role to play in the dynamics of medieval literacy in another sense and that it was they who transferred the reading practice of the clergy into aristocratic households by the acquisition of prayer-books and other devotional texts for their personal use.[5]

---

[1] Walther 20, 3f.; Green, *Listening*, pp. 304–6.   [2] In his introduction, p. 1, to Baker, *Women*.
[3] *Wife of Bath's Prologue* 693–6. Christine, *Epistre* 409–22.   [4] Schnell, *Frauendiskurs*, pp. 190–3.
[5] Clanchy, *Memory*, pp. 251f.

We may best adjudicate between the rival views of Brooke and Clanchy by reverting to the suggestion that there was little private space for personal reading, little opportunity for medieval women to find a room of their own for reading, matching Virginia Woolf's complaint about the lack of space (literally and figuratively) for women in which to write in the twentieth century. That such a 'women's space' existed in the literal sense in the Middle Ages is made clear by frequent references to women's withdrawing chamber (MHG 'kemenâte', 'heimlîch'). These served a patriarchal purpose far from any intention of giving them freedom of scope, for here they could be kept safely secluded and under supervision in a building swarming with young males, here it could be hoped that their most valuable asset in feudal eyes, their chastity, could be kept intact. This private space could therefore be where women were dismissed to and kept apart from the important issues of men's affairs, as in the *Roman de Silence* where the woman is to keep silent and is banished to her room ('Lasciés me faire,/Et vos alés en vostre cambre'). But there is another side to this, for Christine's reading (as well as her writing) took place in her study, where she not merely read Matheolus's misogamous (and misogynous) *Lamentationes*, but also mounted her written counter-attack, thereby anticipating Virginia Woolf and countering her arguments by some centuries.[6] Whether we regard the women's chamber as potentially subversive in this way ('What do the ladies talk about when they are alone?') or as a second-best escape from reality into an imaginative world, this private space provided an opportunity for personal reading by women.

That they could make use of this can be shown briefly by examples from the three vernaculars with which we are concerned. The Anglo-Norman Gaimar relates in his *Estoire des Engleis* that Constance Fitzgilbert, who commissioned his work, often retired into her room to read a history of Henry I by David ('dame Custance en ad l'escrit,/en sa chambre sovent le lit').[7] My other two examples have been mentioned in Chapter 1, but only in passing. Ulrich von Lichtenstein sends a letter to his lady *via* a messenger, but again she withdraws into her private room to read it ('Den brief nam ir wiziu hant/und gie von danne sa zehant/in ir heinlich, da si las,/swaz an dem brief geschriben was' Her white hand took the letter and she forthwith retired into her chamber where she read what was written in the letter).[8] The position is no different with the English example from Chaucer, where Criseyde receives her first love-letter from Troilus and likewise retires to read

---

[6] *Silence* 6406f. *Cité* I 1 (p. 5). See also Brown-Grant's translation, *Book*, p. xvi, for the qualification of Woolf's argument that Christine presents.
[7] Gaimar, *Estoire* 6489f.; Blacker, 'Dame', pp. 109–19.   [8] Ulrich, *Frauendienst* 320, 1–4.

it ('And streighte into hire chaumbre gan she gon/ . . . Ful pryvely this lettre
for to rede'). Here we have pictorial confirmation from an illumination in
the manuscript of one of Chaucer's sources, the *Roman de Troilus*.[9] The
picture is divided into two sections: the larger one on the right shows a
room crowded with people of both sexes and separated by a wall from the
small room on the left in which Criseyde stands alone at a window, reading
the letter to herself. Together, these three examples meet the theoretical
objection that a laywoman could not be imagined having the opportunity
or place for reading a vernacular text, whether a letter or a whole work.
Our task in the rest of this book will be to show that they are by no means
isolated examples.

To do this we have to look at as wide a spread of evidence as possible.
The need for this arises from the fact that the first and most important
class of evidence, references in what may be termed historical works to
actual women reading, by no means gives us enough examples to be really
helpful. It therefore needs to be supplemented by two other classes: first,
suggestions (in historical or fictional works) that women were conceived
by the author as potential readers of his work and, secondly, women as
literary characters in fictional works depicted as readers. The difference
between the first class and the other two raises the question how far the
evidence from fictional, as distinct from historical, works can be regarded
as reliable indicators of medieval reality. However, the difference between
these classes of evidence is not as clear-cut as it might seem. On the one
hand, where historical works refer to a woman reading this is generally to
a patron's wife or to a woman of high rank, where factors such as political
bias, flattery and hyperbole may play a part, but not so much as to be
self-defeatingly implausible. On the other hand, in works of fiction the
mention of a woman reader may be based on actual experience and, even
if a pious hope, could reflect contemporary practice, especially in view of
what historical evidence suggests.

This problem of plausibility has a much wider bearing. It is a difficulty
which faced Bumke in his presentation of court culture, where literary evidence also far outweighs historical. Although this renders acute the question
of credibility, Bumke makes the telling point that the idealisations found
in court literature need not exclude realism in details (especially one which,
as with women reading, plays no decisive part in the narrative action).[10]
Although court authors are not committed to factual veracity, the value of

---

[9] Chaucer, *Troilus* II 1173–6; Coleman, *Reading*, p. 152 (and Fig. 2).
[10] Bumke, *Kultur*, pp. 17–26 (here p. 18).

what they indicate of women reading is not just its truth or untruth, but whether it could have been regarded by their audience as at all conceivable. In this respect Brooke, as a historian of medieval marriage who laudably, if not entirely satisfactorily, includes Wolfram's *Parzival* in his survey makes some valuable observations which have a direct bearing on our subject. He recognises that vernacular fictional literature can tell us things about attitudes to marriage in the Middle Ages that are nowhere else recorded, that it 'opens our eyes to a world which would be unimaginable if we read only the theologians' and that 'to ignore, or voluntarily renounce any use of literature, is an act of austerity or even blindness in the end'. This will prove relevant when we look at Christina of Markyate, and later at wider aspects of marriage in the companion volume. Meanwhile, what Brooke says about his theme is applicable to the question of women readers, given the paucity of non-literary evidence at our disposal. An object-lesson in rescuing the plausibility of literary and artistic evidence is provided by Wolf. After presenting evidence of women reading Psalters from these two spheres he asks how far this can be trusted, whether it may not reflect clerical propaganda or wishful thinking, but then discusses at length what he terms 'positivist' evidence to confirm his earlier examples.[11]

The two chapters that follow endeavour to cover the wider range of women's literary activities in the Middle Ages, not just the bare fact of reading. There are two justifications for this. The first is that reading is involved in one way or another, directly or indirectly, in this range: with women as recipients of literature (they read themselves or are read to), as patrons of works which they are meant to read, reproducers of texts or copyists (especially nuns), and as authors who read prior to or in the act of composition. Dwelling on this wider range has the advantage of breaking away from the post-Romantic preconception that only the creative author is actively engaged in literature.[12] The second justification harks back to Chapter 1 where we saw that precisely this range of activities could be conveyed by the verb *legere* and its vernacular equivalents. Medieval reading was a much wider activity than its modern counterpart.

[11] Brooke, *Idea*, pp. 22, 176, 201. Wolf, 'Psalter', pp. 146–64.
[12] Peters, *GRM* 38 (1988), 35f.; Bennewitz, 'Stimme', p. 69.

CHAPTER 3

Categories of women readers

If there were relatively few woman readers to be considered our task would be simpler, if less rewarding. There are, however, so many as to demand categorisation for the sake of clarity. This creates difficulties, since it would be mistaken to think of these categories as watertight entities. Instead, because of the extreme fluidity of forms of religious women passing from one category to another, taking their reading material and reading habits with them, the categories that follow must all be regarded as permeable in a number of ways.

With the rise of devotional reading for laywomen in the late Middle Ages it often becomes difficult to tell whether a work was meant for religious or for secular women, or indeed for both. With regard to the *Rothschild Canticles* and their intended reader Hamburger observes that in this period it becomes increasingly difficult to draw a line between lay and monastic patronage (and readership).[1] For the English context it has likewise been pointed out that texts meant for religious women gained 'extension of their audience into ranks of the pious noble and gentlewoman' (long before they were addressed to men).[2] A reflection of this is found in the Additions to the rule for Syon Abbey, stipulating that a novice should, among other things, bring her books with her on profession, a possibility which is also attested in Germany, for example, where the books brought by women entering St Catharine's convent from patrician families in Nürnberg made up a substantial part of one of the largest convent libraries of the day.[3]

A similar interplay also frequently occurs between beguines and nuns, in part assisted by the fact that especially in south Germany most beguinages were regularised in the course of time as Dominican convents (e.g. Engelthal, St Katharinental, Ötenbach).[4] In addition to these institutional

[1] Hamburger, *Canticles*, p. 156.   [2] Gillespie, 'Lectio', p. 17.
[3] Syon: Krug, *Families*, p. 153. Nürnberg: Thali, *Beten*, pp. 261, 282f.
[4] Engelthal: Bürkle, *Literatur*, pp. 19, 187. St Katharinental: Janota, *Orientierung*, p. 113. Ötenbach: *ibid.*, 110.

conversions there is no shortage of cases where individual beguines eventually profess as nuns (e.g. Ida of Nivelles, Ida of Louvain, Mechthild von Magdeburg).[5] The same is true lastly of the two-way traffic between anchoresses and nuns, especially in those cases, as with beguinages, where an anchorhold is institutionally converted to a convent (Disibodenberg, Markyate).[6] From this it follows that individual anchoresses, like their beguine sisters, could finish as nuns (Christina of Markyate). However, the opposite is also attested, with some nuns seeking a higher degree of perfection as recluses (Eve of Wilton or the sister for whom Aelred of Rievaulx wrote *De institutione inclusarum*).[7] In view of the frequency of such cases it is unrealistic to imagine that texts read in one walk of life were not also used in the next step of the ladder to spiritual perfection.

WOMEN'S EDUCATION

Despite the work of Riché and others we know very little about how education was conducted in the Middle Ages, especially for women, no doubt because they were educationally marginalised.[8] However, we are not concerned with education at large, but with instruction in reading as an introduction to the world of the book. About this our evidence permits some general comments. Women's instruction in reading is the basis of all that follows in this book.

We start with opposition to the very idea that women should be educated and should read, in which medieval patriarchy could derive support from Paul's injunction that women should not speak in public or teach, but should be content to learn from their husbands at home.[9] This early prohibition of women teaching, accompanied by a restriction on their being taught, informs much of the pressure against their education in the following centuries. Thus, in his *Summa* Henry of Ghent appeals explicitly to this Pauline precedent in hedging the view that all Christians, even woman ('etiam mulier'), must learn in order to be saved with restrictions that diminish the scope for her. She is doubly disqualified: she cannot teach in public, but the weakness of womanly intellect ('debilitas ingenii muliebris') debars her from reaching the requisite knowledge. This late thirteenth-century adaptation of Paul has been described as an object lesson in medieval

[5] Ida of Nivelles: Simons, *Cities*, p. 40. Ida of Louvain: *ibid.*, p. 44. Mechthild: see below, p. 161.
[6] Disibodenberg: Ennen, *Frauen*, p. 117. Markyate: see below, p. 153.
[7] Eve: Olson, 'Women', p. 69. Aelred: Millett, '*Ancrene Wisse*', p. 21. See also Warren, 'Nun', pp. 197–212.
[8] Above all Riché, *Education* and *Écoles*, who breaks off too soon to assist us with vernacular literature.
[9] I Cor. 14, 34f.; I Tim. 2, 11f.

patriarchy's contempt for female intellect.[10] Similar sentiments recur in the vernacular. Less extremely, but still grudgingly. Thomasin argues that if a woman has intelligence ('sin') and education ('lêre') she should on no account display her intelligence, since that would concede authority ('potestât') to her. A man may well possess all kinds of knowledge ('künste'), but it is more becoming that a lady should not have much knowledge ('list'). Simplicity suits her better ('einvalt stêt den vrouwen wol'). It is against such prejudice that Christine de Pizan voices her criticism of men's opposition to women studying.[11] Men's fears about allowing women to know too much include the ability to read, as is sometimes made explicit. In the thirteenth century Philippe de Novare, for example, sees danger in allowing women to read, except in the case of nuns ('A fame ne doit on apanre lettres ne escrire/se ce n'est especiaument por estre nonnain'). One can only assume that he knew nothing of what Carolingian nuns were capable of with their *winileodos*, but even without this historical knowledge Philippe saw where the danger lay, in unsuitable letters, poems and stories. The morbid suspicion that reading for women could open the door to love-letters or dubious reading-matter such as romances is expressed equally pointedly in *Urbain le courtois*: literate women will be better able to deceive their husbands.[12]

This opposition to women's education on two scores (to their being taught at all or to read in particular) was reinforced from about 1200 with the founding of the first universities. The exclusion of women from them meant that they were now deprived of higher education and the high reading on which it was based.[13] This in turn put women educationally at a disadvantage to men, both to the clerical students at universities and to the young noblemen who in the later Middle Ages also acquired a university training when not destined for an ecclesiastical career. With this gender gap the majority of women, with only rare exceptions, were debarred from advanced education and familiarity with intellectual tradition. The universities had an undeniably detrimental effect on the educational status of women.

If this were all to the question of women's education in reading in the Middle Ages, this book could finish unprofitably at this point. There are however a number of factors encouraging their education and reading capability. In the first place, not all theologians went quite so far as Paul. An

---

[10] Schreiner, *Merkur* 44, 1 (1990), 84f.; Blamires, 'Limits', pp. 6f.
[11] Thomasin: *Welscher Gast* 837–49 and Bennewitz, 'Toechter', pp. 32f. Christine: *Cité* II 36 (pp. 139f.).
[12] Philippe: *Ages*, p. 16 and Schreiner, *FMS* 24 (1990), 340. *Winileodos*: Edwards, 'Winileodos', pp. 189–206. *Urbain*: Krueger, *Women*, p. 221.
[13] Lundt, 'Entstehung', pp. 103–18; Bell, *Nuns*, pp. 59, 77.

early dissenting voice was Jerome who encouraged various women with whom he was in close contact to devote themselves to reading, of course of a Christian content. Laeta was to find pleasure not in jewellery or silk, but in sacred writings; Eustochium was enjoined to read as much as possible, so that, when she fell asleep, it was to be with a book in her hand; Marcella must have been a keen reader, too, for whenever possible she overwhelmed Jerome with exegetical questions about the scriptures.[14] In his Rule for nuns Caesarius of Arles was concerned with their education, laying down that girls should be admitted who already know their letters, but stipulating that they should not be admitted simply to be educated. Elsewhere, the precedent set by Jerome can be expressly followed. In one of the sermons that Abelard wrote for the Paraclete, therefore meant to apply to women in particular, he engages with the importance of education for women. He quotes Jerome in arguing that parents should see to the education of their daughters, too, as Susanna's parents had done in the Old Testament, in contrast with parents of his own day.[15] In the following century Vincent of Beauvais includes in his pedagogic treatise *De eruditione filiorum nobilium* remarks about the education of young noblewomen. What he has to say on this he bases on his reading of Jerome's letters: young girls are to learn to read and occupy themselves with the Psalter and sacred writings as a defence against vain pleasures. Humbert of Romans is realistically aware that education for women means essentially instruction for daughters of the rich ('filiae divitum'), recommending them to read the Psalter and other religious texts and quoting as precedents such figures as Agnes, Caecilia, Lucia and Agatha, all of whom had been educated in literacy and for whom pious reading had paved the way to salvation.[16] It is in the fifteenth century with Bernardino of Siena, however, that the full distance between these thinkers and Paul becomes most apparent. Arguing that the age in which he lived no longer resembled the conditions under which the apostle had written, Bernardino admits that in earlier times men may have been educated in spiritual matters and were therefore capable of instructing their wives, as Paul had presupposed, but the men of his day are ignorant and it is they who are in need of being taught by their wives.[17] Bernardino can justify his differences with Paul by arguing that it is the *times* that have changed, but his argument both presupposes a change in women's educational status

[14] Schreiner, *FMS* 24 (1990), 345f.; Ferrante, *Glory*, p. 66.
[15] Caesarius: Ferrante, 'Education', p. 13. Abelard: Ferrante, *Glory*, p. 66.
[16] Vincent: Bumke, *Kultur*, pp. 470f. and Andersen, *Voices*, p. 55. Humbert: Schreiner, *FMS* 24 (1990), 346.
[17] Schreiner, *FMS* 24 (1990), 348.

and justifies it. As a Franciscan preacher Bernardino used the vernacular in his sermons, so it is fitting to conclude with an example that found its way from one vernacular into another. Geoffrey de la Tour-Landry wrote his book for his daughters, arguing expressly against those who oppose women learning to read and write. He accepts that writing may not be necessary for them, but approves of their reading for the conventional religious reason (in Caxton's translation: 'For a woman that can rede may better knowe the peryls of the sowle and her sauement than she that can nouȝt of it').[18]

However important these dissenting voices may be, even more interesting are two contexts in which encouragement for women to read came not from men, but from other women, constituting a feminine solidarity in reading. The first context is the importance of role models for women readers, as with Bernardino's group of holy women. The examples I choose are Mary and her mother Anne. The image of Mary in the act of reading, especially in the Annunciation scene, came very much to the fore in the late Middle Ages.[19] In view of the *imitatio Mariae* at this time the popularity of this image met an obvious need on the part of literate women, justifying their reading practice against any opposition they faced by providing them with an unassailable role model. Significantly, Bernardino was not content to list a group of holy women readers, he could not let the example of Mary escape him, recommending her reading at the Annunciation as a model of pious activity to present-day women which their husbands had every reason to permit.[20] The visual arts depict this role model function of Mary most convincingly. The Primer of Claude of France depicts the young princess, like the infant Mary in front of her by the side of her mother Anne, involved in learning to read. The Buves Hours includes an illumination of the female owner, encouraged in her devotions by an angel, kneeling by an altar on which lies her open Book of Hours, but facing this is the usual Annunciation scene in which Mary is likewise before an altar on which lies her open devotional book, presumably the Psalter.[21] The encouragement to the woman owner is therefore twofold: it comes from the angel, but also from the model of Mary. Clanchy has suggested that the popularity of such pictures from the fourteenth century coincides with the greater availability of private prayer books, so that the scene of Mary at prayer points to how the Book of Hours itself was to be used by its owner. To this it has to be added that literature antedates this scene by

---

[18] Boffey, 'Women', p. 165; Schibanoff, 'Gold', p. 105, n. 34.
[19] Schreiner, *FMS* 24 (1990), 314–68; *Merkur* 44, 1 (1990), 82–8; *Maria*, pp. 116–48.
[20] Schreiner, *FMS* 24 (1990), 347.
[21] Claude: see Fig. 4 and Driver, 'Mirrors', pp. 75, 77. Buves: Fig. 5; Penketh, 'Women', p. 272.

centuries, for in the ninth century Otfrid, in the first vernacular example known to me, has Mary reading the Psalter when Gabriel appears before her.[22] In this earlier case, as we shall see, Mary the Psalter-reader reflects contemporary practice among noblewomen, whereas later it is the other way round, Mary encourages other women. These later images provide 'role-models for mothers and daughters of aristocratic households, who seem to have been at the forefront of new literacy patterns'.[23] Mary's mother also plays a part in this process.[24] Her importance lies in the role she was regarded as playing in educating her daughter, therefore acting as a model for noblewomen to educate theirs. Just as Anne was depicted in a Book of Hours taking Mary to the Temple for schooling, so too was Mary shown taking the infant Christ, complete with ABC tablet, to the Temple.[25] What was referred to above as an *imitatio Mariae* in this respect can also be extended to an *imitatio Annae*. In one scene in the Bedford Hours the owner-patron, the Duchess of Bedford (Anne of Burgundy) kneels before an open book in the presence of her patron saint Anne. What links the Duchess with Anne is not only their shared name, but also what they do, for each has an open book before her.[26]

I call my second context for women supporting each other as readers female reading communities, adapting a term coined by Stock.[27] Examples for this can be regarded in two directions, vertical and horizontal. With the vertical direction we still remain with Anne and Mary, for between them they incorporate the transmission of books and reading from one generation to the next. But the transmission extends beyond Anne and Mary, for whenever the owner is also represented, as in the Bedford Hours, the present is included in this sequence of women passing on literacy to other women. Moreover, to the extent that Anne's and Mary's role in teaching their children is meant as a stimulus to women to instruct their young the transmission continues over untold generations of women. This is borne out in a very tangible way by the evidence of women's wills with instructions that their books, often a Book of Hours, are to be given to their daughter or to a women's religious house.[28] The evidence for this is particularly rich in England, but alongside this we may set a telling detail from Germany. The *Sachsenspiegel* lays down what may legally be bequeathed by a woman in her will. The list includes household goods and objects normally associ-ated with women, including however 'saltere unde alle buke, de to Goddes

[22] Clanchy, 'Learning', p. 37. Otfrid, *Evangelienbuch* I 5, 10 and below, pp. 121f.
[23] Camille, 'Language', p. 35.   [24] Scase, 'Anne', pp. 81–96; Sheingorn, *Gesta* 32 (1993), 69–80.
[25] Alexandre-Bidon, 'Femmes', p. 98 (and Figs. 4 and 5); Clanchy, 'Icon', pp. 47–73.
[26] Sheingorn, *Gesta* 32 (1993), 74f. (and Fig. 11).
[27] Stock, *Implications*, pp. 88–240 ('textual communities').   [28] Penketh, 'Women', p. 271.

denste horet, [de vrowen pleget to lesene]' (Psalters and all the books that belong to divine service, which women are in the habit of reading). These religious books are not meant to be associated exclusively, but primarily with women, so that we cannot read this passage as meaning that only women read, but rather that this ability was more common with them than with men in the lay world.[29]

The horizontal dimension of women's reading communities consists mainly of evidence for women exchanging books with one another, as loans or outright gifts. These exchanges could take place between women's convents (as is well attested between the two communities of Campsey and Barking), but also between lay society and the religious world (suggested in the case of Isabella of Arundel and Campsey, and also in the gift of Mechthild von Magdeburg's book by Margaretha zum Goldenen Ring to beguine houses).[30] This by no means excludes the exchange of books between women in lay society, as has been abundantly documented for England by Riddy and Meale.[31] The dominant subject matter of the books involved may well have been religious, but not to the total exclusion of Arthurian romance, yet hardly enough to justify the alarmist fears of Philippe de Novare.

We approach the acquisition of literacy by women more nearly when we consider what actually constituted their instruction, although this is possible only in very general terms. Given the opposition to women's literacy, we have to ask how far their education included it. When they are described as educated, did this mean instruction in reading as well as the social graces and accomplishments? This twofold nature of education has been discussed, admittedly on a much superior level, in the case of courtier bishops by Jaeger, who sums up the aim of their training as involving *litterae et mores*, letters and manners.[32] However, training in *mores* need not always include *litterae* (Jaeger quotes the example of Barbarossa, 'illiteratus, sed morali experientia doctus'), a restriction which, when applied to women, may explain the detail with which Thomasin describes the social etiquette to which a woman must be educated in contrast to the low valuation he places on her knowledge or need for it.[33] On the other hand, as Jaeger's evidence also makes clear, *mores* can be taught by means of *litterae* as well as by personal example (for William of Conches the reading of 'auctores'

---

[29] *Sachsenspiegel* I 24 § 3.
[30] Campsey and Barking: Wogan-Browne, *Lives*, pp. 10f. Isabella: *ibid.*, pp. 11 (and fn. 16), 153. Margaretha: Andersen, *Voices*, p. 141. If N. Palmer (personal letter) is correct in thinking that this was a bequest, it would be a case of vertical transmission.
[31] Riddy, 'Women', pp. 104–27; Meale, 'Laywomen', pp. 128–58.
[32] Jaeger, *Origins*, pp. 31 (Bernward, Wazo), 213–19.
[33] *Ibid.*, pp. 216f. Thomasin, *Welscher Gast* 391–470.

provided texts from which to draw ethical lessons) and Jaeger rightly says that the 'laity's adoption of courtesy is as closely tied to its literacy as *mores* are to *litterae* in a program of court education'.[34] In view of the ambivalence of such evidence we cannot always tell, when women are mentioned as educated, whether they can actually read.

Concerned with courtier bishops, Jaeger only once includes an example of a woman combining *litterae* and *mores* in the person of Mathilda, the wife of William the Conqueror, of whom Ordericus Vitalis said that she was graced, amongst other qualities, with a knowledge of letters and all beauty of manners and virtues ('litterarum scientia, cuncta morum et virtutum pulchritudo').[35] There are, however, other women for whom the same claim, expressly including their literacy, was made. The first example is indeed an early one, concerning the niece of Theoderic, Amalaberga, sent for marriage to Thuringia as a civilising force and of whom Cassiodorus wrote that she combined a training in letters with instruction in manners ('litteris doctam, moribus eruditam'). Later examples, like that from Ordericus Vitalis from the period when changes in literacy amongst laypeople are well under way, include Hugh of Fleury who dedicates his *Historia ecclesiastica* to the countess Adela of Blois, praising her for her erudition in letters, a great nobility and civilised breeding ('litteris erudita, quod est gentilitium sive civilitas magna'). He further praises her intellectual ability to understand the deepest matters because of her mental application and the elegance of her manners. Geoffrey of Cambrai eulogises Edith, the wife of Edward the Confessor, by listing her intellectual attainments, possible only in one trained as a *litterata* in the liberal arts, but adds to these her 'morum probitas'.[36]

In all this there may well be more than just a streak of courtier fulsomeness, but it would have been equally possible to flatter high-born women without attributing literacy to them in every case. That this accomplishment was included suggests that it was felt to belong to the positive picture of a noblewoman or was even attained in reality, to whatever degree. This has implications for the most illuminating description of a woman's *litterae et mores* in literature, Gottfried's description of the education of the young Isold, first by a court chaplain, then by Tristan himself. Of the literate nature of her instruction there can be no doubt: express mention is made of books ('buoch'), of scholarly learning ('schuollist'), of Latin, and of Isold's ability to read and write.[37] Alongside this, however, the social attainments necessary for a young woman's role at court on which Thomasin laid such

---

[34] Jaeger, *Origins*, pp. 214, 224.　　[35] *Ibid.*, p. 135.

[36] Amalaberga: Bezzola, *Origines* I 15, fn. 2. Adela: *ibid.*, II 2, 378, fns. 1, 2. Edith: *ibid.*, II 2, 404, fn. 4.

[37] *Tristan* 7851, 7971, 7990, 8059.

stress are not neglected. In addition to books Isold is instructed in playing music ('seitespil', 'hantspil') and the peak of her education in *mores* is reached in the teaching of 'moraliteit', instruction in the *morum probitas* of Geoffrey of Cambrai and associated by Jaeger with 'elegantia morum'.[38] Gottfried makes it clear that any woman at court should be instructed in it in youth ('diu kunst diu lêret schoene site:/dâ solten alle frouwen mite/in ir jugent unmüezic wesen').[39] However important, it is combined in Isold's case with book learning and literacy, as it is with the courtier bishops on whom Jaeger concentrates. In her case, as with other women (historical as well as literary), reading formed part of her education.

Prayer-books, to which we now turn, belong here not merely because, amongst their users, women are particularly well attested as reading them, but also because they were employed to teach reading. Although nowadays private prayer can take place inwardly, without voice or text, in the Middle Ages prayer was more closely, if not exclusively, tied to writing and hence to reading.[40] It is true that short prayers could be memorised without recourse to a text (a possibility conceded to the illiterate), but more commonly prayer was by reading a text. This is suggested by the *Klarissenregel* allowing an educated member of the order to say simply the Lord's Prayer if there is a reason for her not to pray from a book, thereby exceptionally permitting her what is normally granted to the uneducated. Reading a prayer from a book can also be made explicitly clear, as in the *Trierer Floyris* ('sie hat al dise naht gelesen/ir gebet an ir buoken' all night she read her prayers from her books), where 'reading' and 'book' reinforce one another, or in the *Vie de Sainte Colette*, where the saint also prayed at night by candlelight, but when a candle fell over, burning her book, she lamented that her prayer had been made imperfect. A similar episode, where light is necessary for reading her prayers at night, is reported of the Viennese beguine, Agnes Blannbekin.[41] The examples I have chosen all concern women reading their prayers, but there are many others to confirm them. The majority of written prayers in German that have come down to us can be shown to be for nuns' use rather than for monks, a disparity which may be due to the latter having a greater command of Latin and no need of a vernacular text.[42] Whether vernacular or not, Hamburger has drawn attention to an illustration of 'La Sainte abbaye', showing nuns processing to Mass, carrying prayer books in hand,

---

[38] *Ibid.*, 7851, 7971, 8006–30. Jaeger, *Origins*, pp. 221f.
[39] *Tristan* 8009–11.   [40] Hamburger, *Canticles*, p. 18.
[41] Memorised: Riché, *Education*, p. 480. *Klarissenregel* and *Floyris*: Green, *Listening*, p. 320. *Colette*: Saenger, 'Books', p. 144. Blannbekin: Ruh, *Geschichte* II 134.
[42] Ehrismann, *Geschichte* II 1, 167–72; Vollmann-Profe, *Wiederbeginn*, p. 118; Janota, *Orientierung*, p. 445. Wolf, 'Beobachtungen', talks of a reading use of such texts by not so highly educated women.

and to a miniature with a Franciscan nun, kneeling with an open prayer book.[43] It would be quite mistaken, however, to restrict these examples to nuns alone, for Hamburger has again connected the rise of the illustrated prayer book in Germany in the twelfth and later centuries with the growth of lay piety, with a seminal role played by women in the development of new habits of prayer, above all in patronage of 'customs that originated in the cloister before passing them on to the laity'.[44]

The most common forms of prayer-book were the Psalter and the Book of Hours, not merely largely read by women, but used for teaching to read. That the Psalter was read for purposes of prayer is repeatedly attested, although this could often be memorised reading, prompted by a written cue. Berthold von Regensburg equates women reading their Psalter with their praying to God, in *Die Klage* Uote reads her Psalter at the canonical hours ('las an ir salter alle ir tagezît), and in Wolfram's *Parzival* Guinevere prays similarly ('an ir venje si den salter las' she read the Psalter kneeling).[45] These examples have been chosen to show that women in particular used their Psalters in this way, and Haubrichs has further shown how in the early Middle Ages, both in historical and in literary records, women are associated with reading the Psalter.[46] Mary is depicted in contemporary medieval terms by Otfrid in the Annunciation scene ('mit salteru in henti, then sang si' with a Psalter in her hand from which she sang) and of Hildegard von Bingen it is reported that she had been taught nothing but the Psalter, after the custom with young noblewomen ('nichil umquam didicerit, nisi solum psalterium more nobilium puellarum').[47] In addition, the Psalter served a double function: to instil the elements of Christian wisdom and ethics (distantly comparable to Jaeger's *litterae et mores*) and at the same time to teach the art of reading. What was demanded of monks was also theoretically applicable to nuns: whoever wished to enter monastic life had to learn to read and did this from the Psalter (even if the reading was memorised reading and what had been learned by heart was not always fully understood). What was common practice in monasteries could be adopted for lay teaching, privately or in schools: as soon as the pupil had learnt the ABC the first reading book was the Psalter. To know how to read was to know the Psalter ('psalteratus').[48]

---

[43] Hamburger, *Visual*, pp. 81 (and Fig. 1.2, p. 45), 380 (and Fig. 7.47).   [44] *Ibid.*, pp. 149f.
[45] Berthold I 253, 18f.: Green, *Listening*, p. 319. *Klage* 3682–5: *ibid.*, p. 143. *Parzival* 644, 23: *ibid.*, p. 319.
[46] *Anfänge*, p. 50. Cf. Wolf, 'Psalter', pp. 141f., 149, 160, and 'Beobachtungen'.
[47] Otfrid: see fn. 22. Hildegard: Küsters, *Garten*, p. 50 and fn. 102.
[48] Monastic education: Küsters, *Garten*, p. 50; Riché, *Écoles*, pp. 38f. Lay teaching: Grundmann, *AfK* 26 (1936), 134; Riché, *Écoles*, pp. 223, 297f., and *Education*, pp. 463f. Examples, textual and pictorial, are

The second form of prayer book, the Book of Hours, flourished in France, England, and the Netherlands, but not in Germany. It arose in the thirteenth century when the Little Office of Our Lady, hitherto an appendix to the Psalter, became detached and formed the basic text of a distinct prayer-book, the Book of Hours, normally of smaller, portable format and meant for private piety and for reading at certain times of the day.[49] This combination of private piety and reading has been seen by Saenger as an important stimulus to silent reading.[50] A well-known depiction of a woman reading is found in the Hours of Mary of Burgundy in an image showing the owner sitting in what appears to be an oratory opening onto the nave of a church.[51] She holds an open book, protected as a valuable object by a rich green cloth. Mary is doing more than just looking down at her book, she is reading it (with closed lips, therefore presumably silently), for with the forefinger of her left hand she follows the text on the left-hand page as she reads it. She recurs again in the body of the church (again with a prayer-book), kneeling in front of Mary with Child – a visualisation of the owner's devotional reading. That such books were popular with women can be seen from the way in which they were often commissioned for them on marriage and occur amongst the objects they leave to other women in their wills.[52] The female context of reading one's prayer in this way is well captured in the *Grandes Heures* of Anne of Britanny, who is shown kneeling with hands together in devotion and with her patron saints, Anne, Ursula and Helena, standing behind her.[53] On the low table before her lies her own Book of Hours, open so as to guide her prayer. This open book in the miniature is identical with the book that Anne would use in her prayers, in which she would be encouraged by this image of herself as a pious woman and by the support of three female saints.

Like the Psalter, the Book of Hours was also used in teaching to read: its common designation as a primer (or elementary schoolbook for teaching children to read) is indicative enough. For example, Isabeau of Bavaria gave one young daughter a Book of Hours and another an alphabet Psalter as teaching aids, while Christine de Pizan in more general terms advises mothers to give their daughters devotional books when they were old enough to

---

to be found in Reynolds, *Reading*, p. 9 (cf. Caviness, 'Anchoress', p. 136 [Fig. 26]); Riché, 'Psautier', pp. 253–6; *Écoles*, pp. 223, 297f.; Alexandre-Bidon, 'Femmes', p. 100 (Fig. 6); Scase, 'Anne', p. 91; *Krone*, pp. 354 (and Fig. 234), 444. If the Psalter was early used for religious instruction (Wolf, 'Psalter', p. 141), then the pedagogic principle *litterae et mores* could easily lend it to teaching to read as well.

[49] Hartham, *Books*, p. 13.   [50] Saenger, 'Books', p. 142.
[51] See Fig. 6 and Penketh, 'Women', p. 266.   [52] *Ibid.*, pp. 270f.
[53] Driver, 'Mirrors', pp. 89f. (and Fig. 47).

begin reading.[54] Illustrated texts, depicting women owners or saints reading provided the kind of encouragement, by women to women, which we considered earlier.

This role played by mothers brings us to the question who assumed responsibility for teaching children or young women to read. First and foremost was the mother herself, as we have seen in the case of Mary being taught to read by Anne. An instructive visualisation of this is provided by the Primer of Claude of France, conveying the message that a child's literacy was the mother's responsibility.[55] On the first page Mary and Claude are presented to Claude's name saint by Anne, but Claude, on the threshold of instruction in reading, holds a closed book in her hand. On the last page Claude kneels as Anne teaches Mary from a book, but this time Claude's book is open as she follows the lesson. At the end of her primer, Claude can now read, but we are meant to realise that it was her mother's responsibility, as it had been with Mary, for Claude's mother was called Anne. In a less sophisticated manner this responsibility is conveyed in the Manesse manuscript with Die Winsbeckin, where the mother is shown instructing her daughter with the conventional gesture of (didactic) speech, but with no indication of a book or reading.[56] An early example of a mother's function as teacher (of her son) is Dhuoda's *Liber manualis*, in agreement with the recommendation of Jonas of Orléans that women should teach their menfolk to mend their ways.[57] In many saints' *vitae* fathers appear to play a minor role in the upbringing of their young, the major responsibility falling to the mother to provide an education in Christian values through personal example and formal study (although it is not always clear how far this included literacy). From Clanchy we are to expect a detailed study of the mother's role in educating the young, especially on the part of pious mothers who could themselves read the Psalter. An English poem connected with Walter of Bibbesworth states categorically: 'Woman teacheth child on book'. For Clanchy the widespread literacy amongst laypeople on which the success of the printed book depended was due to mothers teaching their children the elements of reading in the home, an extension of literacy from its earlier location in the monastery. Alongside the earlier monastic (and male) monopoly of the book he places a female appropriation in the Books of Hours in a sphere of pronouncedly domestic literacy.[58]

[54] Primer: Duffy, *Stripping*, pp. 209–32. Isabeau and Christine: Bell, 'Women', p. 163. Further examples: Alexandre-Bidon, 'Femmes', pp. 97 (Fig. 3), 102 (Fig. 7), 111–15, 116 (Fig. 13); Aston, *Lollards*, pp. 124f.; Sheingorn, 'Mother', pp. 74, 76; Scase, 'Anne', p. 93; McCash, 'Patronage', pp. 22f.; Krug, *Families*, pp. 70–2; Chaucer, *Prioress's Tale* 64f.

[55] Fig. 4 and Sheingorn, *Gesta* 32 (1993), 76 (and Figs. 14, 15, p. 77).   [56] Walther, *Codex*, pl. 71.

[57] Thiébaux, *Dhuoda*, p. 26.   [58] Clanchy, *Memory*, p. 245; 'Learning', pp. 33–9.

Still in the domestic sphere, education could also be provided by a tutor
or court chaplain, although the evidence for this (and its importance?) is
strikingly less. An example comes from Gottfried's *Tristan* in which, before
Tristan takes in hand Isold's education, we are told that this had earlier been
done by a court cleric ('pfaffe'), trained in any number of courtly social
accomplishments, who had also educated Isold's mother.[59] He is described
as the queen's teacher ('der küneginne meister'), but also as responsible
for her daughter's instruction ('die hete er ouch in sîner pflege,/die lêrte
er dô'). However, his instruction goes beyond courtly accomplishments,
it also covers literacy ('beidiu buoch und seitespil'), as was also the case
with Tristan's teaching. Both teachers therefore give instruction in *litterae
et mores*. More commonly, however, the tutor appointed to teach young
women at court is herself a woman ('meisterin'), a precaution that avoided
the scandal arising from Abelard teaching Heloise.[60]

A third possibility was to send the child for education outside the home,
in the case of girls generally to a convent. Here they could be instructed in
Christian truths and ethics as well as taught to read, either as preparation
for a formal profession as a nun or to return to the world as a literate
woman. Many religious houses in Ottonian Germany had schools of this
type that had a high reputation, including important ones such as Essen,
Herford, Gandersheim and Quedlinburg, where the education provided
was certainly much more than respectable.[61] From England we have the
example of Mathilda of Scotland, the wife of Henry I, who had been sent
to a convent for instruction in 'literatoriam artem', which suggests, as in
other cases, not merely reading, but knowledge of Latin. Earlier, Edith, the
wife of Edward the Confessor, had been educated at the convent of Wilton.
From the Low Countries we have the comparable example of Beatrice of
Nazareth who received an early education at a beguine school, whilst in
Germany Hildegard von Bingen learned the Psalter (meaning to read Latin)
from the anchoress Jutta von Sponheim.[62]

One difficulty in determining whether a woman had been educated in
literacy lies in what we may call 'concealed education': she may not be
explicitly said to have been educated, but the evidence implies that this
must have been so or was probably so. Three types of evidence suggest
this. Certainly, there are some cases where mention of a woman's education

---

[59] *Tristan* 7701–20, 7729–31.
[60] Rösener, 'Frau', p. 218, fn. 203; Reuvekamp-Felber, *Volkssprache*, p. 284, fn. 598.
[61] Beach, *Women*, pp. 18f.
[62] Mathilda: Schirmer, 'Rolle', p. 236. Edith: Stafford, *Queens*, pp. 54f. Beatrice: Andersen, *Voices*, p. 35.
Hildegard: Newman, *Sister*, p. 5.

makes it clear that this embraced learning to read, as with Mathilda of Scotland, sent for education to the convents of Wilton and Romsey ('apud Wiltoniam et Rumesium educata, litteris quoque foemineum pectum exercuit') or with Agnes of Weimar's instruction at Quedlinburg ('tam litteris quam diversarum artium disciplinis . . . fuit instructa').[63] But there are many cases where a woman's course of education is not actually mentioned, but can be reasonably deduced from her description as literate. This is true of Mathilda, the wife of William the Conqueror ('litterarum scientia'), of Ida, the mother of Godfrey of Bouillon ('litteris imbuta'), and of Adela of Blois whose interest in verse and in books is commended by Baudri de Bourgueil ('Versibus applaudit, scitque vacare libris'). It may also be true of Judith, the daughter of Ludwig of Thuringia ('litteris et Latino optime eruditam eloquio'), where we cannot tell whether 'eruditam' is a past participle describing the process of her education or is used adjectivally to denote its result, her Latinate literacy.[64] No matter whether education is referred to in these cases or not, there can be no doubt that these women are presented as capable of reading, on whatever level of attainment.

Another concealment of a woman's education, this time calling into question her very literacy, results from the criteria that are being used in medieval sources. Quite apart from the fact that modern scholarship has called into question the simple polarity between 'literate' and 'illiterate' and has suggested a range of terms to denote various shades in between,[65] we find earlier suggestions that *litteratus* was used in a sense going far beyond an ability to read. Already for Sulpicius Severus *litteratus* could mean 'well read' rather than simply 'able to read', while in the twelfth century John of Salisbury demands expertise in a variety of disciplines of a true *litteratus*, claiming that someone ignorant of them is illiterate, even if he knows his letters ('qui enim istorum ignari sunt, illitterati dicuntur, etsi litteras noverint').[66] From such an attitude it follows that anyone of advanced Latinity, as clerics could claim to be, would hesitate to describe as literate those who did not measure up to this standard (as in their eyes women did not), especially when their reading was in the vernacular. We need therefore to be careful how we interpret it when a woman is described in our sources as illiterate.

---

[63] Mathilda: Bezzola, *Origines* II 2, 423, fn. 1. Agnes: Thompson, *Literacy*, pp. 91, 109 (n. 88).
[64] Mathilda: Thompson, *Literacy*, pp. 167, 185 (n. 19). Ida: *ibid.*, pp. 137, 158 (n. 115). Adela: Bezzola, *Origines* II 1, 371. Judith: Thompson, *Literacy*, pp. 100, 115 (n. 155).
[65] Green, *Listening*, p. 328, n. 105.
[66] Sulpicius: Grundmann, *AfK* 40 (1958), 20f. John of Salisbury: *ibid.*, p. 52; Green, *Listening*, p. 328, n. 104.

Thirdly, there are cases where we need to be equally careful when it is the woman who describes herself as illiterate. This occurs mainly in the shape of a humility formula whose conventional nature makes it risky to take it as factual truth rather than as a religious self-deprecation or a deliberate distancing from the values of book learning. If we have by now learnt to suspect the truth of Wolfram's denial of his book learning ('ine kan decheinen buochstap') we need to be equally careful when women say the same of themselves.[67] Despite her range of learning Christine de Pizan plays it down, presenting herself as unlearned in logical subtleties and therefore unable to compete with learned masters, but nonetheless able to debate with those who attack women, as in the debate on the *Roman de la Rose*.[68] More commonly, however, the humility formula is used by or for women not as a rhetorical ploy, but in a religious context, even if just as polemically. Margery Kempe challenges medieval stereotypes about women in meeting the assumption that women were intellectually inferior, unlikely to be formally educated, so that she must be either divinely or devilishly inspired. She of course has no doubt that the former is the case and succeeds at least in impressing lawyers at Lincoln, despite her lack of learning, who are forced to admit: 'we have gon to scole many ʒerys, and yet arn we not sufficient to answeryn as thu dost'.[69] Mechthild von Magdeburg found herself in a comparable position as an uneducated woman ('der schrift ungeleret') confronting trained masters ('wisen meister an der schrift'). As with Christ's reversal of worldly values in revealing himself not to the wise, but to babes, God points out to Mechthild that her lack of education is an advantage. In his eyes the wise are really foolish ('Man vindet manigen wisen meister an der schrift, der an im selber vor minen ögen ist ein tore' There are many masters learned in letters who in themselves are fools in my eyes) and it is the uneducated mouth, inspired by the Holy Ghost, that teaches the learned tongue or man of learning ('das der ungelerte munt die gelerte zungen von minem heligen geiste leret'). A woman, unlearned in the schools but divinely inspired, can therefore teach men whose knowledge, coming only from the schools, makes them really unknowledgeable ('unbekante lúte').[70]

This last paragraph has shown us that women's education, on one level or another, can be presented, by a reversal of gender stereotypes, as superior to men's. In the religious context (Margery Kempe, Mechthild von

[67] Wolfram: Bumke, *Wolfram*, pp. 5–8.
[68] Minnis, *Magister*, pp. 216f. Cf. also Semple, 'Consolation', p. 46.
[69] *Book* 4550f. (p. 269); Watt, *Secretaries*, pp. 38f.
[70] Mechthild, *Licht* II 26 (p. 138) and III 1 (p. 148).

Magdeburg) this depended on a reinterpretation of wisdom (inspiration in place of book learning, *sapientia* instead of *scientia*), but elsewhere this superiority of women is not so surprising, at least before the late Middle Ages, when young noblemen started going to university. The reason for women's superior literacy in the lay world is in part a negative one, namely a divorce from, even hostility to schooling in books and literacy on the part of men for a long period in the Middle Ages, based on a conviction that it was detrimental to the long training necessary for the mounted warrior and the persistence of an oral culture which could adequately provide the historical awareness and ethical norms necessary for the laymen.[71] Thus, for the most part noblewomen acquired some reading ability, whilst their menfolk remained illiterate. An early example of this gender-based difference occurs with Theoderic's daughter who wished for a Roman (lettered) education for her son, but met with (male) disapproval on the grounds that a future ruler should be brought up in the traditional oral manner and not taught to fear the schoolmaster's cane. Of Wiborada it is reported that she learned Latin and the Psalms so well that she seemed in no way inferior to a priest ('nequaquam inferior esse videretur sacerdote'), but we pass from equal to superior literacy on the part of women in other cases. The legend of Catherine of Alexandria presented a noblewoman with a reputation for learning who, like Margery Kempe and the lawyers of Lincoln, defeated learned men in disputation. Peter the Venerable so admired Heloise's intellect that he said she surpassed all women and, with a slight qualification to save appearances, almost every man. The emperor Konrad II was illiterate, whereas his wife Gisela had copies made of Notker's translation of the Psalms and of Job. Hugh of Fleury generalises his point much more widely when he dedicates his *Historia ecclesiastica* to Adela of Blois instead of to illiterate princes who despise the art of literature ('non illiteratis principibus, quibus ars litteratoria spretui est').[72]

Our judgement whether women's literacy was superior to men's depends very much on who the men are with whom they are compared, for their restricted educational opportunities normally made them inferior to clerics, but still superior to most laymen. A similar distinction has to be made when we consider finally women's Latinity where, given the state of research at present, no generalisation (for or against the extent of women's ability) is

---

[71] Green, *Listening*, pp. 23f.
[72] Theoderic's daughter: Bezzola, *Origines* I 19; Green, *Listening*, p. 24. Wiborada: Schulenburg, *Forgetful*, p. 292. Catherine: Orme, *Childhood*, p. 156. Heloise: Baswell, 'Heloise', p. 163. Gisela: Thompson, *Literacy*, pp. 88, 105 (n. 62) and Green, *Listening*, p. 184. Adela: Thompson, *Literacy*, pp. 168, 185 (n. 28).

possible. In the present unsatisfactory state of our knowledge a wide range of possibilities is open, without any overall consensus. These views range from the assumption that women had no Latin at all to the distinction that men had access to Latin, but women only to the vernacular, or to the concession that women understood only a simple Latin (but so did some men, laymen or clerics) or possessed only a limited Latin (as did some clerics) or were barred from expert Latin.[73] Beyond this, there are undoubted cases where some women had a knowledge of Latin, even to a high degree, as presupposed in the liberal arts, engaging in Latin correspondence, commissioning Latin works, translating from Latin for others and composing works in Latin themselves.[74]

Despite the many cases where it is clear that women had some degree of Latinity one qualification has to be made, with important consequences. It is frequently attested that a work was translated from Latin into the vernacular or composed in the vernacular in the first place for a woman or a community of women. This is important in two respects. First, it provides examples of vernacular literacy, breaking free from the monopoly of Latin literacy, as we saw above. Secondly, this state of affairs also encouraged the rise of a vernacular written literature, promoted in various ways by women, as we shall see. These two points enable us to assess the place of women in the dynamics of literacy in the Middle Ages. In addition to their possible, but still gender-restricted access to Latin, women played an important part in the development of vernacular literacy, whether at court, in the religious community or for private devotions. Further, in seeing to the education of their children at home, including instruction in reading for their daughters, women contributed to the domestication of literacy and reading. A process of domestication is also present in another respect, in the adoption of monastic devotional reading (Psalter and the Hours) into the lay context of women's households (what Southern calls the 'conjunction of monastic piety with the religious impulses of great ladies', shaping private devotions).[75] These are points to which we shall recur in the following pages.

---

[73] Only scattered examples are possible in this footnote. No Latin: illustrated by Chauntecleer in Chaucer's *Nun's Priest's Tale* (Martin, *Women*, pp. 2f.). Men's Latin and women's vernacular: Lucas, *Women*, pp. 151f.; Bell, *Nuns*, p. 75, 78; Woods, 'Books', pp. 177f. Simple Latin: Schiewer, 'Möglichkeiten', p. 182. Limited Latin: Thompson, *Literacy*, pp. 88, 144, 145; Orme, *Childhood*, p. 160. No expert Latin: Dronke, *Women*, pp. viii, 168.

[74] Knowledge of Latin: Thompson, *Literacy*, pp. 85, 87, 129, 138f., 146, 167. High Latinity: *ibid.*, p. 138 (Heloise); Riché, *Education*, p. 435, fn. 469. Translating from Latin: Ehrenschwendtner, 'Bildungswesen', pp. 342, 346 (n. 33); Lucas, *Woman*, p. 151. Composing and commissioning works in Latin by women will be treated below.

[75] Southern, *Anselm*, p. 37.

1 Hildegard von Bingen writes her visions, *Liber divinorum operum*

2   Marie de France writes her *Fables*

3 Marie de France peruses her completed book

4 Princess Claude de France learns to read

5 (a) A woman at her devotions

5 (b) The Annunciation

6   Mary of Burgundy reads her Book of Hours

7   Gerburg with Psalter, Naumburg Cathedral

8   Berchta with Psalter, Naumburg Cathedral

9 Tomb effigy of Eleanor of Aquitaine

10   Mary Magdalene reading, by Rogier van den Weyden

11   The Holy Kinship, by Geertgen tot Sint Jans (after restoration)

12 Hedwig of Silesia

13 Baudonivia composes her *Vita Radegundis*

14   Bridget of Sweden receives and transmits her visions

LAYWOMEN

From the often brief references in our sources to a woman reading it is not always possible to tell the precise sense in which 'reading' is used, whether, according to Hugh of St Victor, she reads to herself or to others or whether she is being read to. In any case, reading of one kind or another is involved. One reflection of this uncertainty is the difficulty of judging, when a woman is presented as owning or holding a book in her hands, whether she actually read it.

That owning a book need not always amount to reading it will be admitted by any modern scholar who honestly surveys the unread books in his own library, so that the medieval equivalent need not surprise us. A first example is provided by Priester Wernher's *Maria*: after referring to Christ's birth he states that any woman who possesses a copy of his book and holds it in her hand when in labour will be assured of a painless delivery since this was miraculously the case with Mary.[76] Theoretically, this could imply two senses of reading (either the woman had read the book before or it was read out to her during labour), but neither of these senses is actually stated. Another possibility, with no implication of reading, is equally possible, for there is evidence for the use of amulets, consisting of sacred texts or fragments of them, placed on the stomach or breast of a woman in labour and regarded as a form of white magic to assist her.[77] Mary's miraculous pregnancy and what was regarded as the painless birth of Christ were an obvious precedent for this practice, but another was the saint's legend of Margaret. She could be invoked on such occasions because her martyrdom involved being devoured alive by a dragon, from whose belly she was delivered with ease. Copies of her legend were also given as amulets to pregnant women.[78] Although reading was possible in these cases, it was not necessarily so, since what was regarded as efficacious was physical contact with a sacred text or possession of it in the house.

A second distinction between owning and reading a book comes from a very different source, the Lollards of late medieval England. Our knowledge of the use of books by these heretical groups comes largely from the evidence brought before their trials and makes it clear that not all individual heretics who possessed a book were able to read it. Instead, they depended on

---

[76] Wernher, *Maria* A 2505–38. Cf. Weitlauff, 'Ebner', pp. 344f.; Dinzelbacher, 'Rollenverweigerung', p. 21.

[77] Düwel, 'Buch', pp. 170–93; Schreiner, 'Buchstabensymbolik', pp. 83–93.

[78] Millett and Wogan-Browne, *Prose*, p. xxii; Schulenburg, *Forgetful*, p. 230; Wogan-Browne, 'Women', p. 78, n. 10; Schreiner, 'Buchstabensymbolik', p. 93; Wogan-Browne, *Lives*, p. 126; Düwel, 'Buch', p. 184; Robertson, *Speculum* 78 (2003), 13.

someone else in their community or a wandering heretical preacher to read it out to them, so that, if reading is involved, it is not personal reading by the owner of the book. For example, Joan Smith of Coventry enjoyed temporary ownership of a book by borrowing it, but had to arrange for someone to come to her house to read it to her.[79]

The uncertainty of evidence for ownership of a book as proof of reading is enhanced by the fact that, alongside this negative evidence, there is some for owners as actual readers, including MS pointers to continued readers' use or instructions how to read.[80] This evidence includes the two cases just discussed. Thus, Priester Wernher expects his *Maria* to be read by all true Christians, but specifies them as clerics, laymen and women, so that he envisages women readers alongside those who may use his work to assist childbirth. Similarly, although there were illiterates amongst the Lollard book-owners of Coventry, there was also a noticeable number of literate women who were therefore not dependent on others to read to them.[81] This evidence can be taken further. From the number of Christian authors quoted by Dhuoda in her *Liber manualis* it has been concluded that her passages were not merely derived from florilegia, but point to a collection of books which she herself read (she says expressly that her work was compiled and woven together from other volumes). In the twelfth century Constance Fitzgilbert not merely purchased a copy of the life of Henry I by David, but used to read it in her chamber. From the preface to a religious poem, *The Nightingale*, it emerges that Anne Stafford possessed many books and read them herself, but also arranged for public readings. A similar equation of owning with reading books is reported of Margaret Beaufort by John Fisher, saying 'right studyous she was in bokes whiche she hadde in grete nombre both in Englysshe & in Frensshe'.[82] However, examples such as these do not cancel out those where owners were not actual readers, so that it remains hazardous, without further confirmation, to assume female readership simply on the basis of female ownership.[83]

Similar uncertainty attaches to the presentation of someone holding a book. In his life of Elisabeth of Hungary Osbern Bokenham says that she had no Latin, but nonetheless would often have a Psalter open before her,

[79] McSheffrey, *Gender*, pp. 34f., 70f.
[80] Bodarwé, *Sanctimoniales*, pp. 232–302; Wolf, 'Beobachtungen'.
[81] Wernher, *Maria* A 139–42. Henkel, 'Erzählen', p. 8, refers to the Berlin MS as belonging to the type of devotional book for aristocratic use. McSheffrey, *Gender*, p. 34.
[82] Dhuoda: Riché, *Écoles*, pp. 300f. Constance Fitzgilbert: Gaimar, *Estoire des Engleis* 6489f. Anne Stafford: Krug, *Families*, pp. 78f. Margaret Beaufort: Hutchison, 'Reading', p. 225.
[83] As does McNamer, 'Lyrics', p. 203.

on which she mused as though she were reading.[84] We are not meant to see a difference between the show and the substance of piety here, and other examples confirm that reading need not always accompany a book held in the hand. Prayer books could serve as status symbols as long as only noblewomen could read and afford them. While they were still luxury objects they remained the attributes of noblewomen, tokens of wealth, prestige objects meant to impress, fashionable accessories as well as outward signs of devotional piety. But none of these possibilities necessarily means that they were personally read.

This does not mean of course that books could not also be held for the purpose of reading. When Otfrid describes Mary reading the Psalter at the Annunciation he depicts her holding it ('mit salteru in henti'), like the Sibyl in Veldeke's *Eneasroman* ('ein bûch hete si an ir hant,/dar ane sach si ende las' she had a book in her hand in which she read). Thomasin von Zerclaere (who, like Priester Wernher, anticipates women alongside clerics and laymen amongst his readers) sees his book in the hands of his readers ('begrîfen', 'ze hant'), or lying in their lap ('ûf sîn schôz'). When the author of *Der Saelden Hort* presses the claims of his religious work against the competing ones of court literature on the interests of women readers he sees these secular works in their hands ('fúr Wigoleis, Tristanden/in megten, witwen handen' instead of *Wigalois* and *Tristan* in the hands of maidens and widows), whom he imagines as personal readers of secular and also, he urges, of religious literature.[85] For French examples I quote no more than one for public reading to others (in *Li chevalier as deus espees* a woman reads aloud to others from a romance she holds: 'et si tenoit/Un romant dont ele lisoit') and one for private reading (in Gautier's *Eracle* a woman reads to herself from a book in her hand: 'Un livre tient et si i list'). For another French example, coming from Norman England, we return to David's book owned and read by Constance Fitzgilbert, for our informant, Gaimar, promises to tell more than was written in David's book or held in the hand of the queen of Louvain, for whom it was originally written ('. . . ne la reine de Luvain/n'en tint le livere en sa main').[86]

Although, both with owning and holding a book, the cases suggesting reading are numerous, this cannot simply be assumed with no more ado. A similar range of possibilities can be illustrated, in the case of a woman holding a book, from art-historical evidence. We begin at Naumburg, where

[84] Clanchy, 'Images', p. 110. Cf. Alexandre-Bidon, 'Femmes', p. 93.
[85] Otfrid, *Evangelienbuch* I 5, 10. *Eneasroman* 2714f. Thomasin, *Welscher Gast* 14694–7, 14705–7. *Saelden Hort* 4407–10.
[86] *Chevalier* 8951f. *Eracle* 4244. David's book: Tyson, *Romania* 100 (1979), 192.

in the west choir of the cathedral there stand around the walls a number of statues of aristocratic founders and benefactors of the cathedral, both men and women. Amongst the women two concern us, for they are depicted holding a book: Gerburg holds a closed book and Berchta an open one (in each case probably a Psalter).[87] Even in this latter case we have no assurance that reading is in question, for Berchta holds the book at waist-height and does not look down at it, but straight ahead. If Gerburg carries her book as a status-symbol because it is a hallmark of a woman of rank, the figure of Berchta may suggest a greater degree of devotional piety with her open book, but neither shows an act of reading. A similar uncertainty applies to a twelfth-century French example, the recumbent tombstone effigy of Eleanor of Aquitaine, lying alongside her husband Henry II in the abbey church of Fontevrault.[88] She too holds a book, like Berchta's open and at waist-height, but in her horizontal position she gazes upwards and cannot be said to be reading her Psalter. As with Berchta, this may suggest devotional meditation, possibly after, but not in the course of reading. There are grounds for thinking that Eleanor commissioned these effigies herself, in which case we must assume that such funerary sculpture carried heavy political and religious implications, especially in the church of an abbey to which she herself retired in advanced age. The significance of the book may well be devotional, combined with a suggestion of Eleanor's interest in and encouragement of literature, but hardly, in this setting, the text of the love songs of her grandfather, Guilhem IX, count of Poitiers.[89] That would be adding to the mythology too much of which has accumulated around her person.

In my remaining art historical examples we consider the act of reading from an open book. If we return to the Hours of Mary of Burgundy (fifteenth century), more particularly to the image of her reading in an oratory,[90] it is to emphasise certain details which were absent from Naumburg and Fontevrault. Not merely is Mary's book open, she also holds it higher (well above waist height) and looks down at it. In addition, she can be seen following the text in front of her with her left forefinger on the left page while, visible only to close inspection of the original, the right page has been partly lifted (presumably by the right forefinger, not visible) in readiness to turning it over as reading progresses. The rapt attention with which Mary follows her text conveys meditational reading of a high quality. What was not present in the earlier examples is here delicately suggested. A similar

---

[87] Sauerländer, 'Stifterfiguren', pp. 169–245, especially 198–202. Cf. Figs. 7 and 8.
[88] Nolan, 'Choice', pp. 377–405; Clanchy, 'Images', pp. 116f. Cf. Fig. 9.
[89] Cf. Feld, *Frauen*, p. 76.
[90] Büttner, *Philobiblon* 16, 4 (1972), 103; Penketh, 'Women', pp. 266–8. Cf. Fig. 6.

delicacy informs a fifteenth-century image of Mary Magdalene, painted by Roger van der Weyden on a small panel forming part of what may well have been a larger altarpiece, now surviving only in fragments.[91] Again, the woman holds an open book above waist level, looks down at it closely and with her right hand has already lifted the right page before turning it over. Once more the act of reading has been caught in process. In its setting, however, this painting differs from the Hours of Mary of Burgundy. Instead of an oratory opening out onto a church interior we have now, visible even in its fragmentary state, a household interior, suggesting the domestication of literacy in the late Middle Ages. If this image formed part of an altarpiece the reading matter of Mary Magdalene was almost certainly of a religious nature, suggesting that laywomen could be engaged in devotional reading not merely in a church setting, but also at home.[92]

With a painting by Geertgen tot Sint Jans (fifteenth century) we reach a further degree of explicitness.[93] Its theme is what is known as the Holy Kinship (Anne, Mary and the infant Christ) seated alongside two other women, with men very much in the background in what is again a church interior. Anne seems to dominate this group (Mary sits slightly behind her) and, true to her educational role in teaching her daughter to read, she has an open book in her lap. In that position it would be difficult for her to read it, and she does not look down at it, but instead pensively straight ahead as if divorced from what is going on around her. With these details we seem to be back with Berchta at Naumburg or Eleanor at Fontevrault (open book, but eyes not directed at it), but one detail destroys this illusion, for on Anne's open book lies a pair of spectacles suggesting, as was traditionally characteristic of Anne, that she was a reader, with her reading either just concluded or about to be resumed. (Spectacles had been invented well before the time of Geertgen, after the magnifying qualities of the transparent stone *beryllus*, from which modern German 'Brille' is derived, had been recognised.) Anne not merely taught her daughter her letters, she also habitually read herself.

We conclude this brief survey of a non-verbal medium by turning to the Hedwig codex from Silesia.[94] It contains a picture of Hedwig, the patron saint of Silesia, complete with devotional aids. In her right hand she holds

[91] Penketh, 'Women', pp. 268f. Cf. Fig. 10.
[92] On private vernacular prayer-books, especially for women, see Ochsenbein, 'Privatgebetbücher', pp. 379–98; 'Gebetbuch', pp. 175–99.
[93] Sheingorn, *Thought* 64 (1989), 268–86, especially pp. 281f.; Ruiz-Calvez, 'Religion', pp. 123–55, especially pp. 136–8. Cf. Fig. 11 (after restoration, whereas Sheingorn and Ruiz-Calvez show the spectacles before restoration). I learned too late of *The Holy Kinship: a medieval masterpiece* by A. Wallert *et al.*, Zwolle 2001, to be able to take account of it.
[94] Hamburger, *Visual*, pp. 434–8; *Krone*, pp. 365f. Cf. Fig. 12.

to her breast a small figure of Mary and Child, but in her left hand two other aids, a rosary and a prayer-book. Into the pages of the latter she has inserted her fingers to keep the place in her reading to which she is about to return. Of this momentary, almost snapshot image of a woman reader I can do no better than quote what Hamburger has to say: 'It is as if we, as viewers, had just interrupted Hedwig at her reading, even though it is she and her image who have interrupted ours.'[95]

The context of these examples, from Naumburg through to Silesia, emphatically suggests religious reading matter, and although its precise nature may escape us, it is likely that the books in the early examples were Psalters, while the later ones could be either Psalters, too, or Books of Hours. In view of this and with an eye to the next step in our argument we may interpolate here a few more words on the importance of the Psalter for literate laywomen in the Middle Ages. We saw that Hildegard von Bingen's education in literacy went no further than learning to read the Psalter, but what interests us now is the further remark that in this she was following conventional practice with the daughters of noblemen ('more nobilium puellarum'). That this practice went back much earlier is suggested by the interest in Notker's translation and commentary on the Psalms shown by the Empress Gisela, ordering a copy to be made for herself ('Kisila imperatrix operum eius avidissima psalterium ipsum et Iob sibi exemplari sollicite fecit').[96] The interest of noblewomen in the Psalter is further reflected in the number of ambitious, high-quality Psalters commissioned by them, given to them or otherwise associated with them, such as the Queen Mary Psalter, the Philippa Psalter, the Ingeborg Psalter, the Elisabeth Psalter as well as the St Albans Psalter (although its connection with Christina of Markyate is less clear-cut).[97]

The relevance of this last paragraph to Gabriel's Annunciation to Mary may seem slight, except insofar as Mary can frequently be depicted as holding and/or reading a book, although that is a very loose connection. From early on Mary can be presented as closely engaged with books and reading. Ambrose depicts the young Mary as given to the reading of the holy scriptures, a pseudo-Ambrosian text specifies them as the Books of Moses, while later texts speak alternatively of the prophets, in particular

---

[95] *Ibid.*, p. 438. That this presentation of a devout woman, later canonised, need not be remote from reality is clear from the so-called Hedwig prayer-book (Wolf, 'Psalter', p. 157; *Buch* II.1.4).

[96] Hildegard: see above, p. 92. Gisela: Schützeichel, *Studien*, p. 56.

[97] Queen Mary: Warner, *Queen*, and Stanton, 'Eve', pp. 172–89. Philippa: Stanton, 'Eve', p. 185. Ingeborg: Deuchler, *Ingeborgpsalter*. Elisabeth: Wolter-von dem Knesebeck, 'Nascita', pp. 49–118, and *Elisabethpsalter*, pp. 286–302. St Albans: Pächt *et al.*, *Psalter*, and Geddes, 'Psalter', pp. 197–216.

Isaiah because of what was interpreted as his foretelling of the virgin birth.[98] More significant for our purposes are the cases where Mary reads the Psalms. The pseudo-Ambrosian text mentions these ('carmina Davidica') alongside Moses, Hrotsvitha von Gandersheim likewise sees her as eagerly preoccupied with the Psalms ('carminibus semper studiosa Davidis') while, much later, Bruder Philipp in his *Marienleben* includes the Psalter among the other biblical books, prophetic or otherwise, she read.[99] Whether she is reading the Psalter or not, pictorial representations of Mary at the Annunciation from the fourteenth and fifteenth centuries commonly depict her as reading or surrounded with books, whereas in earlier images she is generally engaged in spinning, not reading. Two points are noteworthy about this late medieval iconography. First, there is no reference to Mary reading at the Annunciation in the gospels (but in the apocryphal tradition), so that some specific influence seems to be at work here. Secondly, the increased association of Mary with reading in the last two centuries of the Middle Ages coincides with the period when Anne is commonly depicted teaching her daughter to read. If Anne served as a role-model for mothers introducing their children to literacy, a similar function can be attributed to the presentation of Mary as a regular reader (not merely at the Annunciation),[100] adding respectability to laywomen occupying themselves with books.

But there is more to this scene than that. For art historians the decisive period for this iconography may be the late Middle Ages with the rise of lay literacy, especially on the part of women, but for literary historians an important precedent is to be found already in the ninth century in Otfrid's description of the Annunciation. The author is quite explicit that the book which Mary is reading is the Psalter ('mit salteru in henti, then sang si unz in enti' with a Psalter in her hand which she sang through to the end), but he also combines this activity with another common practice of hers, making cloth from expensive high-quality thread.[101] Both these activities are absent from this scene in any biblical or patristic source available to Otfrid, but both are occupations in which high-ranking noblewomen were frequently engaged.[102] This suggests that Otfrid was depicting Mary in

---

[98] These and many other examples are discussed by Schreiner, *AGB* 11 (1970), 1437–64, and *Maria*, pp. 116–48.

[99] Vollmann-Profe, *Kommentar*, p. 199; Schreiner, *AGB* 11 (1970), 1442, 1443.

[100] Büttner, *Philobiblon* 16, 4 (1972), 92–126, discusses (with illustrations) the many occasions on which Mary and other women are presented as readers.

[101] *Evangelienbuch* I 5, 11f.

[102] Schreiner *AGB* 11 (1970), 1444, and *FMS* 24 (1990), 322–4. Aelred of Rievaulx also refers to a royal bride, Edith, reading and spinning: Wogan-Browne, 'Women', p. 69, and *Lives*, p. 32.

terms of contemporary Carolingian noblewomen. That this was the case can be seen in the details he adds to this scene. Christ was conceived in the early Middle Ages in terms of power and kingship (Otfrid says that he is to occupy the throne of King David), but his royal descent is traced back not through Joseph (as in Mt 1, 20, Lc 3, 23–31), but through his mother. Accordingly, Mary is referred to as a high-ranking lady of noble birth ('itis frono', 'ediles fróuun'), all her forefathers were kings ('thie fordoron bi bárne warun chuninga alle'), and Gabriel visits her in her palace ('pálinza'), not in the household setting of late medieval Annunciations keeping pace with the domestication of literacy. Otfrid seems therefore to have been led by the contemporary practice of literate noblewomen in his description of Mary, whereas the movement of late medieval iconography was in the opposite direction, with Mary acting as a model for laywomen.[103] In either direction the iconography and literary description of this scene shed light on the reading practice of laywomen at two extremes of the medieval period.

At this point we pass from such general considerations to more particular issues, asking what evidence we have that individual laywomen could and did read. In view of the chronological and geographic spread of this book only a selection of examples can be given, chosen to illustrate laywomen readers over a timespan from the early to the late Middle Ages and to throw light on different aspects of women's reading practice. I divide this brief survey into three parts, looking first at what could be termed historical testimony, statements to the effect that an actual woman was known to be a reader or at least literate. This is followed by two different types of literary evidence, one consisting of remarks by an author showing that he expected certain, but unspecified women in his audience to read his text rather than merely listen to it read out, the other concerning characters in an author's work whom he depicts as readers.

The greatest degree of reliability obviously attaches to the first class of evidence ('historical'), but rather than look at the important, but exceptional, examples of highly literate women such as Margaret of Scotland, Adela of Blois or Margaret Beaufort, I think it more helpful to cover wider ground by considering a greater number of cases.

The evidence for Germany starts early with what has been shown for a number of Carolingian noblewomen leaving books in their wills or borrowing them from ecclesiastical libraries, although more doubt that they

---

[103] *Evangelienbuch* I 3, 17–31; I 5, 7–9 and 28. That Otfrid is unlikely to have meant Mary as a role-model is implied by Wolf, 'Psalter', p. 141, fn. 8.

were meant for personal reading attaches to books of a liturgical nature than to those meant for private devotions, especially Psalters. We have already seen that the Empress Gisela had a copy of Notker's translation of the Psalms made for her own use, but to this has to be added the fact that the Heidelberg MS of Otfrid's *Evangelienbuch* contains a stylus inscription to the effect that a certain Kicila, whether or not the same person as the Empress, read a considerable part of Otfrid's work ('Kicila diu scona min filo las'). (A comparable remark comes from a copy of Augustine's sermons in Merovingian Gaul, to the effect that a certain Juliana read it [and also made it?]: 'Iuliana legit lebrum Iuliana fecit'.)[104] From the Carolingian court we have evidence that Alcuin wrote the treatise *De ratione animae* for Charles the Great's granddaughter Gundrada, urging her also to read Augustine on the subject and referring to other works which, if she finds them among the imperial books, she is to read before sending them on to him. Amongst the women of the Ottonian dynasty it is not only abbesses at Quedlinburg and Gandersheim who are attested as reading Latin, but also laywomen such as Otto I's wife Adelheid ('litteratissima' and 'lectionibus intenta'), his sister Gerberg and his niece Hadwig. Legal rather than historical force attaches to the thirteenth-century *Sachsenspiegel* reference to psalters and religious books bequeathed by women, who it says are accustomed to reading them. From a much later date we have the revealing evidence from St Catharine's convent in Nürnberg that when the widow Katharina Tucherin joined the convent as a lay-sister in the fifteenth century she brought with her a collection of twenty-six manuscripts, suggesting that women in patrician families in the city read religious texts as laywomen which were acceptable additions to the convent's library.[105]

For cases of laywomen reading literature in French we may return to Constance Fitzgilbert who is said by Gaimar to have often retired to her room to read David's history of Henry I ('en sa chambre sovent le lit'), wording that suggests she read it herself and did not have it read to her. In the thirteenth century Isabella, Countess of Arundel, possessed (and read?) a number of hagiographic texts and Matthew Paris dedicated to her an Anglo-Norman version of his own Latin *Vita Edmundi*. The fact that Isabella's texts were copied in the collection of a women's convent exemplifies what we saw with Katharina Tucherin at Nürnberg: the easy continuity

---

[104] Carolingian noblewomen: McKitterick, *Carolingians*, pp. 225f., 247f., 262–4, and 'Frauen', p. 116. Kicila: Schützeichel, *Studien*, pp. 48–58. Juliana: Hen, 'Gender', pp. 222f.

[105] Gundrada: Ferrante, *Glory*, p. 54. Ottonian dynasty: Grundmann, *AfK* 26 (1936), 134f. *Sachsenspiegel*: Wolf, 'Psalter', p. 160. Katharina Tucherin: Thali, *Beten*, pp. 249, 261, 282f.; *Krone*, p. 139.

of reading-material between laywomen (court or city) and nuns.[106] Subject to all due caution about equating ownership of a book with personal readership, it is noticeable how frequently romances occur amongst the books known to have been possessed by women. (Does this lie behind the jibe by Chaucer's Nun's Priest against women who 'holde in ful greet reverence' the story of Lancelot?) In the fourteenth century the will of Isabella of France includes, alongside chansons de geste, a Trojan romance (by Benoît de Sainte-Maure?), Arthurian texts (*de gestis Arthuri*) as well as versions of Tristan and Perceval. Another Isabel, Duchess of York, included a Lancelot book in her will; for Elizabeth Darcy it was a Lancelot and for Elizabeth la Zouche likewise a Lancelot, but also a Tristan.[107] At the very least, details such as these betray an interest in vernacular literature, without informing us whether these romances were read personally by their owners or were read out to them and others. However, the lasting frequency of the double formula *audire vel legere* from classical Latin through to the early modern period and in all the three vernaculars with which we are concerned suggests that both modes of reading were in force and that it would be an oversimplification to opt for one rather than the other.[108]

Because of the multilingual nature of literature in England (Latin, English, French) it is best to look at the problem geographically, rather than linguistically (indeed, some of the romances listed in the last paragraph may have been in English rather than French). Of Mathilda, the wife of Henry I, it is reported that she was not content to hear, but insisted on continually inspecting (reading) the text itself ('non solum audire, sed etiam litteris impressam desideratis jugiter inspicere'). Here we have, if not the concision of the double formula, both modes of reception with particular stress on personal reading. The original audience of the *Ancrene Wisse* (early thirteenth century) was made up of three gentlewomen, all sisters, who had retired to life in an anchorhold. They possessed some basic Latin, were encouraged by the author to read saints' lives and, from internal evidence, were familiar with the conventions of French romances. This literate knowledge they did not acquire as recluses, but brought with them from their secular life, much as Katharina Tucherin brought her manuscripts with her. The earlier life of these sisters had included some considerable degree of literacy. The interpenetration of women's lay and religious worlds which we have observed has been analysed in the case of Margaret Purdans,

---

[106] Constance Fitzgilbert: see fn. 82 above. Isabella: Wogan-Browne, *Lives*, pp. 153–6.

[107] *Nun's Priest's Tale* 3212f. Isabella of France, Isabel of York, Elizabeth Darcy, Elizabeth la Zouche: Meale, 'Laywomen', p. 139.

[108] Green, 'Hören', pp. 23–44, and *Listening*, pp. 93f., 141f., 225–30.

a Norwich widow of the fifteenth century. From her will there emerges a picture of a female literate culture (a reading community) in which books are owned, lent and given by women to women, but which also extends its contacts to the learned clerical culture of Cambridge, to masters and doctors of divinity. Both worlds, laywomen and learned clerics, come together in this reading community and in Margaret's will, more closely than when Katharina Tucherin and the three gentlewomen of the *Ancrene Wisse* left the world for the enclosed life.[109]

In conclusion, we come to the two non-historical classes of evidence, in both of which I shall confine my evidence to German literature. I do this perforce, because the material for French and English has not yet been collected. In her study of women readers in French romance literature Krueger gives an appendix on 'dedications and allusions to woman readers', which in fact contains only two examples of women readers (*Floriant et Florete*: 'an implied lady reader'; *Roman de Silence*: 'with an appeal to women readers'). All the other examples concern a woman commissioning a work, having it dedicated to her or written for her, none of which need mean that she read it personally. We are rather better served by Meale's chronology of women and literature in Britain 1150–1500, for at least a distinction is made between women 'known to have been patrons and/or readers of literature'. Even so, more attention is paid to the first alternative than to the second. Constance Fitzgilbert, for example, is listed because Gaimar wrote for her, but no mention is made of her reading David's work.[110] The first of the classes now to be considered concerns women readers who, unlike the historical cases, are not identifiable for us, but who for the author at least were sufficiently real for him to know or assume that they were literate and whom he could expect with reasonable confidence to read his work. From what we have seen of women's education in reading and the historical evidence of their reading practice this confidence need not have been ill-founded.

Women are included alongside clerics and knights by Thomasin as potential readers of his *Welscher Gast*: these three classes of recipient are envisaged as looking at the work ('schouwen') and as reading it ('lesen'). For all his denial of literacy for himself and disclaimer of bookishness for his work Wolfram acknowledges that, alongside public readings, his *Parzival* may well be read by women ('swelch sinnec wîp,/ob si hât getriuwen lîp,/diu diz

[109] Mathilda: Thompson, *Literacy*, p. 188, n. 46. Three gentlewomen: Robertson, *Speculum* 78 (2003), 2. Margaret Purdans: Erler, *Women*, pp. 68–84.
[110] Krueger, *Women*, pp. 253–8; Meale, *Women*, following p. xi (unpaginated).

maere geschriben siht' whatever intelligent woman, as long as she is sin-
cere, who reads this story). Ulrich von Türheim concludes his *Tristan* with
a reference to the women whom he expects to read it ('swelhe vrouwen
an disem buoche lesen' whatever women read this book) and the same
expectation is voiced as a recommendation by Ulrich von Lichtenstein in
his *Frauenbuch* ('die vrouwen suln ez gerne lesen' women are to read it with
pleasure). We have seen that the author of *Der Saelden Hort* sees his religious
work in competition with romances such as *Wigalois* and *Tristan*, which he
conceives as being held by ladies in their hands as they read them, whilst
in *Lohengrin* an explicit reference to reading is made significantly in close
connection with a reference to ladies ('reine vrouwen'). In his *Weltchronik*,
Rudolf von Ems uses the double formula *lesen und hoeren* (read and hear),
thereby implying reading for some in his audience amongst whom there is
no reason not to include the noblewomen whom he mentions in the same
passage.[111]

To these examples from court literature I add a handful of cases where
laywomen are viewed as potential or probable readers of religious works.
The first two cases have already been mentioned. Priester Wernher may
have meant his *Maria* to be of use as an amulet for women in labour, but
he also confidently envisages a reading reception of his work by three classes
of recipient, including women. *Der Saelden Hort* may also be mentioned
in this context since, by seeing his text in rivalry with romances read by
women, the author hopes to wean them from that kind of reading matter to
his own. Corresponding to what we have seen of Mary and Margaret being
invoked to ease the pains of childbirth, we find Hartwig von dem Hage in his
Margaretenlegende showing the saint praying for those who write or read of
her martyrdom and claiming that childbirth will be made easier wherever his
book is read in honour of the saint. The situation resembles that postulated
by Priester Wernher, but Hartwig differs by expressly mentioning reading,
presumably by women in this context. In his *Marienleben* Walther von
Rheinau uses a double formula in anticipation of readers as well as listeners
and reckons with readers who will peruse his text with critical attention,
but also makes it clear that his audience consists of women as well as men.
As with Rudolf von Ems there is no reason not to include women amongst
these readers.[112]

---

[111]   *Welscher Gast* 14670, 14673–80, and Green, *Listening*, p. 152. *Parzival* 337, 1–3, and Green, 'Rezeption', pp. 277–9. *Tristan* 3658. *Frauenbuch* 2130. *Saelden Hort*: see above, fn. 85. *Lohengrin* 7622f.
Weltchronik 21712, 21729, 21731f., and Green *Listening*, p. 173.

[112]   *Margaretenlegende* 1496f., 1545f., and Green, *Listening*, p. 375, n. 124. *Marienleben* 67, 16152–4,
16237f., and Green, *Listening*, p. 174.

The last class of evidence for woman readers consists of examples which are internal to the literary text itself. They refer not to actual women (real or anticipated), but to fictional characters, yet that does not mean that they are divorced from contemporary experience. However imaginative or idealised this fictional literature may be, it retains a considerable number of links with the reality of its day, amongst which, as we have seen from the first two classes of evidence, may be included the undeniable fact that a considerable number of women could and did read. The depth and extent of their reading may be distorted hyperbolically at times, but this does not call into question the fact that they did read. So many authors present this activity in their works that it is quite improbable that it does not echo, at whatever distance, what was common practice.

Particularly frequent are episodes illustrating an aspect of pragmatic literacy, namely women receiving a letter and reading it themselves (not handing it, for example, to a cleric to read it for them).[113] In Wolfram's *Parzival* Guinevere reads a letter she has received, albeit aloud ('dô ir süezer munt gelas/al daz dran geschriben was' when her sweet mouth read all that was written in it), whilst Gottfried's Isold reads chips of wood with letters inscribed as a missive arranging an assignation with Tristan ('si las Isôt, si las Tristan'). In the *Alexandreis* of Ulrich von Etzenbach Candacis, fully westernised, receives a letter and takes it into her private chamber to read ('dô gienc die saelden rîche/an ir heimelîche,/die schrift selbe sie besach'), just like the lady of Ulrich von Lichtenstein, who acts in the same way ('diu wol gemuote danne gie/in ir heimlich, da si las/swaz an dem brief geschriben was' she then went into her chamber where she read what was written in the letter).[114] The converse of such pragmatic literacy, a lady writing a letter, is equally relevant if we bear in mind a characteristic of medieval literacy, that although it was possible to read without being able to write, writing implied the ability to read. Women characters who are depicted as writing therefore belong here. In Veldeke's *Eneasroman* Lavinia is shown writing a letter and, in slow motion, the name of Eneas; Gottfried's Isold writes her own letter to Tristan; in the *Apollonius von Tyrland* of Heinrich von Neustadt Lucina writes her message on a wax tablet. The lady of Ulrich von Lichtenstein not merely reads the letter she receives, she also writes one in return. Her pragmatic literacy in both directions is confirmation that writing involves the ability to read.[115]

---

[113] On this common practice in letter-writing see Köhn, 'Latein', pp. 340–56.

[114] *Parzival* 650, 23–6. *Tristan* 14678. *Alexandreis* 20273–5. Ulrich's lady: *Frauendienst* 165, 4–6.

[115] *Eneasroman* 10618–30, 10789–93. *Tristan* 15557f. *Apollonius* 2079f. Ulrich's lady: *Frauendienst* 113, 7f.

Women are also shown reading written texts other than merely letters in a secular context. In Veldeke's *Eneasroman* the Sibyl has a book in her hand which she is reading and Lavinia's mother is able to read the name of Eneas which her daughter hesitantly writes out for her. In Hartmann's *Iwein* (as in Chrétien's original) we have the well-known scene of the young aristocratic lady entertaining her parents in the garden by reading aloud to them ('vor in beiden saz ein maget,/diu vil wol, ist mir gesaget,/wälhisch lesen kunde' in front of them sat a maiden who, I am told, was well able to read French). In a more privately feminine context and again with a westernised view of the Orient Wirnt von Grafenberg depicts a scene in *Wigalois* in which a young maiden entertains the princess of Persia in the seclusion of her tent by reading out to her the story of Troy and Aeneas ('ein schoeniu maget vor ir las/an einem buoche ein maere' a fair maiden read a story from a book in front of her). In the *Trojanischer Krieg* of Konrad von Würzburg, Paris secretly declares his love for Helen by writing it in wine on the table in front of her, but she is able to read and understand its import. Helen's literacy also plays a part in the *Göttweiger Trojanerkrieg*, this time in the form of a letter in which Trifon declares his love for her. She is understandably requested to read it herself, which she does ('Heleyna mitt wiplicher tryft/Lass mit züchten die geschrift' as women do, Helen read what was written with good breeding).[116]

Even more frequently women characters can be depicted reading religious texts. We are not surprised that the book in question is often the Psalter, as with Guinevere in Wolfram's *Parzival*, Uote in *Die Klage*, Flordibel in the *Tandareis und Flordibel* of Der Pleier, and, crossing for once into French, Chrétien's Laudine in *Yvain*, mourning after the death of her husband.[117] Although we know from Wolfram's *Titurel* that he conceived of Sigune as literate (she read, if only in part, the inscription on the spaniel's leash) and although he depicts her in *Parzival* as a recluse withdrawn from the world and equipped with a Psalter, we are not expressly told that she read it.[118] But this is likely if her life is conceived as one long prayer, and the phrasing used of her with her Psalter ('Si truoc ein salter in der hant' she held a Psalter in her hand) is reminiscent of Otfrid's words about Mary at the Annunciation ('mit salteru in henti'). What Wolfram may imply, but does not make explicit, is made fully clear in the prose *Lancelot* where a 'clusenerinne' is shown reading her Psalter ('Sie saß darfur und laß yren selter' she sat in front and read her Psalter).[119] Whether still living in the

---

[116] Sibyl and Amata: *Eneasroman* 2714f., 10629f. *Iwein* 6455–7, 6461, 6470 (*Yvain* 5364–6). *Wigalois* 2710–22. *Trojanischer Krieg* 21676–83. *Göttweiger Trojanerkrieg* 4995f.

[117] *Parzival* 644, 23f. *Klage* 3682–5. *Tandareis* 8065f. *Yvain* 1414f.

[118] *Titurel* 144, 1. *Parzival* 438, 1 (cf. 435, 25).   [119] I 550, 15.

world or withdrawn from it as recluses, but not as professed nuns, all these laywomen are shown as literate and engaged in regular devotional reading.

It has been suggested that the exclusion of women from public activity in the spiritual and intellectual life of the ecclesiastic hierarchy may have encouraged them compensatorily to involve themselves more in private devotional reading.[120] Certainly, their role in religious reading was of considerable importance, as the rest of this chapter will show, more in the vernacular than in Latin, although that has interesting implications. The second largest group in women's reading matter was made up of romances and court literature at large but, whatever Chaucer's Nun's Priest may have thought of their predilection, this secular literature, however important historically to us with the benefit of hindsight, occupied a secondary place at the time in a literate culture dominated by religious and didactic writing. An observation made long ago by Grundmann on the thirteenth century has lost none of its significance.[121] He pointed out that women were particularly seized and taken up by the various religious movements of the time and to that extent largely alienated from the values of the court and its literature (Elisabeth of Thuringia is for him an obvious example).[122] We have seen an example of this clash of values, particularly with regard to women's reading, in *Der Saelden Hort*, but it can be detected elsewhere without an express reference to reading. This is the case with the prologue to the *Vies des Pères*, commissioned by Blanche de Navarre, Countess of Champagne. In it the author warns against the example of other ladies of this world who are more concerned with works in rhyme (conventionally the vehicle of untruth) and, turning to the Countess in person, advises her to abandon vain romances ('romanz de vanité') for the sake of spiritual truth and quotes *Cligés* and *Perceval* as texts which should be avoided.[123] By the end of the thirteenth century the Arthurian romance, in Germany at least, had just about run its full productive course, giving way to other genres dominated above all by religious concerns. For that reason the remaining sections in this chapter will be devoted, under various headings, to women's religious reading matter.

NUNS

Since the work of Grundmann we have known what was already apparent to contemporaries, namely that the religious movements of the high

---

[120] Bell, 'Women', p. 160. [121] *AfK* 26 (1936), 156, 159.
[122] Cf. Elm, 'Stellung', pp. 7–28. [123] Mölk, *Literarästhetik*, pp. 94f.

Middle Ages were attractive above all to women, who found in them an answer to their spiritual needs, whether in a regular order, on its fringes (as recluses or beguines) or separated from the Church as heretics. These are the categories that will occupy the following pages. Merely to list these possibilities, to which must be added the range of new orders which were founded in this period and were to some extent open to women, brings home the sheer variety of forms of religious life now available to women. In addition, the women's religious communities that concern us in this section also increased greatly in numbers: for example, in France and England taken together the number of monastic houses for women increased fourfold in the century from the Norman Conquest.[124] Even though a contradiction underlies female monasticism (it provided women opportunities, not least in education, largely lacking in secular life, but still subjected their independence to male, clerical supervision), there is scope enough for us to enquire what opportunities there were for women's literacy and reading in the professed life. I shall include canonesses alongside nuns in what follows, despite the many differences distinguishing them,[125] since the evidence available does not suggest that these differences affected their contact with the book. We shall be concerned for the most part not with individual women, but rather with conventual life at large and the written culture it encouraged.

As our first institutional possibility for women we may take the double monastery, in which men and women formed one community, with nuns in close vicinity to monks and the whole frequently directed by an abbess, even ruling over the monks.[126] These double houses are attested from the early Middle Ages in Anglo-Saxon England (where the leading example of Whitby, under the abbess Hilda, is interesting because of her encouragement of Caedmon to produce the first known example of Christian literature in the vernacular).[127] In Francia there are such renowned centres as Jouarre, Chelles and Faremoutiers. After these early beginnings the double monastery experienced a take-off, however short-lived, only towards the end of the eleventh century, as part of the wider move towards a greater differentiation of religious life in the founding of new orders.[128] In the German-speaking area these double monasteries were especially important; we shall later consider the example of Admont and the way in which the vernacular

---

[124] Variety: *Krone*, p. 344 (on Strassburg in 1400). Number: Staples and Karras, 'Tempting', p. 195, n. 19.

[125] Hamburger, *Canticles*, p. 157; Beach, *Women*, pp. 18f.

[126] Küsters, *Garten*, pp. 142–55; *Krone*, pp. 55f.

[127] Leyser, *Women*, pp. 24–8; Baltrusch-Schneider, 'Doppelklöster', pp. 57–79.

[128] Küsters, *Garten*, pp. 143, 155.

was cultivated in such centres. They clearly granted novel opportunities to women, more so than other new orders which soon grew reluctant to admit women. The best-known example is Fontevrault, founded by the wandering preacher Robert of Arbrissel as part of what he called his 'opus sanctimonialium' in gathering a following of women, including widows and virgins, 'prostitutes and haters of men'.[129] Despite these irregular origins Fontevrault developed into an aristocratic house, constituting a burial place for rulers of Anjou and also, as we have seen, for Eleanor of Aquitaine after she had retired there as a widow. Like other religious reformers Robert was convinced that he was reverting to the practice of the apostles in finding a place for women alongside men in his movement, although it was his focus on women which attracted more scandalised attention in his day. Like most early double monasteries Fontevrault was ruled by a woman and its popularity with women is reflected in the extraordinary number who flocked to it. If they did so in part to escape the constrictions of feudal marriage ('haters of men'), they found a reversal of roles at Fontevrault with men subordinate to an abbess.[130] A similar order, the Gilbertines, meeting comparable needs, was founded in England by Gilbert of Sempringham and was even more pronouncedly female in its membership.[131]

However attractive double monasteries were for women with the opportunities they provided, greater numbers sought entry in other new orders (first the Cistercians and Premonstratensians, then Franciscans and Dominicans). The *cura monialium*, the spiritual care of nuns at first by secular priests, then by the monks of these orders, promised a fruitful spiritual and intellectual exchange between monks and nuns, but because of the numbers of women involved and the drain on the orders' resources this was not easily achieved. Although initially willing to accept this task, these orders, one after another, closed their ranks against this responsibility and were ultimately forced to accept it only under pressure from Rome.

The attitude of the Cistercians to the pressure to accept women was contradictory, varying between an official policy of exclusion, informed by neglect of the task or hostility to it, on the one hand and local informal tolerance or even encouragement on the other. The expansion of the order brought with it a large number of women's convents following the customs of Cîteaux, but without a recognised place in the structure of the order. Attempts to halt this development were unsuccessful, so that in the

---

[129] *Ibid.*, pp. 143, 144; Southern, *Society*, p. 312; Dalarun, *Annales* 39 (1984), 1140–60; Smith, 'Robert', pp. 175–84; Gold, 'Cooperation', pp. 151–66.

[130] Paterson, *World*, p. 244; Gold, 'Cooperation', p. 156.

[131] Grundmann, *Bewegungen*, pp. 490, 522; Leyser, *Women*, pp. 192–5.

thirteenth century the number of Cistercian women's houses in parts of Europe (Germany, Low Countries) actually exceeded that for monks.[132] By contrast the early Premonstratensians included women in their foundations (their founder, Norbert von Xanten, had attracted both men and women by his preaching). Within a short time, however, steps were taken to counter-act what was felt to be a burden, to isolate women (who play no dominant role as at Fontevrault) and deny them further entry to the order.[133] This hardening attitude was justified by emphasising the burden, material and spiritual, and diversion of energies that care of these nuns represented, but the argument of one abbot, Konrad von Marchtal, suggests that misogyny may also have played a part. Basing himself on the unquestioned premise that the wickedness of women surpasses all other wickedness, he rejects acceptance of more sisters as a danger to the monks' souls.[134]

The position is similar with the mendicant orders whose attempts to avoid the responsibility of *cura monialium* were likewise unsuccessful in the thirteenth century.[135] Their failure, too, signals the pressure they faced, the sheer number of women seeking a religious life and Rome's concern to find an institutional answer to this problem, especially in view of the alter-native outlet for these women in heretical movements. Francis of Assisi, despite his encouragement of Clare and her convent, did not want the order he founded to be burdened with the responsibility for women, a refusal which led to conflict between the order and the papacy. Innocent IV met the religious needs of women by imposing on the Franciscans the duty of preaching, taking confession, celebrating Mass and administering sacra-ments in women's convents. He also took steps to incorporate a number of women's houses formally into the Franciscan order, as he did also with the Dominican order.[136] Dominic, like Francis, began in close association with a women's community (Prouille, founded in 1206) before founding his own order, as a means of combating heresy in southern France. Like Fran-cis again, he later discouraged his followers from being involved with the care of women. As with the Franciscans, Rome's concern to supervise the religious women's movement and canalise it safely away from heresy led to the incorporation of women in the Dominican order, frequently in the reg-ularisation of informal laywomen's communities of a religious nature into convents.[137] The function of the Dominicans as preachers and the study necessary as preparation meant that women in this order gained indirect

---

[132] Grundmann, *Bewegungen*, pp. 203–8; Southern, *Society*, pp. 314f.; Gold, *Lady*, pp. 82–6.
[133] Grundmann, *Bewegungen*, pp. 48f., 174f; Southern, *Society*, pp. 312f.; Beach, *Women*, pp. 28f.
[134] Southern, *Society*, p. 314.   [135] Grundmann, *Bewegungen*, p. 311.
[136] *Ibid.*, pp. 253–71, 303–12.   [137] *Ibid.*, pp. 208–52, 284–303.

access to an intellectual world which would otherwise have remained closed to them. Examples of what this could mean in spiritual enrichment are the literary efflorescence at the convent of Helfta (conforming to Cistercian customs, but under Dominican care) and the status of Dominicans such as Eckhart and Seuse as spiritual advisers to nuns, devoting much of their literary work to them.[138]

The difficulty which all these orders faced in coping with this upsurge of women anxious to lead a religious life, together with other possibilities open to women which we shall consider, raises the question of what lay behind this movement. Genuine spiritual needs must have played a considerable part, but these need not exclude other considerations, such as a degree of freedom from patriarchal control in feudal society, the greater possibility of education, and the opportunity to exercise authority as an abbess, which many of noble birth could hope to become. In addition, as the following sections will illustrate and as the companion volume will stress in detail, the difficulties of feudal marriage policy for women cannot be ignored: the strain and dangers of recurrent childbirth, the need to escape an unwanted marriage or, as a widow, a new marriage enforced by kindred or necessity, or a wish to escape from male domination. At a most humdrum level convents provided a refuge for the unmarried (or unmarriageable) woman for whom feudal society had no other ready answer. Although clerical sources have a vested interest in denigrating marriage their propaganda's stress on the nun's escape from matrimony was by no means wide of the mark.[139] In the thirteenth century Yolande of Vianden, the daughter of an aristocratic family in Luxemburg, wished to become a Dominican nun against the strong opposition of her parents, whose plans for a suitable marriage were thereby endangered. How suitable this marriage was is conveyed by the description of the husband-to-be in terms of wealth and status in Bruder Hermann's vernacular *Leben* ('stolz, wolgeboren unde rîch' proud, well-born and rich).[140] By insisting on her vocation the daughter maintains her right to choose for herself against the mother's assumption, in accordance with feudal convention, that it is the family's duty to arrange a marriage by its own criteria. This is a situation which we shall encounter elsewhere, particularly with Christina of Markyate, and has a prehistory going back to early Christian virginity literature (as with Ambrose praising virgins for maintaining their vows against family pressure).[141] However, a topos need

---

[138] Hamburger, *Canticles*, pp. 3, 161; Janota, *Orientierung*, p. 60.
[139] Grundmann, *Bewegungen*, pp. 189–92; Southern, *Society*, p. 311; Newman, *Woman*, p. 6.
[140] Grundmann, *Bewegungen*, pp. 192, 229; Hermann, *Leben* 806.
[141] *De Virginibus* 206–8; Blamires, *Case*, pp. 182f.

not be deprived of historical value by that fact alone, for what underlies this situation was of contemporary relevance in the twelfth century, when the Church upheld the need for *consensus* or free choice on entering marriage. This is what Yolande's parents (like Christina's) were denying her, but what she maintained for herself (again, like Christina) in actively choosing Christ as her bridegroom, as Hermann's *Leben* makes clear with its threefold stress on what she wishes for herself ('*mîn wille* is, herre, daz ich sî/sus vorbaz aller manne vrî/dan eines den ich hân *erkorn*' sir, it is my intention to be free of all men henceforth, apart from the one I have chosen; 'dem *ich enwil nyt ave gân*' I will not be dissuaded from that).[142] The nun therefore escapes an arranged marriage, forced upon her, for the sake of a marriage on which she freely enters. Freedom of choice to reject marriage, it could be suggested by priests preaching against the sins of the flesh, brought with it independence from patriarchal society, from parents and also from husband.

The freedom of scope this entailed, whether or not a nun of noble birth eventually attained the rank and authority of an abbess, seems to have attracted a considerable number of women from the aristocracy in the twelfth and thirteenth centuries. Within a monastery 'a woman could transcend the "weakness" of her sex', as abbess she 'could exercise the political authority which in the secular world . . . was formally monopolised by men'.[143] Hrotsvitha's Gandersheim exemplifies this particularly well: it was a small independent realm of women ruled by women, mainly from the Ottonian dynasty and enjoying undeniable intellectual scope.[144]

Mention of intellectual scope at Gandersheim, like that at the equally Latinate Helfta in the thirteenth century, as well as the exposure to Dominican learning already mentioned, raises the central question of this section. Where did nuns stand with regard to literacy and the world of books, what was their position with regard to Latin and the vernacular? We can discuss this first in general terms with reference to two regions, southern Germany and England.[145]

It is from the Dominican nuns of southern Germany that we obtain at present most information.[146] Although for Dominican monks the standard language was Latin, their sisters in Germany were reminded that the Constitutions were to be read to them in the refectory in the vernacular. This does not allow us to make a gender-specific generalisation about monks and

---

[142] *Leben*, 3737–41 (italics mine).   [143] Nelson, 'Queens', pp. 33f.   [144] Dronke, *Women*, p. 55.

[145] The position at Gandersheim and elsewhere in Ottonian Germany has been discussed by Bodarwé, *Sanctimoniales*.

[146] Ehrenschwendtner, '*Puellae*', pp. 49–71 (vernacular); Ochsenbein, 'Latein', pp. 42–51 (Latin and vernacular). Ehrenschwendtner gives a much fuller treatment in *Bildung*, pp. 119–48.

nuns, because table readings were still often in Latin (even if not understood by some nuns), whilst vernacular table readings were institutionalised by the fifteenth-century reform movement to strengthen the nuns' religious understanding. We have to reckon therefore with both possibilities over time, with a gradual move towards the vernacular, which need not imply a decline in nuns' Latinity, but rather an extension of literacy to embrace the vernacular as well. Not confining himself to Dominicans, Wolf discusses the use of the vernacular in the Rules of monastic orders for women.[147] The reason for this is particularly apparent in the case of the Dominican order, for women were excluded from preaching and hence from the study of (Latin) theology, which would have been superfluous in their case. Throughout her analysis of Dominican nuns' Latinity Ehrenschwendtner stresses this point and attributes to it the difference between the mendicants and the older orders. Still without any absolute distinction, we find that the vernacular was preferred by the nuns for their private prayers and, although Latin was still used for liturgical prayers, short prayers such as the Lord's Prayer and *Ave Maria*, as well as for the Psalms, we cannot tell how much of this went beyond prayers learnt by heart without word-for-word comprehension. In addition, the majority of books in convent libraries were in the vernacular, significantly including translations from Latin as well as original works in German.[148] This is far from a deliberate exclusion of the sisters from knowledge of Latin, but merely a recognition of educational facts. One spiritual adviser says that their salvation will not be jeopardised by ignorance of Latin, but that it would be useful to have some.[149] That this could be realised in practice is shown, for example, by the sister-book of Unterlinden, written in Latin by Katharina von Gebersweiler, for this would have been pointless if the other nuns had not been able to understand Latin.[150] These cases remain exceptional, however, as is borne out by the use of German in other sister-books.

With these Dominican nuns Latin is in use alongside German, but becomes progressively less common. From our point of view, if not from that of a medieval cleric, this does not amount to a loss of literacy, but represents rather an extension from one literacy (Latin) to another (vernacular), which could still grant the nuns access, albeit indirectly, to works of high theology. Like the Latinate nuns of Helfta, they were familiar with Bernard of Clairvaux in extracts, even if they had not read a line of him in Latin, but also with authors such as Augustine and Hugh of St Victor,

---

[147] Ehrenschwendtner, '*Puellae*', pp. 49, 52; *Bildung*, pp. 180–4. Wolf, *Buch* II.1.2.
[148] Ehrenschwendtner, '*Puellae*', pp. 51, 53; *Bildung*, pp. 307, 334f.
[149] Ehrenschwendtner, '*Puellae*', p. 56.   [150] *Ibid.*, pp. 56f.

in short with traditional Latin theology in vernacular guise.[151] It is likely that this preponderance of the vernacular in women's convents was not just realistically tolerated by the monks, but actually supported by them, for in 1242, when the order was still trying to separate itself from the care of these women, the unsuccessful attempt was made to stop the translation of such texts for their use.[152] There is no evidence that these Dominican nuns were denied direct access to Latin texts because they were women, but every suggestion that they made full use of a vernacular literacy instead.

For the literacy of English nuns we can base ourselves on the findings of Bell, a moderate revisionist who likewise takes into account the rise of vernacular literacy in respectability alongside Latin.[153] Again, it is clear that no generalisations can be safely made. For example, at Syon Abbey a number of nuns have been shown as able to read Latin theology and novices may well have been instructed in Latin from the beginning, but, as we saw with the anonymous author of the *Mirror of Our Lady* and with Richard Whytford, even at Syon there were sisters unlettered in Latin, singing without understanding, for whom texts had to be translated into English.[154] A similar situation may be presupposed in the twelfth century for the convent at Barking, where a nun translated Aelred of Rievaulx's *Vita Aedwardi* into Anglo-Norman. She at least had a command of Latin, whilst others were dependent on the vernacular.[155] To confine Latinity to this one translator at Barking is certainly a gross understatement about a house with a long tradition of learning, with similar implications for other centres like Romsey and Wilton.[156] Bell has concluded that although later most nuns would not have been able to understand non-liturgical Latin the minority who could was greater than has been thought.[157] If from the close of the thirteenth century a decline in nuns' Latinity must be postulated for England, as for Germany, this need not always be regarded as gender-specific and yet again it must be emphasised that any decline in Latin literacy was accompanied by a rise in vernacular competence.

The position in England is complicated by the fact that vernacularisation involved two different languages, first Anglo-Norman and then English, as we have seen with Barking and Syon. Into both these languages texts had to be translated for the use of nuns, as they had to be into German for the Dominican nuns we have considered. Some of the Anglo-Norman religious texts are known to have been written for specific nuns or convents, mentioned by name, and some, as we saw with Barking, were written by

[151] *Ibid.*, p. 59. [152] *Ibid.*, p. 60. [153] Bell, *Nuns*, pp. 57–96.
[154] *Ibid.*, pp. 61f. (Latin). *Mirror* and Whytford: see above, p. 32. [155] See below, p. 138.
[156] Bell, *Nuns*, p. 77. [157] *Ibid.*, p. 66.

nuns themselves.[158] Later, when vernacular translations are into English, the evidence from Syon is richly informative, including an impressive list of spiritual works, with a number of continental origin as well as works by English authors.[159] In one important respect these vernacular books at Syon highlight the quality of the reading and intellectual interests shown by the sisters. Many of the texts listed in Syon's holdings are relatively new and up-to-date compositions, the interests they reflect are not restricted to traditional theology, and it has also been argued that Barking was in the forefront of the public for English theology of a recent date.[160] Syon's awareness of new possibilities even extended to taking advantage of printed books at an early stage. In this connection Bell has made a gender-specific point, but reversed its normally antifeminine implication, by pointing out that the nuns' interest in books of the fifteenth century, even though these may have been 'unlearned' because not in Latin, is in 'marked contrast to the unimpressive record of their male counterparts'.[161] Unburdened by a traditional education, as the monks were not, these women's devotional life he judges fuller and more up-to-date, nourished by a vernacular to which, even if they did not know it, the future belonged.

After this wider look at two regions we turn to a highly selective group of specific women's communities, looking at them with regard to the same features: their intellectual standing and their literacy in the perennial tension between Latin and vernacular.

We start with Gandersheim, a community of canonesses, but shall look at one of its most important representatives, the Latin author Hrotsvitha, in a later context. Gandersheim belongs to a remarkable efflorescence of women's communities under the Ottonians, including such culturally important centres as Quedlinburg, Magdeburg, Gernrode and Essen.[162] These communities were imperial foundations whose abbesses were for the most part daughters of the ruling dynasty, closely involved in court politics. Widukind dedicated his history of the Saxons to Mathilda, the daughter of Otto I, when she became Abbess of Quedlinburg, while at Gandersheim Hrotsvitha celebrated in Latin the deeds of that emperor.[163] Gandersheim may have been unique in being exempted from royal authority by Otto I so that it enjoyed a large measure of autonomy, but the authority wielded by its abbess was no different in kind, but only in extent, from that enjoyed by women in charge of other foundations. High birth ensured an education for members of the house: Hrotsvitha writes in Latin for others in

---

[158] *Ibid.*, pp. 69f.   [159] *Ibid.*, pp. 74f.   [160] *Ibid.*, p. 72 (quoting Doyle).   [161] *Ibid.*, pp. 76f.
[162] Bodarwé, *Sanctimoniales, passim*, but on Gandersheim, pp. 15–31, 98–110, 210–12, 238–46.
[163] Leyser, *Rule*, p. 49; Ferrante, *Glory*, p. 76.

her community, and Widukind dedicated his Latin history to the abbess of Quedlinburg. Hrotsvitha's writings imply, on her part and also with her recipients, an acquaintance with Latin authors, pagan as well as Christian.[164] Not far from Gandersheim, at Gernrode, the abbess Hathui (c.1000) commissioned a Latin life of the patron saint Cyriacus, but this community also possessed a vernacular work, a commentary on the Psalms in Old Saxon.[165]

In coming back to the royal abbey of Barking as our next example we must stress, more than we had occasion to before, its tradition of Latinity already before the Conquest and lasting after it. Aldhelm wrote his *De virginitate* for the Anglo-Saxon nuns there in answer to interested questions from them, praised them for their command of rhetoric and intellectual interests at large, and recommended them a reading list including the Bible and the Church Fathers, but also historians and grammarians.[166] However ambitious, this certainly presupposes a high degree of Latin learning at Barking. Even after the Conquest this abbey can boast the largest number of books of Latin learning in any women's community, suggesting at the least continuity in Latin interests.[167] Alongside this, however, room was found for translation from Latin into Anglo-Norman. The author of the *Vie d'Édouard* is anonymous, but refers to herself as a nun at Barking who translated the work from Latin, possibly, it has been suggested, for aristocratic ladies interested in French books.[168] Another work, a life of Catherine, has to be added, whose author names herself as Clemence, a nun of Barking, and with an audience presumably of noblewomen with the same interest in the vernacular as those for the *Vie d'Édouard* (if indeed they are not identical and the two works by the same nun). The *St Catherine* is a stylistic refashioning of an earlier French translation of a Latin *vita*, but since the Barking author refers to translating and putting into the vernacular what the Latin says it is likely that her work was as much a translation from Latin as an adaptation from French.[169] Moreover, in an abbey known for its learning this particular legend, dealing with a learned and aristocratic female saint who bettered in argument a number of pagan 'clercs', was well chosen indeed. If we can accept this as representing a confrontation of a woman's faith and learning with men's 'clergie', whose learning is powerless

[164] Dronke, *Women*, p. 56.   [165] Leyser, *Rule*, pp. 71f.; Haubrichs, *Anfänge*, p. 208.
[166] Latinity: Wogan-Browne, 'Clerc', p. 67. Aldhelm: *De virginitate*, pp. 229f.; Wogan-Browne, 'Clerc', p. 83, n. 41; Robinson, '*Scriptrix*', p. 82; Brown, 'Book-ownership', p. 46; Beach, *Women*, p. 11.
[167] Wogan-Browne, *Lives*, pp. 196, 197, 228, fn. 15.
[168] *Vie d'Édouard* 5299–303; Legge, *Literature*, pp. 60–66.
[169] *St Catherine* 32–5, 2689–91; Legge, *Literature*, pp. 66–72; Damian-Grint, *Historians*, pp. 185, 187f.

without faith, we have here a highly gendered debate, reminiscent, as we shall see, of an episode in Margery Kempe's life concerning the lawyers of Lincoln.[170]

Admont, an Austrian double monastery, is another centre of women's Latinity and literary activity. It has been described as the intellectual centre of its diocese in the first half of the twelfth century and it possessed a school in which the nuns were instructed in reading, grammar and rhetoric, and they were capable of formal letter writing.[171] We are well informed about the books contained in the monastery library in the twelfth century, large enough in its holdings for one of the nuns to be termed librarian ('armaria') and recently reconstructed by Beach in some detail.[172] The 'magistra' of the nuns is sketched in an impressive picture of her intellectual culture: she was well instructed in holy scripture, but also in liberal studies ('studiis . . . liberalibus') and as a teacher at Admont passed on these attainments to her pupils ('quas scholaribus disciplinis instruxit').[173] Letter copybooks from the twelfth century attest a pragmatic literacy, but more ambitious writing is suggested by the case for women's authorship of a number of anonymous literary works, although it will not do to include here, as does Beach, the *St. Trudperter Hoheslied* in the same breath.[174] The case for adducing this commentary on the Song of Songs is a probable one, if by no means certain, but that argument concerns the audience to which it may have been addressed, not its author. A case for authorial activity at Admont, and in Latin, is better made with regard to Gertrud, the 'magistra' who composed a literary text at night which she dictated to a scribe ('nocte litteras composuit et scribenti praedixit'). The literary nature of what she composed is borne out by the mention of its metrical or rhythmical nature ('versus et prosas'), just as the actual process of composition is also suggested in its different stages of dictation ('praedixit'), writing ('scribenti') complete with wax tablets ('tabulas') and eventual reading out ('reddendos').[175] The way in which it is expressly said that what was dictated was not in German ('numquam aliqua theutonica verba protulit'), therefore in Latin, at least suggests the possibility that vernacular composition may not have been unknown at Admont under other conditions. We have every reason to see in the nuns at Admont representatives of a Latin literary culture who

---

[170] Gaunt, *Gender*, pp. 231f.

[171] Knapp, *Literatur*, pp. 74–9; Beach, *Women*, pp. 70f., 75f.; Brunner, *MIÖG* 107 (1999), 271–310.

[172] Beach, *Women*, pp. 77–84. Cf. Seeberg, *Illustrationen*, pp. 21–6.

[173] *Vita Magistrae*, p. 363; Ohly, *ZfdA* 87 (1956/7), 15; Beach, *Women*, p. 70.

[174] Beach, *Women*, pp. 72–77. *St. Trudperter Hoheslied*: ibid., p. 73; Ohly (ed.), *Hohelied*, p. 328; Spitz, *ZfdA* 121 (1992), 174–77. Reservations: Seeberg, *Illustrationen*, pp. 106–8, 120f., 129–32, 143f., 146–50.

[175] Ohly, *ZfdA* 87 (1956/7), 15f.

fully confirm what the abbot Irimbert said of them, that they were learned and wonderfully exercised in knowledge of sacred scripture ('litteratae et in scientia sacrae scripturae mirabiliter exercitatae'). Admont witnesses a move towards vernacular alongside Latin literacy when we come to the production of the bilingual interlinear *Millstätter Psalter*, the *Kuppitzsche Predigten* and (probably) the *St. Trudperter Hoheslied*. (Texts with vernacular elements are also associated with other double monasteries: Benedictine Rules at Zwiefalten and Engelberg, and a breviary at Seckau.)[176]

In the convent Helfta near Eisleben we come to another remarkable centre of Latin learning and visionary piety, with its highlight in the second half of the thirteenth century under the abbacy of Gertrud von Hackeborn. The visionaries in question are Mechthild von Hackeborn and Gertrud von Helfta, both of whom composed their writings in Latin, and Mechthild von Magdeburg, who came to Helfta in later years after living as a beguine in Magdeburg and composed her work in German (the last book probably at Helfta).[177] No writings have come down to us under Gertrud von Hackeborn's name, but we know from Gertrud von Helfta's *Legatus divinae pietatis* what stimulus to reading and learning she must have given to those under her care. She was herself a great reader of scripture and required others to love sacred readings and recite them from memory ('lectiones sacras amarent et jugi memoria recitarent'). She bought books wherever she could and had them transcribed by the sisters, but also encouraged them to study the liberal arts ('et hoc promovebat, ut puellae in liberalibus artibus proficerent'). In accordance with this her biographer, a nun in the same convent, herself quotes a number of early and more recent spiritual writers, whilst Gertrud von Helfta, before a conversion experience, devoted more attention to works of classical literature.[178] Whether classical or religious, the reading this involved was Latin, as were the works written at Helfta (apart from the last book of Mechthild von Magdeburg's *Fließendes Licht*, an exception because it concludes a work begun outside the convent). One feature, confirming the self-confidence and unquestioned Latinity of these nuns, is that they nowhere apologetically refer to the weakness or ignorance of their sex or betray authorial dependence on a spiritual director – this in marked contrast to Mechthild von Magdeburg and other women religious authors in the vernacular whom we shall be considering.[179] The

---

176 Hamburger, *Visual*, pp. 35, 479, n. 3. Vernacular: *Krone*, pp. 308, 319f., 320f., 325, 326, 327. Cf. Hellgardt, 'Handschriften', pp. 103–30, 'Gebetsanweisungen', pp. 400–13, and 'Textensembles', pp. 19–31.
177 Bynum, *Jesus*, pp. 170–262.
178 *Legatus* i, 1–3; Ehrenschwendtner, '*Puellae*', p. 58; Gertrud, *Oeuvres* II 118–20.
179 Voaden, 'Community', p. 82; Hubrath, *Schreiben*, p. 55.

literary activity of the convent was essentially Latinate, from the nuns' initial instruction through their composition of works to the reception of them within the convent. This convent is a convincing example that, contrary to clerical misogynists' negative views of women's intellect and competence in Latin, there was no contradiction between nuns and Latin literacy of a high order.

We move into a different linguistic world, dominated by German, with the Dominican convents of southern Germany of the fourteenth and fifteenth centuries which we have so far considered in general terms, but must now look at with a double focus, first on St Catharine's convent in Nürnberg, then on the nearby convent of Engelthal. In this region and period women's religious literature is essentially Dominican literature (in Germany the female branch had expanded faster than that of the monks and in the south there were nearly as many convents as in all other Dominican provinces together).[180]

St Catharine's (which had adopted the Dominican reform) recruited its members from the patriciate of Nürnberg whose daughters bring their vernacular books with them on entering the convent, so that the literary situation largely builds on the reading habits of Nürnberg laywomen.[181] As previously mentioned, with the Dominican order, more obviously than with any other, we have to reckon with a gender gap between the male members, trained in Latin theology as preachers and increasingly involved with the universities, and the nuns, excluded from preaching and for whom such training was no prerequisite.[182] That fact may have reinforced the vernacular emphasis present at St Catharine's in the recruits from the patriciate, but not to the total exclusion of Latin. For the female scribes identified for this convent the training must have included comprehension of Latin (if writing involves reading, then correct writing can involve understanding of what is written or copied). This is borne out by what has been shown of novices to be trained as scribes: the prioress must see to it that those sisters who know the liberal arts instruct the younger ones in the art of grammar.[183] For both teacher and pupil some degree of Latin must be assumed, but provision is made for the vernacular in the case of laysisters whose inability to read Latin means that texts have to be communicated to them in German.[184] The vernacular comes more pronouncedly to the fore when we consider the convent library, about which we are informed by

---

[180] Ehrenschwendtner, '*Puellae*', p. 50. On the literate culture of these convents see Ehrenschwendtner, *Buildung*.
[181] Thali, *Beten*, p. 247.   [182] Hasebrink, 'Tischlesung', p. 191.
[183] *Ibid.*, pp. 191f., 195.   [184] *Ibid.*, p. 195, fn. 22.

two catalogues drawn up after the reform by the sister in charge of books, Kunigunde Niklasin, one listing books in private ownership and one books held by the convent collectively.[185] Most of these books were in German, only few in Latin, but the importance of this distinction is increased by the fact that the books listed up to the year 1500 number as many as about 350, constituting the largest collection of German books in the late Middle Ages, even if account is taken of duplicates (but even that suggests the possibility of multiple use).[186] This slant towards the vernacular explains, as elsewhere, the notable presence of translations in these holdings and the lack of works of what might be called academic theology. It is also confirmed by the books which came to the convent from patrician families in the city, either donations or brought with them by entrants on profession, for the reading-matter of lay circles, although markedly religious, was vernacular, too.[187]

As in most monasteries, reading at St Catharine's was of two kinds. The books held by the convent provided for table readings in the refectory. As part of the Dominican reform the need for this was reinforced, with the stipulation that these readings could be in German in the morning, but partly German and partly Latin in the evening, whilst the records of these readings show that this was changed in practice to German only.[188] Private reading was also laid down and for this the sisters could make use of books borrowed from the convent library, the linguistic emphasis of whose holdings would again favour vernacular reading.[189] In these two kinds of reading this convent resembled any monastic house in forming a reading community in itself, but it was also part of a reading community extending beyond its walls. The nuns lent books from their own rich holdings for copying at newly reformed convents building up their own libraries (e.g. to St Catharine's at St Gallen) and they also donated books elsewhere (e.g. Altenhohenau and Frauenaurach).[190] The library of this Nürnberg house owed its richness to the Dominican reform, but in its turn it promoted the spread of that reform by assisting the literacy of other houses.

It is one of the merits of Thali's study of the unreformed convent Engelthal to have shown that the reform movement was not indispensable to building up an important library for nuns (even if not so important

[185] Thali, *Beten*, pp. 248–50, 276.
[186] Ehrenschwendtner, 'Library', pp. 126, 127; Thali, *Beten*, p. 276. Ehrenschwendtner, *Bildung*, pp. 275–331, discusses the libraries of these Dominican convents in greater detail.
[187] Ehrenschwendtner, 'Library', pp. 123, 125; *Bildung*, pp. 227–30.
[188] Ehrenschwendtner, 'Library', p. 124; *Bildung*, pp. 176–207.
[189] Ehrenschwendtner, 'Library', p. 124; *Bildung*, pp. 211–37.
[190] Ehrenschwendtner, 'Library', pp. 124f.

as at Nürnberg). Engelthal has rightly been called a literary centre of the
first rank in the fourteenth century.[191] Like St Catharine's, it formed part of
a reading community, lending items to other centres, such as the new foundation of Pillenreuth, to build up their libraries, even to St Catharine's itself
or to Inzigkofen. This exchange traffic could also run in the other direction,
with items at Engelthal coming (or copied) from other houses, for example
from Weiler.[192] With the help of their book holdings the nuns at Engelthal
were in a position to acquire considerable theological knowledge, but we
must be careful how we interpret it when, for example, in the *Engelthaler
Schwesternbuch* a nun is credited with special learning: 'Sie het ein cleine
kunst gelernt unde kom dar zu mit den gnaden gotes, daz sie grozze swerew
buch ze tisch deutet' (She learned little skill and managed with God's grace
to interpret heavy tomes at table).[193] This nun's exceptional learning may
after all be seen as such only by comparison with the weaker achievement
of others, and the reference to her acting 'with God's grace' may suggest
divine inspiration rather than the results of book learning, as is also the case
with other religious women. But that qualification is not meant to diminish
the importance of what we learn about the Engelthal library. It may well
number no more than fifty-four volumes, but in other respects it can be
compared with the Nürnberg library. We learn about its contents from a
fifteenth-century book list made up exclusively of German-language items,
meant both for table reading and for private reading.[194] In one important
respect, however, this library stands out and differs from St Catharine's. It is
remarkable for the variety of items included in the list (biblical and patristic texts, legendaries, legends, devotional and mystical works). Secondly,
however, this collection stands out even more by the quality of the mystical
and devotional literature it contains (Eckhart, Seuse, and Mechthild von
Magdeburg) and particularly by its up-to-date nature, with acquisitions of
works composed only around the close of the fourteenth century.[195] This is
very reminiscent of what we saw with Syon Abbey: together the English and
the German convents suggest that nuns' preference for vernacular reading
matter kept them impressively abreast of the latest developments in spiritual
thought.

We may sharpen our focus on Engelthal still further by looking briefly at
the nun Christine Ebner, known as the author of the *Engelthaler Schwesternbuch*.[196] She has been sketched as a visionary with literary interests,
moreover one who wrote down her own work and must have been for

---

[191] Peters, 'Vita', p. 108.   [192] Thali, *Beten*, pp. 30, 269, 305.   [193] 30, 15–17; Thali, *Beten*, p. 219.
[194] *Ibid.*, pp. 243f.   [195] *Ibid.*, pp. 265–75.   [196] Peters, 'Leben', pp. 402f.

that reason alone literate, at least in the vernacular.[197] She also says that she learnt to read the Psalter when young, but this does not prevent her describing herself as illiterate ('und kan dar zu der schrift niht'), by which she probably meant illiteracy in Latin, but not in German.[198] In this she resembles Mechthild von Magdeburg, as she does also in claiming that she wrote only in obedience to a divine call and in the advice she depends on from her confessor, Konrad von Füssen.[199] In this attitude both these vernacular women authors (one a nun and one who later joined a convent) differ markedly from the Latinate authors of Helfta.

Passing from Engelthal to Töss, we find a fascinating example in Elsbeth Stagel, central to this book in the sense that she cuts across the different aspects of women's engagement with literature we are considering. Active in writing Seuse's *vita*, she represents co-authorship with him, real or pretended, but a miniature of her in the Töss sister-book depicts her authorship in terms of scribal activity.[200] If Seuse was not merely the instigator, but also the recipient of the *vita*, this implies that Elsbeth was encouraged to write that work, but as prioress of Töss presumably undertook the sister-book on her own initiative. These many facets make her a complex literary figure.

For our last example we return briefly to the Bridgettine Syon Abbey, housing a double order of brethren as well as nuns (and also in close relations with Carthusian monks at Sheen).[201] The Bridgettine Rule prescribed daily reading for the nuns, even providing for an unlimited supply of books for study. As at Nürnberg, novices are expected to bring books, amongst other objects, with them when they join (which implies previously acquired literacy on their part), thus adding to the stock of reading-material.[202] A further source of texts were the Carthusians, who provided English translations of works from the continent, amounting, to judge from the books in the Syon library, to an impressive range, including not merely Bernard of Clairvaux, Mechthild von Hackeborn and David von Augsburg, but also even more recent works (Seuse, Ruysbroek). English authors represented in the library include Richard Rolle, Walter Hilton, but also women such as Julian of Norwich and, although not the author herself but the subject, Margery Kempe. (At Nürnberg, too, it was a Carthusian, Erhart Gross,

---

[197] *Ibid.*, pp. 403, 411, 415.
[198] *Engelthaler Schwesternbuch* 1, 11–13; Ehrenschwendtner, '*Puellae*', pp. 54f.
[199] Peters, 'Leben', p. 416.   [200] Hamburger, *Visual*, Fig. 9.24 (p. 466).
[201] Hutchison, 'Reading', p. 215.
[202] *Ibid.*, p. 217; Hutchison, *MS* 57 (1995), 208, 209; Krug, *Families*, pp. 153, 188; Schirmer, 'Reading', pp. 345–76.

who wrote most of his German works for St Catharine's.)[203] Varying what was said of Engelthal, we can say of Syon Abbey that it was a reading centre of the first rank in the fifteenth century, especially in view of evidence that quantity was matched by quality. As with Hugh of St Victor, reading was considered part of meditation, and instructions on how to read devoutly in the *Mirror of Our Lady* stress that, when reading alone, one should read slowly and repeatedly until a passage is fully understood, a typical form of monastic close reading, summed up in the words to 'study bysely'.[204] Inward reading like this underlines the importance of private reading in this house, confirmed by the prevalent use of Books of Hours there, meant above all for personal devotions and solitary reading. The high preponderance of vernacular reading at Syon (represented by the books owned by sisters as distinct from the brethren) does not mean that the nuns were totally divorced from Latin, since some are known by name of whom this cannot be true.[205] Latin could also play a part as a means of feeding into Syon works from abroad, as with the *Liber spiritualis gratiae* of Mechthild von Hackeborn, thought to have been translated into English by a Carthusian for Syon and enjoying some popularity in this guise in late medieval England.[206]

In the Middle Ages convents were the places where women could most easily obtain an education, enabling them to read and engage in the other literary activities considered in the next chapter. How well they could also be equipped intellectually and theologically may be seen from the learned content of the vernacular writings of Dominicans like Eckhart, Seuse and Tauler meant for nuns. This evidence is not confined to what these nuns read, for the theological sophistication of the iconography of the Uta codex or the St Katharinental gradual equals that expected of men and is just as challenging.[207] Nor should we regard these nuns' range of interests as necessarily restricted. The *Hortus deliciarum* makes available, in Latin, the latest theology from Paris, but also includes natural history, world history and something of the liberal arts. This example suggests that the recurrence of the vernacular in women's communities need not always be at the cost of Latin, represented at a high level in many houses (e.g. Barking, Gandersheim, the Paraclete, Admont, Helfta, Unterlinden). After clerics (who had the advantage of education in cathedral schools and universities) these religious women are the main carriers of literate culture in the Middle Ages.

---

[203] Hutchison, 'Reading', p. 216; *MS* 57 (1995), 209–21; Bell, *Nuns*, p. 74. Gross: Steinhoff, *VfL* 3, 273.
[204] Hutchison, 'Reading', pp. 221f.; *MS* 57 (1995), 213.
[205] Hutchison, *MS* 57 (1995), 214; Bell, *Nuns*, pp. 61f.   [206] Barratt, 'Women', pp. 245f.
[207] *Krone*, p. 24 and plates 1 (p. 19) and 4 (p. 23); p. 408 and Figs. 305a–b, 306a–e.

RECLUSES

Almost since its inception Christianity has known various forms of ascetic withdrawal from the world and a corresponding variety of terms for those (in our case, women) who chose this form of life (*reclusa, inclusa, eremita, anachoreta*), but I see no profit in following such distinctions in this section. It was, however, only in the eleventh and twelfth centuries that this form of asceticism became much more common, above all in northern Europe. A growing number of such anchorites, of both sexes, were recruits from the lay world, particularly women, attracted to this form of religious life, as to others, as part of their involvement in the novel religious movements of this period.[208] Contrary to what we imagine by a term like 'hermit', these recluses still retain some contacts with the outside world, they occupy an intermediate position between the world of laymen and the monastery subject to a fixed rule. As a result of monastic orders refusing to accept the flood of women wishing to join, reclusion came to be seen as a way open to women wishing to lead a religious life. Women were more likely than men to embrace this form of life and most of the Rules for anchorites that have survived are accordingly addressed to women.

Although it is difficult to explain the attractiveness of reclusion for women, other than their wish for a religious life, we should not ignore the unattractiveness of married life for many of them, victims of arranged marriages negotiated for reasons of feudal family politics and with little regard for personal wishes. Seclusion provided a measure of independence for them, above all an escape from the marriage plans of parents. Jutta of Huy, married off by her parents and widowed young, evaded their renewed marriage plans for her by having herself enclosed in a cell. Although she entered a beguinage rather than an anchorage Ida of Nivelles illustrates escape from marriage quite literally, climbing out of a window to defeat the marriage plans of her kinsmen after the death of her father.[209] Virginity literature addressed to women couches the traditional contempt for the world in terms of the unpleasantnesses of marriage: domestic labour, the pains of pregnancy and the tribulations of child-rearing.[210] We are not surprised to find the husband listed amongst these disadvantages, as when a fifteenth-century duchess of Braunschweig complains of her hard, unfeeling husband and sees life with him like that of an anchoress in a cell.[211]

---

[208] Küsters, *Garten*, pp. 134–42; Millett, 'Women', p. 89; Wogan-Browne, *Lives*, pp. 24–32.

[209] Jutta: Labarge, *Women*, p. 122. Ida: Ruh, *Geschichte* II 96.

[210] Such considerations were not confined to virginity literature. Cf. the Occitan tenso *Na Carenza al bel cors avinenz* (Bruckner, *Songs*, pp. 96f.).

[211] Busch, *Liber*, p. 779 (quoted by Power, *Women*, p. 28).

The patriarchal nature of arranged marriage politics in feudal society deprived the woman of any say or choice in the matter at a time when the canon lawyers of the Church were arguing the need for *consensus*, freely given assent to marriage in opposition to the dominant practice of the lay world.[212] How this clash of views affected one who became a recluse is particularly clear in the case of Christina of Markyate in the twelfth century. She was the eldest daughter of a wealthy couple in Huntingdon who had arranged what was in their eyes a good marriage for her and of social benefit to them. Christina resisted, having vowed virginity, was constantly ill-treated by her parents and bullied into verbal consent, but sought refuge first with an anchoress, then with a hermit.[213] Christina's vow to remain a virgin is presented in her *Life* as a marriage to Christ (she is termed a *sponsa Christi*), so that her story encapsulates an opposition between two marriages (or rather a prior marriage that overrides a later arrangement).[214] The difference between these two is made clear specifically in terms of *consensus*. In her relationship with Burthred, the man chosen by her parents, it is absent, as Christina underlines in her evidence to the prior Fredebert ('contra voluntatem meam suo compulsu'), a point conceded by her father.[215] By contrast, Christina's vow, amounting to marriage to Christ, not merely comes earlier, but is her own free decision. Christ may have chosen her as his virginal bride, but she also chose him,[216] so that we have here a relationship, freely entered into by each party and resting on *consensus*, which is opposed to what Christina's parents, in conformity to laymen's practice, seek to impose upon her.

Christina's case is not isolated as an appeal to anchoresses. Aelred of Rievaulx, writing for them, says that they have chosen Christ as their spouse and similarly in *Hali Meiðhad* (belonging to the same literary context of the thirteenth century as *Ancrene Wisse*, specifically meant for recluses), it is again the woman who has chosen her celestial lover, escaping thereby from slavery and serfdom to a man in this world. In *Seinte Margarete*, belonging to the same group of texts, the saint is described as having herself chosen God as lover and as suitor ('ha ches him to luue ant to lefmon').[217]

These examples represent clerical propaganda, urging the freedom of celestial marriage over against its absence for women subjected to enforced marriage in secular life. Given this competition, Christ is unsurprisingly

[212] Noonan, *Viator* 4 (1973), 419–34; Brundage, *Law*, pp. 229–324, *passim*.
[213] Leyser, *Women*, p. 122; Cartlidge, *Marriage*, p. 77.
[214] Head, 'Marriages', pp. 116–37.   [215] Christina, *Life*, pp. 60 and 58.
[216] Cf. Hollis and Wogan-Browne, 'Monasticism', p. 38 ('integrity of volition'); Head, 'Marriages', pp. 120, 131f.
[217] *Hali Meiðhad* 4, 16–27. *Seinte Margarete* 46, 9.

shown as surpassing any earthly rival, not merely in the freedom he bestows, but also in his beauty and riches, the high rank he offers the virgin (all advantages that played a role in feudal marriage policy).[218] This presentation of the celestial lover can also draw on the conventions of court literature, using the image of a knight proving his love by knightly exploits, as was the custom of knights once upon a time (but no longer, we are meant to conclude).[219] As a bride of Christ the recluse is given a nuptial ring, a possibility not considered by Wolfram's Parzival when, on seeing the enclosed Sigune's ring, he jumps to the conclusion that she is using her solitude for conducting an affair.[220] In view of this marital imagery applied to the anchoress it is strictly speaking wrong to say that her reclusion is motivated by a flight from marriage, for what she sees herself doing is the renunciation of earthly marriage for the sake of a celestial one.

Newman has observed that virginity literature detailing the unpleasantnesses of marriage in fact makes use of a classical misogamous tradition, amounting to a misogynous one, advising the philosopher not to marry, thereby avoiding the pitfalls of married life and the wickedness of wives.[221] However, virginity literature reverses the thrust of this argument in suggesting that the virgin is to avoid the tyranny of a husband, escape being his slave and undergoing all that he pleases. An originally misogynous tradition has been turned on its head to yield misandry instead. Also important is the fact that the texts in question were written for anchoresses by men who, for all their clerical celibacy, were aware of the problematic nature of patriarchal marriage.[222] We can go much further than this, however, for in the companion volume we shall treat the depiction of marriage in court literature, where we shall encounter, again from the hands of male authors, similar doubts about feudal marriage practice. These authors, like those of virginity literature, also use the technique of 'inverted misogyny', employing traditional misogynous topoi in order to undermine them by showing either their irrelevance or that they more truly imply a criticism of men. An awareness of the shortcomings of patriarchal marriage practice informs both secular and religious texts.

Virginity literature addressed to recluses raises the question how they may have received it: were they literate and were they in the habit of reading? The first question has been analysed by Millett, who traces a continuum between a high level of scholarship through to illiteracy.[223] The high level

[218] Millett and Wogan-Browne, *Prose*, p. xvii.   [219] *Ancrene Wisse* 112, 25–114, 8 and 114, 22–26.
[220] *Parzival* 438, 2–439, 15.   [221] Newman, *Woman*, pp. 32f.
[222] *Ibid.*, p. 33.   [223] Millett, 'Women', pp. 88f.

is exemplified by two works in Latin: Aelred of Rievaulx wrote *De insti-tutione inclusarum* in the twelfth century for his sister, assuming that she could read his and other recommended Latin texts, just as Goscelin in the preceding century wrote his *Liber confortatorius* for Eve, formerly a nun of Wilton, now a recluse in France, and also laid down for her a stiff pro-gramme of Latin reading. Alongside this, however, Aelred takes into account the anchoress who is illiterate ('quae litteras non intellegit'), the author of *Ancrene Wisse* is aware that the recluses who use his work may have a varied educational background (some literate, some not), while in other cases lit-eracy may mean an ability to read the vernacular (English, French), but not Latin.[224]

The second question (the habit of reading) has been touched upon by the reading recommendations made by Aelred and Goscelin, but the evidence reaches further. Reading is one of the activities, but an important one, expected of an anchoress (so much so that it can be valued equally with prayer, the other main activity) or when a daily reading of the *Ancrene Wisse* is advised.[225] In his recommendation of texts for reading by Eve Goscelin suggests that if her cell is too small to contain them, someone could hold the book up to her outside her window and he also recommends her to sharpen her mind on the whetstone of books.[226] From what we have seen of the frequent association of women with Psalters it comes as no surprise that they are often mentioned as reading material, especially since the Psalms were the basis of the recluse's life of prayer (as is implied for Wolfram's Sigune).[227] For Aelred the anchoress's daily routine should be divided between prayer, reading and manual work, while the author of the *Ancrene Wisse* suggests (after Jerome) keeping some holy reading permanently in the hand, going so far as to recommend the recluse sisters he addresses to say fewer fixed prayers in order to accomplish more reading.[228] Other suitable reading matter consisted of saints' lives, especially of women saints who as virgin martyrs appealed to anchoresses, as in the three legends (of Katherine, Juliana and Margaret) in the Katherine group associated with the *Ancrene Wisse*. Chaucer's Criseyde was well aware that an anchoress read such legends in her retreat when, as a widow, she rejects jokingly the idea of dancing and sees the role she should play more in anchoritic terms ('It satte me wel bet ay in a cave/To bidde and rede on holy seyntes lyves'),

---

[224] Aelred: *De institutione*, p. 645f. *Ancrene Wisse*: Millett, 'Women', p. 93. Vernacular literacy: *ibid.*, p. 99.
[225] Wogan-Browne, *Lives*, p. 32; Roy, 'Recluse', p. 121.
[226] Goscelin, *Liber*, p. 80.   [227] Wolfram, *Parzival* 435, 28 and 438, 1.
[228] Aelred, *De institutione*, p. 645. *Ancrene Wisse*: Roy, 'Recluse', p. 121.

equating prayer with reading in a way of which Aelred could only have approved.[229]

The association of recluses with books to read is suggested by a number of further details. Books can be left in wills to or by them (Erler has singled out examples including Margery Pensax and an anchoress who might be Elizabeth Scott).[230] Another link is provided by works written for the benefit of recluses, whether in Latin (by Aelred and Goscelin) or in the vernacular (the *Ancrene Wisse* and associated texts), but to these must be added Richard Rolle's *Form of Living* (written for Margaret Kirkby, a nun who had become an anchoress) and Walter Hilton's *Scale of Perfection* (dedicated to an anchoress).[231] Another way in which a recluse could have contact with books was the manual labour which formed one part of her daily programme, for this could take the form of her copying texts as a scribe. They may do this for their own use, as the *Ancrene Wisse* implies when saying that they should say their Hours from texts which they have written out themselves. Or they may work at copying more 'professionally' on behalf of others and to provide for their upkeep – this was so in the well-known case of Diemut of Wessobrunn, who copied out what amounted to a whole library of well-nigh fifty volumes ('Diemut inclusa, que suis manibus Bibliothecam S. Petri fecit').[232] In all these cases writing out the copy involved the ability to read the exemplar. A last contact if not with books then with literacy is provided by another form of work carried out by anchoresses, namely educating the young. Hildegard von Bingen was taught by an anchoress, Jutta von Sponheim, and the *Ancrene Wisse* acknowledges what may have been an abuse of the practice in advising the recluse not to degenerate into a schoolmistress, turning her cell into a school.[233]

Most of the examples listed could be interpreted as implying personal reading (by the anchoress for herself), but there are also references to group reading (one anchoress reads to another), a religious counterpart to Chaucer's scene of women reading a romance collectively in Criseyde's parlour. The French text of the *Ancrene Wisse* implies reading of this kind ('lego illi') by using the double formula ('E a tret le lisez ou devant vos lire facez') and the anchoresses are to read aloud part of the rule each week to their servants until they know it.[234] That this could have been a

[229] Leyser, *Women*, p. 215; Wogan-Browne, *Lives*, p. 6; Chaucer, *Troilus* II 113–19.

[230] Erler, *Women*, pp. 48, 59, 75.

[231] Leyser, *Women*, p. 218. Rolle: Erler, *Women*, p. 61. Hilton: Voaden, *Words*, p. 65.

[232] *Ancrene Wisse*: Millett, 'Ancrene', pp. 26 and 36, n. 26. Diemut: Beach, *Women*, pp. 32–64.

[233] Hildegard: Newman, *Sister*, p. 5. *Ancrene Wisse* 140, 11f.

[234] Wogan-Browne, *Lives*, p. 38, fn. 72. *Ancrene Wisse* 146, 7f.

more common practice is suggested by the range of educational and reading ability amongst anchoresses, where the *illitteratae* would have needed
vernacular texts read out to them.

In the remainder of this section we look at a number of individual
anchoresses and their reading or literary practice. Our first example, Frau
Ava, comes from twelfth-century Austria and as the author of several religious works she enjoys the privilege of being the first woman author in
German known to us. That she composed her works in German does not
surprise us in view of what we have seen of women and the vernacular.
Although there is no internal evidence of Ava being an anchoress it is generally accepted that she is identical with an *Ava inclusa* whose death is
reported in the annals of the monastery of Melk.[235] On this not completely
certain basis she may be included here. How a laywoman of high social
rank may have acquired her detailed religious knowledge is suggested by
Ava referring to her two sons, presumably clerics, who conveyed to her the
correct understanding ('sin') of the scriptures – an early example of a woman
author writing with clerical assistance or supervision.[236] Some degree of literacy may be assumed for Ava because of her acquaintance with biblical
and apocryphal texts. This may have been acquired indirectly (through
sermons, hymns and from her sons), but there is no compelling reason
to assume that she relied more on an amanuensis than did male authors
of biblical vernacular texts of her day.[237] Unlike some of our following
examples, Ava's works were not addressed to other recluses, for she once
refers to her audience as 'liebe mine herren', implying noblemen and/or
clerics (the latter presumably intended in a reference to possible readers).[238]

With the next two examples (Aelred and his sister, Goscelin and Eve)
we move to the level of Latin literacy, with addressee as well as author.
Aelred wrote *De institutione inclusarum* to provide his sister, formerly a
nun but later a recluse, with instructions on the practices of reclusion
(including the view that, once tested as an anchoress, she would become
a *sponsa Christi*).[239] If Aelred's sister had earlier been a nun, it is probable
that she received instruction in Latin and reading, but in addition Aelred
describes her, together with himself, as educated by their parents ('educati
a parentibus') and refers explicitly to her reading ('Quotiens psallantem vel
legentem').[240] On both counts, therefore, the sister was well equipped to
cope with the far from elementary Latin of Aelred's text, but also with the

[235] Kartschoke, *Geschichte*, pp. 302f.; Knapp, *Literatur*, pp. 117–22.
[236] Ava, *Jüngstes Gericht* 393–5.   [237] Gutfleisch-Ziche, *Erzählen*, pp. 152, 155.
[238] Ava, *Leben Jesu* 297.   [239] Olson, 'Women', pp. 8of. and fn. 51; Head, 'Marriages', p. 126.
[240] Aelred, *De institutione*, pp. 673, 676.

reading programme he devised for her, including other Latin texts such as the lives, rules and miracles of the fathers, which she was to read for herself ('sibi secretius legat').[241] Although Aelred writes specifically for his highly literate sister, his work is also meant as a guide for any woman wishing to seek reclusion, and he is aware that not all of them will be as literate. He refers expressly to not understanding letters ('Illa sane quae litteras non intelligit'),[242] suggesting an uneducated status in Latin and inability to cope with Aelred's work (let alone the whole reading programme), unless it was read out or explained in the vernacular. The need this reveals perhaps explains the existence of two later translations of Aelred's work into Middle English.[243]

The recluse Eve for whom Goscelin composed his *Liber confortatorius* had also once been a nun. When he says that her new schedule as a recluse is much like her conventual one at Wilton (including regular times for Psalter and other readings) he makes it clear where Eve, like Aelred's sister, derived her ability to read Latin.[244] At Wilton, a royal convent that educated noblewomen and by the twelfth century had become a centre for literary women, Eve had every opportunity to become *litterata* in Latin and its literature. Certainly, her ability was demanded (and assumed) in the reading programme Goscelin lays down for her, more ambitious than Aelred's for his sister. Not merely was Eve expected to follow Goscelin's own difficult Latin, she also had to read the scriptures together with commentaries by Jerome, Augustine and Gregory, as well as the lives of the fathers, Eusebius, Augustine's *Confessiones* and *Civitas Dei*, Orosius and Boethius.[245] In all this Goscelin encourages her to be like the women friends of Jerome, referred to as 'Christ's library'.[246] We may not be the only ones to wonder how a cell could accommodate such a library of books, for Goscelin, too, remarks on this when suggesting that, if necessary, someone could hold a book up to her outside the window.[247]

With the *Ancrene Wisse* and associated texts we come back to works in the vernacular. By its very title the leading work in this group shows that it is meant as a work of guidance for recluses at large, even though written for three gentlewomen in particular who had entered reclusion.[248] It is probable that all the works in this group shared the same kind of audience, if not the same actual people. Literacy can be presupposed for some, if not all, when

---

[241] *Ibid.*, p. 645.   [242] *Ibid.*   [243] Olson, 'Women', p. 82, fn. 56.
[244] *Ibid.*, pp. 69 (cf. p. 85, fn. 64), 73f., 80.
[245] Latzke, *MlJb* 19 (1984), 147; Millett, 'Women', p. 88; Leyser, *Women*, p. 88.
[246] Elliott, 'Intimacies', p. 172.   [247] See above, p. 149.
[248] Millett and Wogan-Browne, *Prose*, pp. xif.

the *Ancrene Wisse* gives instructions for the recluse's maidservant 'if she is illiterate' ('ʒef heo ne con o boke'), where the conditional suggests that this was not always the case. Literacy is also assumed when it is stipulated that permission has to be sought if an anchoress is to send letters or receive them or write anything.[249] It is probable that the literacy in question here is vernacular rather than Latin, not merely because of the language in which all these works are written, but also because one of the legends in this group, *Seinte Iuliene*, (if we can indeed generalise beyond this) addresses listeners and is for laypeople who cannot understand Latin.[250] The full range of reading capacity (embracing those who can and those who cannot) may be explained in social terms, since many recluses were relatively high-born and may well have received some education in literacy, whilst others would lack this advantage. The former could read these texts for themselves, but the latter were dependent on someone reading to them.[251] In anchorages at large we therefore find represented all three meanings of *legere* postulated by Hugh of St Victor. Thus, the *Ancrene Wisse* contains references to personal reading ('Of þis boc redeð hwen ʒe beoð eise euche dei') alongside one to reading a section of it to the recluses' women once a week. It has been suggested that the three gentlewomen of *Ancrene Wisse*, together with their servants, formed a reading group made up of personal readers and of those who read to illiterate listeners.[252]

With the *Life of Christina of Markyate* we are dealing with a work not written by or for a recluse (who later became a prioress in charge of a small community), but written about her, presumably by a monk of St Albans, to which her nearby cell was attached. We have looked at the implications of Christina's background and her marital adventures, but may concentrate here on the question of her literacy and reading, as well as her relationship to the book associated with her, the St Albans Psalter.[253] Doubts have been entertained whether she was really literate, but either in general, non-specific terms or by improperly contrasting her with the discernment which wide reading might have gained for a man in the schools.[254] Against this may be set evidence provided by Christina's use of two Psalters, one which she brought with her when she fled from her parents and the other the richly decorated Psalter written for St Albans, but then adapted to her particular situation when it was presented to her. Of the former we are told that it lay open on her lap at all hours of the day for her use and that

[249] 142, 17 and 140, 16f.   [250] Millett and Wogan-Browne, *Prose*, p. xiii.
[251] *Ibid.*, p. xxx.   [252] 148, 9 and 146, 7f.; Robertson, *Speculum* 78 (2003), 14.
[253] On this Psalter: Pächt *et al.*, *Psalter*; Geddes, 'Psalter', pp. 197–216.
[254] Leyser, *Women*, pp. 198f.

her reading and singing of the psalms by day and night ('[lec]ciones ac psalmodia die noctuque') so irritated the devil that he sent her a plague of toads.[255] In the St Albans Psalter drawings of fingers direct the reader's attention to key-words or catch-phrases which the reader then understands by looking at the accompanying picture.[256] If this Psalter was adapted for Christina's personal use, as seems to be the general opinion, this suggests reading by her of text and pictures. But it also suggests that her education in letters did not go very far (here it is justifiable to compare her with Eve or Aelred's sister, rather than with men trained in the schools to which she had no access). The Psalter contains an extract from the letter of Gregory the Great (addressed not to a bishop, but incorrectly to a recluse, adapting it to Christina's position) in defence of pictures as a way of instructing the *illitterati*.[257] Again it is Millett who has interpreted this codex as implying more than one user and a hierarchy of literacy (first at St Albans, then at Markyate?). The Psalter itself could have been used by anyone with elementary literacy, including Christina, but the long Latin gloss on Psalm 1 presupposes a reader who is fully *litteratus*, while the legend of Alexis in French, also included in this compilation, and the French translation of the passage from Gregory suggest a reader with vernacular literacy.[258] The argument of this paragraph depends on the assumption that this Psalter, originally devised for St Albans, was adapted for the use of Christina, but this is borne out by a number of features. Nearly every obit in the calendar refers to members of Christina's family and her friends, while the addition of seven women saints suggests an appeal to her interests, especially since three of them were trapped in difficulties with husband or suitor reminiscent of Christina's own experience.[259] The same is true of the inclusion of the Alexis story, for he too abandoned marriage for virginal asceticism, and the choice of this male saint, rather than any of the female ones included in the Katherine Group, may be connected with the interest in him shown at St Albans, including the dedication of an altar or chapel to him early in the twelfth century.[260] The illustration of the Alexis legend in the Psalter[261] unconventionally shifts the emphasis from Alexis as a pilgrim to the abandonment of marriage, placing the woman in the centre of the composition.

Our last example is the *Book of Showings* of the anchoress Julian of Norwich (c.1343–c.1420) with whom, as with Frau Ava, we return to an

---

[255] *Life*, p. 98; Millett, 'Women', pp. 91f. [256] Geddes, 'Psalter', pp. 202f.
[257] Curschmann, '*Pictura*', p. 218. [258] Millett, 'Women', p. 92.
[259] Cartlidge, *Marriage*, p. 76. [260] Hunt, '*Life*', p. 221.
[261] Reproduced in Fanous and Leyser, *Christina*, plate 5.

anchoress as an author, moreover one who resembles Ava in being the first known woman author in her vernacular. With Julian, too, we face the question whether she was literate and to what extent, particularly in her words that she was uneducated ('that cowde no letter').[262] These words have been taken at face value as admitting that she was illiterate, but *letter*, like Latin *littera* and French *lettre*, was also used in a more restricted sense, meaning 'Latin writing'.[263] In other words, Julian could be denying Latin literacy while still leaving the possibility of vernacular literacy wide open, and, as we have seen with *quasi litterati*, that need not exclude her from access to Latin culture through the intermediacy of clerics. Equally, when she presents herself as a weak and ignorant woman[264] this needs to be weighed carefully, because it could be an expression of Christian humility or a conventional humility topos that should not be taken literally. It could also be, as we saw with Mechthild von Magdeburg, a denial of human knowledge or learning in favour of divine inspiration (this remark is followed immediately by the claim that Julian has received what she says from the supreme teacher). It is presumably considerations of this sort that led the editors of Julian's text to argue on internal evidence that she had been well instructed in Latin, in scripture and the liberal arts and had read widely in the spiritual classics.[265] At the other end of the communication spectrum Julian anticipated personal readers (only they, as with Mechthild von Magdeburg, would have found any use for the list of contents and the summarising chapter headings), but also listeners, as is implied by the use of the double formula ('hear and see') for her recipients.[266]

Julian's allusion to God as the supreme teacher touches on a vital point for, aware of the Church's stand against women teaching and preaching, she emphatically disclaims this role for herself ('God forbede that ye schulde saye or take it so that I am a techere') just before making this more likely by asserting her ignorance.[267] Instead, Julian repeatedly stresses that God teaches, the Church teaches, while she herself is taught and imparts what is given to her.[268] Unlike Mechthild's criticism of learned clerics, Julian avoids such head-on opposition: she believes what the scholars say and recommends her readers to obey the teaching of men of profound learning.[269] Such defensiveness argues that Julian may have been aware that she ran the risk of being accused of heresy, all the more so since she had her difficulties

---

[262] *Book* LT 2.   [263] Spearing, *Julian*, pp. viiif.; *litteral lettre*: see above, p. 3.

[264] *Book* ST 6 ('a woman, le[w]ed, febille, and freylle').   [265] Colledge and Walshe, *Book* I 44f.

[266] *Book* LT 1 (cf. Spearing, *Julian*, p. viii). Mechthild: Palmer, *FMS* 23 (1989), 51, 78. Double formula: ST 6.

[267] *Book* ST 6.   [268] E.g. ST 6.   [269] *Book* LT 80, 86.

with the idea of a fatherly God and put forward the view that God could also be seen in terms of his maternal nature.[270] This in itself need not have incurred any danger (Bynum has emphasised the prehistory of this idea amongst undoubtedly orthodox thinkers),[271] but what could have caused trouble was Julian's extension of this idea to the concept of a motherly, loving and caring God excluding the doctrine of eternal punishment and the concepts of hell and purgatory.[272] In entertaining ideas like this and expressing them in the vernacular where they were accessible to laymen, Julian had every reason to stress repeatedly her orthodoxy and submission to the Church.

SEMI-RELIGIOUS WOMEN

What the Middle Ages regarded as the uncertain position of this category of women (living in the world, but not of it: 'in saeculo non saeculariter')[273] is reflected in the uncertain terminology used of them. Although it is not attested in the Middle Ages, I choose the term 'semi-religious' to bring home the intermediate position of these women. They are attested either as small groups or communities (on the continent commonly known as beguines) or as individuals. Although small groups of such women occur in England they are not known as beguines, so that by using our term we can include both Mechthild von Magdeburg (a beguine before she professed at Helfta) and the essentially isolated figure of Margery Kempe.

Semi-religious women, recognised as a novel phenomenon from the end of the twelfth century, form part, like recluses and heretics, of the wave of religious fervour that affected the lay world of this time, in our case in Northern Europe.[274] Jacques de Vitry, in writing the *vita* of Marie d'Oignies, acknowledged that she and her like constituted a new form of piety ('sanctae modernae in diebus nostris'), so much so that his *vita* has been termed a founding charter of the beguines. Matthew Paris, looking more towards Germany, is struck by the novelty of a movement amongst laypeople, especially women whom he calls beguines, in the Cologne area, leading a religious life without entering a monastery. At about the same time Lamprecht von Regensburg in his *Tochter Syon* expresses more than just surprise at the contemporary development in Brabant (and Bavaria) amongst women whose spirituality exceeds that of wise men ('herre got,

---

[270] *Ibid.*, LT 48, 59, 60, 61, 63. Cf. Spearing, *Julian*, p. xxiv.   [271] Bynum, *Jesus*, pp. 110–69.
[272] Riddy, 'Women', p. 116.   [273] Peters, *Erfahrung*, p. 21.
[274] Degler-Spengler, 'Beginen', pp. 31–91.

waz kunst ist daz,/daz sich ein alt wîp baz/verstêt dan witzige man?' Lord God, what skill is that when an old woman understands things better than learned men?).[275] Lamprecht's reference to Brabant points to the area where this new form of religious life quickly established itself: northern France, Flanders and the Rhineland. The novelty of beguines lies in their midway position between monasticism and the world. They constitute small communities of women living without any officially sanctioned monastic rule, but embracing chastity, devotional practice and good works such as care of the sick, but without a binding vow so that they could at any time return to the world. Such women were neither nuns nor ordinary laywomen.

Amongst the reasons for the rise of this movement (a demographic surplus of women, inability to afford entry into established convents) must be set the dogged reluctance or financial inability of monastic orders to cope with the growing numbers of potential women recruits, an impasse which was finally overcome, under papal pressure, by the mendicant orders assuming spiritual responsibility for beguinages in the vicinity.[276] One particular social group for which beguine life provided a solution was made up of the increasing numbers of unmarried women, not merely in the sense of unmarriageable, but rather as an alternative to (or even escape from) the unattractive features of feudal marriage practice which we observed with recluses. The *vita* of Ida of Nivelles relates that she ran away from home (rather like Christina of Markyate) to escape a marriage arranged by her family. Jutta of Huy may have been forced into marriage by her parents, but after the early death of her husband she succeeded in scotching their plans for re-marriage in order to work for lepers. Marie d'Oignies likewise may not have escaped marriage, but avoided the implications by persuading her husband to live chastely with her, thereby, according to Jacques de Vitry, turning from her earthly husband to Christ, her heavenly spouse. Catherine of Sweden also lived a chaste married life, but was accused by her brother of turning into a beguine and attempting to do likewise with his wife.[277] These examples contain striking parallels with the *Life* of Christina, which raises the question what value we can attach to them as evidence, whether we are not in fact dealing with a hagiographic topos, going back to the early virgin martyr's rejection of marriage to a pagan ruler. This argument has been advanced in the case of Christina, to which it can be replied that although her *Life* may not be biographically true in every factual detail, it is

[275] Jacques: *ibid.*, pp. 16–27; Baldwin, *Language*, p. 9. Matthew Paris, *Chronica* IV 278 and Southern, *Society*, pp. 319f. *Tochter Syon* 2838–43; cf. Ruh, *ZfdA* 106 (1977), 266f.
[276] Grundmann, *Bewegungen*, pp. 319–33.
[277] Ida: Simons, *Cities*, p. 40. Jutta and Marie: *ibid.*, p. 69. Catherine: *ibid.*, p. 70.

historically true in terms of the social conventions of patriarchal marriage. The same has been argued in the case of these semi-religious women.[278]

Despite outwitted parents, disappointed husbands and angry brothers these women did receive support from some men, the clerics who were impressed by them and advocated their cause. Early sympathisers like Jacques de Vitry and Thomas de Cantimpré are obvious examples, persuaded by the model these women were and convinced of their superior standing in spiritual humility. To such individual examples must be added institutional ones like the Cistercian monastery of Villers, interested in the religious and visionary experiences of women already in the person of Hildegard von Bingen.[279] The importance of such support should not be underestimated, for it did much to legitimise the position of semi-religious women, especially valuable when they came to be suspected of heresy.

It was valuable for another reason, too, since these women, anomalous by their position between monastery and world, aroused suspicion and hostility in other clerical quarters. Lamprecht von Regensburg adds to his surprise a contrast between these women's abilities and men's which is not complimentary to the former's intelligence ('ir ringer muot/in einvaltigen sinnen' their foolishness in simple-mindedness) and scorns their lack of self-control in taking the slightest symptom as a sign of divine grace ('ein gnaedelîn' with a mocking diminutive). Bruno von Olmütz complains that beguines use their liberty to escape obedience to two male authorities (priests and husbands), but in his two recommendations ('let them marry or join an established order') he confirms on the one hand that dissatisfaction with marriage may have played a part in their decision and ignores on the other hand that inability to join an order had been thrust upon them. Jean Gerson, like Lamprecht, considers women's enthusiasm unstable and gullible, which is why their teaching should be carefully examined, much more so than men's.[280] That they should teach, especially in public and in the vernacular, aroused further suspicion in the light of Paul's injunction. For Guibert of Tournai their engagement with vernacular texts is suspect when in private conventicles and workshops ('in conventiculis, in ergastulis'), but even more so when in public places ('in plateis').[281] Not all beguines suffered the fate of Marguerite Porète at the stake, but all were exposed to this

[278] Fanous, 'Christina', pp. 53–78; Simons, *Cities*, pp. 71f.
[279] Jacques and Thomas: Peters, *Erfahrung*, pp. 14–27, and Simons, *Cities*, pp. 45–7. Villers: Simons, *Cities*, p. 46.
[280] Lamprecht, *Tochter* 2846f., 2857–9, 2963–70. Bruno: Grundmann, *Bewegungen*, p. 336, and Southern, *Society*, p. 329. Gerson: Watt, *Secretaries*, pp. 35f.
[281] Grundmann, *Bewegungen*, p. 338, fn. 37.

threat, which led finally to the suppression of beguine houses. It is a tragic irony that the accusation of heresy was made against a movement which in its outset, as Jacques de Vitry made clear in the prologue to the *vita* of Marie d'Oignies, was considered as an effective answer to the Albigensian heresy.

If beguines were seen by Guibert as engaged in illicit or suspect teaching they must have received some prior instruction, which brings us to the question of their educational status. For Southern their 'way of life precluded any great development of learning or literature',[282] but this ignores such figures as Mechthild von Magdeburg or Hadewijch who, although exceptional, wrote as beguines. Here we face the same problem as with laywomen's education at large: did it consist of instruction in ethics and behaviour (*mores*) or did it also embrace letters? Both are shown combined already by Jacques de Vitry's reference to their instruction in good morals and in letters ('tam moribus quam litteris'), but elsewhere some degree of literacy can be suggested. This can often imply a modest or restricted ability, thereby confirming Southern's judgment, as with reading the Psalms (was this merely memorised reading and what degree of understanding of Latin was involved?) or with indirect reading ('lego ab illo'), as when her confessor reads out Bernard's sermons on the Song of Songs to the Viennese beguine, Agnes Blannbekin.[283] From what we have seen of the persistence of the double formula, however, hearing a text read need not exclude reading it, as is suggested by Hadewijch in a letter to another beguine ('die woerde die ghi hoert . . . ende die ghi selue leset' the words that you hear and that you yourselves read). Hadewijch goes further, however, in implying the recipient's ability to read in Latin as well as the vernacular ('in dietsche Ochte in latine'), so that in all a wide range of communication is involved (oral and written, vernacular and Latin). Knowledge of Latin is suggested elsewhere. Juliana of Cornillon's teacher, the aptly named beguine Sapientia, taught her to read in the vernacular, but also the Latin works of Augustine and Bernard. Christina Mirabilis may also have possessed a reasonable command of Latin, and Latin prayers occur in Psalters used by beguines in Liège in the thirteenth century.[284]

Although it pays to include these occasional references to the Latin literacy of some beguines in order to complete the picture of their reading

---

[282] Southern, *Society*, p. 326.

[283] Jacques: Galloway, 'Maidens', p. 92, and Simons, *Cities*, p. 82. Psalms: Simons, *OGE* 65 (1991), 23–30, and Oliver and Simons, *OGE* 66 (1992), 249–59. Blannbekin: Köpf, 'Bernhard', pp. 58 and 75, n. 34.

[284] Hadewijch, *Brieven*, nr. 24, 104–7 (I thank Frank Willaert for this reference). Juliana: Simons, *Cities*, p. 42. Christina: *ibid.*, p. 128. Latin prayers: Oliver, *Manuscript* I 5–8.

ability, it remains clearly subordinate to the vernacular. To see the relevance of this let us turn back to Guibert of Tournai's criticism of the beguines' reading practice (that reading in their conventicles is in groups is made clear: 'Legunt ea communiter'). His objection is threefold: that it is women ('mulieres') who meddle with theological subtleties ('subtilitates') beyond their grasp and difficult enough for anyone with training, so that, secondly, heretical errors result from faulty readings ('Haereses et errores'). Thirdly, however, and most important for us, they do this with religious texts rendered into the vernacular ('in communi idiomate gallicata'), including a French Bible ('bibliam gallicatam'). Not merely are these texts read out in public places so that misreadings are 'published' far and wide, but the use of the vulgar tongue runs the risk of demeaning holy scripture ('ne sermo divinus a dictione vulgari vilescat').[285]

If Lambert le Bègue cannot count as the founder of the beguines, his activity as a translator of religious texts for the benefit of laypeople who were able to read in some manner, but not in Latin, is informative about the twelfth-century beguine movement in the Liège area and about clerical doubts about allowing laypeople access to scripture in their own tongue and without priestly guidance.[286] Lambert translated for virgins the *vita* of the virgin martyr Agnes and for his followers the Acts of the Apostles from Latin, which suggests that in his day lay men and women around Liège were in the habit of reading religious texts in the vernacular, French or Dutch, but could not or did not regularly do so in Latin. Since Lambert makes it clear that his translations were for use on feastdays of the Church it seems that they were meant not for individual reading, but to be read out to groups of interested laymen. The fact that in 1242 the Dominicans had to be formally forbidden to translate sermons and other texts into the vernacular suggests stopping an existing practice.[287]

Long ago Grundmann was the first to point to the historical importance of this growth of religious literature transferred from Latin into the vernacular from about 1200, above all for women.[288] What for clerics was their disadvantaged position, their exclusion from Latin literature, was of historical significance since it marked the take-off of religious literature in the vernacular in the late Middle Ages. This vernacularisation presupposes a group, large enough to underpin the whole process, which, like the beguines, occupied a middling position between clergy and lay world: interested in religious literature and keen to read it, but unable to do so in

[285] See fn. 281.   [286] Simons, *Cities*, pp. 24–34.
[287] Grundmann, *Bewegungen*, p. 462.   [288] *Ibid.*, p. 442.

the clerical language Latin. Whether they read themselves or were read to by someone else, the vernacular literacy of these women marks a turning-point in the history of religious literature.

We come now to two specific examples of semi-religious women, one from Germany, Mechthild von Magdeburg, who passed from one community of women to another, the other from England, but with noticeable connections with Germany, Margery Kempe of Lynn, in every sense a 'loner'.

Mechthild, of an aristocratic or at least well-to-do family, spent many years as a beguine before moving to the greater safety of Helfta, home of important religious writing by women in Latin. Mechthild's vernacular work, *Das fließende Licht der Gottheit*, was for the most part composed at Magdeburg, but completed at Helfta, and it has been said that with her the figure of a semi-religious woman about whose experiences a *vita* may have been written by someone else (e.g. Jacques de Vitry on Marie d'Oignies) has been enriched to include the role of authorship.[289] That may be true in the modern sense, but it does not correspond to Mechthild's own view of her function, for she sees herself with humility, but also with a sense of self-defence as no more than a medium, passing on what comes to her from divine inspiration.[290] For the same reason even the suggested term 'co-authorship'[291] fails to do justice to her own view, which resembles that of Julian of Norwich, claiming that she was no teacher, but merely one who transmitted what she was divinely taught. Although such an attitude was not gender-specific, it may well have been gender-aggravated.

Mechthild has been called an educated woman but, as always, this raises the question of what was meant by her education. Her statement about her uneducated status ('wan ich der schrift ungeleret bin' I have not been taught letters)[292] is a standard topos of the *sermo humilis* used by those who minimise their own achievements, but it could also mean more specifically that she was untrained in Latin. This is what she says elsewhere of herself ('Nu gebristet mir túsches, des latines kan ich nit' My German is faulty, I know no Latin),[293] but whereas this is categorically said of Latin, her German is merely insufficient for her purpose, a traditional confession of the mystic before the ineffability of her experience. Mechthild can be termed *illitterata* in the clerical sense of inability to read Latin, while leaving untouched whatever literacy she may have had in German. If the ability to write implies an ability to read, then it is significant that Mechthild,

[289] Bürkle, 'Spiritualität', p. 139, who qualifies herself on the following page.
[290] Palmer, 'Buch', pp. 220, 227. [291] Stadler, 'Sünderin', p. 203.
[292] *Licht* III 1 (p. 148). [293] *Ibid.*, II 3 (p. 82).

as the medium acting between God and the recipients of her work, is presented by Heinrich von Halle, following her own remark, as personally writing down what came to her from God ('. . . ist also getrúwelich hie gesetzet, alse si us von irme herzen gegeben ist von gotte und geschriben mit iren henden' it is arranged here as faithfully as it was given from her heart by God and written with her hands).[294] Heinrich exercises a clerical function in arranging ('gesetzet') in final editorial shape,[295] on the basis of what Mechthild had already written herself ('geschriben'), a double process resembling the illustration of Hildegard von Bingen writing on tablets before Volmar copies the text in book-form.[296] In view of this, to return to Mechthild's statement that she is uneducated, when this is followed by her fears of the consequences of her writing ('ob ich schribe') there is no reason not to accept this verb in its literal sense, thereby implying her vernacular literacy.

Even an *illitterata* in Latin, as Mechthild admits to being, may be *quasi litterata*, since there is internal evidence that she was acquainted with some Latin theological writers, ranging from Augustine to Bernard, a knowledge probably conveyed to her through sermons and her contacts with the Dominicans.[297] We have seen, however, that theological knowledge *per se* did not loom large for Mechthild by comparison with her visionary experience and her sense of having been chosen by God, much as had been the Old Testament female prophets with whom she is compared in the Latin version of her work.[298] If it appears to be gender-specific that God chose to speak through her despite her lowly status as a mere woman, this is reversed when God impresses upon her that this choice was *because* of this and that he had acted similarly in the past with men likewise weak and hesitant such as initially Moses and the apostles. With them, too, things are reversed, 'blŏdekeit' (hesitancy) gives way to 'kŭnheit' (bravery) and it is the weak and simple who are chosen.[299] But it has gender-specific implications when Mechthild stresses not simply her sinfulness, but refers to herself as a 'snŏdez wîp' (wretched woman), but one who has been chosen, so that, 'ungeleret' (unlearned) though she may be, she is enabled to instruct those who are 'geleret'.[300] This is the Christian doctrine of kenosis given a gendered application: 'The disqualification of gender becomes itself a qualification'.[301]

---

[294] *Ibid.*, VI 42 (p. 516). Cf. IV 2 (pp. 236, 238). The attribution to Heinrich is an inference from the Latin translation, not evident from the German text.

[295] Ruh, *Geschichte* II 249.   [296] See Fig. 1.

[297] Grundmann, *Bewegungen*, p. 466; Ruh, *ZfdA* 106 (1971), 269; Andersen, *Voices*, p. 16.

[298] Heimbach, *Mund*, p. 174, fn. 52.   [299] *Ibid.*, fn. 51; Palmer, 'Buch', p. 222 on *Licht* V 12 (p. 346).

[300] *Licht* IV 2 (pp. 236, 238). *Ungeleret*: Heimbach, *Mund*, pp. 162–81.   [301] Bynum, *Jesus*, p. 242.

Despite the assistance and encouragement she received from Dominicans Mechthild met opposition and criticism. As a beguine she was exposed to that in any case, but to this were added the further offences of daring as a laywoman to speak of religious matters, of using the vernacular for this purpose, and of pitting herself, a declared *illitterata* in the conventional sense, against accumulated theological knowledge. Whether because of her beguine status or the views she expresses, she was warned of the danger that her book might be burnt,[302] and it takes little imagination to equate the possible fate of the book with what might befall her, as it did Marguerite Porète. Mechthild was well aware of the corruption of the Church in her day and made no bones about expressing her views, which may have given rise on her part to a sense of being threatened by those she criticised.[303] Although Hildegard von Bingen had been likewise critical, she enjoyed public backing, ecclesiastical as well as secular, no doubt as a nun rather than a beguine.

If the beguine movement has been described as that unique institution in the Middle Ages, created by women and for women,[304] it is equally true that this work by a woman was meant in the first instance for other women, even if Mechthild addresses her fellow beguines explicitly (and critically) on only one occasion.[305] If later in Book VII she addresses her recipients, stressing the books that they are able to consult ('daz vindet ir tusentvalt in iuweren bûchen' you will find that a thousand times in your books)[306] she is likely to have had the highly literate nuns of Helfta in mind, where her work was completed. Whether or not Mechthild's work found its way *via* a translation into High German to southern Germany through beguine channels, once it arrived in the south it came into the hands of beguines (and nuns).[307] Her fellow beguines, confined to vernacular literacy, were the readers Mechthild had primarily in mind. It is such readers who are recommended to work through her book the requisite number of times and for whose convenience in the process of reading the text is divided into books and sections with headings to indicate themes,[308] as was the case for a similar purpose with Julian of Norwich's *Book*. Whether we call Mechthild an author or not, a woman whose literacy was divorced from Latin wrote for women whose reading ability was confined to the vernacular. In this they were anticipating the future course of literary development.

---

[302] *Licht* II 26 (p. 136).   [303] Bynum, *Jesus*, pp. 231, 237; Andersen, 'Mechthild', p. 85.
[304] Cf. Galloway, 'Maidens', p. 93 ('essentially female nature').
[305] *Licht* III 15 (p. 192).   [306] *Ibid.*, VII 21 (p. 572).   [307] Haas, 'Mystik', pp. 246f.
[308] *Licht*, pp. 10, 12; Palmer, *FMS* 23 (1989), 43–88, especially 77f.

Margery Kempe stands at a beginning in another sense, for she wrote the first known autobiography in English, one which plots not merely a life of adventurous journeying (to the Holy Land, Rome, Santiago and the Baltic), but also spiritual experiences. Like Christina of Markyate she avoided the implications of marriage, not by escaping from parental control, but by persuading her husband to lead a life of chastity together, as other women in her position succeeded in doing (Marie d'Oignies, Bridget of Sweden, Dorothea von Montau). As with these other women, it is wrong to say that Margery escaped from marriage, for she exchanged one union for another. Christ may say that she is free from her husband, but only in the sense that, with a frankness of erotic imagery, he has made her body freely available to himself.[309]

Like other women (Mechthild, Julian) Margery says point-blank that she is uneducated,[310] but that does not relieve us of the task of determining what she meant by this. We have already seen that she was completely dependent on others (men) for the physical act of writing down her experiences which she dictated to them, but not from a draft or tablet of her own.[311] Here, too, we need to employ the concept *quasi litterata* to account for the fact that the religious knowledge she displays was not restricted to her literate scribes, but shared by them with her. We have already seen something of the extensive knowledge she must have possessed, but what is relevant here is the way in which she acquired it, by hearing books read out to her on many occasions, making of her an indirect reader. When referring to some of these books she talks of hearing them read and, in connection with a priest who came to Lynn, she says that he read many devotional works to her, including the Bible and commentaries.[312] Nor was knowledge restricted to English devotional literature, for she refers to Bridget of Sweden and had associations with Germany and the Low Countries (many mystics of these regions were known in England). Margery's journey to the Baltic region included a visit to Danzig at a time when the cult of Dorothea von Montau flourished.[313] Like Margery, Dorothea described herself as illiterate, managed to live in chastity with her husband, was influenced by the example of Bridget, and had her life written by a cleric. It is tempting to think that she belonged to the continental range of Margery's considerable devotional knowledge.

[309] Kempe, *Book* 6059f. (pp. 331f.), 7148–54 (p. 375).
[310] *Ibid.*, 4290 (p. 257).   [311] Dinshaw, 'Kempe', p. 226.
[312] *Book* 4800–5 (p. 279), 4818–21, 4826f. (p. 280), 4920f. (p. 284). See also Windeatt, *Book*, pp. 15f.
[313] Windeatt, *Book*, pp. 17, 21. Dorothea: Triller, *VfL* 6, 60f.

Margery resembles Mechthild in claiming that God commanded her to write her revelations, but her illiteracy was such that, unlike Mechthild, she did not write herself. She uses the phrase 'have a book written', others offer to write for her, and when, after the lapse of many years, she consents to written form, she again has to 'have it written'.[314] The line of authorisation is the same as with Mechthild (God – visionary – scribe(s) or cleric(s) to act in that capacity), but whereas Mechthild herself incorporates the transition from orality (God's word to her) to writing, with Margery the stage of writing is reached only with her scribe(s). Although Margery was therefore dependent on someone to write for her, that does not necessarily mean that she was at his mercy as a potential censor. She says that she spent considerable time with her scribe and, as we have seen, he read the text out to her, she intervened over any difficulty and was well aware of what was in the written text.[315]

From the *Book* it is clear that Margery was exposed to much criticism by laypeople and clerics alike, not merely because of her ecstatic fits, uncontrolled weeping and unconventionally free style of living and travelling far and wide. Perhaps inevitably this criticism focused on her possible heresy. Although there is no reason to regard her beliefs as anything but orthodox, she aroused the suspicion of Lollardy by her claim to have had direct communication with God, by her freespoken attitude to ecclesiastical authority, and by travelling around the country proclaiming God's word very much as if she were an itinerant preacher.[316] Nor were these simply abstract criticisms. At Canterbury she is threatened by a crowd with burning as a Lollard and elsewhere on her travels she is repeatedly arrested and interrogated by clerical or secular authorities as a heretic.[317] Despite grounds for suspicion there can be no doubt about Margery's orthodoxy: her piety includes many features rejected by the Lollards (confession, pilgrimage, submission to the Church) and she meets the accusation of preaching by saying that she never entered a pulpit.[318]

Not merely in the independent manner in which she conducted her life, but also in the spirit in which she comported herself under interrogation Margery belongs to that small, but far from negligible group of women who challenge contemporary stereotypes about the position and nature of women.[319] Her lack of any formal education, greater than with Mechthild, made no difference to her conviction that what she had to say had been communicated to her by God. Mechthild had been similarly convinced,

---

[314] *Book* 76–87 (pp. 46f.); Johnson, *Speculum* 66 (1991), 834.
[315] Johnson, *Speculum* 66 (1991), 835.   [316] Watt, *Secretaries*, pp. 37–50; Dinshaw, 'Kempe', p. 228.
[317] Windeatt, *Book*, pp. 11, 13f.   [318] *Book* 4213 (p. 253).   [319] Watt, *Secretaries*, p. 38.

but at least enjoyed some degree of literacy to support her. Nonetheless, the lawyers of Lincoln were surprised by Margery, admitting that she was superior to the learning they had acquired in the schools, so that, coming from others and not from herself, we find in her a contrast between divine inspiration and human learning such as we saw with Mechthild.[320] That this contrast was gender based is also clear from the advice she is given in an examination at York to give up her manner of life and take up spinning and carding like other women.[321] It could even be suspected that she was providing a dangerous example for women by objecting for sectarian ends to the institution of marriage, as when the mayor of Leicester accuses her of coming to lure away their wives from them and lead them off with her.[322]

Despite their differences Margery and Mechthild share two important features. They do not hesitate to criticise the shortcomings of the clergy and they both do this out of a conviction that, unlettered though they may be, what they have to say comes to them from God and is superior to human learning. They thereby confirm positively what Lamprecht von Regensburg had meant negatively in contrasting semi-religious women and wise men. They also show how women, assailed by criticism and threats, could maintain their freedom of choice against the odds. From a clerical point of view their literacy may have been imperfect, but this did not prevent them from finding expression for their experiences, spiritual and autobiographical, in literary form.

HERETICS

In this section it is time to look more systematically at what we have so far encountered only in passing, at the reading practice of women who were or could be suspected of being heretics. We have seen that suspicions were harboured against figures such as Mechthild von Magdeburg and Margery Kempe, but also against untrained laywomen occupying themselves with religious texts, running the risk of remaining prisoners to a literal understanding, and led astray by the conceptual shortcomings of a vernacular to which most of them were confined.

There is no shortage of clerical voices expressing concern over these dangers, especially from fifteenth-century England disturbed by Lollardy, whereas it had escaped earlier heresies on the continent. Although offence

---

[320] *Book* 4550 (p. 269). Margery also contrasts her illiteracy with the knowledge of learned men, 4288–91 (p. 257).
[321] *Ibid.*, 4330f. (p. 258). 　　　[322] *Ibid.*, 3841f. (p. 236).

is caused by male as well as female laypeople or heretics it is the women who attract shrill attention. Speaking of heretics, Henry Knighton complains that the women who can read are like swine trampling on the pearl of the gospel. Bishop Pecock makes a point of criticising the arrogance of women heretics who, having looked at the scriptures, cling to an inadequate biblicism, disregard the clerical exegesis of centuries and see themselves as superior to clerics. For Thomas Netter this study of the scriptures by laypeople has led women to daring to read and teach the sacred text to a congregation of men (thereby ignoring the Pauline injunction to avoid precisely this). In the eyes of Roger Dymmok, simple uneducated women were an easy prey for Lollards. In the early fifteenth century the poet Hoccleve resembles Lamprecht von Regensburg in the thirteenth in contrasting the thin and feeble wits of these uneducated women with the art and knowledge of clerics in expounding scripture, telling these women to abandon what does not pertain to them. Hoccleve's patriarchal advice to them also resembles that given to Margery Kempe at York, for they are likewise put in their place: 'sittith doun and spinne,/And kakele of sumwhat elles'.[323] Behind such statements lies the fear that heresy enabled women to preach and teach, even though traditional clerical misogyny regarded them as the root of heresy, debarred from preaching because of their unfitness to teach correctly and the facility with which they seduce ('ineptitudo ejus ad recte docendum et ad seducendum facilitas').[324] Talking of heretics (even though he may not mention women expressly), Gerson makes a related point in equating the use of vernacular translations of the Bible by laymen with a literal understanding of the naked text, disastrously divorced from the further exegesis that only trained clerics can supply ('tamquam credenda sit in suis nudis terminis absque alterius interpretis vel expositoris admissione').[325]

The heretical movements we shall be looking at are three in number, and to do justice to their relevance to the subject of this book we must look at them under three headings. First, what is the connection between heresy and women? Secondly, how far is heresy tied up with questions of reading and literacy? Thirdly, in what respects do women heretics play a part in reading and what is the nature of their literacy?

That women were particularly prone to heresy could be argued in the Middle Ages on biblical authority: the view that in the last days it was

---

[323] Knighton: Aston, *Lollards*, pp. 49f. Pecock: *ibid.*, p. 51, and Krug, *Families*, p. 115. Netter: Aston, *Lollards*, p. 65, and Krug, *Families*, p. 115. Dymmok: Somerset, 'Mulier', p. 245. Hoccleve: Aston, *Lollards*, p. 51.

[324] Hanna, *MLQ* 51 (1990), 328, and Blamires, *Viator* 26 (1995), 135.

[325] Copeland, *Pedagogy*, p. 105.

women in particular, demeaned as silly (*mulierculae*), who would be led away captive, incapable of ever coming to the truth.[326] The misogyny which the medieval interpretation of this biblical passage betrays is present in other respects in the early Church. It was scandalised, for example, by the freedom to teach which the Montanist heresy afforded to women in the second century and Tertullian, a leading opponent of this heresy, complained of the audacity of such women in going even further, including the right to baptise. Bishop Irenaeus likewise registers that women in particular are attracted to these heretical groups, even acting as priests serving the Eucharist and acting as prophets. Jerome follows this tack, accusing women of helping to spread heresies, commenting on their attraction to the heresy of Pelagius and quoting Irenaeus on the spread of another heresy especially amongst women.[327] Unsurprisingly against this background, medieval sources are convinced of the connection of women with heresy. In the twelfth-century *Glossa Ordinaria* a comparison is made between the physical attraction of a prostitute and the verbal seductiveness of heretical doctrines, a comparison which is more than simply figurative in such a well-known case as Solomon, seduced to worship idols by love of foreign women. Implicit in this is what became the traditional association of women with idols and lusting after them with idolatry, as argued by the Dominican Holcot in a series of lectures at Cambridge 1334–36.[328] How well this topos of Solomon lent itself to clerical misogyny can be seen in the *Speculum humanae salvationis* where the exemplum of Solomon, for all his wisdom, being seduced to worship idols for love of women ('Salomon propter amorem mulierum idola adoravit') is used as a warning to all men to beware the blandishments of women.[329] Reverting to another form of misogyny, Bishop Pecock undermines the arrogant claims of heretical women by gender stereotyping them, seeing their vernacular biblicism as ultimately betraying their stronger 'affeccioun or wil' and weaker 'intelleccioun or resoun'.[330]

So far we have listened to the opposition (which may have exaggerated the feminine element for polemical reasons), but what was it that undoubtedly attracted women, alongside men, to heresy? Economic reasons suggested (a search for security or increased survival chances from greater prosperity) cancel each other out, while the Marxist explanation (an escape from the

---

[326] II Tim. 3, 6. Cf. Biller, 'Cathars', p. 64; Grundmann, *Bewegungen*, p. 36, fn. 46; Somerset, 'Mulier', pp. 265, 274, n. 22.

[327] Montanists: Bloch, *Misogyny*, p. 72. Tertullian: *ibid.*, p. 74, and Pagels, *Signs* 2 (1976/77), 299f. Jerome: Blamires, *Viator* 26 (1995), 135.

[328] Ferrante, *Women*, pp. 21f.; Camille, *Idol*, p. 298.

[329] *Speculum* I 43, quoted by Schnell, *Causa*, p. 477.   [330] Blamires, *MÆ* 58 (1989), 236.

oppression of women as part of class oppression at large) runs up against the objection that heresies, while granting women new opportunities, were not free from misogynous tendencies.[331] Nonetheless, if the Church offered women little scope in its intellectual or organisational life, some heresies offered more (Cathars recognised 'perfectae' and the Waldensians the possibility of women priests). Even so, it is dangerous to interpret this in terms of self-emancipation on the part of women, since heresies seem to have attracted families as a whole rather than individual members. Certainly as regards teaching (at times hardly distinct from preaching) heresies offered opportunities withheld by the Church from laymen at large and from women in particular.[332] This activity, shared by heretics of both sexes, could be justified by an appeal to the precedent of the apostles, but this did not prevent derision and criticism, as when Hugh of Rouen refers to these women heretics with the diminutive *mulierculae* and insinuates less than spiritual motives by stressing that they were neither wives nor relatives of the men they accompanied ('sub contubernio private libidinis').[333] To justify their preaching heretics claimed that they had been sent to do this by God, to which an official response was given by Robert of Basevorn (no unauthorised layman, and no woman at all, may preach, saying that he was sent by God, for that is what heretics claim).[334] A heretic justifying herself in this way was using the same kind of argument, and facing the same sceptical opposition as Margery Kempe saying that she had been ordered to write by God and Mechthild von Magdeburg presenting herself as the medium for God's words. Not by chance were these two women seen on the fringes of heresy.

With our second heading (the connection of heresy with literacy) we approach the theme of this book. Officially, the Church insisted that there was no connection, as in the words of a German inquisitor ('O vos illitterati haeretici'),[335] thereby contrasting the unlettered ignorance of their opponents with the accumulated knowledge in writing of the orthodox. For the Anonymous of Passau the lines are clearly drawn between the poor, workmen, women and *ydiote* on the one hand and princes, philosophers and *litterati* on the other. But in religious terms this was a dangerous argument to use, not merely because of the social contrast between the powerful and the weak, but also in view of literacy or its lack, for Christ had chosen his disciples from amongst unlettered fishermen, a form of kenosis known to Mechthild von Magdeburg in defence of her lack of Latin

---

[331] Wessley, 'Guglielmites', p. 299; Koch, *Frauenfrage*.
[332] Wessley, 'Guglielmites', p. 300.   [333] Grundmann, *Bewegungen*, p. 36 and fn. 46.
[334] Blamires, *Viator* 26 (1995), 149.   [335] Biller, *Waldenses*, p. 169.

literacy.[336] In addition, it has become clear that the designation of the heretic as *illitteratus* was a topos used polemically by the Church which need not always correspond to reality (in much the same way, an author's use of the topos 'non cognovi litteraturam' cannot automatically be taken literally).[337] We must therefore expect with heretics, as with other groups, no clear-cut distinction between literacy and illiteracy. There are suggestions of a lack or only modest degree of literacy, as with the stress placed on memorising the scriptures by heretics, an obvious advantage in the face of persecution, where frequently the possession of a vernacular book was taken as proof of heresy.[338] Another token of illiteracy (from a clerical viewpoint) was the heretics' dependence on translations from Latin into the vernacular, although for us this could point to literacy of another kind. In 1199 the Bishop of Metz reported to Rome that heretical men and women were reading translations of the scriptures into French to each other, to which Innocent III replied that the translators at least could not be entirely uneducated.[339] To this qualification we may add that those who read out these translations possessed vernacular literacy and those who listened to them can be classed as indirect readers. With the persecution of Lollardy in England to own or read a text in English could of itself be incriminating, but when Aston says that literacy pointed an accusing finger towards heresy this has to be qualified as vernacular literacy.[340] For Richard Ullerston at the beginning of the fifteenth century the prospects held out by vernacular translations were grimmer than, but similar to those seen by Lamprecht von Regensburg. These texts would allow any old woman ('vetula', cf. Lamprecht's 'alt wîp') to take over the role of teacher, leading to a world 'in which women (*mulierculae*) talk philosophy and dare to instruct men'.[341]

The indirect reading suggested by Innocent III's letter takes firmer shape when we look at it from the heretics' position. From a group of Lollards in fifteenth-century Norwich we learn something of their reading practice. Margery Baxter invited two women to come secretly to her house to hear her husband read to them a text which he was accustomed to read to her, but the words used point unmistakably to their indirect reading.[342] A book is mentioned ('librum'), the husband reads to them ('legere . . . eisdem') and to her ('legere eidem') and is heard ('audiret'). Frequent attendance at such readings (certainly in the case of Margery Baxter) could make of

[336] *Ibid.*, pp. 169f.   [337] *Ibid.*, pp. 169–88.
[338] Copeland, *Pedagogy*, pp. 9f. on the Lollards. Cf. Aston, *Lollards*, p. 207.
[339] Copeland, *Pedagogy*, p. 9. Bishop of Metz and Innocent III: Grundmann, *Bewegungen*, pp. 97–9.
[340] Aston, *Lollards*, p. 207.   [341] Watson, *Speculum* 70 (1995), 843.
[342] Copeland, *Pedagogy*, p. 12.

a listener as much a *quasi litterata* as it did of Margery Kempe and the Wife of Bath. We should not regard these listeners as merely passive, for they make what they hear part of their mental equipment and actively discuss it with others (as is also reported of the *quasi litteratus* Baldwin of Guines). The wife of the Lollard Thomas Man, together with others, is reported as discussing books of scriptures with other Lollards.[343] More informative is a passage from a Lollard sermon, perhaps by an itinerant preacher, suggesting that he left copies of it with various groups on his way, expecting a discussion of it on his return, which presupposes that they peruse it ('ouerse') in his absence, so that some at least in these groups were literate independently of him.[344] Even though these examples have been taken from the English heresy, there is enough support elsewhere to show that, in opposition to the polemical dismissal of heretics as ignorant and unlearned, their connection with books and reading was undeniable. Not merely are the books of earlier authors condemned for heresy frequently mentioned, but Stephen of Bourbon associates books with heretical sects and there are references to the books of Waldensians and Albigensians, as there were for the Lollards.[345] The range of what is meant by reading and literacy is as broad for heretics as it is for their orthodox counterparts.

The third point in our argument is the importance of literacy and reading for women heretics and is best discussed with regard to the three heretical movements, from the twelfth century on, with which we shall be engaged. There is however a fourth heresy which we must leave on one side, the so-called Guglielmites.[346] This is unfortunate since potentially this movement is of the greatest relevance to women, maintaining as it did a doctrine of salvation through women, based on a female incarnation and the founding of a new Church under a female pope. This millennial movement, with its links with Joachim of Fiore, represents a reaction against the male priesthood of the established Church, a specifically female criticism of the Church which parallels, but goes heretically far beyond Hildegard von Bingen's criticism of her times as a 'muliebre tempus', when women are called on to make good the shortcomings of the male clergy.[347] Despite the promise of this movement for our subject it yields nothing, not simply because of its restricted scope (it was confined to Italy and lasted for only one generation in the thirteenth century), but especially because of the lack of testimony on the role of books and reading amongst its followers.

[343] Baldwin: see above, p. 21. Discussion of religious reading: Cross, 'Reasoners', p. 369; Paterson, *World*, p. 252; Copeland, *Pedagogy*, p. 12.
[344] Copeland, *Pedagogy*, pp. 127f. [345] Biller, *Waldenses*, pp. 172f.
[346] Wessley, 'Guglielmites', pp. 289–303. [347] Newman, *Sister*, p. 3.

With that we turn to the first heretics who do promise us something, the Cathars, especially at home in southern France after their repression in the north, in the Low Countries and the Rhineland. Against what has been rightly called a myth surrounding the special role of women in this heresy (their position has been regarded as a Marxist extension of exploitation from class to gender)[348] we have to set the misogynous strain within this heresy. Its rejection of the flesh led to a rejection of marriage which, as often with misogamy, issued in misogyny. Indeed, the growing preoccupation of the twelfth-century Church with marriage and procreation, unenthusiastic though it may have been, has been seen as a reaction to and a way of combating Catharism.[349] These heretics' rejection of the flesh led them to view original sin as intercourse (with Eve primarily responsible), Mary as not truly feminine, Christ not really incarnate, and women as taking on male form on death in order to enter paradise.[350] These views did little to impede the presence of women amongst the Cathars, even an active one. Esclarmonde, an aristocratic 'perfecta' (a status that gave her precedence over others in the sect, including men), took part in disputations between Cathars and Catholics, receiving on one occasion the stock clerical rebuke to go home and spin threads, since it was not becoming for a woman to participate in religious discussion.[351] Although 'perfectae' are not often described as preaching, the fact that they could and did take this opportunity at all sets them well apart from women in the Church.[352] A Cathar meeting at which both male and female members preached to the congregation would have been unthinkable with the orthodox.[353]

The ability of Cathar women to preach raises the question of their educational or literate status and the role played by books in this heresy. The ritual use of a book in administering the *consolamentum* is as little indicative of reading as its Catholic employment as a talisman in childbirth, and the standard inquisitor's question whether 'credentes' held or possessed a book is for us as open regarding literacy and reading as with orthodox women holding Psalters.[354] More telling are the observations that Cathar teaching could not be achieved without books and that it was addressed to aristocrats (including literate women) and to social groups whose professional

[348] Biller, 'Cathars', pp. 72, 76; Abels and Harrison, *MS* 41 (1979), 216f.
[349] Duby, *Knight*, pp. 107–20.   [350] Biller, 'Cathars', pp. 84–99.   [351] Shahar, *Estate*, p. 259.
[352] Abels and Harrison, *MS* 41 (1979), 239f.; Blamires, *Viator* 26 (1995), 138; Biller, 'Cathars', pp. 62f.
[353] Abels and Harrison, *MS* 41 (1979), 239f.
[354] *Consolamentum*: Hamilton, 'Wisdom', p. 46; Biller, 'Cathars', p. 73. Inquisitor's question: Biller, 'Languedoc', p. 71.

training included reading.[355] That books formed part of the Cathars' doctrinal equipment is suggested by one of their sermons in which the text ('littera') of the 'perfecti' came from God whilst that of the Catholics came to them from the devil ('carta diaboli').[356] Bookishness is also present in the account by Stephen of Bourbon of the ordeal by fire of two books (of Dominic and the Cathars), incorporating the opposing faiths.[357] These books of the Cathars, however, were not just tokens, they were there to be read, in various ways. These could include reading to others, as when in Languedoc men and women in a knight's hall listen to a reading of the Passion or when for Durand of Huesca the 'perfecti' are 'doctores', having books and treatises which they read to their followers in conventicles.[358] Private reading to oneself can also be involved. To see someone reading was a reason for suspecting that he was a 'perfectus' ('Vidit ipsum legentem in quodam libro . . . suspicatus tunc ipsum esse haereticum').[359] Amongst the passages signalling Cathars' contact with written material one finds not merely wording suggesting reading aloud to others (*legere* + dative or *audire legentem*), but also a construction implying personal reading (*legit in libro*) with no hint of listeners.[360] However, amongst all the depositions concerning Cathars there is not one mention of a woman reading a book, either to others or for herself.[361] If we are to remain suspicious of the universal truth-value of the official topos of the heretic as *illitteratus*, then we must regard women Cathars, as far as our evidence goes, as no more than indirect readers or at the most as *quasi litteratae*.

About the position of literacy in the Waldensian heresy we are informed from the beginning in what is reported of the conversion in the twelfth century of its founder Valdes, a merchant of Lyons. He commissioned a translation into the French vernacular of the Bible and certain patristic passages from two clerics.[362] His literary historical importance lies in stimulating religious writing in French, but the statement by Stephen of Bourbon that Valdes was 'non multum litteratus' needs careful assessment.[363] If 'litteratus' is here used by a cleric in the sense of an ability to understand a Latin text, then the addition 'non multum' means that Valdes's command of Latin was modest. What Stephen could not mean by 'litteratus', but what concerns us, is the fact that it can imply Valdes's vernacular literacy: he could read (and use for his own preaching) the translations, but not readily enough their Latin originals. How far the clerical establishment was

---

[355] Paolini, 'Catharism', p. 97. [356] Biller, 'Languedoc', pp. 78f.
[357] Biller, *Waldenses*, p. 174. [358] Biller, 'Languedoc', pp. 75, 81. [359] *Ibid.*, p. 79.
[360] E.g., Biller, *Waldenses*, p. 176, fn. 49. [361] Biller, 'Languedoc', pp. 81f.
[362] Patschkovsky, 'Literacy', p. 113. [363] *Ibid.*, p. 117.

from recognising this novel departure is shown by Walter Map's designation of Valdes's followers as 'homines ydiotas, illiteratos'.[364] This may be the topos we have encountered, but it also reflects a cleric's attitude towards a layman's improper recourse to the vernacular. By one count, therefore, Valdes was considered an *illitteratus*, but by another he was literate, even if not adequately in Latin.

In this ambiguity Valdes sums up the Waldensians at large, whose relation to literacy is complex and varying. Bernard Gui divided their 'magistri' into two groups, some able to read ('sciunt legere'), others not. Durand of Huesca demonstrates what could be achieved by the former group, a good command of Latin and literacy in the highest sense.[365] Where the language used by Waldensians was Latin, especially as a bridge between one vernacular and another, this has been taken as an indication that there was little educational difference between a Catholic priest and a Waldensian preacher. With the Waldensian 'magistri' interrogated in the 1390s the typical comment is that, although not ordained priests, they were *litterati* or *doctores litterati*.[366] This stress on reading and literacy is hardly surprising in a movement founded on a literal reading of scripture and rejecting any interpretation going beyond it, so that its members needed to be able to read or to have access to those who could. On the other hand, Waldensians interrogated by Peter Zwicker in the late fourteenth century set very little store by the value of university education,[367] thereby distancing themselves from formal learning in much the same way as Mechthild von Magdeburg and other marginalised women. Perhaps polemically distorted by those who had converted to Catholicism, there is a telling contrast between the (oral) mutterings of Waldensians in corners ('garrulitas in angulis') and the thousand volumes of the fathers and modern doctors.[368] In this movement as a whole there is an interplay between Latin and vernacular, reading and memorising, just as there had been in its founder, who had a little Latin, but insufficient to dispense with a vernacular translation which he both read and memorised.[369]

As regards the position of women in this movement, the *De Inquisitione hereticorum* stresses that women as well as men preach and that every attempt is made to attract noblewomen to their ranks. (They may be termed 'potentes' socially, but by gender they can be classed with the weak to whom the Anonymous assigns these heretics.) Bernard Gui reports

---

[364] *Ibid.*, p. 118.   [365] Gui: Biller, *Waldenses*, p. 175. Durand: Patschkovsky, 'Literacy', pp. 119f.
[366] Biller, *Waldenses*, p. 181.   [367] Patschkovsky, 'Literacy', p. 125.
[368] Biller, *Waldenses*, p. 180f. and fn. 64.
[369] *Ibid.*, p. 184. Cf. Grundmann, *Bewegungen*, p. 446, fn. 14 ('legeret et cordetenus firmaret').

the heretics' view that any layman in their sect may perform priestly functions, adding that they even believe this of women.[370] None of this bears directly on women as readers, who play as negligible a part as with the Cathars,[371] unless we take into account what has been described as the entry of the book into households where women were likely to play a more active part, a domestication of literacy which we have encountered before.[372]

With Lollardy, a more popular and often less learned version of Wycliffe's teaching, we are dealing with a heresy that towards the end of the fourteenth century arose in England, a country that had escaped the earlier movements we have been considering. That sentence encapsulates the position of this movement within our problem, for what began as an intellectual heresy at the university of Oxford became a popular movement amongst the middle classes and artisans, open to women and moving from Latin learning to include the vernacular. That in itself renders the attempt to distinguish between literacy and illiteracy difficult. True to its academic origins Lollardy attached importance to books throughout its history and, although it maintained that the vernacular was the language of religious instruction, Latin still played a role with the academically trained.[373] This movement of a heresy that attached importance to books from the academic world to a popular audience brought with it an opening to the vernacular and may even have encouraged vernacular literacy within its wider audience, in origin still largely illiterate.[374] This is how opponents saw the danger, as when Henry Knighton accused Wycliffe, because of his translation of the gospel into English, of having made it accessible to laypeople and the feeble-witted ('laicis et infirmioribus personis'), amongst whom he includes women who know how to read, whereas previously it had been read safely by well-read clerics.[375] This is no isolated awareness of the danger as the Church perceived it, for the sustained attempt to hunt down and destroy the writings of Wycliffe and his followers has been described as if it were an attempt to take the topos seriously, to push those exposed to these vernacular writings 'back into the stereotype of the *laicus illiteratus*'.[376] Legislative steps seek to control the situation: in 1401 *De heretico comburendo* sees the making of dangerous books as a characteristic of the heretic, and in 1407 the Constitutions of Archbishop Arundel forbid the ownership of vernacular biblical texts without episcopal permission.[377]

---

[370] *De inquisitione* and the Anonymous: Biller, 'Cathars', p. 65. Gui: Aston, *Lollards*, p. 67.
[371] Biller, 'Women', pp. 181f.   [372] Biller, *Waldenses*, p. 188.
[373] Hudson, 'Laicus', pp. 228, 230.   [374] *Ibid.*, p. 229.   [375] Aston, *Lollards*, p. 206.
[376] Hudson, 'Laicus', p. 232.   [377] *Ibid.*

In view of this it is difficult to interpret some of the evidence. Did the authorities, in calling heretics illiterate, still cling to the convention that only Latin literacy counted as literacy or were they wishfully attempting to restore an earlier situation? Conversely, when heretics are presented as literate, is this an accurate reflection of reality or does it register, in exaggerated form, the alarm felt by the establishment? When Henry Knighton refers to women who know how to read was this a fact of heretical life or was he imagining a worst-case scenario ('Things must be really bad if even women have access to these writings')?

The importance attached by the Lollards to books and reading did not diminish the role of memorising or reading aloud to a small gathering of like-minded. Partly because of illiteracy, but partly for security reasons (given the danger of being caught with a prohibited vernacular text) learning by heart and recital from memory played an important role in Lollard communities.[378] This practice could involve longer texts (parts of the Pauline epistles or even the whole Apocalypse), so that Alice Colyns, for example, who was particularly gifted in this, would be sent for when conventicles were held. She would attend very much like a 'walking book', but less incriminating than a book and, in the case of illiteracy, a substitute for a book.[379] Those who attended these conventicles, whether they were themselves literate or not, were on these occasions indirect readers, but this is also the case on more intimate, private occasions. John Claydon was illiterate, paid to have a work copied, and listened to it read out to him by the scribe and later by servants who could read. Margery Baxter owned a Lollard book, but in this case, too, owning is not synonymous with personal reading, for her husband read it to her (and also held other readings in their house). Alice Rowley of Coventry may have been illiterate, but owned a few books (and was responsible for passing on others) and listened to her husband reading them to her.[380] All this reinforces the mixed status of literacy in these Lollard communities: some are literate and read for others ('lego illi'), while others, whether expressly illiterate or not, are indirect readers ('lego ab illo').

The importance of collective readings at conventicles tends to push out of sight the practice of personal reading to oneself ('lego librum'). That it must have taken place is clear from those cases where we are informed of the literacy of individual heretics. Walter Brut, the author of some Lollard tracts, may say of himself that he knows no letters ('non cognovi litteraturam'), but

---

[378] Cross, 'Reasoners', p. 371. [379] Aston, *Lollards*, p. 201.
[380] Claydon: Hudson, '*Laicus*', pp. 230f. Baxter: Krug, *Families*, pp. 144f. Rowley: Cross, 'Reasoners', pp. 366f.

in his case, too, we do well not to take this humility formula at face value.[381] The factual truth of this is belied by his detailed knowledge of canon law and of the Bible, from which he often quotes at considerable length and with verbatim accuracy. His reading ability must rest on much more than the scribal activity of reading what one writes ('lego scriptum') and he has been called a heretic who is a 'laicus litteratus'.[382] Another heretic, William Swinderby, describes himself in slightly different, but comparable terms as 'bot sympully lettered', but this, too, is contradicted by his knowledge of canon law (even greater than Brut's), his erudite arguments and his quoting of sources in Latin.[383]

Not merely these perhaps exceptional cases of advanced literacy amongst Lollards, but also the more commonly attested and more modest attainments of literate Lollards who read to others which we have mentioned have one thing in common: they are confined to men. This highlights the fact that, although there is evidence that some Lollard women could and did read, it is remarkably scarce. In part this may be because to conceal or deny one's ability to read was a good defence against the charge of heresy, as was the case with Juliana Young at Coventry, who later admitted that she could read.[384] However, it would be rash to generalise this negative evidence in order to produce a crop of Lollard women able and accustomed to read, for Margery Kempe, undoubtedly illiterate, was accused of reading the gospels as a Lollard because she knew them so well.[385] When we turn to positive evidence the position is hardly more favourable to the case for women's reading activity in these circles. The evidence for women, as opposed to men, is exceedingly rare (seven cases out of approximately 270), with a distinct focus on Coventry, where an active group of literate women is clearly visible, unique because of the unique Alice Rowley.[386]

This example from Coventry shows that it was not impossible for women readers to play a part in this heresy, but that it was nonetheless a rare phenomenon. This ties up with the Cathars and Waldensians, where the evidence is similarly negative. Taken together, this further undermines the myth that heresy, however much it may have granted women new opportunities, also encouraged activity by them as readers, whether in public or in private. As far as our evidence goes, the opposite appears rather to be the case: any reading the majority of these women practised was indirect, they listened to others reading to them. As some compensation, however,

[381] Hudson, '*Laicus*', pp. 225f.   [382] *Ibid.*, p. 226.   [383] *Ibid.*, pp. 226–8.
[384] Cross, 'Reasoners', p. 367.   [385] *Book* 4208f. (p. 252).
[386] McSheffrey, 'Literacy', pp. 159–61. Coventry: McSheffrey, *Gender*, pp. 29–33.

these heresies provide further confirmation of the domestication of literacy in the late Middle Ages, its extension from the monastery to the household where conventicles gathered more safely than in public places and where women were likely to be present and affected by the world opened up by the book.[387]

[387] Aston, *Lollards*, pp. 203, 205; Copeland, 'Women', p. 272.

CHAPTER 4

Women's engagement with literature

In this concluding chapter we adopt a wider approach, passing from women as readers to other ways in which they were engaged with literature, assisting its spread and development. The four sections that follow are arranged symmetrically. The first and last deal with writing in the two senses considered earlier: women as scribes (copyists) and as authors. The second and third sections are concerned with women's role in the composition of works by others: in having literature addressed or dedicated to them and in actively encouraging or commissioning it themselves. Together, these sections trace a closer engagement of women with literature in various ways.

WOMEN AS SCRIBES

In this section 'writing' is used in the physical sense of making meaningful signs on wax tablet or parchment by means of stylus or pen. Our main concern will be with women who act as scribes, generally as members of a scriptorium, but since this presupposes a literacy that embraces writing as well as reading we shall also consider briefly more general indications that women could be conceived as able to write for personal ends as well as for a scriptorium.

Although the existence of some female scribes has long been recognised, the conventional scholarly view has been that the copying of books was the task of monks rather than nuns. It is symptomatic that Bodarwé has to begin her chapter on nuns as writers by dealing with questions whether women could write, whether there were scriptoria in their convents and whether it was not rather clerics who did the writing. The conventional view has its forerunners in a commentary by Irimbert of Admont which he says was copied by two nuns, who are however replaced by a monk in a manuscript of that work and in an English translation of Mechthild von Hackeborn's *Liber specialis gratiae* in which her nun-scribes are rendered by masculine pronouns.[1] What we cannot safely do, given this situation and the preponderant scribal anonymity of medieval book-production, is to seek to remedy this conventional bias by postulating a female hand, supposedly more delicate or light, even irregular.[2] Instead of this approach, informed by a modern scholar's view of women, we do better to look for more reliable pointers from medieval sources. The most important of these is the presence of a colophon in which the scribe names herself. A twelfth-century volume from Munsterbilsen (near Maastricht) gives the names of all eight nuns who collaborated in producing it, and a thirteenth-century antiphonal from the convent of Nazareth (Belgium) identifies Agnes as the scribe and Christina as responsible for the musical notation.[3] Sometimes the pointer to female scribes may be external to any work they are known to have copied, as when a necrology records their names and adds 'scriba' or 'scriptrix'.[4] If in such cases it is often impossible to match name with any specific work copied, we shall see that the position is quite different with two book-lists recording in detail works copied by Diemut at Wessobrunn and confirming her grave-plaques' statement that she built an entire library with her hands.

We can also reliably postulate a woman scribe, even if anonymous, as responsible for a change of hand within a quire whenever the earlier hand is identifiable with a named woman scribe in an enclosed community, so that the two would have collaborated in producing the work.[5] If not an individual named scribe, then at least convent scriptoria can be presumed for women's communities, for example, in late medieval Westfalia from their purchases of parchment and colouring from markets at Münster, Deventer and Zwolle.[6] However, we shall see that the pictorial evidence for women scribes is much richer. At this point we may mention one example only, giving the nun's name as Guda. The colophon in question takes the form of a self-portrait accompanied by the statement that, a sinful woman, she copied and painted this book ('Guda peccatrix mulier scripsit que pinxit hunc librum').[7] There is nothing about the portrait to indicate a scribe, but the figure is veiled as a nun and the lettered caption she holds makes her function clear.

[1] Bodarwé, *Sanctimoniales*, pp. 87–96; Beach, *Women*, pp. 4f. and fn. 10; Hamburger, *Visual*, p. 35; Voaden, 'Hand', p. 62, fn. 34. Graf, *Bildnisse*, p. 35, adduces a similar example.

[2] Bruckner, 'Schreibtätigkeit', p. 441–8; Robinson, 'Scriptrix', p. 79; Beach, *Women*, p. 5; Bodarwé, *Sanctimoniales*, p. 95.

[3] Munsterbilsen: Robinson, '*Scriptrix*', p. 88. Nazareth: Oliver, 'Worship', p. 106. Further examples: *Krone*, pp. 506f. (items 453, 456) and Wolf, 'Beobachtungen'.

[4] Beach, *Women*, p. 7.   [5] *Ibid.*, pp. 6, 96.   [6] Gleba, 'Klosterreformen', p. 112.

[7] Reproduced in Graf, *Bildnisse*, Fig. 1.

Amongst the difficulties we face in interpreting the evidence for women scribes in our written sources two stand out. The first consists in the need to determine whether we have *scribere* in the sense that concerns us here, to write physically, or meaning to compose as an author. As we saw in Chapter I, both senses can be involved, as when an author composes a work by writing a first draft onto tablets (as did Hildegard von Bingen) before writing it (or having it written) in more permanent form on parchment. Similarly, Elsbeth Stagel, who compiled Seuse's *Exemplar*, can be depicted not just as an author, but also as a scribe, if not in the act of writing, then ruling her parchment in preparation.[8] In linguistic, rather than pictorial form we find these two activities conjoined in what is said of the Empress Kunigunde in her *vita*: that she both composed and wrote a letter ('Ipsa per se . . . composuit et scripsit'). Very much earlier in Merovingian Gaul, Fortunatus implied the same of verses composed by Radegund by the addition that she had written them on tablets ('In brevibus tabulis mihi carmina magna dedisti'). Even more revealing is the case of Baudonivia, the author of a seventh-century *vita* of Radegund, now lost. A late eleventh-century portrait depicts Baudonivia in the act of writing with stylus and tablets. Between them, this author's lost work and the later portrait exemplify both senses of *scribere*.[9]

The other difficulty may be described as indirect writing (through the services of another), corresponding to what we have seen of indirect reading. It is not unknown today when someone, employing a secretary, says that he is writing a letter when all he does is to append a signature. A twelfth-century example is found in Priester Wernher's *Maria*, where pious women amongst his readers are requested to spread knowledge of his work far and wide by copying it (themselves?) in MS C² ('daz si ez abe schrîben'), whereas MS A more explicitly talks of having it copied ('si haizzen ez ab schreiben').[10] We have encountered the same contracted phrasing with Margery Kempe, whose prologue likewise varies 'to write' with 'to have written' ('don . . . wryten').[11]

To be persuaded that many women, not just a few exceptions, could be involved in scribal activity we need to realise that although in the Middle Ages literacy did not always include writing there are indications enough that many women were trained to write. The evidence for this, as it was for their reading ability, is both historical and literary. Under the former

---

[8] Hildegard: Graf, *Bildnisse*, pp. 92–122. Elsbeth: Hamburger, *Visual*, pp. 465f. (and Fig. 9.24).
[9] *Vita Cunegundis*, MGH SS 4, 822. Fortunatus: *Carmina*, Appendix XXXI (p. 290). Baudonivia: see Fig. 13; Smith, '*Scriba*', p. 31; Graf, *Bildnisse*, pp. 83–91; *Krone*, pp. 230, 245f.
[10] C² 3049–55; A 2557–63.   [11] Kempe, *Book* 78f. and 81f. (p. 46), 161–4 (p. 51).

heading we have seen that both Radegund and Kunigunde were presented as able to write, but to these we may add Almode, countess of Toulouse, who made out a deed to Cluny containing words (if only two!) in her own hand.[12]

As with women reading, the evidence for their writing is much richer in literary texts, but not implausible for that reason alone. A woman's literacy may well not have been of interest to a chronicler, but an author of court literature addressed to readers as well as listeners at a time when lay and vernacular literacy was achieving a breakthrough, had a greater interest in presenting a cultivated woman as literate in every sense. A number of women figures are therefore shown writing as well as reading. This is true of Gottfried's Isold: not merely does she read messages on chips of wood, but she also twice writes a letter to Tristan ('si schreip unde sande/einen brief Tristande'). Similarly, the lady of Ulrich von Lichtenstein may read the letter he sends her, but also in turn writes and sends him a reply ('wan sa do si den brief gelas/und ouch diu liet, do schreip si wider,/seht, einen brief' as soon as she had read the letter and also the poems she wrote a letter in reply). In Veldeke's *Eneasroman* Lavinia's mother Amata can read the name Eneas which her daughter hesitantly writes out letter by letter, but is also able to compose and write a letter with her own hands to Turnus ('einen brief sie selbe tihte,/den si mit schônen worden vant,/und screib in mit ir selber hant' she composed herself a letter with fine wording and wrote it with her own hand).[13] On the other hand, there are cases where a woman is shown writing without our always being expressly told that she can read, but this means nothing if we accept the fact that writing is not possible without the ability to read. Thus, Veldeke's Lavinia writes out the name of Eneas for her mother, using a tablet and stylus for this simple task. She is also capable of composing and writing a longer letter which she conveys to Eneas attached to an arrow. For this purpose she prepares ink and parchment, writes like an educated medieval lady in good Latin and, having written it, reads it through again, thus showing that she commands both literate abilities ('dô siz gescreib und uberlas').[14] Without a hint of reading ability Lucina in Heinrich von Neustadt's *Apollonius* uses a tablet to write, but if she anticipates surprise on the part of the recipient this is not because a woman should be able to write, but because of what she writes.[15] To move to French literature: Marie de France concludes the lai *Milun*

---

[12] Thompson, *Literacy*, pp. 129f.

[13] Gottfried, *Tristan* 14677f., 15557f., 16305f. Ulrich, *Frauendienst* 113, 6–8. Veldeke, *Eneasroman* 10628–30 and 4351–3. Other examples of women writing: Reuvekamp-Felber, *Volkssprache*, pp. 245f.

[14] 10618–27, 10789–93. [15] 2079–91.

(in which a woman writes her story in a letter) by expressing satisfaction at having put it into writing ('e jeo que le ai mis en escrit'). In view of this double stress on a woman writing it is perhaps fitting that the Arsenal manuscript of Marie's *Fables* should open with a miniature of Marie seated at a desk and writing her book, but close with another miniature in which she holds up for inspection the completed text. Together these two images suggest that 'while the reader has been reading, the book itself is being written, and the illuminations have implicated the author and the reader together in the action of reading and writing'.[16]

This last example shows that we cannot afford to neglect pictorial evidence for women writing, as we have seen already with Elsbeth Stagel. The evidence for this up to the beginning of the thirteenth century has been discussed by Graf, who usefully correlates pictorial with textual evidence.[17] In looking at images of women engaged in the act of writing we have to bear in mind the iconographic model from which they descend, depictions of the evangelists seated at their desks and writing the gospels. As regards the sense in which they write (scribally or authorially) they write as scribes what God dictates to them, they do not compose in any sense as independent authors. This is already clear in the Old Saxon *Heliand*: what they write is a book ('endi mid iro handon scrîban/ berehtlîco an buok' and with their hands they write clearly in a book) with divine help and inspiration ('thia habdon maht godes,/helpa fan himila, hêlagna gêst,/craft fan Criste' they had the power of God, assistance from heaven, the Holy Ghost, strength from Christ).[18] The evangelists' role in transmitting what comes to them from above underlies the authorisation claimed by women visionaries, writing not just at the command of God, but what he passes on through them. Hildegard von Bingen argues in this way in *Scivias* to justify her gift of prophecy: she writes no more than what she receives ('accipis'), what she sees and hears ('scribe quae vides et audis').[19] It is this function of Hildegard and other women visionaries and mystics as a medium which makes it doubtful whether they can even be called co-authors with God and which justifies the inclusion of religious women writing in this section rather than in the fourth (women as authors).

This iconography, religious in origin for most of the Middle Ages, could be adapted to secular ends. Christine de Pizan is depicted in several of her

---

[16] *Milun* 535. Arsenal: Ward, 'Fables', pp. 191, 196. See Figs. 2 and 3.   [17] Graf, *Bildnisse*.
[18] *Heliand* 1–9. On portraits of the evangelists cf. Nordenfalk, *WJbK* 36 (1983), 175–90; Graf, *Bildnisse*, pp. 170f., 177 (and on Gregory the Great's inspired writing pp. 33, 175f. and Figs. 52, 55, 57). Cf. also Meier, *FMS* 34 (2000), 338–92.
[19] *Scivias* I, Preface, p. 3.

books after the iconographic model of the scribe, seated alone in her room at her desk, equipped with pen and knife and writing in a codex. Although the portrait of Reinmar von Zweter in the Manesse codex concerns a male author who dictates, his words are taken down at a first stage by a male scribe onto a tablet, but then by a woman scribe in the more permanent form of a parchment scroll.[20]

There is therefore enough evidence, textual and pictorial, to show that many women could not only read, but also write, either for personal purposes or as a scribe copying another work. Their writing activity can be considered in two ways, either as individual writers or as members of an established convent scriptorium. About the latter we are much better informed, but the individual cases must be briefly considered because they include two important figures: a highly productive woman scribe, Diemut of Wessobrunn, and a woman author, Hildegard von Bingen, who tells us about the act of her physical writing.

We learn of the scribal activity of Diemut, a recluse at Wessobrunn active 1080–1120, not from any colophon, but from two grave-plaques recording her name and creation with her own hands of a library for St Peter's ('Diemut inclusa, que suis manibus Bibliothecam S. Petri hec fecit').[21] More detailed information comes from two book-lists, giving the books she is said to have provided, more than forty in number. The earlier list was drawn up by a nun-scribe who had first-hand knowledge of Diemut and begins with an explicit attribution of the works that follow to her ('Isti sunt libri, quos scripsit et sancto Petro tradidit Diemot, ancilla Dei'). The second list dates from the early thirteenth century and begins with a similar attribution, so that together these lists confirm what the plaques say.[22] If the typical Benedictine day was divided into prayer, reading and work it is likely that for Diemut monastic work took the form of copying texts and must have occupied much of her time in contributing to the rapid growth of the Wessobrunn library.[23] A life of seclusion can only have benefited her scribal labours.

Our second example, Hildegard, is a very different case: certainly no copyist, but in our eyes an author in her own right, yet one who tells us something about the process of writing. The Lucca manuscript of her *Liber divinorum operum* contains an image of Hildegard, in the tradition going back to the evangelists, receiving illumination from above and herself

[20] Christine: Smith, '*Scriba*', pp. 26f. Reinmar: Walter, *Codex*, plate 112.
[21] Beach, *Women*, pp. 32–64 (here p. 32, fn. 1).
[22] *Ibid.*, pp. 40–5 (with Table 2.1).   [23] *Ibid.*, p. 39.

writing in her tablets,[24] but she makes the same point in her own words. By itself, her remark that she wrote *Scivias* ('Cum librum Scivias scriberem') is not enough for us, since it could mean authorial composition or be a telescoped phrase (indirect writing).[25] The position is different, however, when writing is mentioned specifically by hand ('manus tandem ad scribendum tremebunda converti'), a physical writing which is confirmed by two other testimonies, by Godfrey ('scribendi opus, quod non didicerat, adtemptavit') and Theoderic ('manu propria scripsit').[26] Hildegard's education must have included some form of writing as well as reading. However, this is only one aspect of the production of Hildegard's works, for she also dictated orally to a secretarial help who, as a cleric, was able to correct her Latin grammar.[27] In addition, Hildegard had assistance from other sisters to whom she also dictated,[28] but who presumably were not so well equipped as a cleric was to improve her Latin. Women scribes are therefore active in two senses at Rupertsberg: Hildegard as her own scribe and other nuns to help her. Just how emphatically Hildegard invites us to regard her in this light, and not as the author she is nowadays seen to be, is clear from the command she says she received from God to write only what he communicates to her and not what she may invent or anyone else conceive ('Itaque scribe ista non secundum cor tuum, sed secundum testimonium meum, . . . nec per te inventa, nec per alium hominem praemeditata').[29] As she presents herself, Hildegard is not even a co-author, but simply a scribe recording what God says.

Scribal activity without a hint of authorship is what is found in the nuns' scriptoria to which we now turn. Copying of this kind can be done for the convent's own internal use (as with Diemut at St Peter's) or for the benefit of other communities, amounting to a women's reading community in the horizontal sense (as with some of the southern German Dominican houses). This scribal activity has a long prehistory going back to the early Church. Origen employed girls trained in writing to provide copies of his commentaries, and Melania was praised for the accuracy of her copying, which enabled her to correct any errors made by the woman reading out to her ('ut etiam emendaret eam quae legebat'), so that woman reader is here supplemented by woman copyist, as later with Hildegard at Rupertsberg.[30] The practice of using literate nuns for this purpose is attested also in early medieval Gaul: the *vita* of Caesarius of Arles reports that in the community

---

[24] See Fig. 1.   [25] *Vita sanctae Hildegardis* 2, 5 (p. 29).
[26] *LDO*, p. 46. *Vita* 1, 3 (p. 8) and 2, 1 (p. 20).   [27] *Vita* 2, 1 (pp. 20f.).
[28] Ferrante, 'Hildegard', p. 111 ('puellis quae ex ore meo excipiunt').
[29] *LDO*, p. 45.   [30] Robinson, '*Scriptrix*', p. 80.

of his sister the nuns, alongside psalmody and readings, copied sacred books most skilfully, having learnt this from the abbess ('libros divinos pulchre scriptitent virgines Christi, ipsam matrem magistram habentes').[31] In northern Francia an important centre for nuns' copying was Chelles, mainly during the time when its abbess was Gisela, the sister of Charles the Great. A number of *scriptrices* there are known to us by name as collaborators on a work of Augustine for the Archbishop of Cologne. Bischoff has underlined the radiation of works copied by nuns at Chelles to Cologne (high-quality copies betraying the Latin literacy of the copyists), but the influence of Chelles could also extend to England, as when Bertila, its first abbess, sent manuscripts to newly founded abbeys in this country.[32]

That is important in another respect, since it suggests the role these women scribes could play in the mission-field, not merely in England, but also in Germany as part of the Anglo-Saxon mission there. From the German mission-field Boniface writes back to England, to the abbess Eadburga, thanking her for books she has already sent and requesting the epistle of Peter as a new item. That we are not dealing here with an 'interlibrary loan', but with a fresh copy that Boniface knows can be produced at Thanet is clear from his also sending writing materials.[33] The presence of two German women's names, Gunza and Abirhilt, in the margins of two manuscripts produced in the late eighth century near Würzburg (a centre of the Anglo-Saxon mission) has been interpreted as suggesting that German *scriptrices* may also have worked at producing texts required in the religious frontier-zone, but that depends, as was also the case with Eadburga, on our taking these names as indicating scribes, rather than owners. Ottonian nuns' scriptoria have been discussed in detail by Bodarwé.[34]

As in so many other respects, the twelfth century is important for our question. The need felt at Wessobrunn for the expansion of its library in which Diemut played such a part has been attributed to the monastic reform movement.[35] Monastic reform and an upsurge of religious writing, hence the need for scribes, have been discussed in general terms by Schreiner and for a later period by Hamburger. For Schreiner a monastic reform in the high and late Middle Ages worked as an impetus towards a written culture and brought forth new forms of writing, while for Hamburger manuscript production, the result of copyists' writing, is a sign of

[31] *Vita sancti Caesarii* I 58, MGH SRM 3, 481.
[32] Bischoff, *Studien* I 17–35; *Krone*, p. 240; Beach, *Women*, p. 14.   [33] Beach, *Women*, p. 14.
[34] McKitterick, *Francia* 19, 1 (1992), 22; Beach, *Women*, p. 15. Bodarwé, *Sanctimoniales*, pp. 98–110 (Gandersheim), 110–65 (Essen), 165–88 (Quedlinburg).
[35] Beach, *Women*, p. 39.

spiritual renewal which he sees exemplified in the convent Unterlinden in Colmar, a centre of the Dominican order's reform north of the Alps.[36] The earliest reformed Dominican monastery in northern Europe was, however, Schönensteinbach, from which the reform spread to Colmar, but also further afield, including St Catharine's convent in Nürnberg, reformed with nuns from Schönensteinbach. At Nürnberg, as we have seen, the nuns' copying of manuscripts, mainly in the vernacular, helped produce a large collection of books in their library, copied and corrected to high standards.[37] Not merely in the twelfth century, but also subsequently, monastic reform endeavours encouraged book production and the scribal activity of nuns.[38]

For the twelfth century we must restrict ourselves to two scriptoria only, both German for reasons given at the end of this section. With the first of these we return briefly to the double monastery of Admont, this time with regard to scribal activity centred on the works produced by abbot Irimbert. In this he was assisted by nuns to whom he dictated as they wrote for him, although whether they can be designated with the overused term 'co-authors' is another matter.[39] About their scribal work, however, there is no doubt. Irimbert reports first that without his knowledge they committed to parchment what he had preached ('sorores Admuntenses capitula quedam . . . a me audierant, que me nesciente ipse in membranis exceperant').[40] That cannot have been the abbot's only kind of contact with nun-scribes, for he elsewhere expresses gratitude to two sisters who took down on tablets what he said to them ('que continue et diligenter transcriberent, que a me dicta in tabulis excipi potuissent').[41] Whether known to Irimbert or not, the nuns seem to have been involved at two stages in the production of his work, to judge at least by the mention of tablets and parchment.

To Beach we also owe a discussion of women scribes at another Bavarian centre, the Premonstratensian abbey of Schäftlarn.[42] This order's stress on the importance of manual labour and the view that scribal activity was a form of labour meant that there was a place here for the copying of books by women. We know of three women scribes by name in twelfth-century Schäftlarn: one is recorded in a necrology and two give their own names.[43] These latter not merely name, but identify themselves as scribes. Sophia does

[36] Schreiner, 'Verschriftlichung', pp. 37–75; Hamburger, *Visual*, p. 313.
[37] Hamburger, *Visual*, pp. 427, 460.
[38] On this question see the work of Williams-Krapp, 'Ordensreform', pp. 41–51; 'Frauenmystik', pp. 301–13; 'Observantenbewegungen', pp. 1–15.
[39] Beach, *Women*, p. 72, referring to Borgehammar, 'Admont', pp. 47–51.
[40] Beach, *Women*, p. 85, referring to Braun, *FMS* 7 (1973), 319.
[41] *Ibid.*, pp. 86 and 320.   [42] Beach, *Women*, pp. 104–27.   [43] *Ibid.*, p. 108.

this twice in a subscription ('scripsit Sophya' and 'Sophia scripsit'), while Irmingart's name appears twice in colophons ('Iste liber . . . quem scripsit soror Irmingart obtentu Domni Hainrici prepositi').[44] In Schäftlarn, to judge by the corrections called for, the level of Latinity and hence the nuns' understanding of what they were called on to write were respectably high.[45]

We conclude with a brief look at women scribes in the southern German Dominican convents. Here too the level of Latin was high enough to allow the nuns to copy Latin as well as vernacular texts (as early as 1249 the Dominicans had to be forbidden to allow nuns and other women to copy Psalters and other texts for them).[46] There is indeed evidence of scribal activity in these communities. At Töss Elsbet von Cellinkon and Willi von Constanz are numbered amongst these scribes, and the scriptorium at Ötenbach was a major production centre, providing not merely *scriptrices*, but also illuminators and painters of manuscripts.[47] At St Catharine's convent in Nürnberg a number of nun-scribes have been identified whose work gives evidence of a thorough basic education, including knowledge of Latin. The same is even more true of Unterlinden convent, not simply because of its rarity in producing a sister-book in Latin, but also in view of what we learn of the Latin interests and copying ability of individual nuns there (Gertrud von Rheinfelden, Elisabeth Kempf). We can apply this beyond the case of Unterlinden, for in Germany nuns produced large numbers of liturgical manuscripts which had to be accurate, had a complex layout and demanded considerable knowledge of Latin. Examples of the fine quality of this work are the Gisle codex and the Seligenthal gradual.[48] Of scribal facilities at Medingen we learn from a letter of Heinrich von Nördlingen to Margaretha Ebner in which he informs her that he has sent a copy of a Latin work, the *Horologium Sapientiae*, to the prior of the Cistercian house at Kaisheim and recommending her to borrow this copy and arrange for it to be copied for the convent at Medingen ('das haiss dir lihen . . . und schribent es den ab dem convent, das es allzeit bei euch belib' Have it loaned to you and copy it so that it may remain with you for good).[49] This letter illustrates in some detail the traffic in book loans in the late Middle Ages, but also the involvement of women's communities in this traffic, resting on their interest in Latin theology and ability to produce a copy from their own scribal resources as much as was possible for the men at Kaisheim.

[44] *Ibid.*, pp. 120f., 124f.   [45] *Ibid.*, p. 117.   [46] Grundmann, *Bewegungen*, p. 462.
[47] Lewis, *Women*, pp. 273f.; Ehrenschwendtner, *'Puellae'*, p. 63, n. 40; *Bildung*, pp. 287–90.
[48] Hasebrink, 'Tischlesung', p. 191; Ehrenschwendtner, *'Puellae'*, pp. 56f.; *Krone*, pp. 420f., 421f.
[49] Strauch, *Margaretha*, pp. 228f. (Brief XXXV).

The copying of religious texts could be regarded not merely as a form of the monastic labour required of every monk or nun, but also throughout the Middle Ages as a form of silent preaching ('muta praedicatio'), an apostolate of the pen. Peter the Venerable says of the (male) copyist that he preaches without opening his mouth and the library catalogue of a Cistercian abbey of the fourteenth century says that although monks cannot preach by word of mouth, they can proclaim the truth with their hands by writing books.[50] In a similar vein Jean Gerson argues that the man who writes (in the sense of copies) books of sacred doctrine may be termed a preacher, for he preaches with his hand when his tongue is silent.[51] The authors of these passages had male scribes in mind, but the evidence we have considered shows that the idea was also applicable in practice to woman scribes, indeed with greater force since they were debarred from speaking or preaching in public. Whether this equation of their writing activity with the otherwise forbidden preaching acted as a consolation or even encouragement for them or whether it aggravated a sense of being dismissed to a second-best alternative escapes us.

A merit of Beach's book is that it makes clear the frequent evidence for women scribes in Germany, more than seems to be the case elsewhere. This is why this section has largely concentrated on this one country, but we need more work on the position in France and England to confirm this impression and explain why this should be so. Also needed are studies of women's involvement in commercial book-production of the kind done for Paris since 1200.[52]

WOMEN AS DEDICATEES

With this and the following section we face the problem we confronted in Chapter 3, where the uncertain boundaries between categories of women readers made allocation difficult. Here the difficulty arises from the frequency with which laywomen as well as religious women practised devotional reading, so that a religious text could be meant for either class of woman (or both). An example is provided by the fourteenth-century *Christus und die minnende Seele*, meant for devotional and mystical meditation and equipped with pictures. One such illustration presents the soul (feminine in Latin and German) shooting the arrow of love at Christ's heart. In the Donaueschingen codex she is depicted as a secular woman,

---

[50] Ep. I 20, PL 189, 98; de Poorter, *Catalogue*, p. 10. Both in Leclercq, *Love*, p. 128.
[51] Gerson, *Oeuvres* IX 424; Schreiner, *ZHF* 11 (1984), 262, fn. 12.   [52] Rouse, *Illiterati*.

in corresponding garb, but the Einsiedeln codex shows her unmistakably as a nun. This work, like many other devotional texts, could have been meant for either class of reader. A similar weakening of boundaries occurs with a translation of the *Hieronymus-Briefe* by Johann von Neumarkt for Elisabeth Markgräfin of Moravia and ladies of the Prague court, but with a marked concentration of about fifty manuscripts of this work on women's monasteries.[53]

Even more acute is the need to distinguish between this section (works written for women) and the next (women as sponsors of literature). In theory, the distinction is clear-cut, depending on where the initiative comes from. In this section women's role is more a passive one (works are dedicated to them, written for their benefit, addressed to them, and are hoped to be of interest to them), but as sponsors they play a more active role (commissioning works or otherwise assisting or encouraging their production). Women's activity as sponsors can often be made explicit. Chrétien makes it clear at the opening of *Lancelot* that he composes it on the instructions of the countess of Champagne ('Puis que ma dame de Champaigne/vialt que romans a feire anpraigne') and the position is made equally clear in Gaimar's *Estoire des Engleis* ('Ceste estorie fist translater/Dame Custance la gentil').[54] Where a pointer of this nature is lacking it is difficult to tell what position a work reflects, a reservation to be borne constantly in mind in these two sections.

Things can be made more complicated by the interplay between dedication and commission: the former may not register the latter as a fact, but could express a hope for it in the future. The two possibilities may even be combined with reference to different people, as in a *vita* by Ralph Bocking, written at the request of Archbishop Kilwardby, but dedicated to Isabella, Countess of Arundel. How do we interpret a case like Aldhelm's *De virginitate*, written in response to questions put to him by nuns at Barking whom he praises for their scholarly interests?[55] In their questioning the nuns show a form of initiative, but can it be said to constitute a commission or does the impetus rest with Aldhelm? In many cases we must remain content with an either-or, as is frequently the case in art historical terms in the catalogue of an exhibition in 2005 in Germany ('works of art commissioned by and for religious women's communities').[56] In other cases, however, a decision

---

[53] *Christus*: Keller, *Secret*, pp. 256f. (with reproductions). *Hieronymus-Briefe*: Janota, *Orientierung*, p. 449.
[54] *Lancelot* 1f. *Estoire* 6430f.
[55] Bocking: Legge, *Literature*, p. 270. Aldhelm: Hollis, *Women*, pp. 75–7.
[56] Graf, *Bildnisse*, pp. 38–52. *Krone*, p. 32 (Hamburger: 'Kunstwerke, die von und für religiöse Frauengemeinschaften in Auftrag gegeben wurden').

is possible, as with the contrast between the copy of Notker's Psalms which the Empress Gisela ordered to be made for herself ('sibi exemplari sollicite fecit') on the one hand and the St Albans Psalter on the other, originally made for St Albans, but then adapted when presented as a gift to Christina of Markyate.[57] A further problem lies in wait if we consider the possibility that invoking a woman (as dedicatee or as sponsor) may be no more than a fiction (as with Ulrich von Lichtenstein's lady).[58] But such a fiction may not be totally divorced from reality, for behind the pretence could lie the hope for real sponsorship and the frequency with which women are referred to is an indication of their involvement in literature.[59]

The suspicion of a fictive stance is most apparent when in court literature it is claimed that the author's work is a form of love-service of his lady, who is thus the occasion of his text. Wolfram refers to this, but rejects it in his own case, thereby acknowledging that it was a contemporary convention.[60] What he has to say in this context is even more relevant to the distinction we seek to establish between dedicatee and patron. The conclusion of Book 6 of *Parzival*, with all the appearance of an epilogue, has been interpreted as symptomatic of a break in Wolfram's work, possibly due to a change in patronage. The context of this epilogue is decidedly feminine (it is concerned with women recipients and women characters in the work), so that it has been concluded that the patron-to-be is a woman.[61] This conclusion rests on two hypotheses, however, and in any case the woman sponsor is not a fact, but a hope expressed tentatively: Wolfram would proceed further if only a certain mouth would give the word ('ich taetz iu gerne fürbaz kunt,/wolt ez gebieten mir ein munt').[62] By listing examples of his speaking sympathetically of women in his work Wolfram hopes to justify this hope, but it remains no more than a wish yet to be fulfilled. Even the true epilogue to *Parzival*, at the close of Book 16, does not resolve the matter, for although Wolfram now refers explicitly to a woman, her role in the completion of his work is tantalisingly expressed in the conditional ('ist daz durch ein wîp geschehen')[63] and we are still left uncertain what is meant by 'done for a woman's sake'. At no point is a woman as patron presented as a fact, rather than as a possibility, so that we do better to regard her, for want of harder evidence, as a dedicatee, not as the actual sponsor.

In referring critically to poetry as a form of love-service of a lady Wolfram most probably had the poets of Minnesang in mind, but this convention is also attested in narrative literature. A number of French romances from

---

[57] See above, pp. 120 and 153f.   [58] Ruh, *Geschichte* III 468.   [59] Scholz, *Hören*, p. 210.
[60] *Parzival* 115, 13f.   [61] Bumke, *Mäzene*, pp. 19f.; *Wolfram*, p. 14.
[62] 337, 27f.   [63] 827, 29.

the late twelfth century address the woman whom the author claims to be courting by name instead of any patron, while the author of *Reinfried von Braunschweig* implies that his work was composed in the love-service of the woman whose name he gives in an anagram.[64] Composition as a way of courting a woman rather than in obedience to her commissioning the work can also occur at one stage further removed when Rudolf von Ems suggests that his *Willehalm von Orlens* was written not on behalf of his own lady to pay her a compliment, but instead indirectly in the service of Konrad von Winterstetten, his real patron, in the hope that the latter's lady may reward him for his constancy ('Daz si in frôden riche/ Und daz si siner stâte/Durch ir tugende raete/Ze gûete an im gedenke' That she may enrich him in joy and virtuously think kindly of him for his constancy).[65] The distinction here between patron and lady resembles that between Kilwardby and Isabella in Bocking's *vita*, mentioned above, and suggests that composition on behalf of a woman, even when named, need not always imply that she was the patron. The same could also be true of the unnamed woman in Wolfram's *Parzival*.

After this glance at the difficulties in distinguishing the women who belong to this section from those who fit into the next we must consider selected examples of the former. These are arranged, for the sake of clarity but with no claim for an exclusive allocation, under the same headings as in Chapter 3, but with regard to the secular or religious nature of the works in question. This should permit a coherent survey of a large number of cases, deliberately large to bring out the sheer quantity of texts addressed to women. What follows, in tune with this book as a whole, is meant as a factual survey of women's position within the world of the book in the Middle Ages, whilst any consideration of their role in court literature, its appeal to their interests, its attempted presentation of their point of view and its composition with them in mind must be reserved for the companion volume.

A first entry into surveying the range of works dedicated to women, at least up to 1200, is provided by Bezzola's monumental history of court literature in Europe.[66] Certain recognisable centres of gravity emerge from his history. Two examples come from the Merovingian period: Venantius Fortunatus presents a poem to Radegund and dedicates another to the Queen mother Ultrogotha.[67] Carolingian literature offers a richer crop of works destined for women. Alcuin sends letters and poems to the Emperor's

---

[64] French romances: Ferrante, *Glory*, pp. 126f.; 'Voice', p. 14. *Reinfried*: Janota, *Orientierung*, p. 199.
[65] 2314–17, 15613–24. Bumke, *Mäzene*, p. 242; *Kultur*, p. 706.
[66] *Origines* I–III.   [67] *Ibid.*, I 49, 50.

daughters, in particular to Rotruda, Gisela (the abbess of Chelles, to whom he dedicates his commentary on the gospel of John) and Gundrada, to whom he sends his *De animae ratione* as well as a poem.[68] Gundrada also received a poem from Dungal, who further addressed a letter to Theodrada, another daughter of Charles, on her profession as a nun, whilst Theodulf of Orléans devoted a poem to Queen Liutgardis.[69] The praise of the Empress Judith was sung by Walahfrid Strabo (but was this addressed to her directly or not?) and she was also presented with a volume of the world history of Freculf, Bishop of Lyons, and had dedicated to her two biblical commentaries by Hrabanus Maurus (one very appositely on the biblical Judith). Another woman of the Carolingian dynasty, Bertha, had three poems dedicated to her by Sedulius Scotus.[70]

Bezzola's third focus is the Ottonian dynasty. Under this heading he refers to Liutprand's multiple dedication of his *Relatio de legatione Constantinopolitana* to Otto I and Otto II, but also to the Empress Adelheidis. He also mentions the dedication by Widukind of Corvey of his *Res gestae saxonicae* to Mathilda, the daughter of Otto I, but in addition, from a later period, another multiple presentation, this time of a new redaction of the Michelsberg chronicle by Bishop Erlung of Würzburg to the royal couple Heinrich V and Mathilda of England.[71] With that example Bezzola has reached a date (1114) when his fourth centre of gravity, concerned with the Anglo-Normans, was beginning to show its importance for the flourishing of court literature. We learn from an external source that archdeacon Ingelramnus addressed a poem to Adela, the daughter of William the Conqueror, on the exploits of her father. Baudri de Bourgueil dedicates his life of Robert of Arbrissel to Petronilla, the first abbess of Fontevrault, and Hildebert of Lavardin devotes a poem, almost as a poet laureate at the English court, to the Empress Mathilda.[72]

All the works dedicated to women covered so far in Bezzola's survey are in Latin, but it is in his fourth period, from about 1100, that a change arises which is decisive for his theme, and also for ours, as now for the first time vernacular works are dedicated to women. The first of these is the *Voyage of St Brendan* by Benedeit, written in connection with a woman to whom manuscripts give two names, one identified as Adeliza of Louvain, whom Henry I married in 1121, the other as Mahalt (Maud).[73] Behind this double

---

[68] *Ibid.*, p. 131.   [69] *Ibid.*, p. 132.

[70] Strabo: *ibid.*, p. 160. Freculf: Ferrante, *Glory*, p. 74. Hrabanus: *ibid.*, pp. 55f. Sedulius: Bezzola, *Origines* I 177.

[71] Liutprand, Widukind, Erlung: Bezzola, *Origines* I 217, 251, 299.

[72] Ingelramnus, Baudri, Hildebert: *ibid.*, II 379f., 386, 433.

[73] Benedeit: *ibid.*, p. 427; Legge, *Literature*, pp. 8–18.

attribution there lurk considerations of marriage politics (the king's wish to strengthen his position by marrying a princess from the old English royal house), but significantly in each case it is the woman's name that is given. To the same Adeliza, once she was Queen of England, Philippe de Thaon also dedicated his *Bestiaire*, a vernacular version of a Latin *Physiologus*.[74] This work, too, has a variant dedication (one manuscript refers to Eleanor of Aquitaine), which suggests that the work retained its popularity over some years, but again a vernacular work is seen in connection with a woman. About the middle of the twelfth century Samson de Nanteuil dedicates a translation, the *Proverbes de Salemon*, to Aelis de Condé, related to the Constance Fitzgilbert we have already encountered and described by Samson as well educated and delighting in religious writings which, with the double formula, she both reads and hears read out to her ('Molt volonters les ot et lit').[75] Gautier d'Arras in a long dedication presents his *Ille et Galeron* to Beatrice of Burgundy after her marriage to Friedrich Barbarossa, but also addressing women at large, urging them not to envy her, but to take her as an example. The anonymous author of *Guillaume de Palerne* dedicates his work to Yolande, the wife of the Count of Saint-Pol.[76] Soon after this point Bezzola's chronological framework brings his survey to a close, but not without making clear the historical continuity of writings dedicated to noblewomen, first in Latin and then, in addition, in the vernacular, with the twelfth century as the turning point in an innovation in which women were closely involved from the beginning.

The important role played by women in literary activity in the Middle Ages can be taken further than Bezzola's findings. Since he was mainly concerned with literature at the secular court what he has to tell us is largely confined to secular literature addressed to laywomen, so that we may start with this before considering what has so far been largely left on one side, works of religious literature written both for laywomen and for religious women.

Given the continuity with which women repeatedly occur as dedicatees of literature it does not surprise us that their role in the production and judgment of literature should be so stressed by Bumke in his work on court culture. He points out that in the *Wartburgkrieg* it is taken for granted that a literary performance at court demands the presence of ladies in the audience ('wilt uns diu maere künden vürebaz, wir müezen nâch den vrouwen allen senden' if you intend to tell us more of this story we

---

[74] Bezzola, *Origines* II 428, III 286; Legge, *Literature* pp. 22–6.
[75] Samson: Bezzola, *Origines* II 455f.; Blacker, 'Portrait', pp. 116f.
[76] Gautier: Bezzola, *Origines* III 419. *Guillaume: ibid.*, p. 430.

must send for all the ladies).[77] This is also reflected in the way in which the audience can be so divided into its constituent members as to bring out the presence of women. Thomasin sees the same three groups: knights, ladies and clerics ('vrume rîtr und guote vrouwen/und wîse phaffen') as does Hadloub ('edel frouwen, hôhe pfaffen, ritter guot').[78] If it had not been felt desirable to highlight women it would have been simpler to exclude them by referring to laymen and clerics or to knights and clerics. Or to take one specific example: Wolfram's composition of *Parzival* is accompanied throughout by a troubled preoccupation with one woman (and through her with women at large) at the end of Books 2, 6 and 16. We may therefore expect to find traces of secular literature addressed specifically to women.

In view of the emergence of evidence for the vernacular hesitantly in the first half of the twelfth century it is only to be expected that earlier evidence will be for Latin, as it was for Bezzola. For our earliest evidence it will pay also to take epistolary literature into account, as does Ferrante in her survey of women's roles in medieval literature or Constable on letter collections, and not to dismiss it as merely pragmatic letter writing.[79] The justification for this is that skilled letter writing could be regarded as an art to be learnt (*ars dictaminis*), that letters could be composed according to the rules of rhetoric and were frequently in verse form. However, the transmission and survival of such letters is very much a one-sided affair, with many more written by men to women coming down to us than the converse. This disparity bedevils any search for women authors in this field, but is fortunately irrelevant to our present concern and allows us a close insight into what could be expected of them by their correspondents, both stylistically and in Latinity. Although this Latin correspondence was between men and women religious, its themes are of a secular nature, often playful and on the verge of the erotic, so that we may include it here before treating religious literature addressed to women.

Early examples come from the Merovingian and Carolingian periods. Venantius Fortunatus exchanged poems with Radegund and Agnes but, as Ferrante points out, his complaints when they do not send him poems in return and his pleasure when they do are evidence that this poetic correspondence was two-sided. From the later period Lull writes a grateful letter

---

[77] *Wartburgkrieg (Rätselspiel)* 33, 2–3; Bumke, *Kultur*, pp. 704f.

[78] Thomasin, *Welscher Gast* 14695f. Hadloub: Bartsch, *Minnesänger*, p. 288 (2, 52). Cf. Green, '*ritr*', pp. 7–26.

[79] Ferrante, *Glory*, pp. 10–35; Constable, *Letters*; Wand-Wittkowski, *Briefe*.

to an abbess, apologising for any grammatical errors and leaving it to her and her nuns to correct them.[80]

Richer and much more important is the evidence we have from the Latin poetry of the school of the Loire valley, treated by Bond and constituting in the late eleventh and early twelfth centuries a veritable network of poets, men and women.[81] The men included high clergy and the women aristocrats or nuns, with Latin as their natural means of poetic exchange. A focal point of this literary activity seems to have been Adela of Blois. It is to her that literary praise and written works are directed, not from her that, as with the nuns of this remarkable group, poetic replies are expected. Although we are not informed whether she actually commissioned his work, Hugh of Fleury knew her interests well enough to dedicate to her an ecclesiastical history which is in effect a universal history including the deeds of ancient emperors up to Charles the Great, an 'appropriation of Roman history and historiography which characterized the authors patronized by her father to legitimize his rule'.[82] More in the vein of the Loire school is the flattery lavished on Adela by Baudri de Bourgueil in his highly decorative Latin which, as was the case with Hugh, she is confidently (or flatteringly?) expected to understand and appreciate.[83] Although it has been suggested that at an early age Adela began to commission laudatory poems ('poemata . . . quae directa sibi filia regis habet') the wording is not clear enough to warrant this. It could equally well mean that she had them sent to her and the verbal construction lacks the explicitness of one with *facere*. It may well be the case that Adela wished to be praised poetically for secular attributes such as her birth as the daughter of a king and her beauty, but that alone does not mean that she actually commissioned all the praise-poetry which she attracted. Knowledge of her interests, as with Hugh of Fleury, could have proved incentive enough. That some scope remained for the author to dedicate, rather than be commissioned, is suggested by another work of Hugh, the *Liber modernorum regum francorum*, which he originally promised to Adela (does that necessarily mean in obedience to her command?), but later dedicated to Empress Mathilda, Adela's niece, married to Heinrich V.[84]

Other women in this region were recipients of Latin works of literature. They include a poem addressed to Constantia, a nun at Le Ronceray, by Baudri de Bourgueil, who makes it clear that the initiative comes from his busily composing trifles for her ('nugas, quas scriptito sedulus ad te'),[85] quite

---

[80] Ferrante, *Glory*, pp. 30f.
[81] Bond, *Subject*. Other Latin examples are the letter collections from Tegernsee and Regensburg.
[82] Adela: *ibid.*, pp. 129–57. Hugh: *ibid.*, pp. 154f.
[83] *Ibid.*, pp. 144f., 150.   [84] *Ibid.*, p. 261, n. 66.   [85] *Ibid.*, pp. 170–80 (quotation: v.3).

apart from the inconceivable possibility of a nun commissioning a poem from a bishop. As a nun Constantia can be expected to cope with reading Latin herself: it is she who is to open the letter and read it through by herself ('Perlege sola meos uersus'). In this case at least we have the reply given by Constantia in her Latin verse, confirming that she had indeed often read his words ('Ergo consumpsi sepe legendo diem').[86] The polygynous Baudri also addressed a poem to an English nun, Muriel, praised by Hildebert of Lavardin for her skill in verse. Lastly, and once more linking the Loire region with England, Marbod of Rennes addressed a poem to Mathilda of England, *Ad reginam Anglorum.*[87]

The period in which this Latin literature, exchanged between men and women, flourished was also the time when the vernaculars made a tentative début and it is this secular literature addressed to women in the vernacular which we must now consider. Authors can address works specifically to women either in the plural (suggesting the wider audience they have in mind) or in the singular (one woman, the occasion of the work). We earlier considered cases where women were expected as readers of the work in question, but now we widen out to regard them as addressees at large. Hue de Rotelande explicitly addresses women in the conclusion of his *Ipomedon* (which has prompted Krueger to speculate how they may have reacted to the work).[88] At the end of his *Troilus* Chaucer addresses women in his audience, apologising for its possibly antifeminine implications (as if, by a typically misogynous generalisation, the shortcomings of one woman could be held against them all), but then reverses these implications by warning women against the treachery of men.[89] In Germany women are frequently addressed explicitly by authors. Ulrich von Lichtenstein envisages them in connection with his *Frauendienst* ('Ditz buoch sol guoter wîbe sîn' This book is meant for good women), but also specifically as readers of his *Frauenbuch*, while Heinrich von dem Türlin claims that his *Crone* was undertaken on their behalf ('Ir vrouwen . . . /Dirre arebeit wil ich iu jehen,/Wan ich ir durch iuch began' Ladies, I mean this labour for you, since I began it on your account), where 'on your account' is by no means precise enough to indicate patronage by one woman alone.[90]

Rather less common are addresses to one woman. Ulrich von Türheim begins his *Rennewart* in God's name and for the sake of a good woman ('und

---

[86] *Ibid.*, pp. 182–92 (quotation: v. 6).   [87] Baudri: Jaeger, *Love*, pp. 94f. Marbod: PL 171, 1660.
[88] *Ipomedon* 10571–80; Krueger, *Women*, p. 81.
[89] *Troilus* V 1772–85; Mann, *Chaucer*, pp. 15f. This authorial address to women has to be set against the recent trend to regard Chaucer's audience as predominantly male.
[90] *Frauendienst* 1850, 1. *Frauenbuch* 2130. *Crone* 29990–6.

ouch durch ein gûtes wîp'), where the same qualification has to be made
as with Heinrich von dem Türlin. Similarly, Herrand von Wildonie claims
in *Der nackte Kaiser* that a woman asked him to compose the work ('dô bat
ein frouwe minniclich mich,/daz ich ez tihte'), which he did for her sake
('durch si'), where the wording is just as ambiguous for our purpose.[91] Nor
should it be thought that addressing one woman contradicts an appeal to
womankind at large. This is demonstrated most convincingly by Wolfram
in the three passages in *Parzival* where he alludes to his relationship with
one woman, but sees this in terms of how he stands in the eyes of all
women. In his so-called self-defence at the end Book 2 his reference to
this one woman ('einer', 'gein einem wîbe') is set against the backdrop of
praising women in the plural ('swer nu wîben sprichet baz').[92] Similarly,
in the provisional epilogue at the close of Book 6 singular and plural are
linked more closely together in the author's argument that he could praise
or speak better of women than what he sang about one individual one ('ich
kunde wîben sprechen baz/denne also ich sanc gein einer maz').[93] Finally,
in the very last lines of the work its author implies that his completion
of the task was accomplished for the sake of one woman ('ist daz durch
ein wîp geschehn') and deserves the approval of all good women ('guotiu
wîp, hânt diu sin,/deste werder ich in bin').[94] Whether or not we attach
any biographical truth-status to what Wolfram says of his relationship to
this woman, the impression he conveys is that he composed his work with
her reaction constantly in mind, and that of other women, too, especially
those in his audience who would read his work and with whom he sought
to ingratiate himself at the close of Book 6.

The romance was a narrative genre which was felt to have a special
appeal for women: most of our recent examples come from this genre in
the widest sense and Chaucer could make fun of this in referring to the
Lancelot story as one which women admire in particular. In her discussion
of questions of gender in the French romance Krueger lists some of the
French works with which women were or are considered to have been
involved, ranging from early representatives of what may technically be
called romances (*Roman de Brut*) through central cases like Thomas's *Tristan*
and Chrétien's romances, down to later works.[95] These match what we have
seen in German literature and show that women and the romance genre
go closely together in England, France and Germany. How persistent this
association could be is shown even by the devout Margaret Beaufort, given

---

[91] *Rennewart* 140f. *Kaiser* 8–11.   [92] 114, 5, 8 and 15.   [93] 337, 5f.   [94] 827, 25f. and 29.
[95] Chaucer: see above, p. 124. Krueger, 'Questions', p. 135.

to religious reading, for Caxton dedicates his *Blanchardyn and Eglantine* to her in 1489. Admittedly, Caxton says that he translated (and printed?) the book at her 'commandement', but this could be no more than an advertising boost, for he also says that this same book, which she is said to have commissioned, was long before sold by him to her.[96] Finally, if we may take not the romance itself as a genre attractive to women, but instead two authors influential in that genre, many of the French adaptations of Ovid or Andreas Capellanus are dedicated to women. This is true of Drouart la Vache's *Livres d'amours*, but also of *La Clef d'Amours* (a translation of the *Ars amatoria*) by an unknown author, and of *L'art d'amors*, another translation of the same Latin work, by Jacques d'Amiens.[97]

In addition to Latin literature and court literature in the vernacular, works meant for women cover a third field, best described as pragmatic writing. The first group under this heading includes what may be termed deportment books (teaching *mores* rather than *litterae*). Two well-known books of this kind were written by men for women, instructing them how to behave in their future status as wives: *Le Ménagier de Paris* by the husband for his young wife and the *Livre du Chevalier de la Tour Landry* for his daughters. The popularity of the latter is attested by the number of different manuscripts and by translated versions in German and in English, but both, as might be expected by their didactic tone, adopt a patriarchal attitude, whether by father or by husband, in their view of how women should behave in marriage.[98] A different attitude is adopted by Christine de Pizan in her *Livre de trois vertus*, likewise providing rules of conduct for women and dedicated to Margaret of Burgundy, recently married at a tender age.[99] Concerned more with education at large, for girls as well as for boys, Vincent of Beauvais was probably conscious of the mother's role in the education of the young in dedicating *De eruditione filiorum* to Queen Marguerite of France.[100]

In a second pragmatic field, domestic economy, we find no less a figure than Grosseteste, Bishop of Lincoln, writing an Anglo-Norman treatise, the *Reules seynt Roberd*, for the countess of Lincoln, widowed and therefore presumably in need of such practical advice on running her estates. Still pragmatic in its aim is the rhyming French vocabulary composed by Walter Bibbesworth for Denise de Montchensy in the thirteenth century, specifically to help her teach her children the vocabulary of 'husbondrie

---

[96] Summit, 'Caxton', pp. 152, 154.   [97] Krueger, *Women*, pp. 194f.
[98] Carruthers, 'Wife', p. 27; Bennewitz, 'Toechter', pp. 38–41; Shahar, *Estate*, pp. 72f., 104.
[99] Labarge, *Women*, pp. 41f.   [100] Robertson, *Speculum* 78 (2003), 17.

manaungerie' (management).[101] A fourteenth-century English medical treatise addresses women especially, not merely because it is attributed to Trotula (supposedly a twelfth-century woman doctor of Salerno) or because
women were responsible for family medical care, but especially because,
like some of the work of Trotula, it is concerned with gynaecological
questions.[102] Finally, women's non-aesthetic interests could include history,
as we have seen with the Anglo-Norman Constance Fitzgilbert. Nicholas
Trevet therefore dedicated his Anglo-Norman chronicle to Mary, daughter
of Edward I, and Queen Emma had a history of Cnut addressed to her, to
name only two examples.[103]

However significant for future developments these works with secular
themes, especially in the vernacular, intended for women may be, over the
whole medieval span women's concern as readers was much more with
religious and devotional literature, whether as nuns or as laywomen. We
have seen how permeable were the boundaries between laywomen and
religious women in reading and it is on these boundaries that religious
writers concentrated in their attempts to wean women away from romance
literature towards their own themes. The author of *Der Saelden Hort* is
explicit in naming the romances (*Tristan*, *Wigalois*) he wishes ladies to put
on one side in favour of works like his own, as are also the author of
the *Vies des Pères* in addressing Blanche de Navarre (*Cligés*, *Perceval*) and
Robert of Greatham, the author of the *Evangiles des domnees*, hoping to lead
Aline away from fables, amongst which he includes *Tristran*. Denis Piramus
begins his hagiographic *Vie de saint Edmund* by proposing its virtues in
place of secular court literature (*Partenopé*, the lais of Marie de France)
which he condemns as so many lies. That women need to be converted
from this literature is suggested not so much by his mention of a woman
author as by his emphasis that Marie's lais are popular with women ('solent
as dames pleire').[104] In addition, the occurrence of legends in German
literature from the middle of the twelfth century may have been associated
with the rise of court literature at that time and as a reaction to the novel
presentation of a secular ideal.[105] There are reasons enough, then, for the
composition of religious works addressed to laywomen.

[101] Grosseteste: Power, *Women*, pp. 39f.; Labarge, *Women*, p. 75. Bibbesworth: Power, *Women*, p. 75;
Clanchy, *Memory*, p. 198.
[102] Power, *Women*, p. 78; Green and Schleissner, 'Trotula', *VfL* 9, 1083–88.
[103] Trevet: Labarge, *Women*, p. 105. Emma: Riché, *Écoles*, p. 129.
[104] *Saelden Hort*: see above, p. 117. *Vies des Pères* 1–135. Robert: Legge, *Literature*, p. 213. Piramus, *Vie*
1–48.
[105] Green, *Listening*, pp. 103f.

To illustrate this in small compass I can do no more than give an array of examples selected from different periods and regions, so as to demonstrate something of the wide spread of this literary practice. In common with women's predilection for the Psalter, the Countess Hoda (a miswriting for Dhuoda?) had a commentary on the Psalter composed for her by the monks Richer and Rathelm. The case of Hrabanus Maurus is a little more complicated: to the Empress Judith he dedicated two biblical commentaries (one aptly on Judith, the other on Esther), but later re-dedicated these works to the Empress Irmingard, possibly for political considerations, but in either case addressing commentaries on biblical women to women, rather than their husbands.[106] Anselm of Canterbury plays a double role in this survey, presenting a copy of his *Orationes sive meditationes* to Adelaide, the daughter of William the Conqueror, but also to Mathilda of Tuscany.[107] The life of Margaret of Scotland, depicted by Turgot with hagiographic elements as if she were a saint, is dedicated to her daughter Mathilda, the wife of Henry I of England. In the following century Matthew Paris was active in writing saints' lives for aristocratic women. He composed a life of Edward the Confessor for Eleanor of Provence, the wife of Henry III, but also one of Edmund of Abingdon and possibly of St Alban for Isabelle, the Countess of Arundel, so that he has been said to run 'a kind of circulating library among his aristocratic friends'.[108] In the fifteenth century Osbern Bokenham wrote a life of Elisabeth of Hungary for Elizabeth de Vere and Lydgate his *Virtues of the Mass* for Alice, Countess of Suffolk, assuming that she would be able to follow the celebration of the Mass in her private book.[109] Since we began this paragraph with a German, if not in the German language (Hrabanus Maurus), we may conclude it by making this good in referring to Grundmann's observation that the first Dominican known to be active in Germany, Prior Heinrich of Cologne, wrote devotional letters to pious women of this city, that another Dominican prior of the same name (from Basel) wrote German verse ('rithmos theutonicos') for women,[110] and that, as we saw, *Der Saelden Hort* was addressed expressly to women.

---

[106] Hoda: Thiébaux, *Dhuoda*, p. 10. Hrabanus: Stafford, *Queens*, p. 20; Ferrante, *Glory*, p. 55; de Jong, 'Bride', pp. 202–4.
[107] Anselm: Olson, 'Reading', pp. 13–21. Adelaide: Gameson, 'Gospels', p. 156. Mathilda: Olson, 'Women', pp. 90f.
[108] Turgot: Gameson, 'Gospels', p. 157. Matthew Paris: Legge, *Literature*, pp. 268f.; Wogan-Browne, 'Clerc', p. 78, n. 5; *Lives*, pp. 55, 155–72.
[109] Bokenham: Erler, *Women*, p. 22. Lydgate: Rubin, *Corpus*, p. 158.
[110] Grundmann, *Bewegungen*, pp. 459–61.

In turning finally to religious literature addressed to and composed for nuns, where we find the richest range of examples, we must be aware that, spread over the three countries and four languages covered in this book, it is so vast that we must confine ourselves to no more than a few representatives from three classes. These are: convents for whose use works were composed, authors who wrote for nuns, and specific works composed for nuns.

Four convents for which works were meant may be cited. It was for Heloise's community of the Paraclete that Abelard wrote not simply a Rule, but a discourse on the study of scripture, the *Problemata*, a collection of sequences, hymns and homilies, in fact a rich contribution including the major works of his later years. For the community of nuns at Hohenburg (Landsberg) their abbess Herrad designed an encyclopaedic work, the *Hortus Deliciarum*, comprising extracts from the Bible, twelfth-century theologians such as Honorius Augustodunensis and a large number of sermons and poems, illustrating what intellectual (and Latinate) demands could be made of the nuns.[111] At Barking abbey, Aldhelm dedicated his *De virginitate* to the abbess Hildelith and her nuns, whilst after the Conquest the nun Clemence would seem, if we follow Gaunt's suggestion, to have meant her Anglo-Norman *Sainte Catherine* for her own community. Another English community was Syon Abbey where Thomas Berson, the librarian of the men's community, wrote a treatise for women preparing to enter the house, and Richard Whytford a text for the abbess Elizabeth Gibbs.[112]

Under authors who wrote works for nuns we may again confine ourselves to four cases, in addition to those implied in the last paragraph. The vernacular *Leben des heiligen Ulrich*, based on a Latin *vita*, was written by Albertus for nuns of the Augsburg monastery where the saint lies buried. From the division of the works written by the Franciscan David von Augsburg into Latin and German it has been concluded that he wrote the former mainly for theologically trained brethren in his own order, but the latter for other members, for laybrothers, but also nuns and tertiaries.[113] Like David, the Dominican Seuse wrote according to the needs of specific audiences and composed his *Exemplar* in German for nuns in his order, whilst his Latin *Horologium* (which in this international language found its way into other countries) was addressed to clerics and male members (although Heinrich von Nördlingen recommended Margaretha Ebner to procure a Latin copy). In England we learn from a colophon in a manuscript of Osbern

[111] Paraclete: Dronke, *Women*, p. 134; Newman, 'Authority', p. 137; Clanchy, *Abelard*, p. 153. Hohenburg: R. Green *et al.*, *Herrad*; Curschmann, 'Herrad', *VfL* 3, 1138–44; Graf, *Bildnisse*, pp. 63–7.

[112] Barking: Schulenburg, *Forgetful*, pp. 98f.; Gaunt, *Gender*, pp. 228–32. Syon: Krug, *Families*, pp. 198f.

[113] Albertus: Küsters, *Garten*, pp. 150, 174f.; Geith, *VfL* 1, 114–16. David: Heinzle, *Wandlungen*, pp. 74f.

Bokenham's *Legendys of Hooly Wummen* that it was written in Cambridge and presented to a nunnery.[114]

With an obvious overlap we move under our last heading to works that were written for nuns. We have seen that, although it was composed by an anonymous, probably male author, the *St. Trudperter Hoheslied* is likely to have been intended for a community of nuns, whether or not we locate this at Admont. The same is true of the *Rheinisches Marienlob*, meant for use in a Rhenish nuns' convent (the author interprets his theme in the presence of all God's brides: 'vür allen godes brüden') and probably composed by a cleric charged with their spiritual care.[115] The German *Alexius* A legend was composed by a woman (to judge by the conclusion of MS G) and, since it seems to have been at home in a female context (a convent of the Poor Clares in Eger and a double monastery in Seckau), appealing to nuns in much the same way as did the same saint's legend to Christina of Markyate in the St Albans Psalter. *The Rothschild Canticles*, as Hamburger has shown, were addressed to a female recipient (suggested by the feminine gender of 'peccatrix'), probably a nun or canoness in a convent of the area of Flanders and the Rhineland.[116]

However selective it had perforce to be, the catalogue with which this section has finished should convey some idea of the ubiquitous role played by women in the world of the medieval book, both secular and religious. The evidence is not always explicit enough to tell us whether dedicating, addressing or presenting a book to a woman conceals her role as actual patron or merely expresses a hope for possible patronage but, taken together, this and the following section establish women's important role in the production and reception of books in the Middle Ages.

WOMEN AS SPONSORS OF LITERATURE

With this section we reach a turning point not just in this chapter, but in the whole book. We saw that the difference between works written for women and women as sponsors lay with where the initiative came from, so that only now in this section can women be seen as in some measure in control of what they read. But this difference extends further than between these two sections. On the one hand, literary initiative also lies outside women in the first section of this chapter (they copy what others have composed) and in the whole of Chapter 3 (they read what others have written), whilst on the

[114] Seuse: Ruh, *Geschichte* III 442; Newman, *God*, pp. 206f., 209. Bokenham: Riddy, 'Women', p. 105.
[115] *Hoheslied*: Ohly, *Hohelied*, p. 328. *Marienlob*: Heinzle, *Wandlungen*, p. 149; Green, *Listening*, p. 129.
[116] *Alexius*: Rosenfeld, *VfL* I, 226f. *Canticles*: Hamburger, *Canticles*, pp. 3, 30, 101, 155.

other hand the initiative lies with them not merely when they sponsor works of literature, but more so when, as we shall consider in the next section, they themselves compose them. This is much more than a distinction between theoretical categories, for it means that from this point on women must be granted not merely an important, but even a central role, in medieval literary practice. The sponsor of a work can be said to play a creative role in literature as well as the author himself, but sponsorship plays a much wider role than this. In the Middle Ages it was one of the few realms where women were allowed a public voice, even if only indirectly, an opportunity which enabled them to exercise cultural, and at times political, influence.[117]

In what follows I use the term 'sponsorship' at times in preference to 'patronage' in order to convey the wide sense of this engagement of women with literary production. Just as in the last section we looked at women's passive role in various ways (works dedicated to them, addressing them and of potential interest to them), so must we now grant their active contribution a variety of forms of expression (they not merely reward or pay for the production of a work, they can also encourage, request, even command it, without necessarily commissioning it). From this range of possibilities I have excluded women as dedicatees, treated in the last section, because of the passive nature of that role and because, although it may conceal an act of sponsorship, it is not of itself enough to establish it. Although Ferrante includes dedication in her survey of women's literary patronage, I agree with her suggestion that we need to operate with a wider concept (what I term sponsorship), including the active encouragement of a written work (especially of a religious nature) by asking questions or requesting further explanation.[118] Our wider concern, women's engagement with literature, must find room for more than what is commonly meant by commissioning a work for some form of reward, although it must clearly include that. This means that we cannot be content with the narrow conception of literary patronage shown by Broadhurst in her discussion of Henry II and Eleanor of Aquitaine.[119] We may agree with her distinction between commissions and dedications, but still insist that her essentially negative conclusion is reached by her confining herself to literary patronage in the restrictive sense of 'the remuneration bestowed by the patron on the author', to the exclusion of any other encouragement or display of interest in literary production. To restrict ourselves to such a view, working with documentary evidence as the only reliable indicator of patronage, is inadequate for our purposes by ignoring or downplaying what the literary texts themselves

---

[117] McCash, 'Patronage', pp. 1f.   [118] Ferrante, *Glory*, pp. 39f.   [119] *Viator* 27 (1996), 53–84.

say. It reminds us of the criticism by Brooke that the historian of medieval marriage who ignores the literary evidence is depriving himself of a rich source of information which is not available anywhere else.[120] Nor will it do when Benton, engaged on the parallel task of questioning the role of the court of Champagne in literary patronage, seeks support in doubting whether a given author was 'regularly a member of the court'.[121] Our concern is not with that, but whether he was required, in this case by Marie de Champagne, to compose a particular work, as Chrétien says he was.

That women could be actively involved in the production of literature without actually commissioning it has been well documented by Ferrante in her discussion of male authors encouraged or 'pushed' in different ways to write their works. She begins her survey with Jerome and Augustine, who wrote various works in response to women, and proceeds as far as Abelard, who was prompted to write in answering theological questions raised by Heloise. Ferrante calls these women 'patrons' (although I prefer the wider term 'sponsors') on the grounds that 'they caused the work to be written and supported the writer with intellectual, emotional, and sometimes financial help'.[122] By implying that the last form of help was given only sometimes she makes clear the difference between her position and Broadhurst's and it is this wider-ranging concept of encouragement that tells us more about women's activity in the field of literature. Jerome was urged into writing by the questions that arose in the studies of women like Marcella, Paula and Eustochium, but the way in which he defends himself for this is revealing (he would not be doing so if men were to ask him such questions about scripture). In the case of Augustine, two works that are preliminary studies for the *Civitas Dei* were written at the request of women, Italica and Paulina, in answer to questions that they, too, had raised.[123]

Centuries later, the position is little different in the Anglo-Saxon mission to Germany, for Boniface has to apologise to Bugga for his delay in finishing the text she had asked for, and responds to a comparable request from the abbess Eadburga. A sister and daughter of Charles the Great, Gisela and Rotruda, strengthened their request to Alcuin for a commentary on John by reminding him that Jerome had responded positively to similar requests from women. When Alcuin says that he had wanted to write this commentary for thirty years he makes it clear that it is thanks to them that he eventually got round to it. At the request of the Emperor's granddaughter, Gundrada, he also composed *De ratione animae*.[124] Ferrante

---

[120] Brooke, *Idea*, p. 176.   [121] *Speculum* 36 (1961), 552.   [122] Ferrante, 'Voice', p. 4.
[123] Jerome: Ferrante, *Glory*, pp. 48–52. Augustine: *ibid.*, pp. 52–4.
[124] Boniface: Ferrante, 'Role', p. 77. Alcuin: Ferrante, *Glory*, pp. 28, 54f.; *Krone*, pp. 230, 236.

concludes her survey of these productive literary relationships between male authors and female instigators by harking back to her starting point in saying of the collaboration between Abelard and Heloise that it came closer than other cases to Jerome's relationship with his women friends. To this could be added a further agreement for, like Jerome, Abelard sees the spiritual interests of Heloise and her nuns as accomplishing and making good what men fail to achieve.[125] It is to them and the intellectual problems they raise with him that Abelard owed the impetus to compose many of the works extant under his name, including a Rule suitable for women and a history of women's monasticism. In summary, none of these instances can be remotely conceived as commissioning of a work by a patron; they illustrate instead the genesis of literature as the result of gentle insistence, intellectual pressure or even a touch of emotional blackmail. They show sponsorship in the widest sense.

In view of this wider conception it is fitting to recall that women's support of cultural and religious activity was itself many-sided and that the literary form which is our concern is part of a much greater whole. This includes the sponsorship of artistically decorated and illuminated Psalters and Books of Hours, but also the lavish support by aristocratic women of female monasticism. Outstanding examples of this are Agnes of Prague, Hedwig of Silesia and Elisabeth of Thuringia, but with forerunners going back to the Ottonians. This sponsorship represents women's encouragement of female monasticism, but also of the artistic and literary activity of these houses.[126] Parallel with this, but with an intellectual as well as a spiritual emphasis, is a phenomenon known in England in particular, the founding and support of a college by a wealthy noblewoman, even if the education provided there was for men, not for women. Continental examples include Jeanne of Navarre's founding of the College of Navarre and possibly Mechthild von der Pfalz in the case of Tübingen, but it is in Cambridge that this role played by women is striking.[127] Here Elizabeth de Burgh founded Clare Hall, while Queens' College was founded by Margaret of Anjou and later supported further by Elizabeth Woodville and Anne Neville. Margaret Beaufort went further in not merely establishing a professorship, but also founding two colleges, Christ's and St John's. It is Margaret Beaufort who best illustrates the connection between benefactions to found colleges (here the provision

[125] Ferrante, *Glory*, pp. 28f., 44–6; 'Role', pp. 80f.
[126] Hamburger, *Visual*, pp. 58–71; *Krone*, pp. 229–306, 381–422, 503–31.
[127] Navarre and Tübingen: Rashdall, *Universities* I 491, II 1, 273. Cambridge: McCash, 'Patronage',
      p. 32; Michalove, 'Education', p. 134; Rashdall, *Universities* II 2, 563f., 575; Pevsner, *Cambridgeshire*,
      pp. 39, 120.

of land and funds justifies the term 'patronage') and sponsorship of literature (she had connections with both Caxton and Wynkyn de Worde and was praised for her devotional reading). In praising her for the latter, Bishop John Fisher coined a phrase which sums up both her spheres of activity: she was for him 'a veray patroness'.[128]

Another way in which women could encourage literary activity was joint patronage, in which the woman was active with someone else, normally her husband, a necessity arising from the fact that most married women lacked the legal or financial independence to exercise cultural patronage alone. (Exceptions there may have been, but they remain exceptions, and even the most striking case, Eleanor of Aquitaine, can also be shown active alongside her husband.) How this may have worked in practice is well illustrated in the case of Hedwig of Silesia who, together with her husband, founded the Cistercian convent of Trebnitz. This is recounted in the *Legenda maior*, in which the caption to an image tells us that Hedwig prevailed on her husband to build the convent and that he endowed it on the advice of his wife ('induxit maritum suum, ut de propriis sumptibus suis construi faceret monasterium').[129] We are left in no doubt that the initiative came from her, but also that it worked only through him. A parallel in the vernacular is the *Rolandslied* whose author makes it clear that Henry the Lion, with whose religious praise the work concludes, ordered the book to be read out ('daz bûch hîz er vor tragen'), but adds that, given the work's French source, the initiative (presumably in obtaining a copy of the source) came from his wife requesting this to be done ('Des gerte di edele herzoginne').[130] Henry's wife Mathilda, the daughter of Henry II of England and Eleanor of Aquitaine, leads us to the Anglo-Norman realm from which other examples of joint patronage are available. Although Henry I was known as Henry Beauclerc and has been seen as a sponsor of literature at court, it is more likely that it was his two wives who stood behind this encouragement. Although it may well have been Henry II who commissioned the *Roman de Rou* from Wace, nonetheless the author takes care to praise his wife Eleanor, significantly including generosity amongst her virtues.[131] Gautier d'Arras wrote his *Eracle* for Marie de Champagne, another daughter of Eleanor, and for her brother-in-law, Thibaut of Blois ('par lui le fis . . . et par le contesse autresi'), and his *Ille et Galeron* for Beatrice of Burgundy and Thibaut, again emphasising that he could not have done this without either of them ('. . . se il ne me feïst/ E ele ausi'). Likewise, the frontispiece

---

[128] Summit, 'Caxton', pp. 151f.
[129] Hamburger, *Gesta* 31, 2 (1992), 117, 129, n. 100; McCash, 'Patronage', pp. 8f.
[130] *Rolandslied* 9022–4. [131] Henry Beauclerc: Huneycutt, '*Proclaiming*', p. 155. Wace, *Rou* 24–36.

of a *Bible moralisée* depicts a queen and king (possibly Blanche of Castile and Louis IX) presiding over the production of the text which they can be assumed to have jointly commissioned.[132]

In many cases women became identifiably active as patrons only when they were widows, which suggests that, before this, they were so dependent on their husbands for access to resources that a woman's legal identity was submerged in her husband's.[133] The result could be that a work was attributed to both of them, or even to him alone, although the controlling impetus came from her. 'Women encourage, men pay'.[134] Here we may indeed ask, reverting to Hedwig of Silesia and to the *Rolandslied*, whether the women in these two cases would have been mentioned at all if there had not been a compelling reason. With Hedwig, this was her hagiographer's need to stress her role in founding a convent and, with the *Rolandslied*, Henry the Lion's political interest to stress the royal descent of his wife ('aines rîchen chuniges barn'), as in the coronation scene in the Gospel book of Henry the Lion.[135] Although this suggests that the women's role in such cases runs the risk of being expunged from the record (as we shall see this is also the case with their role as authors) this does not give us the right to generalise and claim that behind every male patron there stands a wife with whom the true initiative lay. Instead, we have to register this as a real, but unquantifiable factor. In many cases, therefore, women's role as patrons may be visible to us only indirectly; like so many Victorian wives they operated behind the scenes, persuading their husbands to provide financial support, but nonetheless playing a direct role in suggesting what was to be encouraged. A non-literary example of our need to look behind the scenes is the *Abingdon Chronicle's* mention of the gift of a reliquary to the abbey, claiming that it was commissioned by King Cnut, whereas the report of the inscription on it makes it clear that in fact it was a joint enterprise by Cnut and Queen Aelfgifa, both of whom ordered the reliquary to be made ('Rex Cnut hanc thecam, necnon Aelfgiva regina cudere jusserunt').[136] In this as in other cases the woman may be mentioned second, but present she is (and may even have played a primary role).

As distinct from joint patronage by two people we must also take into account what may be termed collective patronage, where more than just

---

[132] *Eracle* 6551f. *Ille et Galeron*: Bezzola, *Origines* III 421. *Bible moralisée*: Caviness, 'Anchoress', p. 136 (and Fig. 27).
[133] Jambeck, 'Patterns', pp. 244f.; Hen, 'Gender', pp. 228f.
[134] Paterson, *World*, p. 258.
[135] *Rolandslied* 9025. Gospel-book: Rösener, 'Frau', pp. 193f.; Schneidmüller, *Welfen*, plate 2 (facing p. 293).
[136] Caviness, 'Anchoress', pp. 124f. and 149, n. 50.

two are involved. An important form of this, as we shall see with Eleanor of Aquitaine, is the exercise of patronage by or in families, the evidence for which is rich from late medieval England. Four 'family profiles' of patronage have been established in detail by Jambeck: the families of Elizabeth Berkeley, Countess of Warwick, of Blanche, Duchess of Lancaster, of Joan FitzAlan, Countess of Hereford, and of Joan Beaufort, Countess of Westmoreland.[137] From the last-named a rich ramification of patronage can be traced. Joan Beaufort was herself a patron of literature, but so were her daughters Cecily and Anne Neville. Furthermore, her sisters are also known to have encouraged writing: Eleanor (who commissioned the Edinburgh Psalter) and Mary de Bohun. We go further with Eleanor's daughter Anne, Countess of Stafford, who patronised Lydgate's well-chosen invocation to St Anne, and still further with Anne's daughter, another Anne, who patronised another work by Lydgate, his *Legend of St Margaret*.[138] At an earlier date the same kind of 'matrilineal patronage' can be found on the continent with Gisela (the wife of the illiterate Konrad II) whom we have encountered commissioning a copy of Notker's translation of the Psalms and who took care that her son married Agnes of Poitou, so that cultural patronage was continued in their marriage.[139] These examples of literary patronage by women through the generations are reminiscent of what we saw earlier of their vertical reading communities, with one woman passing on reading material to her daughter or to other women, but whereas in this earlier phenomenon women played a passive role (as readers, recipients of what was passed on to them), now they are more active as patrons, choosing what should be made available in book form.

Another form of collective patronage exercised by women is made up of works commissioned by a convent for its own use, generally by an abbess on behalf of the community at large. Already in Merovingian Gaul a number of female saints' *vitae* are commissioned by abbesses of communities with which these saints were associated (e.g. Dedimia's commissioning of the *Vita Radegundis* from Baudonivia, a nun of Radegund's own monastery in Poitiers).[140] In the tenth century a picture of the abbess Hadwig of Essen shows her as the donor of a manuscript containing the *vitae* of Cosmas and Damian, the patron saints of Essen, and in Regensburg on behalf of the canonesses of Niedermünster the abbess Uta commissioned a manuscript containing the Rule of Caesarius of Arles for nuns and the Benedictine Rule (grammatically adapted with feminine endings). This same Uta also

---

[137] Jambeck, 'Patterns', pp. 233–9.   [138] *Ibid.*, pp. 239–42; Michalove, 'Education', p. 134.
[139] McCash, 'Patronage', pp. 14f.   [140] Hen, 'Gender', p. 225.

commissioned the so-called Uta codex.[141] Eberhard's *Gandersheimer Reim-chronik*, written in defence of the community's exemption from control by the Bishop of Hildesheim, was most probably commissioned by the abbess Mechthild, embroiled in that struggle for independence at the turn of the thirteenth century. Finally, as an even later example, the *Engelthaler Schwesternbuch* appears to have been commissioned by the prioress of the convent, possibly from Christine Ebner.[142]

At this point we abandon these general considerations for more particular examples, including important cases of female patronage with the aim of illustrating its continuity and frequency throughout the Middle Ages, although I shall focus more on the twelfth century. Limitations of space mean that I can give only a few examples before we concentrate on the richly informative evidence of Anglo-Norman and Angevin literature of the twelfth century.

Under religious themes it is no surprise to find women commissioning a Psalter (Gisela and Notker's Psalter, Eleanor de Bohun and the Edinburgh Psalter), so much so that women are responsible for many of the finest examples (also of Books of Hours) in the closing centuries of the Middle Ages.[143] The permeability of laywomen's and religious women's reading matter means that, although these last cases concern laywomen, religious texts of a more general nature are also largely commissioned for use in convents (Abelard wrote so many of his religious works at the request of Heloise, and a Middle English translation of the Pseudo-Augustinian *Soliloquia* was requested by a convent of women).[144] The same permeability can be seen with saints' lives, another genre popular with women patrons. The *Visio Tnugdali* was commissioned by the abbess Gisela for the nuns of a Regensburg convent and the *Leben des heiligen Ulrich* was composed for nuns ('geistlichen kint') in Augsburg who had requested it.[145] On the other hand, laywomen are known to have encouraged such works: Agnes von Loon and Veldeke's *Servatius* legend or Margaret Beaufort's commission of a book of prayers in Latin and English from Caxton.[146] How common to women patrons in both walks of life this religious literature was is suggested by Alber's German *Tnugdalus* legend, written at the request of three named 'frouwen', who could be nuns, but could equally well be noblewomen.[147]

---

[141] Hadwig and Uta: Beach, *Women*, p. 22. On Uta cf. *Krone* plate 1 (p. 20), plate 4 (p. 23), pp. 24f., 186 and plate 26 (p. 187).

[142] Eberhard: Heinzle, *Wandlungen*, p. 133. *Schwesternbuch*: Thali, *Beten*, pp. 28f.

[143] Meale, 'Laywomen', p. 137.   [144] Olson, 'Women', p. 95 and fn. 101.

[145] *Visio Tnugdali*: Bumke, *Mäzene*, p. 231; *Ulrichsleben*: ibid., p. 232.

[146] *Servatius*: ibid., pp. 116f., 238; Bumke, *Kultur*, p. 669. Margaret Beaufort: Krug, *Families*, p. 99.

[147] Bumke, *Mäzene*, p. 231.

Under secular themes it would be mistaken, despite what Chaucer reports of women's fondness for the Lancelot story, to regard their literary interests as confined to romance fiction. Noticeably frequent is their sponsorship of works of history: Gundeperga and Theodelinda both play a part in having the early history of the Langobards written, Gerberga commands Hrotsvitha to compose the *Gesta Ottonis*, Aethelweard writes his *Chronicle* for his cousin Mathilda, abbess of Essen, and William of Malmesbury his *Gesta regum Anglorum* for Queen Edith.[148] Although not always easy to distinguish from history, encomiastic literature may also be included here (Emma commissions the *Encomium Emmae Reginae* to urge the claims of her son against a rival half-brother, and Baudri de Bourgueil implies something like dependence on Adela of Blois as a patron by adding to his lengthy praise of her a request for a gift).[149] Female patronage of romance literature may be illustrated by the involvement, albeit chequered, of Margaret of Cleves in the production of Veldeke's *Eneasroman*, by Gérard d'Amiens composing *Escanor* at the command of Eleanor of Castile, the wife of Edward I, and by Adenet le Roi praising two ladies in the prologue to *Cléomadès* (one of whom is Marie de Brabant) who requested this work from him, a patronage relationship illustrated in the miniature accompanying the prologue in the Arsenal manuscript.[150]

Drastically compressed though the last two paragraphs have been, they should suggest the range of women's patronage of literature before we change our focus to consider some cases in greater detail. For the first we turn to Adela of Blois whom we have considered as one to whom literature was dedicated, but now we look at the counterpart of her actually commissioning literature. Taken together, these two aspects not merely illustrate the uncertain, not always clarifiable boundary between dedications and commissions, they also suggest that a woman known to be a patron could attract works dedicated to her in the hope of extended patronage. Adela's position was assisted by the political power she wielded (during the absence of her husband on crusades, then after his death as regent on behalf of her sons), so that as a patron she enjoyed the advantages of widowhood before she became a widow.[151] (The position is little different in the fifteenth century, when Elisabeth von Nassau-Saarbrücken and Eleonore of Austria,

---

[148] Gundeperga and Theodelinda: Pohl, 'Gender', pp. 37–9. Gerberga: Dronke, *Women*, p. 36; Ferrante, *Glory*, p. 78. Aethelweard and William of Malmesbury: Ferrante, *Glory*, pp. 83, 100.
[149] Emma: Ferrante, *Glory*, pp. 90f.; McCash, 'Patronage', pp. 16f. Baudri: Ferrante, 'Role', p. 86.
[150] *Eneasroman*: Bumke, *Mäzene*, pp. 113–16; *Kultur*, p. 669. *Escanor*: Ferrante, 'Voice', p. 17. *Cléomadès*: Hindman, 'Authorship', p. 52; Ward, 'Fables', pp. 196f. (and Fig. 88).
[151] Bond, *Subject*, p. 129; LoPrete, 'Adela', pp. 42f.; Ferrante, *Glory*, p. 97.

of Scottish birth, are both active as authors in the absence of husbands or in their widowhood.) Whether or not they imply actual patronage, the words of Godfrey of Reims that already as a young woman Adela had poems sent to her ('quae directa sibi filia regis habet') certainly suggest that she was interested in panegyrics addressed to her. Baudri de Bourgueil makes it clear, however, that her role was not merely passive (as a dedicatee), but also active in that she sent a message wanting to have his poems, approved of them and urged him to continue. He also makes it clear that she is informed enough to prefer some poems to others, a fact of crucial importance at a court which attracted the rivalry of competing *versificatores*, and that she knew how to reward those whom she favoured.[152] Hugh of Fleury may well dedicate his *Historia ecclesiastica* to her, but amongst the eminently courtly qualities for which he praises her, he gives first place to her well-known generosity ('generositate preclara'), of more importance in a patron than in a dedicatee, even though there is no indication that Adela commissioned his work. Hugh has every reason to address his work to Adela rather than to illiterate princes who despise the art of literature.[153]

We turn now to women's patronage of literature in the Anglo-Norman realm founded by Adela's father, William the Conqueror, for what this brings is support of literature in the vernacular, whilst the works encouraged by or addressed to Adela are, to our knowledge, all in Latin. Here too we have to do with some of the names mentioned in the preceding section, but now, as with Adela, in the active context of encouraging, not merely receiving literature, although it is often difficult to distinguish these. In this new departure an important role was first played by Adeliza of Louvain, the second wife of Henry I. We have already seen that, as reported by Gaimar, she was the patron of David's poem on that ruler, but she is also addressed by name and title in the first version of Philippe de Thaon's *Bestiaire*, whereas the second was meant for Eleanor of Aquitaine.[154] In addition, Adeliza is presented by Benedeit as the patron of his *Voyage of St Brendan*, which he undertook at her command ('Que comandas ço ad empris' and 'Esi cum fut li teons cumanz'). One of the manuscripts admittedly refers instead to 'Mahalt' or Maud, probably Henry I's first wife, Mathilda, so that, as with Philippe de Thaon's *Bestiaire*, a change of name makes no difference to the fact that in every case the initiative is shown coming from a woman.[155] Samson de Nanteuil names Aelis de Condé as the patron of his *Proverbes de Salemon*, saying that she entreated him many times to do this

[152] Godfrey: Bond, *Subject*, pp. 145f. Baudri, *Carmina* 134, 37–66; Bond, *Subject*, pp. 131f.
[153] MGH SS 9, 349, 353.   [154] David: Gaimar, *Estoire* 6483–6. Philippe, *Bestiaire* 5–11.
[155] Benedeit, *Voyage* 1–13; Legge, *Literature*, p. 9.

('Ki mainte feiz l'en out preiéd').[156] With Constance Fitzgilbert we return to David's life of Henry I, for although she may not have been his patron she at least commissioned a copy of it to be made ('Dame Custance en ad l'escrit') for her personal use as a reader. However, Constance comes fully into her own as a patron of Gaimar's *Estoire des Engleis*, who describes in unusual detail how she took trouble in procuring source material for his work. Although the source book (almost certainly Geoffrey of Monmouth's *Historia regum Britannie*) was loaned to Constance's husband it is she, not he, who provided Gaimar with it ('Dame Custance l'enpruntat/de son seignur'), so that the author has every reason to say that but for her he would never have accomplished his task.[157]

We conclude with the Angevin court of Henry II and Eleanor of Aquitaine, together with the latter's patronage ramifications in France and Germany as well as England, so that in her person the three countries with which this book deals are brought together. Whereas Henry is known also to have supported literature in Latin, the works associated with Eleanor are all in the vernacular, so that in this she continues what we saw of female patronage in the last paragraph.[158] Furthermore, whilst Henry's interests as a patron lay with historiography and statecraft, those of his wife were more of a literary nature, with fictional works or ones with what could be called entertainment value.[159] Even with all due reservations about some of Lejeune's more wishful arguments[160] (yet without falling victim to Broadhurst's restrictive view of patronage) it is at Eleanor's court that the move from history-writing to the composition of romances was first made and through her daughters that some of these romances (with Tristan and Arthurian themes) were cultivated on the continent. In his *Roman de Brut*, a vernacular adaptation of Geoffrey of Monmouth, Wace does not mention Eleanor, but the later version of Layamon associates Eleanor with Wace's work. Moreover, in his *Roman de Rou*, a history of the Normans appealing to Henry, Wace says that both Henry and Eleanor rewarded him for his work.[161] If we assume the same for the *Roman de Brut* and bear in mind that Henry's historical interests appear not to have extended to Arthur and the Britons,[162] it would seem that joint patronage could include divergent interests: Norman history for the king, Arthurian history, verging on the fabulous, for Eleanor.

---

[156] *Proverbes* 194–8; Legge, *Literature*, p. 37.
[157] Gaimar, *Estoire* 6489, 6439–52; Blacker, 'Portrait', pp. 110f.
[158] Schirmer and Broich, *Studien*, pp. 198f.   [159] *Ibid.*, pp. 195f., 202f.
[160] Lejeune, *CN* 14 (1954), 5–57; *CCM* 1 (1958), 319–37.   [161] Layamon, *Brut* 39–44. *Rou* 17–21.
[162] Schirmer and Broich, *Studien*, p. 91.

Benoît de Sainte-Maure, a rival of Wace who eventually ousted him from royal favour, includes a eulogy of Eleanor in his *Roman de Troie*, referring to her as 'Riche dame de riche rei', making a pointed reference to her generosity and fearing lest he might offend her taste ('criem g'estre blasmez').[163] The reason for his fear is that he has just recounted the episode of the inconstancy of Briseïs and, like Chaucer with his Criseyde, anticipates female objections. Benoît's placing of his praise of Eleanor has been called a backhanded apology to his patroness,[164] but it can rather be seen as a subversion of misogyny, a literary technique that will occupy us in the companion volume. Benoît's praise works by contrast and he carefully blocks off any negative generalisation about women from the one case of Briseïs alone by stressing the virtues incorporated by Eleanor ('En cui mesfait de dames maint/sont par le bien de li esteint').[165] An appeal to Eleanor need not have excluded Henry from interest in this work, for he was probably encouraged by the wish, shared by other medieval rulers, to propagate a Trojan origin for his Anglo-Norman realm, a consideration that has been extended to the possible genesis of the *Roman d'Enéas* under Angevin auspices, so that these 'romans antiques' have been seen to provide the dynasty with historical legitimation.[166] Whether Eleanor shared these dynastic interests in these works we do not know, but the greater role they grant to women characters and the treatment of love alongside warfare may have made their own appeal to her. The same could be true of two other works, romances of the *matière de Bretagne*, thought to have been composed for the same court. In Thomas's *Tristan* the theme of love dominates, but the extended praise of London probably appealed to a ruler who had his court there, while in *Erec*, the first romance of Chrétien and one with undeniable associations with England, the final coronation scene at Nantes is reminiscent of the politically important court held there by Henry II in 1169.[167] In all these cases the king and queen may work together as patrons, even if each finds something different in the works to attract their interest and support.

With Eleanor's eldest daughter from her first marriage, Marie, the wife of Henry the Liberal of Champagne, we return to women's patronage on the continent. Like Adela of Blois and for similar reasons (the death of her husband and regency on behalf of her sons) Marie exercised political power and also enjoyed freedom of patronage as a

---

[163] *Roman de Troie* 13457–70.   [164] Krueger, *Women*, p. 6.
[165] *Troie* 13463f.   [166] Green, *Beginnings*, pp. 155, 160.
[167] Thomas: Lejeune, *CN* 14 (1954), 33–5; Bezzola, *Origines* III 302. *Erec*: Schmolke-Hasselmann, *Versroman*, pp. 190–201.

widow.[168] Before this, however, husband and wife presided over a court renowned for the scholars and authors it attracted. These include none other than Chrétien, but also Evrat and Gautier d'Arras, all of whom make express reference to the patronage they received. Thus, at the start of his *Lancelot*, Chrétien refers to Marie as the Countess of Champagne and makes it quite clear that he writes at her command ('Puis que ma dame de Champaigne/vialt que romans a feire anpraigne'). Moreover, so much is Marie in command as patroness that she suggests not merely the (Arthurian) theme, but also how it should be interpreted ('matiere et san li done et livre/la contesse'), which may explain Chrétien's abandonment of an uncongenial task, handing it over to Godefroi de Laigny for completion.[169] We move to quite a different context with Evrat's lengthy verse-translation of Genesis which he says was required of him by a countess who is elsewhere specified as of Champagne ('De la gentis contesse/Ki l'estoire en romans fist feire').[170] The third work to be written for Marie is another biblical text, *Eructavit*, a verse paraphrase of Psalm 44. Although there is no outright statement, as in the first two works, that Marie ordered the translation to be made, the unknown author addresses her and presents his work to her.[171] Finally, although Gautier d'Arras began his *Eracle* with praise of Marie's brother-in-law, Thibaut of Blois, he later widens this remark by saying that he put this work into rhyme for Thibaut and also for Countess Marie.[172] Benton, whose analysis of the court of Champagne I follow with reservations in this paragraph, concludes by contrasting the literary tastes of Henry and Marie: the former, well educated but conservative in his interests, and the latter with tastes more avant garde (*Lancelot* and an erotic subplot in *Eracle*).[173] Marie's fame as a patroness of literature rests essentially on her encouragement of Chrétien's Arthurian romance and it is probably this that accounts for her (fictive, not historical) role as an adjudicator in matters of love in the *De Amore* of Andreas Capellanus.[174]

Eleanor's younger daughter Mathilda (from her marriage to Henry II) takes us back to Braunschweig, to the court of her husband, Henry the Lion. Aware now that she came from what at the time was one of the most cultured courts of Europe and from a highly literate family, we need no longer be surprised that she was involved in providing source material

---

[168] Benton, *Speculum* 36 (1961), 554.
[169] *Lancelot* 1f., 26f. The Guiot manuscript underlines this pictorially with a miniature of Marie alongside the prologue. Cf. Hindman, *Parchment*, p. 54 (and Fig. 41, facing p. 77).
[170] Benton, *Speculum* 36 (1961), 563, fn. 41 (this text is as yet not published).
[171] *Ibid.*, p. 566.   [172] *Eracle* 1–94, 6548–93; Benton, *Speculum* 36 (1961), 568.
[173] *Speculum* 36 (1961), 585f., 587f. Cf. Bezzola, *Origines* III 369, and Broadhurst, *Viator* 27 (1996), 80.
[174] E.g., *De Amore*, pp. 150–5, 273.

and encouragement for the German *Rolandslied* or indeed that the author, amidst his praise of the duke's patronage, finds it necessary to imply that the initiative in this joint patronage came from her, not so much for the act of translation (suggested for Marie de Champagne) as for the promotion of the work itself. As was the case with Henry II and Eleanor, the joint patronage of her daughter with Henry the Lion was fully acceptable to the Welf duke, above all since the imperial and crusading implications of the work could easily be adapted to his own political ambitions.[175] Nor are we justified in essentialising what we may regard as typically feminine literary interests and arguing that these implications cannot have interested Mathilda. She too had an interest in the strengthening of her husband's political and territorial position and we have seen that laywomen's patronage could be just as well directed towards historical as to literary themes. (The widespread literary activity of Elisabeth von Nassau-Saarbrücken consisted in adapting not French romances, but chansons de geste.) The example of Mathilda's half-sister in Champagne is enough to show that a woman patron's interests could embrace such widely different topics as a romance of adultery and biblical texts. If we look for different interests on the part of Mathilda, for themes even including adultery, we need go no further than what, despite long-lasting scholarly disagreement, is still the most likely placing of the *Tristrant* of Eilhart von Oberg as a work commissioned by the Braunschweig court shortly after the duke's marriage to the English princess.[176] The author was a ministerial from near Braunschweig who is documentarily attested at that court, the source for his *Tristrant* (like that for the *Rolandslied*) is likely to have come from England,[177] and his acquaintance with French (as well as German) literature of the day points to an up-to-date awareness of literary developments such as are attested both for Mathilda's mother and for her half-sister. Whether we associate both these works with Mathilda's influence or only the *Rolandslied*, her literary role as a patron stands out in yet another respect, for she played an important role in opening the way to French influence on German literature with all that this was to mean for more than a century afterwards.[178]

We may sum up what we have seen of Eleanor, Marie and Mathilda by saying that together they constitute a triangle of patronage (London,

---

[175] Bumke, *Mäzene*, pp. 88f., 143–6.   [176] *Ibid.*, pp. 109–13; Mertens, *Literatur*, pp. 207–9.

[177] Bumke, *Mäzene*, p. 146. Cf. Mertens, *Literatur*, p. 205, on the precedent of encouraging vernacular literature. Wolf, *Buch* II.2.4, discusses links between the *Rolandslied* and England, but also the Anglo-Norman origin (connected with Eleanor and her son, Richard Lionheart) of sources for two other German works (II.3.2.1).

[178] Bumke, *Mäzene*, p. 236.

Troyes, Braunschweig), the most important example we have of 'matrilineal patronage' on an international scale. Furthermore, all three can be seen as actively promoting the beginning of the court romance and the genesis of literary fiction in the vernacular. Lastly, and most importantly, they help to demonstrate not merely the extent of women's patronage, as traced very selectively in the rest of this section, but also the quality of their literary taste and their awareness of the latest developments.

There are broader questions in the background of this section, too large to be dealt with in its compass. There is a history of women's sponsorship of literature to be written, with regional and chronological variations. How do women in this field compare with men? Did women's sponsorship contribute to their playing a more significant social role? How do we account for their frequency as sponsors by contrast with their rarity as authors? In view of the predominance of religious literature for women, what lies behind their encouragement of the romance? All this still needs to be done.

WOMEN AS AUTHORS

In view of the difference between medieval and modern conceptions of authorship, especially when women are involved, it will pay to start with a number of general considerations before looking at chosen examples. Since women's authorship was devoted much more to religious than to secular themes, what follows is largely concerned with the difficulties they faced in 'talking about the things of God'.[179]

We have seen that Chaucer's Wife of Bath and Christine de Pizan make a comparable point. The Wife contrasts the mass of men's writings with the rarity of women's ('By God! if wommen hadde writen stories,/As clerkes han withinne hire oratories'), just as Christine admits the same in her *Epistre*.[180] For both women this explains the overwhelming bias of literature against women, but for us their 'if only' stance suggests the infrequency of women writers, although not so drastically as these two women's rhetoric implies and certainly not so far-going as the restriction to six examples in this section which reasons of space impose.

There are grounds for thinking that the rarity of evidence may be more apparent than real, even without appealing to the dangerous assumption of 'lost' examples of women's work. One such reason puts the blame for this

---

[179] Minnis, *Theory*, 'Talking': cf. the title of Riddy, 'Women'.
[180] Chaucer: *Wife of Bath's Prologue* 693f. Christine: *Epistre* 409–22. Jaeger, 'Epistolae', pp. 144f., quotes the extravagant praise of Muriel by Hildebert of Lavardin, calling her unique in an age with few women poets.

situation fully in our court, for the modern tendency to assign 'literature' or a 'work of literature' to belles-lettres contrasts with the medieval view of *litteratura* as 'writing' or anything in written form. As a result, modern scholarship for long neglected works which fell outside its view of literature (e.g. the religious or devotional texts with which women were so largely engaged), but which were central to the medieval view. In doing so we have also failed to pay due attention to women authors of such works. Admittedly, this distortion is now being rectified (in German studies in the wide remit of the second edition of the *Verfasserlexikon* and of Hein-zle's literary history, focused on 'Schriftlichkeit' or *litteratura* in the wide medieval sense).[181] Our modern canon of literature, in marginalising what was not marginal in the Middle Ages, has therefore tended to obscure the activity of women (and men) authors in the fields it excluded. Although Marie de France has long attracted scholarly attention, this cannot be said so confidently of women's correspondence (to which Ferrante has begun to alert us)[182] or to their devotional literature (although this is now being remedied for England and Germany). It is revealing that with the discovery of printing a number of works were not rescued into permanent printed form and were hence lost to view until their rediscovery and scholarly pub-lication. Such belated members of a new literary canon include outstanding figures like Hadewijch, Mechthild von Magdeburg, Julian of Norwich and Margery Kempe.[183]

The loss of women writers to view is even more telling when it appears to be deliberate and a woman's authorship of a work is denied or concealed. An anonymous nun-poet of the early twelfth century rails against not merely a slanderer of poetry ('lacertor carminis'), but also the view that a religious woman should not compose verse or concern herself with Aristotle ('Non est sanctarum mulierum frangere uersus,/Quaerere nec nostrum quis sit Aristoteles'). This would-be exclusion of women from literary composition, even to the point of plagiarism, is seen as a danger by Marie de France when in the epilogue to her *Fables* she names herself as author to guard against clerics appropriating the work for themselves ('Put cel estre que clerc plusur/Prendreient sur eus mun labur./Ne voil que nul sur li le die').[184] In *Lavision Christine* (de Pizan) it is suggested that clerics forge works for her, for they could not come from a woman, but this is realised in practice when another work by Christine, on chivalry, circulated in some versions with her name and sex suppressed, since the subject of warfare was not fitting for a

---

[181] Ruh (ed.), *Verfasserlexikon*; Heinzle (ed.), *Geschichte*.
[182] Ferrante, *Glory*, pp. 1–35.   [183] Newman, *God*, p. 315.
[184] Nun-poet: Bond, *Subject*, pp. 166–8, vv. 45f., 55. Marie: *Fables*, Epilogue 4–6.

woman.[185] Translation, or the extraction of a work from its original context, also provided an opportunity for expropriation. In English translations of Christine's works they were ascribed frequently to their male translators, a Middle English translation of Mechthild von Hackeborn circulated under the name of a male author, while, somewhat differently, Marguerite Porète's *Mirouer des simples ames* appeared in translation anonymously, thereby shedding the name of a heretic, but also of a woman.[186]

This medieval practice of expropriating women authors is not unknown in modern scholarship. Without wishing to disparage his learning Newman has drawn attention to a continuity in Benton's work in minimising the patronage of Eleanor of Aquitaine and Marie de Champagne, in arguing that the correspondence between Abelard and Heloise was in fact the man's work, and that Trotula was not the author of the medical works attributed to her. Another example of what has been called a systematic elimination of women from the medieval corpus is Huchet, who has questioned the authorship of *trobairitz* (in favour of male lyric poets), Heloise and Marie de France.[187] Although this is no argument against their scholarship, one cannot help wondering about the psychological motivation of such sustained attempts. A weaker reflection of the same attitude can be found in the conventional titles given to some medieval works, excluding women characters. Dronke has pointed out how, despite Hrotsvitha's stress on women characters in her dramas, the titles given them by Conrad Celtis refer to men, and suggests that we revert to her practice. The same attitude informs Celtis's doubt about Hrotsvitha's authorship and its echoes in modern scholarship.[188]

Underlying this, and not confined to medieval sources, is an inclination towards criticising women's right or ability to compete on the literary scene. For example, when Mechthild von Magdeburg states her quandary (fearing God if she keeps silent and fearing men if she writes) she reveals in the latter fear her expectation of opposition to her writing as an untrained ('ungeleret') woman, while the assurance of her translator in the prologue to the *Revelationes* that there is after all nothing scandalous or offensive in her writing ('nullum scandalum . . . vel offendiculum') implies that there are others who might read it in that light.[189] Much more explicit is Gerson's full-scale attack on women visionaries (he has above all Bridget of

[185] *Lavision*, p. 143. Christine: Ferrante, *Glory*, pp. 177, 208, 263, n. 5.
[186] Christine: Newman, *God*, p. 315. Marguerite: Johnson, *Speculum* 66 (1991), 827.
[187] Benton: Newman, *Woman*, pp. 48f., 263, n. 15. Huchet: Bruckner, *Speculum* 67 (1992), 867, fn. 10.
[188] *Writers*, p. 294, n. 11; Nagel, *Hrotsvit*, pp. 15f.; Bodarwé, *Sanctimoniales*, p. 89, fn. 17.
[189] Mechthild, *Licht* III 1 (p. 148), *Revelationes* II 436.

Sweden in his sights), denying them the right, by quoting Paul, to teach in public on the basis of their revelations, whether in speech or in writing ('seu verbo seu scripto'). If Gerson approves of Jerome's women friends, Paula and Eustochium, it is because they at least did not presume to write ('nulla [scripta] praesumpserunt'). The twofold reference to women writing shows that this is where their offence lies for him.[190]

Echoes of this attitude, questioning more women's ability than their actual right, can be heard in modern scholarship. Neumann's editorial work on Mechthild von Magdeburg did not stop him summing up her book as 'ein sehr fraulich unsystematisches Werk'. We may agree that it is unsystematic, but to add that that is very much like a woman gives the game away. Thali has assembled a collection of such judgments from past scholarship, including not merely 'naive', but such gems as 'sickly', 'pathological', 'hysterical' and even 'nymphomaniac'. On quite a different level, and concerning a different genre, Carl von Kraus argued that in *Minnesangs Frühling* woman's voice was detectable by its lack of artistry, although we are left uncertain how far this was his judgment or that of the male authors of the poems in question.[191]

Further general considerations to which we now turn can apply mostly to men as well as women, but more tellingly to the latter if we take into account the medieval conviction of their weakness (intellectual and ethical as well as physical) and their educational marginalisation. These considerations concern the demeaning use of diminutives to 'put these women authors in their place', women's self-deprecating admission of ignorance to suggest instead a higher source of inspiration, their claim to act as a medium for God's message, their ambiguous position, at once inferior, but also superior to the spiritual directors involved in their writing, and finally their writings as a form of public teaching, traditionally forbidden to their sex.

The weakness which medieval patriarchy imputed to women could theoretically be given a positive Christian interpretation going back to Paul's argument that God has chosen the foolish things of the world ('stulta mundi') to confound the wise ('sapientes'), the weak ('infirma') to overcome the strong ('fortia').[192] One common linguistic way of expressing a lowly status of weakness was to use a diminutive which, indicative of a general Christian truth, was applicable to men as well as women. A diminutive which in the eyes of the world was demeaning could therefore be used positively of or by men to convey their Christian humility. Hrabanus Maurus

[190] Gerson, *Oeuvres* IX 467f.; Newman, *God*, p. 289.
[191] Neumann, 'Beiträge', p. 226. Thali, *Beten*, pp. 50f., 57. Kraus, *Untersuchungen*, pp. 92, 168.
[192] I Cor. 1, 27.

sees himself as a little man ('homunculus') and his work as no more than little commentaries ('commentarioli'), just as a commentator on the Song of Songs refers to himself as a Cistercian monk of whatever little importance ('quantuluscumque').[193] Self-abasing diminutives of this type can also be used of women. Urban VI calls Catherine of Siena a little woman, but adds that he does not say this out of contempt for her, but in recognition that her fragile sex has proved itself stronger than men, a reversal of stereotypes which the diminutive is meant to highlight by contrast. Goscelin employs another religious diminutive of Eve ('Christi paupercula'), but with equally positive intent.[194]

More commonly a patriarchal view of women as insignificant or contemptible can be expressed by such diminutives. We have already come across examples of women heretics being dismissed in this way as 'little women' ('mulierculae') or of women at large branded as prone to heresy by the same diminutive,[195] but its use goes much further than this. In one of Hrotsvitha's dramas the pagan emperor, confident that no danger lies in the coming of mere women, dismisses them contemptuously with a double diminutive ('tantillarum adventus muliercularum'). Elsewhere, women can be disregarded because of their foolishness ('fatuitatem muliercularum'), their unserious levity ('leves mulierculae'), and by now we should not be surprised to find Gerson in this company, referring to the sex forbidden to teach in public as so many 'mulierculae'.[196] As an indication that the mentality using such negative diminutives dies hard Newman has seized upon DW Robertson referring patronisingly to Heloise, of all people, as 'poor Heloise' or even 'little Heloise'.[197]

It is this demeaning use of diminutives, putting women in their proper place, especially when they presume to think that in their lowly, ignorant state they can teach others, that some women writers seek to subvert by using these diminutives of themselves in a novel way. They do this either by irony (suggesting a discrepancy between the diminutives and the learning that informs their work) or by arguing, in the spirit of Paul's letter to the Corinthians, that their foolishness, a disqualification in the eyes of men, is what qualifies them in the eyes of God as fit to transmit his message to others. This they do either by word of mouth or in writing, and it is here

[193] Hrabanus: Coon, 'Word', p. 280. Commentator: Ohly, *Hohelied-Studien*, p. 188.
[194] Urban: Watt, *Secretaries*, pp. 26f. Goscelin, *Liber*, p. 104.
[195] See above, pp. 167f, 169. Cf. also p. 170.
[196] Hrotsvitha, *Passio (Sapientia)* I 3. I place in brackets the conventional name. Foolishness: Elisabeth von Schönau, *Visionen* 5, 7. Levity: PL 204, 185. Gerson, *Oeuvres* IX 467.
[197] Newman, *Woman*, p. 49.

that the express reference to both forms of communication by the critic Gerson is significant with regard to women as authors of written works.[198]

This subversion of the negative diminutive, amounting to an inversion of misogyny, is already to be found with Hrotsvitha, whose frequent use of diminutives has often been observed. She refers to herself in her prefaces as 'muliercula' and also to her writings with similar forms such as 'libellum', 'opusculum', 'aliquantulum tinnitum', 'dictatiuncula'.[199] If we juxtapose these examples with others where Hrotsvitha presents herself self-deprecatingly as a mere slave ('famula') or the last of the last ('ultima ultimarum'), all these terms suggest traditional Christian humility.[200] But in the years since Curtius we have learned that the stronger a traditional topos may be, the stronger will the effect be when it is unexpectedly overturned, as Dronke has established with Hrotsvitha. For him her topos of humility is 'almost presumptuous through sheer over-insistence', her declared inadequacy as a writer is undermined by a deliberate use of recherché terms, and her 'admission of weakness is inseparable from an impulse of self-assurance'.[201] All this makes of her use of diminutives as a modesty topos much more than simply a topos, as is best seen in her description of herself as 'muliercula', for this same word is used derisively by the pagan tyrant of the women who as Christian martyrs eventually defeat him. The words with which Hrotsvitha sums this up are significant: womanly weakness is victorious and manly force is confounded ('feminea fragilitas vinceret et virilis robur confusioni subiaceret').[202] In hagiographic tradition the conflict was between paganism and Christianity. It is that with Hrotsvitha, too, but to it she has added a contest between men and women in which womanly weakness emerges as strength.

Undermining of diminutives is also found with Hildegard von Bingen. She, too, uses them of herself in Christian humility, but with pointed reference to her feminine sex, stressing therefore her poor, small and weak form ('paupercula et imbecillis forma'), seeing herself as a poor little thing ('paupercula') and a simple person ('simplicem hominem'), but also as one whose lowly status is intrinsic to her softness as a woman ('paupercula mollis forma').[203] Without calling into question the genuineness of her Christian humility, we need to place these statements in two different contexts. On the one hand, such protestations of weakness and lowliness come from a visionary and author with an international reputation in her own

[198] See above, fn. 190, and below, p. 231.
[199] Details with Dronke, *Women*, pp. 72f., 74, 78; Ferrante, *Glory*, p. 179; 'Postures', p. 222.
[200] Wilson, *Hrotsvit*, p. 12.   [201] Dronke, *Women*, pp. 64, 66.   [202] 2. *Praefatio*, 5 (p. 234).
[203] *LDO*, p. 46; Ferrante, 'Scribe', p. 110; *Epistolarium*, ep. 217.

day, who has the ears of Pope and Emperor and takes them to task when she regards them as neglecting their duties, and who, far from the 'imbecillitas' patriarchally attributed to women, displays in her writings a wide knowledge of the philosophical and scientific thought of her day.[204] On the other hand, the combination of self-effacement (presented in diminutives) with self-assurance (displayed in her attitude towards the powerful of her day) is reminiscent of what Dronke saw in Hrotsvitha: an employment of diminutives to new ends.[205] In Hildegard's case, this is to show that a woman, weaker and lower in status, may yet be chosen by God to accomplish what men have failed to do.

Both these examples of women confronting current prejudices and establishing their status as writers have concerned Latin literature, so that it is fitting also to take account of a vernacular example. Safeguarding herself against ecclesiastical censure by protesting that she is no teacher, Julian of Norwich supports her claim by using not a diminutive, but a womanly modesty topos, apparently disqualifying her from any teaching function, for she is a weak, uneducated woman ('I am a woman, lewed, febille and freylle').[206] Here, too, the facts belie what the topos says for, as her editors have shown, Julian is anything but uneducated and ignorant and, far from not being a teacher, she teaches what God has taught her. He is the 'soverayne techere' and she maintains her duty to pass on what she has received from him.[207]

With another humility topos, an author's apology for not knowing anything of letters ('non cognovi litteraturam'), we touch upon what is often a particular aspect of womanly weakness, her apparent disqualification as an author. As we have just seen, Julian of Norwich couples her womanly weakness expressly with her uneducated ignorance ('lewed'), the former embracing the latter. As was the case with lowly status and weakness, the Christian revaluation of ignorance as opposed to worldly knowledge goes back to Paul, whose contrast of weakness with power also embraced one between the foolish and the wise and who elsewhere reinforces this with the saying that the letter kills, but the spirit gives life.[208]

In the wake of this Christian revaluation of worldly wisdom, not meant as gender-specific (even though regarded as more readily applicable to women), we find this topos used by and of men writers. It has been well studied in the case of Wolfram's statement in *Willehalm* that he has had no book education ('swaz an den buochen stêt geschriben/des bin ich künstelôs

---

[204] Cf. Meier, 'Eriugena', pp. 466–97; 'Scientia', pp. 89–141.   [205] Ferrante, *Glory*, p. 158.
[206] *Book* ST 6.   [207] See above, p. 155; Greenspan, 'Autohagiography', p. 222.
[208] I Cor. 1, 26–9; II Cor. 3, 6.

beliben' I have remained ignorant of what is written in books), but that what artistry he possesses comes from the gift of grace that inspires him ('wan hân ich kunst, die gît mir sin').[209] Although we have no concrete information about Wolfram's book education (he was certainly not as 'künstelôs' as he suggests), we do know that Veldeke's Latinity was good enough to enable him to cope with Virgil, as well as a French source, in composing his *Eneasroman* and in providing a vernacular version of the *Servatius* legend. This makes it significant that in his legend Veldeke presents himself, in a topos that goes against the facts, as *illitteratus* ('want ich ein sundech mensche bin,/ane maht ende ane sin,/ungeleret ende ungerecht' for I am a sinful man without ability and intelligence, unlearned and unjust)[210] so that, weak and uneducated like Julian of Norwich, he is as dependent on divine help from the saint as she was on God's teaching. This legendary conjunction of lack of learning and divine inspiration stands at the beginning of vernacular biblical literature in England as well as Germany: in the former with Bede's account of the miraculous gift of song to the illiterate Caedmon, in the latter with the parallel account in the *Praefatio* to the Old Saxon *Heliand* with its legendary details of an illiterate, but divinely called poet.[211] We also find the topos outside the legendary context: not merely in Wolfram's adaptation of the formula in his *Parzival* ('ine kan decheinen buochstap' I know nothing of letters), but also with the English Lollard Walter Brut, who claims equally 'non cognovi litteraturam', even though this is belied by his undeniable status as a *laicus litteratus*.[212]

We are more concerned with women writers who make this claim of themselves, likewise with a grain of salt, and for them we turn to three figures. Hrotsvitha, for example, deprecates her ability not merely by diminutives, but straightforwardly, referring to her ignorance ('inscientia') and weak capacity ('meum posse licet minime'), and if she uses diminutives to refer to her genius ('ingeniolum') and the grace she receives ('gratiola'), these diminutions present her literary activity from the point of view of a patriarchal society, while still suggesting, with a mixture of self-deprecation and self-assertion, that she does possess genius and does receive the gift of grace.[213] However revealing Hrotsvitha may be, the evidence for Hildegard von Bingen is even richer, with whom we find a contrast between lack of formal education and divine inspiration. A contemporary hagiographer

[209] *Willehalm* 2, 19–22; Ohly, *ZfdA* 91 (1961/62), 1–37; Eggers, 'Litteraturam', pp. 162–72.
[210] *Servatius* 183–5, 193–8.
[211] Caedmon: Bede, *Historia* IV 24. *Heliand* ('Versus de poeta'): Haubrichs, *Anfänge*, p. 274.
[212] *Parzival* 115, 27. Brut: Hudson, 'Laicus', p. 225.
[213] Ferrante, *Glory*, p. 177; Dronke, *Women*, p. 82.

says that, although not trained in letters ('nullis litteris . . . erudita') except in the Psalms (and we know how elementary that could often be), she produced great volumes under instruction by the Holy Ghost ('per Spiritum sanctum edocta'). Hildegard also resembles Caedmon in the plainsong she composed, making a point of saying that she was not taught this and acquired this gift not by human intelligence but from God, and we shall see that she makes a similar claim for miraculously acquiring an understanding of Latin. Hildegard sums this up, contrasting the absence of external with the presence of internal (spiritual) teaching, with a pointed opposition between *indoctus* and *docta* ('homo sum indoctus de ulla magistratione cum exteriori materia, sed intus in anima mea sum docta').[214] It is possible that, in wishing to stress divine inspiration, Hildegard played down the extent of her education by the recluse Jutta who seems to have conducted a *schola* in literacy not confined to the Psalter.[215] In doing this Hildegard, like others who used this topos of ignorance, could rely on established precedents, for Augustine had conceded that, as if by a Whitsun miracle, understanding of the scriptures could be attained without literacy ('sine ulla scientia litterarum') and more recently Peter Damian had made the same point ('cui sensus incolumis est, litteras non requirit').[216] Although this argument was not gender-specific, its undervaluation of a formal education from which women were largely debarred must have had an attraction for them. This appeal to divine inspiration could invite a potentially dangerous gender-specific response, as when Robert of Basevorn, arguing in 1322 against unauthorised preaching, makes special mention of women and adds that it is not enough to argue commission by God, for that is what heretics say.[217]

This was not a danger faced by Hildegard, but it was by Mechthild von Magdeburg. She not merely proclaims her (Latin) illiteracy ('wan ich der schrift ungeleret bin'), but sees herself in this unlearned state as a receptacle for inspiration over against those whose learning comes from the schools ('. . . das der ungelerte munt die gelerte zungen von minem heligen geiste leret' that the unlearned mouth teaches the learned tongue through my Holy Ghost). Mechthild faces a quandary, commanded by God to pass on her revelations, yet fearing the result (as a beguine, lacking the authorisation enjoyed by Hildegard) if she writes ('Nu vôrhte ich got, ob ich swige, und

---

[214] Hagiographer: *Vita S. Gerlaci, AASS* Jan. I 309; Newman, 'Hildegard', p. 23. Plainsong: *Vita Sanctae Hildegardis* II 2 (p. 24). *Indoctus*: PL 197, 190.
[215] Newman, 'Hildegard', p. 197, n. 18.   [216] Ohly, *ZfdA* 91 (1961/62), 9, 10f.
[217] Blamires and Marx, *JML* 3 (1993), 45.

vórhte aber unbekante lúte ob ich schribe' I now fear God if I remain silent, but fear people lacking in understanding if I write).[218]

These are not the only examples of women writers, disqualified as such in the eyes of the world by their ignorance, claiming a higher qualification for themselves: Ekbert presents Elisabeth von Schönau as apparently disqualified by lack of education and by ignorance how to speak, but makes pointed reference to two Old Testament prophets (Moses, Jeremiah) who were similarly reluctant because of slowness of speech. He thereby insinuates a similar divine command for Elisabeth's prophetic function.[219] Thomas of Cantimpré says of the saintly nun Lutgard that, although outwardly she was uneducated and simple, her wisdom was enough to make himself appear stupid.[220] We must also take it as assumed modesty when Julian of Norwich presents herself as a simple, unlettered creature, an uneducated woman, for this is amply belied by her acquaintance with the Bible and exegetical tradition, and her command of rhetoric. But to draw attention away from the education lying behind this is, as with Hildegard, a way of emphasising that what she writes comes, as she says, from the sovereign teacher.[221] The common view of women's inferior intellect, together with their exclusion from formal education, informs the reaction of the steward of Leicester to his questioning of Margery Kempe, for he assumes that she must therefore be supernaturally inspired, either by God or by the devil.[222]

If a woman religious writer qualified herself as such by claiming inspiration from above, this confronted her with another difficulty, for it had the anomalous effect of disqualifying her, in her own eyes if not always in ours, as an author. Provided that she escape the kind of objection raised by Robert of Basevorn, a woman who affirmed that she wrote at God's command or at the command of her confessor could hope to validate her work, as attested for Mechthild von Magdeburg.[223] The essential point is not so much that the woman is commanded to write, but that she is to write what God speaks, not what she has to say. To see this we may revert to Elisabeth von Schönau, for to her reluctance to speak the Lord is reported, with an allusion to Luke 10, 16, as replying: 'Open your mouth and I shall speak, and whoever hears you hears me too' ('Aperi os tuum, et ego dicam, et qui audit te, audit et me'). Mechthild von Magdeburg

---

[218] Mechthild, *Licht* II 26 (p. 138), III 1 (p. 148).   [219] Clark, 'Woman', pp. 41f.

[220] *Vita Lutgardis, AASS* Jun. IV, I 1, 15; Coakley, *CH* 60 (1991), 457.

[221] *Book* ST 6, LT 2; Johnson, *Speculum* 66 (1991), 831f.; Greenspan, 'Autohagiography', pp. 221f.

[222] *Book* 3743f. (p. 231); Watt, *Secretaries*, pp. 38f.

[223] *Licht* IV 2 (pp. 236, 238). Cf., more generally, Dillon, 'Women', p. 137. Robert: see above, p. 225.

similarly disclaims authorship for herself in saying that her book comes from God and not from human thought ('menschlichen sinnen').[224] The Benedictine nun Umiltà of Faenza justifies her preaching in similar terms, saying that her prophetic words are not her own, but come from God.[225] Hildegard von Bingen gives us the most explicit formulation of her role as a medium, acting as God's voice and conveying what he tells her. In her *LDO* she describes God's command, telling her expressly not to write anything according to her own opinion ('Itaque scribe ista non secundum cor tuum, sed secundum testimonium meum') and not to invent anything ('nec per te inventa'). This passage is meant to highlight Hildegard's humble function as a mere medium and to exclude her from any authorial role, restricting her to being no more than God's scribe or secretary.[226] Even this diminished role, pictorially present in the Lucca miniature in which Hildegard records her divine revelations in temporary form on wax tablets, is taken one step further in another pictorial example, concerning Bridget of Sweden, from Marienbaum, a Bridgettine house near Xanten. A miniature in a manuscript from there is divided into two registers: in the upper one Christ in heaven hands down to Bridget a text which she receives with one hand and simultaneously passes on with the other further down to two clerics, whilst in the lower register these two men present the book to royalty. Here Bridget's role as a medium is seen simply in terms of her handing on a celestial text, her function as a writer (let alone a composer or inventor) has been visually excised altogether. In different ways both Hildegard and Bridget are presented as non-authors and it cannot even be claimed that they are co-authors with God. The one acts as his secretary, the other literally, and more drastically, as his 'Handlangerin'. That this denial of authorship was not gender specific can be seen from the remark of Honorius Augustodunensis that the Holy Ghost was the author (*auctor*) of the Song of Songs and Solomon the writer (*scriptor*).[227]

It is not only from God's authority that the scope for women's religious authorship can be restricted, for the command to write can also come from their spiritual director, as is clear from Mechthild von Magdeburg.[228] Accordingly, with regard to the pastoral authority the director may have exercised over the woman and also because whenever he functioned as scribe

---

[224] Elisabeth, *Visionen*, p. 33; Clark, 'Woman', pp. 41f. Mechthild, *Licht* IV 2 (p. 238).
[225] *Vita S. Humilitatis, AASS* May V 213.   [226] *LDO*, p. 45.
[227] Lucca: see Fig. 1. Bridget: see Fig. 14 and *Krone*, pp. 465–7. Honorius: PL 172, 347f. and Graf, *Bildnisse*, p. 12.
[228] *Licht* IV 2 (pp. 236, 238).

or redactor he could act in a 'nihil obstat' manner, it has been questioned in many cases how far we may be confronted with a male-authored view, rather than direct access to the women's voice. Such doubts, put forward in their most sceptical form by Peters, have been criticised by many, most recently by Bynum,[229] but there is no denying that these clerics may have also had personal or institutional interests in mind which could have affected their version of a woman's text or, in the case of a *vita* written by them, their picture of a holy woman. In such cases, as opposed to what we saw in the last paragraph, co-authorship (between man and woman) can be entertained, restricting from a different angle the latter's authorial role. There is no doubt that these clerics exercised spiritual authority over the women in their care. Ekbert's biographer makes it clear that with Elisabeth he put into writing what he felt to be appropriate, but omitted other things, and the hagiographer of Beatrice of Nazareth, although presenting his work as a translation of her vernacular notes, admits to rhetorically 'colouring' his Latin version.[230] The Latin preface to Mechthild von Magdeburg's German text makes it clear that a particular picture of a woman visionary is promoted from a male Dominican viewpoint. Behind all this lie different interests which the confessor had in promoting his picture of a woman visionary: to enhance the reputation of his order (most frequently the Dominicans), of a region (such as Prussia in the case of Dorothea von Montau) or even his own personal advancement. In all such cases the appropriation of a woman for possible canonisation cannot be excluded as a driving motive.

The privileged position of these women, it has been observed, introduces ambiguity into the friars' authority over them, amounting to a qualification of the extent they could colour their presentation and even raising the question 'Who leads whom?'.[231] We have seen Thomas of Cantimpré's sense of inferiority to Lutgard's (uneducated) wisdom, but Guibert of Gembloux is no less convinced of the same with Hildegard von Bingen, for he repeatedly turns to her with his questions as a theological authority.[232] This means that, contrary to what we saw in the last paragraph, some of these women are by no means devoid of control over the text for whose final form they may be dependent on clerical assistance. The revision of her text by Julian of Norwich, ranging over years from a short to a long text, suggests that she paid attention to the way in which it was drawn up, and the same is

[229] Peters, *Erfahrung* (and also her pupil, Bürkle, *Literatur*). Bynum: *Krone*, pp. 120–5. Cf. also Poor, *Mechthild*, pp. 6–12.
[230] Emecho, *Vita Eckeberti*, pp. 448f.; Clark, 'Woman', p. 37. *Vita Beatricis*, prologue (p. 14); Wiberg Pedersen, 'In-carnation', pp. 64f.
[231] Coakley, *CH* 60 (1991), 450; Elm, 'Stellung', p. 16.   [232] Guibert, *Epistolae*, ep. 19–21, 23–5.

likely with Margery Kempe (the length of time she spent with her scribes over the text suggests her awareness of what was in it in her name).[233]

Two other cases go much further in illustrating how far these women writers could exercise control over what was written for them by others. For the first case we go back to Hildegard's statement of her role as God's medium for his message, for to God's injunction that she is not to insert any inventions of her own into what he has said to her she adds that this applies equally (or even more?) to other people ('nec per alium hominem praemeditata'). This is reflected in her insistence that Volmar, in producing a final version, confine his corrections only to grammatical points in her imperfect Latin, and his caution about her censorship in this ('censoris eius cautelam exhibens').[234] All this suggests that Hildegard saw to it that no one tampered with what she regarded not as her text, but as God's. If God's command to her deprives her of any role as an author, it equally denies any part to others to exercise control over her text as co-authors. Co-authorship in which the man's role is as much circumscribed as was Volmar's is found with Angela of Foligno and her scribe, who does not shrink from showing how she regarded his shortcomings. He reports that she often rejected his Latin translation of what she had dictated to him in Italian, when he read it back to her, complaining that his words distort her meaning.[235] This example illustrates how a clerical translator felt at liberty to make his own alterations, but also that some of these women, whether we call them writers or authors, were still able to maintain control over their (or God's) text.

A further obstacle to their authorship which women had to overcome can be traced back to Paul. His remarks on two occasions prohibiting women from speaking cover a number of points.[236] The prohibition concerns speaking on religious matters in public (in church), it is equated with teaching and usurpation of authority over men, to whom they should instead be obedient and from whom they should learn at home. Although theoretical distinctions could be made in the Middle Ages between teaching and preaching, in practice Paul's *docere* was used as the wider term to embrace preaching, so that Chaucer, for example, can talk about Cecilia's activity, using both 'teche' and 'preche'.[237] The fact that the Pauline statements concerned religious knowledge imparted in church made this equation all

---

[233] Julian and Margery: Johnson, *Speculum* 66 (1991), 829, 835. Margery: Watson, 'Making', p. 400.

[234] *LDO*, p. 45; Ferrante, 'Scribe', p. 109. Volmar: *ibid.*, pp. 103, 108f.

[235] Arnold, *Libro*, pp. 170–4; Newman, 'Hildegard', p. 29; Coakley, *CH* 60 (1991), 458.

[236] I Cor. 14, 34f.; I Tim. 2, 12.

[237] Blamires and Marx, *JML* 3 (1993), 39f. Chaucer, *Second Nun's Tale* 342f.

the more understandable. From the twelfth century with the rise of the Waldensian heresy which allowed women the right to preach this problem became a matter for urgent debate amongst orthodox theologians. What caused them difficulty was the fact that in Christian tradition there were women saints who had been preachers and acknowledged as such.[238] Since Mary Magdalene had been the first to see and report the risen Christ to the apostles she came to be known as the apostle of the apostles, but hagiography developed this further, taking her to Marseilles, where she preached ('praedicare') to the pagans and converted them. The other precedent concerns public debate rather than preaching (but still goes against Paul's prohibition), for Cecilia and Catherine were recognised hagiographically as having defeated unbelievers in disputes with pagan philosophers. Somehow these precedents had to be accommodated with the official prohibition and this was done by arguing that, although not sent by a prelate to authorise them, these women had been sent by the Holy Ghost ('missae a Spiritu Sancto').[239] This is a form of argument which parallels what we have seen with women's educational shortcomings, where the problem was similarly side-stepped by moving from the human to the metaphysical.

These two precedents open the door to possible exceptions. One way of accounting for these exceptions was to appeal to a lack of priests in the early Church or the need to deal with the failings of clerics, as is implied by Hildegard's *muliebre tempus*, a degenerate age in which women had to step in where men had failed.[240] This does much more than explain how Hildegard, casting off the Pauline stereotype, went on preaching tours in which she addressed the clergy; it also explains how she could contrast herself with wise men (clerics) guilty of vainglory, while she, like Moses, was sent to preach by God.[241] On her travels Margery Kempe can also be accused of teaching or preaching to the people. In Yorkshire the Archbishop accuses her of the former, while a cleric uses the latter term in upbraiding her for going against Paul (who used only *docere*), an accusation met by Margery by the literalist claim that she never entered a pulpit.[242] Clearly, in the eyes of some a woman preaching was dangerously close to heresy, especially after a Lollard rising in 1414.

So far, the possibility of a woman preaching or teaching in public may have seemed remote from a woman writing, but we approach the latter if we

---

[238] Blamires, *Viator* 26 (1995), 142–5; Kerby-Fulton, 'Women', pp. 31–55.

[239] *Ibid.*, p. 148 and fn. 65.

[240] Blamires and Marx, *JML* 3 (1993), 40; Blamires, *Case*, p. 193; Bériou, 'Right', pp. 138f.; Kerby-Fulton, 'Women', pp. 38, 41, 52, n. 21.

[241] Hildegard, *Epistolarium*, ep. 103 R, 44–52; Ferrante, 'Scribe', p. 104.

[242] *Book* 4194f. (p. 251); 4210–13 (p. 253); Blamires, *Viator* 26 (1995), 150.

recall a point made in the first section of this chapter, where the activity of a copyist (frequently carried out by women) was termed a silent preaching ('muta predicatio').[243] If one meaning of the verb *scribere* (to act as a scribe) can be seen in that light, there is no difficulty in conceiving the same for its other meaning (to compose a work). There are several indications that preaching could be seen as carried out by word of mouth or in writing. Hildegard illustrates this well, for Guibert of Gembloux defends her public teaching, but refers to her writings ('scriptis') and to her books and sermons ('libris et sermonibus'). Meister Eckhart, in meeting the objection that he was teaching the unlearned (and therefore employing their vernacular), refers not just to teaching, but specifically to writing ('. . . sô enmac nieman lêren noch schrîben' thus no one can teach or write). Like Guibert, but with a critical intention aimed specifically against women, Gerson refers to women teaching orally and in writing and is suspicious of both, arguing that every teaching by women, in speech or writing, is to be suspected and tested more rigorously than the teaching of men.[244] If one of the points in Paul's prohibition was that women should not teach in public, it could be argued that the situation he had in mind (by word of mouth in a church) was made far worse in the context of writing, which made it possible for their teaching to spread much further, to be made public or to be 'published' far beyond the walls of a building. This was the case with the spread of continental women's visionary and mystical literature in translation to late medieval England or, in a narrower geographical context, with the transposition of Mechthild von Magdeburg's work into Latin and into High German.[245] It is this spread of her work, if not its actual translation, that Mechthild herself had in mind when she asked God to reward 'his scribe' who would copy out this work after her ('. . . dinen schriber, der das bůch na mir habe geschriben').[246] Mechthild teaches far more publicly than was ever anticipated by Paul and in a manner which implied, even if it was not intended, a challenge to priestly privilege.[247]

After this survey of the difficulties facing women authors we may consider a handful of specific examples, women writing in Latin and the vernacular, on secular and religious themes. Comments are confined to what is known of their education, literacy and position between Latin and the vernacular, but include signals to what may have particularly interested them and

---

[243] See above, p. 189.
[244] Guibert, *Epistolae*, ep. 18, 240–55. Eckhart, *Deutsche Werke* V 60. Gerson: Brown, *Pastor*, p. 223; Blamires and Marx, *JML* 3 (1993), 47.
[245] Continental literature: Voaden (ed.), *Prophets*.   [246] *Licht* II 26 (p. 138).
[247] Blamires and Marx, *JML* 3 (1993), 46; Dillon, 'Women', pp. 128f.

distinguished them from male authors. We have already in passing looked at several examples, such as the Latin women poets of the Loire valley, and in the vernacular Frau Ava, Clemence of Barking, Julian of Norwich, and Mechthild von Magdeburg. In the following pages our Latin women authors include Hrotsvitha, Hildegard von Bingen, Elisabeth von Schönau (all with religious works, although the first two also deal with a secular subject) and for authors in the vernacular we look at Marie de France, Mechthild von Magdeburg (but now from a different point of view) and the southern German sister-books (Marie composed one religious work alongside her secular products, the others deal with religious themes).

Our first example of women writing in Latin is Hrotsvitha von Gandersheim. She is one of the many literate women, secular or religious, of the Ottonian period, more noticeably interested in learning than their menfolk. Her community is likewise one of several active in matters of literacy, of which Gandersheim, Quedlinburg and Essen, recently studied in depth, are the most noteworthy, but not the only examples.[248] Hrotsvitha stands out as the leading woman author of the early Middle Ages by the sheer range of her output, including eight legends, six dramas modelled in competition with the comedies of Terence, and two histories, all intended for her own community (and the *Gesta Ottonis* for the court?). Unsurprisingly with a woman author writing for a predominantly female audience her works have a pronouncedly feminine slant. This is most obvious in the legends in which it would be short-sighted to see the virgin martyrs as no more than victims of misogyny, rather than as triumphant over their male persecutors, as we have seen in the overturning of the diminutive *mulierculae* and explicitly in the *Praefatio* to the dramas.[249] Hrotsvitha uses the diminutive *muliercula* of herself, but also has the pagan tyrant use it contemptuously of the women who are about to defeat him. It is not just their chastity or religious conviction that brings them victory, but also their intellectual and ethical superiority. This equation of the author, a self-confessed *muliercula*, with the ultimately triumphant so-called *mulierculae* suggests that Hrotsvitha did not regard herself demeaningly any more than she did the women characters in her dramas. In other words, she does much more than show sympathy with these women characters, she also undoes the conventional view about women's weakness by showing it to be a misreading of their inner strength, capable of overcoming men's brute force.[250] That this is

---

[248] McKitterick, *EME* 2 (1993), 67f., and especially Bodarwé, *Sanctimoniales* (on Hrotsvitha, pp. 303–15).

[249] See above, p. 222; 2. *Praefatio* 5 (p. 234).

[250] Blamires, *Case*, pp. 154, 158; Dronke, *Women*, p. 78; Ferrante, 'Postures', pp. 223f.

true of Hrotsvitha's work at large has been suggested as her aim in displaying thematically women's strength in three of the categories in which they were conventionally placed (virgin, wife, prostitute). It has been proposed that in so widening the feminine scope of her writing (embracing author, recipients and characters) Hrotsvitha was perhaps presenting 'an ideal of feminine bonding, sceptical of men'.[251] Her references to women's weakness and her use of the diminutives that enshrine this view must be seen as highly ambiguous.[252] One way in which this finds expression and which we have encountered elsewhere in virginity literature is the resistance of women to the idea of marriage, as with Constantia in the drama *Gallicanus* and with Agape, Chloria and Hirenia in the *Passio (Dulcitius)*, where the plot concerns the attempt to impose conversion, but also marriage on these three sisters. Rejection of marriage may be an obvious topos of virginity literature, but Hrotsvitha gives it renewed force by combining it with the dubious role played by men.

Scepticism about men and solidarity with women are not enough to make of Hrotsvitha a feminist or even a protofeminist (just as many feminists have reservations about including Heloise or Christine de Pizan in their canon), but they suggest that she was profeminine. Blamires includes her in his 'case for women' in medieval culture, above all because her argument goes beyond the particular cases she treats and has 'broader objections to dismissive misogynous stereotyping'. For Blamires this is apparent in the last of her dramas, in the female solidarity, the communal voice of women against male oppression.[253] If we follow him in seeing amongst these women characters a sense of sisterhood, moreover one shared by the author and the feminine audience she addressed, this might explain how it was that the only comprehensive manuscript of her writings was preserved in the women's community at St Emmeram, Regensburg, where Hrotsvitha's abbess Gerberga had been educated.[254]

Solidarity of another kind amongst women and a focus on their role rather than men's can be found in *Maria*, the first of Hrotsvitha's legends.[255] Here it is a case of showing not that women's weakness is in fact strength of a different kind, but rather that they show themselves superior to men, a different subversion of antifeminine stereotyping which will occupy us in the companion volume (with the interesting variation there that the works in question are male-authored). Hrotsvitha's legend deals with the birth and youth of Mary and employs a double contrast between the sexes. On

---

[251] Blamires, *Case*, pp. 158f.   [252] Dronke, *Women*, p. 66.
[253] Blamires, *Case*, pp. 154–9 (quotation p. 157).
[254] *Ibid.*, p. 231. Dronke, *Women*, p. 83.   [255] Ferrante, *Glory*, p. 180.

the one hand, Mary and her mother Anne are praised for their devotion by contrast with the arrogance of the priests and the shortcomings of their husbands, both of whom have difficulties, not shared by their wives, in dealing either with taunts for sterility or with an unexpected pregnancy. Moreover, the royal status conferred on Mary in this legend is attributed to her descent through her parents from David, not as in the gospels through Joseph, her husband. We saw that this was also the case with Otfrid, but that does not mean that the Carolingian poet was endeavouring to elevate women above men. Instead, Otfrid utilised the dominant conception of Christ as king as an opportunity to depict Mary, reading her Psalter at the Annunciation, like any royal or aristocratic lady of his day. For Hrotsvitha the opportunity presented was quite different.

The sense of superiority to men conferred by Hrotsvitha on virgin martyrs and on Anne and Mary can also be detected in her self-awareness as an author, even though any comparison with men in her case may only be implicit, correcting men's patriarchal dismissive view of women's abilities. This was accomplished by her overturning of negative diminutives, but one of the ways to do this was to go against their surface meaning. Contrary to the stance of self-abasement she implies, she is quite prepared to show that she does possess literary skill. In her epistle to the *sapientes* who may judge her work she expresses satisfaction that they acknowledge that she has some knowledge of the arts ('arbitrantes mihi inesse aliquantulam scientiam artium') and has surpassed what might be expected of a woman's ability ('muliebre ingenium').[256] The crucial point is that she has done better than these *sapientes* expected from a woman and that what she refers to elsewhere as her *inscientia* is here replaced by *scientia*, qualified somewhat only by *aliquantulam*, just as likewise *ingenium* takes over from what is elsewhere merely *ingeniolum*. In praising these *sapientes* for their superior judgment she is of course indirectly praising herself as the author of whose work they approve. Ferrante has illustrated how virtually every pose of humility is countered by an opposing assertion which converts the negative into a positive.[257] But, as she adds, Hrotsvitha's best defence of her undertaking is to claim God's support for it. At the beginning of the legend *Maria* she compares herself with the ass whom God made speak, but more positively with Mary's conception of Christ, but sees herself equally as informed and instructed by God, who loosens her tongue ('Si placet, ipse meam potis est dissolvere linguam').[258] In arguing on behalf of her

---

[256] *Epistola eiusdem ad quosdam sapientes* 3 (p. 235).
[257] *Glory*, pp. 177f.   [258] *Ibid.*, p. 178; *Maria* 29–37 (p. 49).

poetic composition Hrotsvitha is suggesting that her talent as an author comes to her from God. She may not see herself as a passive medium for God's words, so that she can still justifiably be termed an author in her own right, but she claims instead that her ability to speak is a gift of God. With her at least there is no conflict between what she had learned in the school (her knowledge of Latin and classical literature) and what she receives from God, no playing down of the one in favour of the other.

The range of literary activity of Hildegard von Bingen is even greater than that of Hrotsvitha. This astonishing polymath was responsible not only for visionary and mystical writings, but also for a variety of other subjects, including the composition of poetry and music, but she was also active as a playwright and author of a medical encyclopaedia. My use of the word 'author' in this latter context, as distinct from her own statements about her responsibility for divinely inspired writings, shows that she occupies a divided position in this section: a medium or secretary of God on the one hand, but also an author on the other. In the latter works she writes in her own words and with personal authority (hence authorship),[259] so that acting as a medium for God in some works does not exclude her role as author in others. In all her works Hildegard writes in Latin, even though she may rely on clerical assistance to improve it grammatically (but is resistant, as long as possible, to stylistic embellishment). This confronts us with the question of what is reported as her miraculous acquisition of Latin, even though she says her education at the hands of a recluse had taught her no more than the Psalms, with little grammatical comprehension.[260] This linguistic miracle parallels what Hildegard claims for her musical ability: in her *vita* she says that, untaught by any human being, she acquired the gift of composition and plainsong from God.[261] Divine inspiration of this nature is no peculiarity of Hildegard's and is reported of men as well as women, although women's educational marginalisation made it more apposite to them. Two examples must suffice to illustrate this.[262] In the Latinate community of Unterlinden Tuda von Colmar is enabled by divine grace to understand scripture even though she had never been taught by anyone ('. . . persensit sanctarum intelligenciam litterarum, cuius ante omnino ignara erat, nec ab homine aliquando litteras didicerat'). With reference to the vernacular, it is similarly said of Mechthild von Wangen at

---

[259] Ferrante, 'Scribe', p. 108.
[260] *Scivias*, preface (p. 3). Cf. also Millett, 'Women', pp. 90, 101 (n. 24).
[261] *Vita* II 2 (p. 24). On the status of Hildegard's autobiographical writings see Klaes, *Vita*, pp. 17*–156*.
[262] These and others are given by Ochsenbein, 'Latein', p. 46. Further examples: Ehrenschwendtner, *Bildung*, pp. 109, fn. 213, 126, 129, 130f., 132; Newman, 'Thoughts', pp. 234f.

St Katharinental that she never learned Latin or how to write, yet wrote in German with her own hand ('gelernet nie latin noch schriben und schreib doch die vier passion in tútsch mit ir hant').[263] In the case of Hildegard we are to assume that if, as she says, she wrote as God spoke to her, then God's Latin must be as 'simple' as hers (*sermo humilis*) and that he did not speak as the philosophers do. Like others of whom a similar claim is made, Hildegard's inspiration from above is contrary to and replaces human instruction, or at least plays it down, as when she minimises the extent of the education she received from Jutta.[264] In order to side-step Paul's injunction by arguing for her inspiration she therefore maintains that, other than the Psalms, she had been given no formal education ('indoctus de ulla magistratione cum exteriori materia'), but had been taught internally in her soul ('sed intus in anima mea sum docta'), even though there are grounds for thinking that Jutta's instruction was not so elementary as this implies.[265] These two points are combined in Hildegard's description of her miraculous inspiration when the heavens opened and she understood the whole range of scriptures, for to this is added the observation that the woman who had taught her had herself little literary knowledge.[266]

By arguing in terms of inspiration from above Hildegard is enabled to maintain that she writes on the command of God. Subject to the tests or suspicions advocated by Robert of Basevorn or Gerson, women visionaries who were granted prophetic status, as was Hildegard, were allowed a voice that would be listened to because of the source from which it ultimately came, especially when accompanied by a 'Schreibbefehl', an injunction not to keep the vision to themselves, but to publicise or pass it on for the benefit of others. In doing this in her writings, and on her preaching tours, Hildegard diverges most pointedly from Paul's view on women teaching, which may account for Guibert de Gembloux justifying this by the exemption granted by her being instructed by the spirit and, more pointedly, calling her, like Paul himself, a chosen vessel ('vas electionis').[267] Similarly, Theoderic of Echternach confirms Hildegard's prophetic status by comparing her with the Old Testament prophetess Deborah, whilst Hildegard repeatedly likens herself to other Old Testament precedents, male as well as female (Joshua, Joseph, Job, Jeremiah, Jonah, but also Susanna).[268] Nor does she stop short of comparing herself, more explicitly with her prophetic role in mind, with Moses and John the Evangelist, leading prophets of the Old

---

[263] Unterlinden: *Vitae Sororum*, p. 49. St Katharinental: *Schwesternbuch*, p. 121.

[264] Newman, 'Hildegard', p. 197, n. 18.   [265] *Epistolarium* I (p. 4).   [266] *Vita* II 2 (p. 24).

[267] *Epistolae* 18 (p. 232) and 22 (p. 249).   [268] *Vita* II 6 (p. 30); Newman, 'Hildegard', p. 24.

and New Testaments.[269] Legitimation of Hildegard's position by biblical precedent is taken a daring step further by Guibert, when he addresses her in terms from the angelic greeting laden with religious import: 'Hail, full of grace after Mary, the Lord is with you, blessed are you among women, and blessed the speech of your mouth' ('Ave, ergo, post Mariam gratia plena, Dominus tecum, benedicta tu in mulieribus, et benedictus sermo oris tui'). Not merely does her admirer compare Hildegard with Mary (but safeguards himself by inserting the words 'post Mariam'), he also replaces the biblical 'fruit of your womb' with 'the speech of your mouth'. By that substitution he suggests a comparable role for both women, the one giving birth to the Son of God (the Logos), the other giving expression to the word of God, directly communicated to her.[270]

The care to justify her position taken by Hildegard and the men who support her probably results from the tension felt by any woman in her situation (as is also evident with Mechthild von Magdeburg) between God's command to write (and thereby teach or preach) and the opposition she can expect to any woman publicly teaching men, including clerics. In this woman's case teaching was indeed synonymous with preaching, whether in writing or in her public preaching widely in Germany, a drastic gesture given the Pauline injunction and the Benedictine demand for *stabilitas loci*, especially on the part of nuns.

What may be called a gendered approach to Hildegard, involving not just the problems posed for her literacy and Latinity by restrictions on women's education, but also their right to speak publicly, can be justified by the attention she pays to the relations and differences between men and women. In this her views can be critical of men, as will be paralleled in the companion volume in the gendered discussion of this problem in court literature. Hildegard can invert an antifeminine stereotype (Adam, made from earth, is strong, but Eve, made from his flesh is soft and weak) by concluding that, not pulled down by the weight of earth, Eve's mind is sharper.[271] To the conventional view that man is to woman as soul is to body she gives a novel twist by saying that man signifies the divinity, woman the humanity of the Son of God ('Et vir divinitatem, femina vero humanitatem Filii Dei significat'), a telling stress at a time when incarnational theology, focusing on the humanity of Christ, was coming to the fore.[272] In arguing for equality in marriage she reformulates Paul's words arguing the superiority of the man ('For the man is not of the woman; but the woman of the man. Neither was

---

[269] Newman, 'Hildegard', p. 24. Moses: Graf, *Bildnisse*, pp. 106f.
[270] *Epistolae* 22, 18–20; Ferrante, '*Scribe*', pp. 123f.; Graf, *Bildnisse*, pp. 181–3.
[271] PL 197, 963; Cadden, *Meanings*, p. 75.   [272] *LDO*, p. 243; Cadden, *Meanings*, p. 191.

the man created for the woman; but the woman for the man'). Hildegard changes this in *Scivias*, saying instead that in marriage woman was created for the man and from the man, man for the sake of woman and from woman. ('Mulier propter virum creata est et vir propter mulierem factus est'.)[273] Finally, the visionary's choice of adjective to castigate her age as womanish[274] has often been interpreted as an internalisation on her part of a negative view of woman's weakness. This is to ignore the two-pronged nature of her criticism: her age is deficient because it is men who have become weak and effeminate, so that the tasks they have neglected now fall to women. Behind the internalised use of 'muliebris' to suggest weakness there stands a criticism of men, rather than women.

Our third example of a Latinate woman writer is Elisabeth von Schönau. Like so many women visionaries, her possible authorship was under pressure and even called into question from two angles. On the one hand, in a family relationship similar to Frau Ava's dependence on her sons, Elisabeth's education was less than that of her brother Ekbert, who had studied in Paris, so that, on abbot Hildelin's order, it was he who was to record her visions.[275] It was he who translated into Latin the revelations she had had in German, but proceeded very selectively in what he chose to set down. Although it may be possible to detect traces of Elisabeth's self-presentation as distinct from what her brother put forward,[276] we are still left with a collaborative enterprise or co-authorship in which the woman's role may not be expunged, but is still qualified. The position is more extreme when we turn to God's role in Elisabeth's visions. The command to write comes to her through a divine emissary, upbraiding her for keeping her revelations to herself and scourging her in punishment, but whether Elisabeth's writing as a result of this command can be called 'co-writing' is as dubious as the concept 'co-authorship' whenever God, as distinct from another human being such as Ekbert, is involved.[277] How little Elisabeth regarded herself as an author, rather than the vessel of God's words, is clear from her confession of slowness of speech ('nescio loqui, et tarda sum ad loquendum'), which recalls Moses and Jeremiah, whom God had likewise chosen to act on his behalf.[278] The disqualification of a woman for this task also rests on Elisabeth's lack of adequate Latin and education, ultimately meant to

---

[273] Paul: I Cor. 11, 8f. Hildegard: *Scivias* I ii, 11f. (p. 21); Cadden, *Meanings*, p. 193; Ferrante, *Glory*, p. 159.

[274] PL 197, 1005; Newman, *Sister*, pp. 138–40.   [275] Clark, 'Woman', p. 37.   [276] *Ibid.*, pp. 38f.

[277] Blamires, *Case*, p. 194 and fn. 99. 'Co-writing': Voaden, 'Women', pp. 57f. (cf. the title of her essay, p. 55).

[278] *Visionen*, p. 33; Clark, 'Woman', pp. 41f. Cf. Ex. 4, 10 and Jer. 1, 6.

establish her divine call to speak.[279] Ekbert is fully aware of an antifeminine resistance to the kenosis of God condescending to speak through a weak woman ('Hoc illos scandalizat, quod in his diebus plurimum in sexu fragili misericordiam suam dominus magnificare dignatur').[280] He conducts his counter-argument, as was the case with Hildegard, by adducing Old Testament female precedents (Huldah, Deborah, Judith, Jael and others) but, again like Hildegard, interprets these women as praiseworthily stepping into the breach where men had failed in their lethargy ('quando viris socordie deditis, spiritu dei replete sunt mulieres sancte, ut prophetarent').[281] With an example such as Deborah Elisabeth was following, but adapted to her own ends, the kind of remark made earlier by Ambrose that the Jews had chosen her to rule them at a time when the judges failed to govern them with manly justice or defend them with manly strength.[282] That, too, was a 'muliebre tempus', brought about by the weakness of men. It is not merely the case that Old Testament prophetesses are called upon to legitimise medieval women visionaries, for underlying this parallel is a gendered argument, the need for women to accomplish what men had neglected to do; to show that, in overcoming the indolence of men, women's weakness is really strength.

The first of our women authors in the vernacular is Marie de France. She occupies a unique position in the second half of the twelfth century as a woman writing mainly on secular themes in a vernacular in which the field was otherwise dominated by male authors.[283] She was aware of the competition this provoked, as is suggested by the care she takes to give her name as author to guard against men claiming her work as their own. For us Marie's position is unique within the gendered discourse of the twelfth century in providing a genuinely female voice to contrast with the predominance of male authors.[284] The sense of independence which Marie's position and competition with men forced upon her is reflected in the absence of the humble stance or self-deprecating diminutives in her work which we find in the spiritual writing of other women. She does not admit any ignorance of Latin (real or assumed), but instead lets us know that before writing her lais she had considered, but rejected, the possibility of translating from Latin into the vernacular (which in fact she did in her *Espurgatoire*).[285] She also betrays acquaintance with a Latin grammarian (Priscian) as well as Ovid. Subject to none of the authorial constraints imposed on religious women writers, Marie was conscious of herself as a

[279] Clark, 'Woman', p. 45.   [280] *Visionen*, p. 40; Clark, 'Woman', pp. 40f.
[281] *Visionen*, p. 40; Newman, *Sister*, p. 39; Blamires, *Case*, p. 193.   [282] Blamires, *Case*, p. 8.
[283] Krueger, 'Marie', p. 177.   [284] Baldwin, *Language*, p. 30.   [285] Green, *Beginnings*, p. 198.

writer, putting into written form themes from oral tradition and taking delight in doing so.[286] Here Marie regards writing in the sense of authorial composition, but the other meaning of *scribere*, putting a pen to parchment, is attributed to her in a miniature of the Arsenal manuscript, showing her at a desk in the act of writing.[287]

The female voice which Marie brings to the transmission of the *matière de Bretagne* is heard in her choice of themes and the point of view from which she treats them. Although the marginalisation of women characters in male-authored romances is not always as pervasive as has been maintained, Marie's lais grant them an undoubtedly central role, taking the initiative and displaying an independence and intelligence which well become their author. More revealing is the position from which we are allowed to see them putting these qualities into practice, for a recurrent theme with Marie is marriage, seen specifically from the woman's point of view. In this she has been compared with Heloise and with Marie de Champagne (at least as presented by Andreas Capellanus), for these two are also presented as fully aware of the constraints of feudal marriage and what they mean for women subjected to them with no choice in the matter.[288] Accordingly, a major theme in Marie's lais is the *mal mariée*, the unhappy lot of a woman caught in an unwanted marriage or denied the marriage she desires. Thus, a daughter can be refused marriage by a jealous father (*Les deux amanz*) or forced into a disastrous marriage by the father's choice (*Milun*) or handed over by her relatives to an old man (*Yonec*). These pictures of a variety of arranged marriages present a series of unhappy women, trapped in what feudal marriage practice meant in many cases. The symbol of these women's unhappiness is imprisonment, either literally in a castle, admittedly luxurious, but with a guarded exit (*Guigemar*, with a German parallel in Eilhart's *Tristrant*)[289] or in the form of close surveillance by a jealous husband (*Laüstic*). Given the recurrence of these unhappy arranged marriages there is no tale of happy love in Marie's lais, and it is in this divorce, even contradiction between love and marriage that she comes closest to Heloise's argument against marriage or to the dictum attributed to Marie de Champagne ('. . . amorem non posse suas inter duos iugales extendere vires').[290] With such themes in her lais and with this female approach to them we can understand why Denis Piramus, in describing

---

[286] Marie, *Milun* 535f.
[287] Ward, 'Fables', p. 196. See Fig. 2. On the pictorial presentation of Marie as author (not translator) see Hindman, 'Cock', pp. 47f.
[288] Baldwin, *Language*, p. 230.   [289] *Tristrant* 7916–39.
[290] Bloch, *Misogyny*, p. 172. Marie: Andreas, *De Amore*, p. 153.

the popularity of Marie's lais at court, stresses how much pleasure they gave to women. This also suggests why her *Fables* may have been kept in the libraries of women like Marie de Brabant and Marie d'Autriche.[291]

For our second example of a woman writer in the vernacular we come back to Mechthild von Magdeburg, looking at her afresh in the context of this section. In this light her significance lies in her use of the vernacular, a fact made clear from the beginning of her work ('. . . wart dis bůch geoffent in tůsche von gotte einer swester' this book was revealed by God to a sister in German) and from the reference in the Latin version to composition in a barbarous tongue.[292] Where the linguistic kenosis of God's revelation to Hildegard meant that he spoke to her in her own simple Latin, not in the language of philosophers, with Mechthild it goes a step further 'downwards', addressing her in her mother tongue. The novelty of this departure in using the vernacular lies in its contrast with the Latin visionary writings of women such as Hildegard von Bingen and Elisabeth von Schönau, but this novelty exists beyond the German language area, for a similar move had been made earlier in the thirteenth century, geographically and linguistically close to Mechthild's Low German, with Beatrice of Nazareth's and Hadewijch's use of Dutch.[293] These parallels confirm the novelty of Mechthild's choice of the vernacular, as does *ex negativo* the continued use of Latin at Helfta.

Although Mechthild may follow the instructions of her confessor (and God) in putting her revelations into written form, she does this herself and is not dependent on clerical assistance with Latin, as Hildegard and Elisabeth had been. In this sense the vernacular freed her from this degree of supervision, for the contribution of Heinrich von Halle appears not to have gone beyond organising the layout of what she had written. On the other hand, Mechthild's authorial role is restricted from another angle, for she resembles other women mystics in being not merely commanded by God to write, but acting as a conveyor of his message, not as a woman author in her own right. Acting as the chosen vessel of God's message is the time-honoured function and justification of prophets, an idea present in the mind of the author of the prologue to the Latin version when he referred to the Old Testament prophetesses Deborah and Huldah.[294] The comparison with what we have already seen goes further for, like Hildegard's criticism of her *muliebre tempus* and Mechthild's condemnation of abuses in her own day, these Jewish precedents from the fragile sex ('sexus fragilis') were likewise chosen so that the weak might confound the stronger ('Elegit

[291] Jambeck, 'Reclaiming', p. 136.   [292] *Licht*, p. 12; *Revelationes*, p. 437.
[293] Köbele, *Bilder*, pp. 33f.; Poor, *JMEMS* 31 (2001), 216–19 and *Mechthild*, pp. 17–56.
[294] *Revelationes*, pp. 435f.

namque persaepe infirma mundi omnipotens Deus ut fortiora salubriter erubescant').[295] The failure of (male) authority, both in the Jewish past and in the Christian present, is what triggers God's intervention, his choice of the weak to convey his message and hence the authorisation of their words.

With the so-called sister books of German Dominican convents as our last vernacular example we deal with a quite different type of literary authorship by women. They constitute a unity both geographically (southern Germany) and chronologically (from the first half of the fourteenth century, although often based on earlier tradition) and each book is made up of a series of short *vitae*, relating visionary and other religious experiences of nuns from the convent in question. Nine such compilations have come down to us, only one of which is in Latin (from Unterlinden). Compiled and added to over the years, with contributions by a series of authors or redactors and based on several texts originally written by different women, these books represent a form of collective authorship[296] (just as convents could also exercise a form of collective patronage). Even the most obvious suggestion of a named individual author (Elsbeth Stagel at Töss) has been seen as more peripheral to the production of 'her' book, as one of a number of layers in its compilatory genesis.[297] These books are interesting in the role played by women in them: they are the subject and the intended audience, but also the authors (in the special sense just mentioned). A monograph devoted to them therefore bears the title *By women, for women, about women*.[298] Although these books may contain a short outline of the foundation and early history of the community, the nuns' *vitae* are not historical themselves, since their concern is with the inner, spiritual life of the sisters they deal with, rather than external events in their lives.[299]

Another feature of this group of texts, distinguishing them from other religious writing by women in the vernacular, is the absence of any suggestion that their spiritual directors played any part in the production of these books which therefore, however collective their authorship may be amongst the nuns, cannot be described as co-authored by nuns and confessors.[300] The absence of the confessor from the process of writing these books, in other words the independence of the women writers, has been seen as a defining feature, so that the phrase 'by women' in the title of the monograph just quoted remains unimpaired.[301] Against the independent

---

[295] *Ibid.*   [296] Bürkle, *Literatur*, p. 237; Langer, *Mystik*, p. 293; *Krone*, pp. 112–14.
[297] Grubmüller, *ZfdA* 98 (1969), 171–204.   [298] Lewis, *Women*.
[299] Langer, 'Existenz', p. 51; Hubrath, *LiLi* 27, Heft 105 (1997), 31; Vassilevitch, 'Schwesternbücher', p. 224.
[300] Bürkle, *Literatur*, p. 264; Lewis, *Women*, p. 198.   [301] Peters, *Erfahrung*, p. 133.

authorship of these women which this appears to suggest must be set the fact that we are not dealing with individual or personal, but with collective authorship.

If we turn finally to another phrase in this same title ('for women'), it is to ask how the sisters for whom these books were intended received them, what kind of access they had to them. A telling indication is the use of the double formula in many of these books (thus, Anna von Munzingen, who copied the Adelhausen book in Freiburg, refers to those who read this book or hear it read).[302] This suggests, as elsewhere throughout medieval literature, that two forms of reception were regularly envisaged, personal reading and listening to the text read out (in the refectory or the chapter house).[303] This implies literacy on the part of these nuns (including the training of novices in the convent school, a series of readers to perform daily in the refectory, and private devotional reading).[304] The fact that all the sister books but one are written in German, rather than Latin, suggests a far from negligible move towards vernacular literacy by the fourteenth century.[305]

In addition to the six women writers we have considered others could easily be included (say, Dhuoda and the Latin production at Helfta or, in the vernacular, Christine Ebner, Elisabeth von Nassau-Saarbrücken and Christine de Pizan). If reasons of space have forced us to restrict ourselves to no more than six, this has the advantage of underlining the undeniable fact that, by comparison with men and also in contrast with women's frequency amongst readers, copyists, dedicatees and patrons, we find markedly fewer women writers. For this a number of reasons have been advanced.

In her study of women's literary practice in late medieval England Krug concludes by asking the pointed question why so few women, even literate ones like Margaret Beaufort and others who knew how to read and write, wrote texts which form part of a recognised literary tradition.[306] In asking this she aligns herself with the Wife of Bath and Christine de Pizan, so that the question is far from being posed only by modern feminists. To the extent that this was already a medieval question we must seek an answer in medieval conditions, where a number of explanations are possible. An obvious candidate is the marginalised position of women educationally. It is not enough to say (as does Krug) that many women could read and write, for literary composition was a learned activity in the Middle Ages, requiring

---

[302] *Adelhausener Schwesternbuch*, p. 192. For another example (Kirchberg), see above, p. 11, fn. 20.
[303] Ehrenschwendtner, *Bildung*, pp. 176–237.   [304] *Ibid.*, but also pp. 82–118.
[305] *Ibid.*, pp. 119–48 on the relationship between Latin and the vernacular.
[306] Krug, *Families*, pp. 207f.

a knowledge of rhetoric and poetics, hence a training in the liberal arts not available to most laywomen and by no means central to the predominantly spiritual education of nuns. Even when women received a literate education, there was a bias towards their learning to read, but not to write, as with the recommendation of the Chevalier de la Tour Landry that they need not learn to write.[307] As a result, women authors must have been aware that they were entering a male preserve and attempting to insinuate themselves into a literary tradition dominated by men, as the Wife of Bath and Christine make clear in complaining that women's 'bad press' is to be expected from a literature composed by men. This situation is reflected linguistically in the Latin terms *auctor* and *auctoritas*, implying that an author was someone to whom authority could be attributed not merely by the simple act of writing a work, but one which could be acknowledged as wise and truthful, conveying a lesson of value.[308] Such a view of an *auctor* put many medieval authors at a disadvantage by comparison with classical ones, but women in particular, whose subordinate position in patriarchal society removed them from much exercise of authority (intellectual or otherwise) and against whose active role in teaching the Pauline prohibition continued largely to hold sway. Such opinions could be internalised by women: even Margery Kempe, who eventually had her experiences put into writing, shrank from doing this at first when urged by the Bishop of Lincoln.[309] Newman has spoken of 'the female writer's perennial need for authorization', a need confirmed by Gerson's remark that the written revelations of women in particular have to be scrutinised with critical care.[310] That the reluctance to grant authority to women could amount to denial of their authorship and continue into modern scholarship is evident from the protracted debate over whether Heloise, rather than Abelard himself, was really the writer of her letters in their correspondence.[311] One way out of this quandary for women religious writers was to seek an alternative, higher authority by claiming that they were transmitting God's words, but we have seen, most decisively with Hildegard von Bingen, that this claim for authority amounted to a loss of their authorship in favour of God's. Loss of authorship (or at least of what we nowadays regard as individual authorship) also comes into play when we recall the collective composition of sister books, added to by individual writers over a period of time so that the resulting work cannot be attributed to any one author.[312]

---

[307] Krueger, 'Voices', p. 31.   [308] Minnis, *Theory*, pp. 10–12; Poor, *Mechthild*, Index, s.v. 'authority'.
[309] Kempe, *Book* 1066–75 (p. 105).   [310] Newman, *God*, p. 312. Gerson: see above, p. 231.
[311] Newman, *Woman*, pp. 46f.   [312] Thali, *Beten*, p. 58.

One of the reasons for the paucity of women authors adduced by Krug was their sense of subordination to all forms of male authority.[313] An example of this, reinforced by religious humility, is found in the Anglo-Norman *Vie d'Edouard le Confesseur* by an anonymous nun. The author withholds her name on purpose, revealing only that she is a nun at Barking and claiming her unworthiness to be named in a book in which she has written the holy name of Edward. So far, that is the conventional humility to be found in hagiographic or religious writings at large, where male authors likewise cloak themselves in anonymous humility. But to this topos the author gives a gendered twist by expressing the hope that those who hear her work will not despise it because a woman has written it and will pardon her presumption. To Christian humility this woman author therefore adds an awareness that she is moving onto ground where women are not usually found. Although conscious of their divinely bestowed authority, Hildegard von Bingen and Elisabeth von Schönau feel the need to reconcile it with their gender.[314] All this is revealing, but we should hesitate to generalise it. Another nun at Barking adopts a different stance in naming herself in the epilogue to her *Life of St Catherine*, and an otherwise unknown author (probably also a nun) of the *Vie sainte Audrée* names herself in her epilogue ('Ici escris mon non MARIE,/Pur ce ke soie remembree'). From these two examples it does not follow that their authors were 'less modest' and sought literary renown, for they could equally well be following conventional hagiographic practice in seeking to be remembered in their readers' prayers.[315]

There is also a postmedieval side to the rarity of women authors, lying more with our view of literature and our failure to recognise how different the medieval view was. At issue here is the long-lasting exclusion of certain genres of women's writing from medievalist teaching and research which has only recently begun to be rectified. Frau Ava and Marie de France may have long attracted attention, but the same was not always true of women's devotional literature. Historically, as late as 1867 it was still possible to hold that a woman of such literary education as Hrotsvitha could not have been possible in the tenth century, so that she was regarded as a fabrication of her sixteenth-century editor, Conrad Celtis.[316] Parallel with this has gone the exclusion of certain types of literature (and of their women authors) from consideration because they do not correspond to our modern idea of literature, in other words an anachronistic equation of what was

[313] Krug, *Families*, p. 208 (quoting Barratt).
[314] *Vie* 5296–320; Legge, *Literature*, p. 61; Bell, *Nuns*, pp. 70f. Newman, *Sister*, pp. 34–41.
[315] *Catherine* and *Audrée*: Legge, *Literature*, pp. 68, 265.   [316] See above, p. 219.

understood by *litteratura* in the Middle Ages with the modern sense of imaginative literature. The latter was not unknown earlier, but was much less common, so that devising a canon of literature according to the modern sense excluded much that was central to medieval interests. It also excluded women authors other than such rare examples as Marie de France and Christine de Pizan, whilst to pay due attention to the medieval sense of *litteratura* (Latin learning in written form) meant applying a yardstick of literate education to which women had much less access than men. In either case women authors were edged into a marginal position and their contribution to written culture was seen as small.

To put these comments, suggesting a paucity of women writers, into a proper perspective it is time to widen out from women's role as writers to embrace also their activity considered in other parts of this book, as readers, copyists, dedicatees and patrons of literature. To judge women's contribution primarily in terms of authorship is to grant that role a prominence which it has assumed above all since Romanticism's stress on the creative author. This approach for long informed the principles of textual criticism with its search for an original version, as it had supposedly come from the hands of the author, with a consequent neglect of what preceded the act of composition (the patron's commission of the work, the acquisition of sources) and followed it (the repeated and varying copying of the text, its reception on different occasions in different forms). This variability of textual transmission, even in written form, has led Bumke to observe that, alongside the wishes of a patron and ability of the author he commissions, we must take into account the contribution of copyist and redactor in producing the text in the various forms in which it is transmitted.[317] To these different aspects of the literary scene we must also add the recipient, above all in our case the reader. In this wider context women are much more prominent than they are as authors.

Even as authors, despite all the qualifications just made, they are not to be ignored. Within Latin literature, for reasons that have not yet been explained, Germany occupies a special place in that it produced in the twelfth century three outstanding women writers of the highest rank (Hildegard von Bingen, Elisabeth von Schönau, Herrad von Hohenburg), alongside whom only Heloise could be set from France or England, Moreover, Germany can also boast of a woman writer in Latin from as early as the tenth century (Hrotsvitha) and of two in the thirteenth (Gertrud von Helfta and Mechthild von Hackeborn). If we turn to women authors in

[317] Bumke, *ZfdPh* 116 (1997), 112.

the vernacular the yield is much less impressive, even if we were to take into account Occitan women lyric poets, the *trobairitz*, whose number is restricted and who are not paralleled in northern France or Germany. Old English literature offers us two surprisingly early examples, *The Wife's Lament* and *Wulf and Eadwacer*, but it is uncertain whether what we have here are women authors or no more than male-authored women's voices. Beyond that, if we resist the temptation to attribute any number of anonymous works to women simply because some women authors are known to have been expropriated, we can come up with Clemence of Barking (as a translator), Marie de France and Christine de Pizan, all using French, and Elisabeth von Nassau-Saarbrücken (in German). These cannot compensate us for this meagre crop.

The position in the vernacular is changed drastically when we turn to religious literature where, in revelatory writings by women, we have striking examples like Hadewijch, Mechthild von Magdeburg and Marguerite Porète, and it is here that any focus on imaginative literature with a secular theme is most in danger of failing to do justice to women's authorship. The role played by women in religious literature at large is clear in what is termed 'vernacular theology',[318] emerging in the thirteenth century and involving a range of religious genres in the vernacular, often written by and also for women, so that with this we pass from women authors to their wider field of literary activity. Not only was mystical literature written in the vernacular by women, it was also addressed to them by male authors such as Meister Eckhart, Tauler and Seuse. All this may represent a relatively circumscribed field within the whole span of medieval literature, but one with a rich representation of women, including authors as well as readers. What needs to be stressed is the part played by the vernacular in this field. Since Grundmann it has been clear that the replacement of Latin by the vernacular in religious literature is directly connected with the emergence of women's mystical interests. In this respect Ruh has drawn attention to vernacular commentaries on the Song of Songs in the twelfth century such as the *St. Trudperter Hoheslied* in German and the paraphrase of Landry of Waben in French.[319] These works are meant for women whose deficient Latin made the vernacular necessary, and the former work is followed by women's mystical literature of the thirteenth century, likewise illustrating a vernacular freed from dependence on a direct Latin source. Moreover, it was not only in religious literature that women recipients are involved with the vernacular, for we have seen the role they played as readers of

[318] Newman, *God*, pp. 295f.   [319] Ruh, *Geschichte* I 17. Landry: Ohly, *Hohelied-Studien*, pp. 281f.

court literature, but also in commissioning or otherwise encouraging its production. It may be a critical commonplace, but it is still a truth worth emphasising that 'the demands and influence of a female public helped to shape and foster the twelfth-century new vernacular literature'.[320] It is as readers and as encouragers, if not as authors, that women exercised an influence on the course of literature. That may be an order of priorities different from ours, but one which has to be acknowledged as still granting them a significant role.

The tone of the last few paragraphs may have sounded apologetic, providing excuses for the paucity of women authors, but the case for women became stronger as we widened our survey of their engagement with literature. It becomes much stronger still if we concentrate on the innovations which can be attributed to them. As patrons of literature, as we saw with Anglo-Norman literature in the twelfth century, they play a groundbreaking role in the encouragement of the vernacular alongside Latin.[321] As readers of literature they, rather than their menfolk, are prominent in court literature of the twelfth century, but also, as laywomen or religious, in spiritual literature, especially from the thirteenth century. These points can be taken further, but to do this we must no longer look at women individually, as readers, patrons or authors, but more generally, with regard to their position in literary history, asking about the innovations behind which they stand.

In asking this we must be careful how we phrase our question. For example, it will not suffice to say that Marie de France was the first (known) woman author in French or that Christine de Pizan was the first professional woman author in French (earning her living by the pen). Such claims invite the misogynous response that men had been active long before in these capacities, that these women typically lagged behind them in these respects and that it is not they who are the ground-breakers. The case of Hrotsvitha illuminates how the question should instead be formulated, as when Beach says that she was 'the first known author of Christian drama, poet, and the first woman historian of Germany'.[322] The last of these epithets is irrelevant to our concern, since it can again be countered by the observation that she was preceded as a historian by men. The same cannot be said of her as the first author of Christian drama, where she indeed had no predecessor and can be classed as an innovator. (This cannot be said of Lucas's remark

[320] Krueger, 'Misogyny', p. 395. Extending this to the thirteenth century Wolf, 'Beobachtungen', regards the association of women with the book as a key to the establishment of a vernacular written culture for the laity.
[321] McCash, 'Patronage', pp. 25f.   [322] Beach, *Women*, p. 19.

that Hrotsvitha, in addition to being the first known dramatist after the fall of Rome, was also the earliest poet known in Germany, for that rests on simple ignorance of the earliest German literature.)[323] From Hrotsvitha we learn therefore that the kind of question to ask is not 'Who was the first woman to do X?', but rather 'What innovation in the field of literature was brought about by a woman (acting as author, patron or reader)?'. In asking this type of question, perforce selectively, I divide the material into four headings: new literary genres encouraged by women; innovations in secular literature; new departures in religious literature; women's role in the vanguard of literary development. The result will be to show how great women's influence in medieval literature actually was, in contrast to the numerical paucity of women authors.

Under new genres inaugurated by women we may briefly mention again Hrotsvitha as the first Christian dramatist known to us as an individual author (indebted, if only negatively, to Terence and not to the Christian liturgy). A new genre of mystical revelatory literature was introduced into the German vernacular by Mechthild von Magdeburg, an innovation underlined by the parallels of Beatrice of Nazareth and Hadewijch in the Dutch vernacular.[324] These three women are at the beginning of vernacular theology and are also responsible for composing the earliest prose works in the vernacular which are not in any sense dependent on a Latin model which they merely translate.[325] To Mechthild we also owe the first attempt at an autobiographically structured work, albeit of an inward spiritual nature, in German, while in English similar innovations were made in their works by Margery Kempe and Julian of Norwich. Although they may owe something to the Latin male model of the *vitae fratrum*, the southern German sister books present a biographical structure of a different kind for the first time in the vernacular.[326] If we disregard the isolated example of the prose *Lancelot*, Elisabeth von Nassau-Saarbrücken and Eleonore of Austria can be seen as initiating the tradition of the German 'Prosaroman'.[327]

A wide range of novelties in secular court literature, above all in the innovative twelfth century, are the result of women's influential encouragement. The Anglo-Norman *Voyage of St Brendan* which with its tale of fabulous wonders and despite its hagiographic sounding title has been called the

---

[323] Lucas, *Women*, p. 143.
[324] Ortmann, 'Buch', p. 158; Poor, *Exemplaria* 12 (2000), 442f.; *JMEMS* 31 (2001), 216–19.
[325] Bürkle, *Literatur*, p. 21; Langer, *Mystik*, p. 235; Wiberg Pedersen, 'In-carnation', p. 67.
[326] Vollmann-Profe, *Mechthild*, p. 681; Langer, *Mystik*, p. 235; Heinzle, *Wandlungen*, p. 79; Menuge, *Women*, p. 59.
[327] Steinhoff, *VfL* 2, 488.

first ancestor of the court romance had as its first patron Mathilda, the wife
of Henry I, but then, when he married again, also Adeliza of Louvain.[328]
Whether the author Benedeit was commissioned twice or only once (and
then dedicated his work to the second queen), it is significantly women
whom he had in mind as recipients. We move closer to the great thematic
innovation of twelfth-century literature, the *matière de Bretagne*, with the
lais of Marie de France. Where she stands precisely in dating with regard to
Chrétien, the founding father of the Arthurian romance, may be uncertain,
but she is rightly held to be a founding author of this new literary world.[329]
On quite a different tack, the first chronicles in French of which we have
any knowledge were both initiated by women: one dealing with Henry I
by David, commissioned by Adeliza of Louvain, and the other the *Estoire
des Engleis* by Geoffrey Gaimar, commissioned by Constance Fitzgilbert of
Lincolnshire.[330] With our next example we turn to a (pseudo) history which
opened the way to Arthurian material, for the *Historia regum Britannie* of
Geoffrey of Monmouth was first rendered into the vernacular by Gaimar,
again at the command of Constance Fitzgilbert. If we look at Geoffrey of
Monmouth's work not for what it purported to be, as history, but for what
twelfth-century literature made of it, namely a backdrop for romances of
love and adventure, then the first vernacular version which begins to do
this justice is the *Roman de Brut* by Wace, presented by him to Eleanor of
Aquitaine.[331] To her, too, Benoît de Sainte-Maure dedicated his *Roman de
Troie*, a romanticised version of what was regarded as the historical origins
of the Britons, descended from the Trojans, hence seen as the prehistory
of what Geoffrey of Monmouth had recounted of their insular history.[332]
Falling outside the realm of Arthurian literature in this widest sense, two
other works in this sudden efflorescence of the vernacular were likewise
encouraged by women: the *Bestiaire* of Philippe de Thaon, the first bestiary in French, by the ubiquitous patronage of Adeliza of Louvain, and the
Proverbes de Salemon of Samson de Nanteuil for Aelis de Condé, another
'first' since it is the earliest known instruction for the young in French, and
apposite for women, responsible for the earliest upbringing of children.[333]

Women also acted as literary innovators in religious or devotional literature, where I can name only a few examples, the first two of which concern
the Song of Songs. In the late eleventh century John of Mantua wrote a
letter of spiritual guidance, based on this biblical book, to Mathilda of

[328] Legge, *Literature*, pp. 8f., 11f.   [329] Bloch, *Marie*, p. 6.
[330] Legge, *Literature*, p. 28; Damian-Grint, *Historians*, pp. 49f.
[331] Legge, *Literature*, pp. 28, 45.   [332] Damian-Grint, *Historians*, p. 59.
[333] Legge, *Literature*, pp. 23, 42.

Tuscany, noteworthy because it is the first case (since patristic times) in which the Song is interpreted in terms of the bride or *sponsa* as the individual soul (rather than as the Church or Mary), an individualised focus which came to inform the use of the Song in later mystical literature, especially for women.[334] This innovation is continued in the twelfth century by the *St. Trudperter Hoheslied*, meant for a community of nuns rather than an individual, but the novelty of this text is that it is the first work of German mysticism, where 'German' has to be taken in the linguistic sense (whereas John's letter to Mathilda had been in Latin).[335] Quite apart from the stimulus it received from the Song of Songs, German mysticism (again in the linguistic sense) is, if not an actual innovation by women, a product of the *cura monialium*, the combined result of Dominican theology and their spiritual care of women in need of devotional reading-matter in the vernacular. This combination gave birth to the efflorescence of the vernacular mysticism of women in the thirteenth century, and hence of mysticism in German or Dutch at large.[336] It only appears anomalous if we include under this heading the involvement of a woman, as its occasion, in the first known example of private letter writing in German, since it took place between Margaretha Ebner and the secular priest Heinrich von Nördlingen and is concerned with devotional, but not mystagogical, matters.[337]

Women are more than just involved in new developments, they are active in the vanguard in many respects. The first attested readers of German literature are both women: the Kicila recorded as reading the ninth-century work of Otfrid and the same-named (and identical?) empress who had copies of Notker's works made for her personal use.[338] With a jump to the twelfth century we may sum up women's role in Anglo-Norman literature in three points: at this time France was in the cultural lead in Europe, but within that frame it was the Anglo-Norman authors who were the pioneers in French literature, whilst behind them there lay decisively the patronage and readership of women in the Norman realm.[339] Hilda, the abbess of Whitby in the seventh century, encouraged the earliest Christian poetry in Anglo-Saxon (Caedmon), while the Mathilda for whom Benedeit wrote about St Brendan is the first patron of French literature whom we know by name.[340] French literary influence also spread to Germany, where it influenced court literature of the twelfth and thirteenth centuries, but

---

[334] Riedlinger, *Makellosigkeit*, pp. 106f.; Hamburger, *Canticles*, p. 158.
[335] Riedlinger, *Makellosigkeit*, p. 226.
[336] Grundmann, *Bewegungen*, *passim*; Haas,'Mystik', p. 239; Hamburger, *Canticles*, p. 3.
[337] Haas, 'Mystik', p. 298; Janota, *Orientierung*, pp. 125f.
[338] Schützeichel, *Codex*, pp. 55–8.   [339] Legge, *Literature*, p. 7.   [340] Lucas, *Women*, pp. 170, 172.

again the initiative came from a woman, from Mathilda, the wife of Henry the Lion, in transposing the first French themes to Germany (*Rolandslied, Tristrant*).[341] In these works encouraged by her the vernacular is present in double strength, for they are the first examples of works translated into German not from Latin, but from another vernacular. Again we can cap this with other examples, this time concerning women authors. Marie de France claims that she translated her *Fables* from English into French (whether the English source was the work of King Alfred, as she implies, does not affect the linguistic issue) and Elisabeth von Nassau-Saarbrücken and Eleonore of Austria base their literary activity as authors on French models.[342] To conclude with a later period and with literature meant for nuns, it has been shown that the sisters of Syon Abbey were quick to make use of the new possibilities of printing and it was they who showed 'the greatest interest in this vernacular literature, it was the nuns, not the monks, who stood at the fore-front of English spirituality'. In support of this for another community, the same leading role in English theology has been argued for the abbey of Barking in the fifteenth century.[343]

These examples, which are by no means all that could be cited, cover a wide range, a point which must be emphasised. They are drawn from all the three vernaculars with which this book is concerned and they cover a wide time span, extending from the abbess Hilda in the seventh century as far as Syon Abbey into the sixteenth. They also illustrate the many ways in which women were involved in literature: not merely as authors, but more frequently as patrons, encouragers of literature, dedicatees, addressees and, not least for us, also readers. Their spread embraces both secular and religious literature, and the range of genres, indicative of women's wide interests, is impressively large (drama, biography, letter writing, pedagogic literature, the *matière de Bretagne*, the romance, bestiary literature, historiography, mysticism and devotional texts). The extent of this spread (over time, languages and genres) can hardly be by chance, it reveals that women's innovative role in literature cannot be dismissed as a one-off affair. It is a constant feature, even if it is much more pronounced from the twelfth century onwards.

Common to all these examples is the ubiquity of the vernacular, revealed in different ways: as vernacular literacy distinct from Latinity, as works translated from Latin or from another vernacular, or as texts composed in the vernacular in the first place. It might be possible to raise the kind

[341] See above, pp. 215f.   [342] Bloch, *Marie*, p. 7. Steinhoff, *VfL* 2, 470–3, 482–8.
[343] Bell, *Nuns*, pp. 74, 75f. (Syon), 72 (Barking).

of antifeminine criticism of these women's vernacularity which I sought to avoid by the way in which I formulated my question about women's innovations, in other words to argue that women's vernacularity was yet another symptom of their inferior literacy. This is to fall victim to the medieval cleric's vested interest in maintaining that literacy was confined to his Latin cultural world, to fail to see that historical changes over the medieval period undermined what had been a static view of literacy.[344] The twelfth century saw the beginnings of the slow shift from orality to literacy, but also the rise of lay literacy and, more cogently in the present context, of vernacular literacy. The women with whom we have been concerned cannot have known it, but the future in literary and cultural terms lay with the vernacular, not with the hitherto dominant Latin. To this vernacular literacy women gave an impetus whose significance we are only now coming to realise.

For a woman to depend on vernacular literacy (even of necessity) and thus to go against the accumulated prestige of Latin, moreover for her to enter into the male domain of authorship and to claim authorisation from God when engaged in religious writing demanded considerable self-confidence and daring, given the opposition and prejudice she faced. How far these virtues reached can be shown in the opening scene of the *Livre de la Cité des Dames* by Christine de Pizan, an author who has not played as great a part in this book as she deserves. In what follows I depend on an interpretation by Kolve which I use to show how this scene sums up a number of issues that have emerged in our argument.[345]

The scene depicts Christine seated in her study, reading the *Lamentationes* of Matheolus, a diatribe against marriage and women. Her despair on reading this is interrupted by the appearance of three allegorical female figures who inform her that God has chosen her to write a book to rectify these false views and, like a city, defend women from such attacks.[346] That seems straightforward enough, but into this account Christine has inserted a number of biblical reminiscences which cumulatively become clearer until, at the climax, they are confirmed by an explicit quotation from the Annunciation to Mary. The appearance of the three ladies, miraculously through closed doors and windows, is heralded by a beam of light (equally inexplicable given the time of day) shining into the study.[347] The Bible knows of no such light on this occasion, but it is depicted frequently in the visual arts of the Middle Ages, falling on Mary's breast or face, but

---

[344] Green, *Listening*, pp. 9f.   [345] Kolve, 'Annunciation', pp. 171–91.
[346] *Cité* I 1–7 (pp. 5–16).   [347] *Ibid.*, I 2 (pp. 7f.).

more pointedly on Christine's lap. Theological allusions also suggest that the apparition of the ladies before Christine is a trinity: they are called celestial beings and daughters of God, they are described as one and the same; what one decides the second puts into effect and the third completes.[348] More pointedly, these figures do not simply tell Christine of their errand, they announce it to her ('adnoncier'), stress that what she is to do has been decreed by God, who has chosen her for this purpose (alone of all women).[349] In her response to this annunciation Christine presents herself as saying that the sweet rain and dew of the ladies' words have sunk into her arid mind and refreshed and replenished her thought, an unmistakable reference to Gideon's fleece, a traditional prefiguration of the Annunciation.[350] The climax of explicitness, where biblical text and medieval fiction come together, occurs when Christine accepts the task laid on her, saying 'Behold your handmaiden, ready to do your bidding. I will obey your every command, so be it unto me according to your word.'[351]

This astonishingly daring equation by a woman author of her conceiving a book with Mary's conception of Christ takes up a number of points touched on in our argument. It starts with Christine surrounded by books and reading in her study, so that she joins the women whom we saw at the start of Part II, enjoying privacy for solitary reading. Virginia Woolf's complaint about the absence of such privacy for modern women had to do with their ability to write, not to read, but that is precisely what Christine goes on to do. In moving from reading in her study to writing her own work she reflects the course of our argument, which began with women readers and has ended in this section with their function as writers. This combination of reading with writing also concerns the role of Mary, her adaptability to both purposes. We saw that Mary as a reader, especially in the scene of the Annunciation, could be presented as a precedent for women readers in the late Middle Ages, legitimising an activity in which many obstacles were put in their way. By making use of allegory Christine further empowers herself as an author, using religious imagery connected with Mary to grant herself authority as well as authorship. In both literate activities, reading as well as writing, women could find a role model in Mary.

We can go a step further in conclusion, for Christine's self-authorising by an appeal to Mary has a precedent in Hildegard von Bingen. Coming not from her, but from what Guibert de Gembloux said of her, there is also

---

[348] *Ibid.*, I 3 (p. 10), I 6 (pp. 14, 15).   [349] *Ibid.*, I 3 (p. 11), I 4 (p. 12).
[350] *Ibid.*, I 7 (p. 15).   [351] *Ibid.*, I 7 (p. 16).

the daring comparison of Hildegard, vowed to virginity, giving birth to the words of her visions with Mary giving birth to Christ, the Logos.[352] In blessing the speech of Hildegard's mouth, in place of Gabriel's blessing of the fruit of Mary's womb, Guibert's biblical allusion was to the archangel's salutation, whereas Christine's biblical quotation refers to Mary's response, so that both illustrate the Annunciation from complementary points of view. Behind this parallel between two women writers, authorising their activity, there lies a difference. This comparison of Hildegard with Mary was not made by the German writer herself, but by someone else, a male admirer, editorial assistant and would-be stylistic embellisher, whereas it was Christine who made her own comparison. When Hildegard sought authorisation it was by deriving it from God whose words she claimed to be simply transmitting as his mouthpiece, whilst Christine's use of the Annunciation model was an act of self-authorisation. Where Hildegard's words were in the sacred language of Latin and meant as religious truth, Christine's were a fiction put forward in the vernacular. If the word 'daring' can be used of the Annunciation model to legitimise the writing of these two women, it belongs more to Christine who in the fifteenth century exemplifies the self-confidence that by then some women could acquire in their engagement with literature.

[352] See above, p. 237.

Conclusion

Although this book's survey has had to be selective, omitting much of interest and importance, it has taken us on a long haul through three countries and four languages and a timespan from Radegund in the sixth century to Margaret Beaufort at the start of the sixteenth. Although over this long period a number of changes have been identified, it may seem like an anticlimax to observe that the marginalisation of women, in literature and in society, persisted into the early modern period and, as Virginia Woolf argued, much more recently. If little seems to have altered it is all the more important to stress what shifts can be registered in our earlier period.

In looking at the peculiarities of medieval reading we saw the importance of figurative alongside literal reading and that the former had a special bearing on the meditational or devotional reading in which women, religious and lay, were closely involved. It has become clear that the number of women readers was far greater than has been commonly assumed, especially when account is taken of women's spiritual reading-matter. After clerics and monks, religious women are important as the main bearers of a written culture and its expansion during the course of the Middle Ages. It would, however, be too restrictive to confine women's role in written culture to reading alone, for the last chapter has shown that, in addition to this receptive function they were active in encouraging the composition of texts by others and producing some literature for themselves. They were not merely recipients, but also initiators.

Other points that have emerged go much further. We have seen, especially in religious literature, that what was traditionally regarded in the patriarchal world as feminine weakness (including woman's intellectual or educational inferiority) could be converted into a sign of her strength (as a chosen vessel for conveying God's message). This amounts to a subversion of misogyny, a feature which will play a large part in the companion volume in works of court literature by male authors, but with women in their audience largely in view. The concluding chapter has also emphasised the innovative force latent in women's preoccupation with literature, their lead in encouraging new genres and changes of various kinds. To these belong a number of important developments to which the future belonged. These include the extension of literacy from religious life to the lay world, where it could also be practised by men, but more commonly by women. Also important was the domestication of literacy, its expansion from the monastery to the household, particularly in the education of the young in reading and the laywoman's use of prayer books and devotional reading matter in the home as well as in church. Lastly, perhaps most significant of all was women's part in the vernacularisation of literacy, the encouragement of mother tongues to the extent that they eventually rivalled and then ousted the Latin language from which they had learned so much and which had long overshadowed them. Women were by no means the sole agents in these changes in the cultural landscape, but of the importance of their role there can be little doubt.

The approach to women readers in this book has been textual, although this needs to be supplemented from two other angles. Text must be seen further in conjunction with image (as in Hamburger's work on women's devotional meditation on illustrations in texts), but also with palaeography and codicology (as in Wolf's aptly named *Buch und Text*). Much remains to be done.

Bibliography

PRIMARY SOURCES

Works are listed by author, where known, or by title of the work.

Adelhausener Schwesternbuch, J. König (ed.) *Freiburger Diözesan-Archiv* 13 (1880), 129–236

Aelred of Rievaulx, *De institutione inclusarum*, C. H. Talbot (ed.), in Aelred of Rievaulx, *Opera omnia*, A. Hoste and C. H. Talbot (eds.), Turnhout 1971, pp. 637–82

Alanus ab Insulis, *De planctu naturae*, N. M. Häring (ed.), *Studi Medievali* 19, 2 (1978), 797–879

Aldhelm, *De virginitate*, MGH AA 15, 209–323

Ambrose, *De virginibus*, PL 16, 187–232

Ancrene Wisse, quoted from Parts 7 and 8, B. Millett and J. Wogan-Browne (eds.), *Medieval English prose for women. Selections from the Katherine Group and Ancrene Wisse*, Oxford 1992, pp. 110–49

Andreas Capellanus, *De amore*, E. Trojel (ed.), Munich 1964

Annolied, E. Nellmann (ed.), Stuttgart 1986

Anselm of Canterbury, *Orationes sive meditationes*, F. S. Schmitt (ed.), *Opera omnia* III, Edinburgh 1946

Arnold, Friar, *Il libro della beata Angela da Foligno*, L. Thier and A. Calufetti (eds.), Rome 1985

Asser, *Life of King Alfred*, W. H. Stevenson (ed.), Oxford 1904

Ava, Frau, *Das Jüngste Gericht* and *Das Leben Jesu*, F. Maurer (ed.), *Die religiösen Dichtungen des 11. und 12. Jahrhunderts*, Tübingen 1965, II 498–513 and 308–49

Bartsch, K., *Die Schweizer Minnesänger*, Darmstadt 1964

Bede, *Historia ecclesiastica*, C. Plummer (ed.), Oxford 1975

Benedeit, *Voyage of St Brendan*, E. G. R. Waters (ed.), Oxford 1928

Benoît de Sainte-Maure, *Roman de Troie*, L. Constans (ed.), Paris 1904–12

Béroul, *Tristran*, A. Ewert (ed.), Oxford 1967

Berthold von Holle, *Demantin*, K. Bartsch (ed.), Stuttgart 1875

Berthold von Regensburg, F. Pfeiffer (ed.), Berlin 1965

Book of Privy Counselling, P. Hodgson (ed.), *The Cloud of Unknowing and related treatises on contemplative prayer*, Exeter 1982, pp. 75–99

Busch, Johannes, *Liber de reformatione monasteriorum*, K. Grube (ed.), Halle 1886

Chaucer, *Works*, F. N. Robinson (ed.), London 1968
  The Book of the Duchess, in *Works*, pp. 266–79
  The House of Fame, in *Works*, pp. 280–302
  The Nun's Priest's Tale, in *Works*, pp. 198–206
  The Parliament of Fowls, in *Works*, pp. 309–18
  The Second Nun's Tale, in *Works*, pp. 207–13
  Troilus and Criseyde, R. K. Root (ed.), Princeton 1954
  The Wife of Bath's Prologue, J. Winny (ed.), Cambridge 1965
Li chevalier a deus espees, W. Foerster (ed.), Halle 1877
Chevalier à l'épée, R. C. Johnston and D. D. R. Owen (eds.), Edinburgh 1972
Chrétien de Troyes, *Lancelot*, M. Rocques (ed.), Paris 1963
  Yvain, W. Foerster (ed.), Halle 1926
Christina of Markyate, The life of, C. H. Talbot (ed.), Oxford 1959
Christine de Pizan, *L'epistre au dieu d'amours*, M. Roy (ed.), *Oeuvres poétiques* II
  1–27, Paris 1891
  Livre de la Cité des Dames, trans. R. Brown-Grant (*The Book of the City of
  Ladies*), Harmondsworth 1999. References to this translation, rather than to
  the edition of M. C. Curnow, available only in microfilm.
Clemence of Barking, *The life of St Catherine*, W. Macbain (ed.), Oxford 1964
The Cloud of Unknowing, P. Hodgson (ed.), Exeter 1982
Dante, *Inferno*, C. S. Singleton (ed.), *The Divine Comedy* I, London 1971
Dhuoda, *Liber manualis*, M. Thiébaux (ed.), Cambridge 1998
Ebernand von Erfurt, *Heinrich und Kunigunde*, R. Bechstein (ed.), Quedlinburg
  1860
Eckhart, Meister, *Die deutschen Werke*, J. Quint (ed.), Stuttgart 1936–76
Eilhart von Oberg, *Tristrant*, F. Lichtenstein (ed.), Strassburg 1887
Einhard, *Vita Karoli*, O. Holder-Egger (ed.), Hanover 1922
Elisabeth von Schönau, *Die Visionen der heiligen Elisabeth und die Schriften der
  Äbte Ekbert und Emecho von Schönau*, F. W. E. Roth (ed.), Brno 1884
Emecho von Schönau, *Vita Eckeberti*, S. Widmann (ed.), *Neues Archiv der
  Gesellschaft für ältere deutsche Geschichtskunde* II (1886), 447–54
Engelthaler Schwesternbuch, K. Schröder (ed.), Tübingen 1871
Fleck, Konrad, *Flore und Blanscheflur*, F. Sommer (ed.), Quedlinburg 1846
Floire et Blancheflor, J.-L. Leclanche (ed.), Paris 1980
Fortunatus, Venantius, *Carmina*, MGH AA 4, 1, 7–292
Froissart, *L'Espinette amoureuse*, A. Fourrier (ed.), Paris 1963
Frutolf von Michelsberg, *Chronica* (ed. as part of Ekkehard von Aura, *Chronicon
  Urspergense*), MGH SS 6, 33–265
Gaimar, *Estoire des Engleis*, A. Bell (ed.), Oxford 1960
Gautier d'Arras, *Eracle*, G. Raynaud de Lage (ed.), Paris 1976
Geistlicher Herzen Bavngart, H. Unger (ed.), Munich 1969
Gerson, Jean, *Oeuvres complètes*, vol. 9, Glorieux (ed.), Paris 1973
Gertrud von Helfta, *Legatus divinae pietatis*, in *Revelationes Gertrudianae ac Mechtil-
  dianae* I, Paris 1875
  Oeuvres spirituelles (I: *Le héraut*), P. Doyère (ed.), Paris 1968

Goscelin of Saint Bertin, *Liber confortatorius*, C. H. Talbot (ed.), *Studia Anselmiana* 37 (1955), 1–117

Göttweiger Trojanerkrieg, A. Koppitz (ed.), Berlin 1926

Gottfried von Strassburg, *Tristan*, P. Ganz (ed.), Wiesbaden 1978

Gower, *Confessio Amantis*, G. C. Macaulay (ed.), Oxford 1901

Gregory the Great, *Registrum epistularum*, D. Norberg (ed.), Turnhout 1982

Guibert de Gembloux, *Epistolae*, A. Derolez (ed.), Turnhout 1988/89

Guibert de Nogent, *De vita sua*, PL 156, 838–962

Hadewijch, *Brieven*, J. Van Mierlo (ed.), Antwerp 1947

Hali Meiðhad, B. Millett and J. Wogan-Browne (eds.), *Medieval English prose for women. Selections from the Katherine Group and Ancrene Wisse*, Oxford 1992, pp. 2–43

Hartmann von Aue, *Armer Heinrich*, F. Neumann (ed.), Wiesbaden 1958

Iwein, G. F. Benecke, K. Lachmann, L. Wolff (eds.), Berlin 1968

Hartwig von dem Hage, *Margaretenlegende*, W. Schmitz (ed.), Göppingen 1976

Heinrich von dem Türlin, *Die Crone*, G. H. F. Scholl (ed.), Amsterdam 1966

Heinrich von Freiberg, *Tristan*, A. Bernt (ed.), Hildesheim 1978

Heinrich von Neustadt, *Apollonius von Tyrland*, S. Singer (ed.), Berlin 1906

Heinrich von Veldeke, *Eneasroman*, D. Kartschoke (ed.), Stuttgart 1986

Servatius, T. Frings and G. Schieb (eds.), Halle 1956

Heldris de Cornuälle, *Le Roman de Silence*, L. Thorpe (ed.), Cambridge 1972

Heliand, O. Behaghel (ed.), Halle 1933

Herbort von Fritzlar, *Liet von Troye*, G. K. Frommann (ed.), Amsterdam 1966

Hermann, Bruder, *Leben der Gräfin Iolande von Vianden*, J. Meier (ed.), Breslau 1889

Herrand von Wildonie, *Der nackte Kaiser*, H. Fischer and P. Sappler (eds.), *Vier Erzählungen*, Tübingen 1969, pp. 22–43

Hildebrandslied, in W. Haug and B. K. Vollmann, *Frühe deutsche Literatur und lateinische Literatur in Deutschland 800–1150*, Frankfurt 1991, pp. 10–14

Hildegard von Bingen, *Epistolarium*, L. Van Acker (ed.), Turnhout 1991–2001

Liber divinorum operum, A. Derolez and P. Dronke (eds.), Turnhout 1996

Scivias, A. Führkötter and A. Carlevaris (eds.), Turnhout 1978

Hrabanus Maurus, *De universo*, PL 111, 9–614

Hrotsvitha von Gandersheim, *Opera*, H. Homeyer (ed.), Paderborn 1970

Hue de Rotelande, *Ipomedon*, A. J. Holden (ed.), Paris 1979

Hugh of Folieto, *De bestiis*, PL 177, 15–154

Hugh of St Victor, *Didascalicon*, PL 176, 741–838

Isidore of Seville, *Etymologiae*, W. M. Lindsay (ed.), Oxford 1910

Sententiae, PL 83, 558–738

John of Salisbury, *Metalogicon*, C. C. I. Webb (ed.), Oxford 1929

Julian of Norwich, *A Book of Showings to the Anchoress Julian of Norwich*, E. Colledge and J. Walshe (eds.), Toronto 1978

Kaiserchronik, MGH *Deutsche Chroniken* I, 1

Kempe, The Book of Margery, B. Windeatt (ed.), Harlow 2000

Kirchberger Schwesternbuch, F. E. W. Roth (ed.), in *Alemannia* 21 (1893), 103–23

Die Klage, J. Bumke (ed.), *Die 'Nibelungenklage'. Synoptische Fassung aller vier Fassungen*, Berlin 1999

Konrad von Würzburg, *Trojanischer Krieg*, A. von Keller (ed.), Stuttgart 1858

Lambert of Ardres, *Historia comitum Ghisnensium*, MGH SS 24, 557–642

Lamprecht von Regensburg, *Die Tochter Syon*, K. Weinhold (ed.), Paderborn 1880

Lavision Christine, M. L. Towner (ed.), Washington D. C. 1932

Layamon, *Brut*, F. Madden (ed.), London 1847

Lohengrin, T. Cramer (ed.), Munich 1971

Marie de France, *Espurgatoire seint Patrice*, K. Warnke (ed.), Halle 1938

   Fables, C. Brucker (ed.), Louvain 1998

   Lais, A. Ewert (ed.), Oxford 1963 (*Milun*, pp. 101–15)

Mechthild von Magdeburg, *Das fließende Licht der Gottheit*, G. Vollmann-Profe (ed.), Frankfurt 2003

   Revelationes, L. Paquelin (ed.), *Revelationes Gertrudianae et Mechtildianae*, Vol. II, Poitiers 1877

Münchner Oswald, M. Curschmann (ed.), Tübingen 1974

Nibelungenlied, H. de Boor (ed.), Wiesbaden 1961

Notker, *Boethius de Consolatione Philosophiae*, E. H. Sehrt and T. Starck (eds.), Halle 1933–34

Otfrid von Weissenburg, *Evangelienbuch*, O. Erdmann (ed.), Halle 1882

Otte, *Eraclius*, W. Frey (ed.), Göppingen 1983

Paris, Matthew, *Chronica majora*, H. R. Luard (ed.), London 1872–83

Paulinus of Nola, *Epistulae*, W. de Hartel (ed.), Prague 1894

Peter the Venerable, *Epistolae*, PL 189, 62–472

Philipp, Bruder, *Marienleben*, H. Rückert (ed.), Quedlinburg 1853

Philippe de Novare, *Les quatre âges de l'homme*, M. de Fréville (ed.), Paris 1888

Philippe de Thaon, *Bestiaire*, E. Walberg (ed.), Lund 1900

Piramus, Denis, *La vie saint Edmund le rei*, H. Kjellman (ed.), Geneva 1974

Der Pleier, *Garel von dem blühenden Tal*, W. Herles (ed.), Vienna 1981

   Tandareis und Flordibel, F. Khull (ed.), Graz 1885

Prosalancelot, H.-H. Steinhoff (ed.), Frankfurt 1991. Quotations from parts where this edition is not complete are from the edition of R. Kluge, Berlin 1948–74

Rolandslied, F. Maurer (ed.), Leipzig 1940

Rudolf von Ems, *Weltchronik*, G. Ehrismann (ed.), Berlin 1915

   Willehalm von Orlens, V. Junk (ed.), Berlin 1905

Der Saelden Hort, H. Adrian (ed.), Berlin 1927

Samson de Nanteuil, *Proverbes de Salemon*, P. Meyer (ed.), *Romania* 37 (1908), 212–15

Secretum Secretorum, R. Möller (ed.), Berlin 1963

Seinte Margarete, B. Millett and J. Wogan-Browne (eds.), *Medieval English prose for women. Selections from the Katherine Group and Ancrene Wisse*, Oxford 1992, pp. 44–85

Seuse, Heinrich, *Deutsche Schriften*, K. Bihlmeyer (ed.), Frankfurt 1961

Speculum humanae salvationis, J. Lutz and P. Perdrizet (eds.), Leipzig 1907

St. Katharinentaler Schwesternbuch, R. Meyer (ed.), Tübingen 1995

St. Trudperter Hoheslied, F. Ohly (ed.), Frankfurt 1998

Der Stricker, *Daniel von dem blühenden Tal*, M. Resler (ed.), Tübingen 1983

Theodulf of Orléans, *Libri Carolini*, PL 98, 941–1350

Thomas, *Tristan*, B. H. Wind (ed.), Geneva 1960

Thomasin von Zerclaere, *Der welsche Gast*, H. Rückert (ed.), Quedlinburg 1852

Twinger von Königshofen, Jakob, *Deutsche Chronik*, in *Die Chroniken der ober-rheinischen Städte, Straßburg I*, Leipzig 1870

Ulrich von Etzenbach, *Alexandreis*, W. Toischer (ed.), Tübingen 1888

Ulrich von Lichtenstein, *Frauenbuch*, C. Young (ed.), Stuttgart, 2003

    Frauendienst, F. V. Spechtler (ed.), Göppingen 1987

Ulrich von Türheim, *Rennewart*, A. Hübner (ed.), Berlin 1964

    Tristan, T. Kerth (ed.), Tübingen 1979

Väterbuch, K. Reissenberger (ed.), Berlin 1914

Vie d'Édouard le Confesseur, Ö. Södergård (ed.), Uppsala 1948

Vie Sainte Audrée, Ö. Södergård (ed.), Uppsala 1955

Vies des Pères, quoted P. Meyer, *HLF* 33 (1906), 293

Virgil, *Aeneid*, H. R. Fairclough (ed.), London 1930

Vita Beatricis, L. Reypens (ed.), Antwerp 1964

Vita s. Caesarii, MGH SRM 3, 433–501

Vita s. Cunegundis, MGH SS 4, 821–8

Vita sanctae Hildegardis, M. Klaes (ed.), Turnhout 1993

Vita, ut videtur, cuiusdam magistrae monialium Admontensium, in *Analecta Bollandiana* 12 (1893), 356–66

Vitae Sororum (Unterlinden), J. Ancelet-Hustache (ed.), *Archive d'histoire doctrinale et littéraire du moyen âge* 56 (1930/31), 317–513

Von dem übeln wîbe, K. Helm (ed.), Tübingen 1955

Wace, *Roman de Rou*, A. J. Holden (ed.), Paris 1970–3

Walther von der Vogelweide, F. Maurer (ed.), Tübingen 1955/6 (I have retained Lachmann's conventional numbering for easier reference)

Walther von Rheinau, *Marienleben*, E. Perjus (ed.), Åbo 1950

Wartburgkrieg, T. A. Rompelman (ed.), Amsterdam 1939

Wernher, Priester, *Maria*, C. Wesle (ed.), Halle 1927

Wirnt von Grafenberg, *Wigalois*, J. M. N. Kapteyn (ed.), Bonn 1926

Wolfdietrich A, H. Schneider (ed.), Halle 1968

Wolfram von Eschenbach, *Parzival*, K. Lachmann (ed.), Berlin 1926

    Titurel, H. Brackert and S. Fuchs-Jolie (eds.), Berlin 2003

    Willehalm, K. Lachmann (ed.), Berlin 1926

Zwiefaltener Benediktinerregel, C. Selmer (ed.), *Middle High German Translations of the Regula Sancti Benedicti*, Cambridge MA 1933, pp. 13–47

SECONDARY SOURCES

Footnote references in this book give a key word (normally the first noun in the title), permitting recognition of the entry in the bibliography.

Abels, R. and Harrison, E., 'The participation of women in Languedocian Catharism', *MS* 41 (1979), 215–51

Alexandre-Bidon, D., 'Des femmes de bonne foi. La religion des mères au moyen âge', in J. Delumeau (ed.), *La religion de ma mère. Les femmes et la transmission de la foi*, Paris 1992, pp. 91–122

Andersen, E. A., 'Mechthild von Magdeburg: her creativity and her audience', in L. Smith and J. H. M. Taylor (eds.), *Women, the book and the godly*, Cambridge 1995, pp. 77–88
    The voices of Mechthild of Magdeburg, Bern 2000

Arnulf, A., *Versus ad picturas. Studien zur Titulusdichtung als Quellengattung der Kunstgeschichte von der Antike bis zum Hochmittelalter*, Munich 1997

Aston, M. *Lollards and reformers. Images and literacy in late medieval religion*, London 1984

Auerbach, E., 'Sermo humilis', in Auerbach, *Literatursprache und Publikum in der lateinischen Spätantike und im Mittelalter*, Bern 1958, pp. 25–53

Baker, D. (ed.), *Medieval women*, Oxford 1978

Baldwin, J. W., *The language of sex. Five voices from northern France around 1200*, Chicago 1994

Balfour, M., 'Francesca da Rimini and Dante's women readers', in L. Smith and J. H. M. Taylor (eds.), *Women, the book and the worldly*, Cambridge 1995, pp. 71–83

Balogh, J., 'Voces paginarum. Beiträge zur Geschichte des lauten Lesens und Schreibens', *Philologus* 82 (1927), 84–109, 202–40

Baltrusch-Schneider, D. B., 'Die angelsächsischen Doppelklöster', in K. Elm and M. Parisse (eds.), *Doppelklöster und andere Formen der Symbiose männlicher und weiblicher Religiosen im Mittelalter*, Berlin 1992, pp. 57–79

Barratt, A., 'Continental women mystics and English readers', in C. Dinshaw and D. Wallace (eds.), *The Cambridge Companion to medieval women's writing*, Cambridge 2003, pp. 240–55

Bartlett, A. C., *Male authors, female readers. Representation and subjectivity in Middle English devotional literature*, Ithaca 1995

Baswell, C., 'Heloise', in C. Dinshaw and D. Wallace (eds.), *The Cambridge Companion to medieval women's writing*, Cambridge 2003, pp. 161–71

Bäuml, F. H., 'Autorität und Performanz. Gesehene Leser, gehörte Bilder, geschriebener Text', in C. Ehler and U. Schaefer (eds.), *Verschriftung und Verschriftlichung. Aspekte des Medienwechsels in verschiedenen Kulturen und Epochen*, Tübingen 1998, pp. 248–73

Beach, A. I., *Women as scribes. Book production and monastic reform in twelfth-century Bavaria*, Cambridge 2004

Bell, D. N., *What nuns read: books and libraries in medieval English nunneries*, Kalamazoo 1995

Bell, S. G., 'Medieval women book owners: arbiters of lay piety and ambassadors of culture', in M. Erler and M. Kowaleski (eds.), *Women and power in the Middle Ages*, Atlanta GA 1988, pp. 149–87

Bennewitz, I., '"Darumb lieben Toechter/Seyt nicht zu gar fürwitzig . . ." Deutschsprachige moralisch-didaktische Literatur des 13.–15. Jahrhunderts', in E. Kleinau and C. Opitz (eds.), *Geschichte der Mädchen- und Frauenbildung* I, Frankfurt 1996, pp. 23–41

'Die obszöne weibliche Stimme. Erotik und Obszönität in den Frauenstrophen der deutschen Literatur des Mittelalters', in T. Cramer *et al.* (eds.), *Frauenlieder. Cantigas de amigo*, Stuttgart 2000, pp. 69–84

Benton, J. F., 'The court of Champagne as a literary centre', *Speculum* 36 (1961), 551–91

Bériou, N., 'The right of women to give religious instruction in the thirteenth century', in B. M. Kienzle and P. J. Walker (eds.), *Women preachers and prophets through two millennia of Christianity*, Berkeley 1998, pp. 134–45

Bezzola, R. R., *Les origines et la formation de la littérature courtoise en Occident (500–1200)*, Paris 1958–63

Biller, P., 'The Cathars of Languedoc and written materials', in P. Biller and A. Hudson (eds.), *Heresy and literacy, 1000–1530*, Cambridge 1994, pp. 61–82

'Women and texts in Languedocian Catharism', in L. Smith and J. H. M. Taylor (eds.), *Women, the book and the godly*, Cambridge 1995, pp. 171–82

'Cathars and material women', in P. Biller and A. J. Minnis (eds.), *Medieval theology and the natural body*, York 1997, pp. 61–107

The Waldenses, 1170–1530. Between a religious order and Church, Aldershot 2001

Bischoff, B., *Mittelalterliche Studien* I, Munich 1965

Blacker, J., '"Dame Custance la gentil"; Gaimar's portrait of a lady and her books', in E. Mullally and J. Thompson (eds.), *The Court and cultural diversity*, Cambridge 1997, pp. 109–19

Blamires, A., 'The Wife of Bath and Lollardy', *MÆ* 58 (1989), 224–42

'The limits of bible study for medieval women', in L. Smith and J. H. M. Taylor (eds.), *Women, the book and the godly*, Cambridge 1995, pp. 1–12

'Women and preaching in medieval orthodoxy, heresy, and saints' lives', *Viator* 26 (1995), 135–152

The case for women in medieval culture, Oxford 1997

Blamires, A. and Marx, C. W., 'Women not to preach. A disputation in British Library MS Harley 31', *JML* 3 (1993), 34–63

Blank, W., 'Zu den Schwierigkeiten der Lancelot-Rezeption in Deutschland', in M. H. Jones and R. Wisbey (eds.), *Chrétien de Troyes and the German Middle Ages*, Cambridge 1993, pp. 121–36

Bloch, R. H., *Medieval misogyny and the invention of Western romantic love*, Chicago 1991

The anonymous Marie de France, Chicago 2003

Bodarwé, K., *Sanctimoniales litteratae. Schriftlichkeit und Bildung in den ottonischen Frauenkommunitäten Gandersheim, Essen und Quedlinburg*, Münster 2004

Boffey, J., 'Lydgate's lyrics and women readers', in L. Smith and J. H. M. Taylor (eds.), *Women, the book and the worldly*, Cambridge 1995, pp. 139–49

'Women authors and women's literacy in fourteenth- and fifteenth-century England', in C. M. Meale (ed.), *Women and literature in Britain, 1150–1500*, Cambridge 1996, pp. 159–82

Bond, G. A., *The loving subject. Desire, eloquence, and power in Romanesque France*, Philadelphia 1995

Borgehammar, S., 'Who wrote the Admont sermon corpus – Gottfried the abbot, his brother Irimbert, or the nuns?', in J. Hamesse and X. Hermand (eds.), *De l'homélie au sermon. Histoire de la prédication médiévale*, Louvain 1993, pp. 47–51

Braun, J. W., 'Irimbert von Admont', *FMS* 7 (1973), 266–323

Brilliant, R., 'The Bayeux Tapestry: a stripped narrative for their eyes and ears', *WI* 7 (1991), 98–126

Broadhurst, K. M., 'Henry II of England and Eleanor of Aquitaine: patrons of literature in French?', *Viator* 27 (1996), 53–84

Brooke, C. N. L., *The medieval idea of marriage*, Oxford 1989

Brown, D. C., *Pastor and laity in the theology of Jean Gerson*, Cambridge 1987

Brown, M. P., 'Female book-ownership and production in Anglo-Saxon England: the evidence of the ninth-century prayerbooks', in C. J. Kay and L. M. Sylvester (eds.), *Lexis and texts in early English*, Amsterdam 2001, pp. 45–67

Bruckner, A., 'Weibliche Schreibtätigkeit im schweizerischen Spätmittelalter', in J. Autenrieth and F. Brunhölzl (eds.), *Festschrift Bernhard Bischoff zu seinem 65. Geburtstag*, Stuttgart 1971, pp. 441–8

Bruckner, M. T., 'Fictions of the female voice: the women troubadours', *Speculum* 67 (1992), 865–91

Shaping romance. Interpretation, truth, and closure in twelfth-century French fictions, Philadelphia 1993

Bruckner, M. T. *et al.* (eds.), *Songs of the women troubadours*, New York 2000

Brundage, J. A., *Law, sex, and Christian society in medieval Europe*, Chicago 1990

Brunner, K., 'Quae est ista, quae ascendit per desertum. Aspekte des Selbstverständnisses geistlicher Frauen im 12. Jahrhundert', *MIÖG* 107 (1999), 271–310

Bumke, J., *Mäzene im Mittelalter. Die Gönner und Auftraggeber der höfischen Literatur in Deutschland 1150–1300*, Munich 1979

Höfische Kultur. Literatur und Gesellschaft im hohen Mittelalter, Munich 1986

'Autor und Werk. Beobachtungen und Überlegungen zur höfischen Epik (ausgehend von der Donaueschinger Parzivalhandschrift G⁸)', *ZfdPh* 116 (1997), 87–114

Wolfram von Eschenbach, Stuttgart ⁷1997

Die Blutstropfen im Schnee. Über Wahrnehmung und Erkenntnis im 'Parzival' Wolframs von Eschenbach, Tübingen 2001

Bürkle, S., 'Weibliche Spiritualität und imaginierte Weiblichkeit. Deutungsmuster und -perspektiven frauenmystischer Literatur im Blick auf die Thesen Caroline Walker Bynums', *ZfdPh* 113 (1994), Sonderheft (*Mystik*), 116–43

Literatur im Kloster, Historische Funktion und rhetorische Legitimation frauenmystischer Texte des 14. Jahrhunderts, Tübingen 1999

Büttner, F. O., 'Mens divina liber grandis est. Zu einigen Darstellungen des Lesens in spätmittelalterlichen Handschriften', *Philobiblon* 16, 4 (1972), 92–126

Bynum, C. W., *Jesus as mother. Studies in the spirituality of the High Middle Ages*, Berkeley 1982

Cadden, J., *Meanings of sex difference in the Middle Ages. Medicine, science and culture*, Cambridge 1993

Camille, M., 'Seeing and reading: some visual implications of medieval literacy and illiteracy', *AH* 8 (1985), 26–49

'The language of images in medieval England, 1200–1400', in J. Alexander and P. Binski (eds.), *The age of chivalry: Art in Plantagenet England 1200–1400*, London 1987, pp. 33–40

The Gothic idol. Ideology and image-making in medieval art, Cambridge 1989

'Philological iconoclasm: edition and image in the *Vie de saint Alexis*', in R. H. Bloch and S. G. Nichols (eds.), *Medievalism and the modernist temper*, Baltimore 1996, pp. 371–401

Capua, F. di, 'Osservazioni sulla lettura e sulla preghiera ad alta voce presso gli antichi', *Rendiconti della Accademia di Archeologia, Lettere e Belle Arti*, n.s. 28 (1953), 59–99

Carruthers, M. J., *The book of memory. A study of memory in medieval culture*, Cambridge 1990

'The wife of Bath and the painting of lions', in R. Evans and L. Johnson (eds.), *Feminist readings in Middle English literature. The Wife of Bath and all her sect*, London 1994, pp. 22–53

Cartlidge, N., *Medieval marriage. Literary approaches, 1100–1300*, Cambridge 1997

Caviness, M. H., 'Anchoress, abbess, and queen: donors and patrons or intercessors and matrons?', in J. H. McCash (ed.), *The cultural patronage of medieval women*, Atlanta GA 1996, pp. 105–54

Chazelle, C. M., 'Pictures, books, and the illiterate: Pope Gregory I's letters to Serenus of Marseilles', *WI* 6 (1990), 138–53

Chinca, M., *History, fiction, verisimilitude. Studies in the poetics of Gottfried's Tristan*, London 1993

Clanchy, M. T., 'Learning to read in the Middle Ages and the role of mothers', in G. Brooks and A. K. Pugh (eds.), *Studies in the history of reading*, Reading 1984, pp. 33–9

From memory to written record, England 1066–1307, Oxford ²1993

Abelard. A medieval life, Oxford 1999

'Images of ladies with prayer books. What do they signify?', in R. N. Swanson (ed.), *The Church and the book*, Woodbridge 2004, pp. 106–22

'An icon of literacy: the depiction at Tuse of Jesus going to school', in P. Herrman (ed.), *Literacy in medieval and early modern Scandinavian culture*, no place 2005, pp. 47–73

Clark, A. L., 'Holy woman or unworthy vessel? The representation of Elisabeth of Schönau', in: C. M. Mooney (ed.), *Gendered voices. Medieval saints and their interpreters*, Philadelphia 1999, pp. 35–51

Coakley, J., 'Gender and the authority of friars: the significance of holy women for thirteenth-century Franciscans and Dominicans', *CH* 60 (1991), 445–60

Coleman, J., *Public reading and the reading public in late medieval England and France*, Cambridge 1996

Colledge, E. and Walshe, J., *A Book of Showings to the anchoress Julian of Norwich*, Toronto 1978

Constable, G., *Letters and letter-collections*, Turnhout 1976

Coon, L., 'What is the word if not semen? Priestly bodies in Carolingian exegesis', in L. Brubaker and J. M. H. Smith (eds.), *Gender in the early medieval world. East and West, 300–900*, Cambridge 2004, pp. 278–300

Copeland, R., 'Why women can't read. Medieval hermeneutics, statutory law, and the Lollard heresy trials', in S. S. Heinzelman and Z. B. Wiseman (eds.), *Representing women. Law, literature and feminism*, Durham 1994, pp. 253–86
Pedagogy, intellectuals, and dissent in the late Middle Ages. Lollardy and ideas of learning, Cambridge 2001

Crosby, R., 'Oral delivery in the Middle Ages', *Speculum* 11 (1936), 88–110

Cross, C., '"Great reasoners in scripture": the activities of women Lollards 1380–1530', in D. Baker (ed.) *Medieval women*, Oxford 1978, pp. 359–80

Curschmann, M., 'Herrad von Hohenburg', *VfL* 3, 1138–44
'Hören – Lesen – Sehen. Buch und Schriftlichkeit im Selbstverständnis der volkssprachlichen literarischen Kultur Deutschlands um 1200', *PBB* 106 (1984), 218–57
'*Pictura laicorum litteratura?* Überlegungen zum Verhältnis von Bild und volkssprachlicher Schriftlichkeit im Hoch-und Spätmittelalter bis zum Codex Manesse', in H. Keller *et al.* (eds.), *Pragmatische Schriftlichkeit im Mittelalter. Erscheinungsformen und Entwicklungsstufen*, Munich 1992, pp. 211–29

Curtius, E. R., *Europäische Literatur und lateinisches Mittelalter*, Bern 1948

Dalarun, J., 'Robert d'Arbrissel et les femmes', *Annales* 39 (1984), 1140–60

Damian-Grint, D., *The new historians of the twelfth-century renaissance. Inventing vernacular authority*, Woodbridge 1999

Degler-Spengler, B. 'Die Beginen im Rahmen der religiösen Frauenbewegung des 13. Jahrhunderts in der Schweiz', in C. Sommer-Ramer (ed.), *Die Beginen und Begarden in der Schweiz (Helvetia Sacra IX 2)*, Basel 1995, pp. 31–91

Deuchler, F., *Der Ingeborgpsalter*, Berlin 1967

Dillon, J., 'Holy women and their confessors or confessors and their holy women? Margery Kempe and continental tradition', in R. Voaden (ed.), *Prophets abroad. The reception of continental holy women in late medieval England*, Cambridge 1996, pp. 115–40

Dinshaw, C., 'Margery Kempe', in C. Dinshaw and D. Wallace (eds.), *The Cambridge Companion to medieval women's writing*, Cambridge 2003, pp. 222–39

Dinzelbacher, P., 'Rollenverweigerung, religiöser Aufbruch und mystisches Erleben mittelalterlicher Frauen', in P. Dinzelbacher and D. R. Bauer (eds.), *Religiöse*

Frauenbewegung und mystische Frömmigkeit im Mittelalter, Cologne 1988, pp. 1–58

Draesner, U., *Wege durch erzählte Welten. Intertextuelle Verweise als Mittel der Bedeutungskonstitution in Wolframs 'Parzival'*, Frankfurt 1993

Driver, M. W., 'Mirrors of a collective past: reconsidering images of medieval women', in L. Smith and J. H. M. Taylor (eds.), *Women and the book. Assessing the visual evidence*, London 1997, pp. 75–93

Dronke, P., *Women writers in the Middle Ages. A critical study of texts from Perpetua (†203) to Marguerite Porete (†1310)*, Cambridge 1984

Duby, G., *The knight, the lady and the priest. The making of modern marriage in medieval France*, London 1984

Mâle moyen âge. De l'amour et autres essais, Paris 1988

Women of the twelfth century, II: Remembering the Dead, Cambridge 1998

Duffy, E., *The stripping of the altars. Traditional religion in England c.1400–1580*, New Haven 1992

Duggan, L., 'Was art really the "book of the illiterate"?', *WI* 3 (1989), 227–51

Düwel, K., 'Ein Buch als christlich-magisches Mittel zur Geburtshilfe', in M. Stausberg (ed.), *Kontinuität und Brüche in der Religionsgeschichte*, Berlin 2001, pp. 170–93

Edwards, C., '*winileodos*? Zu Nonnen, Zensur und den Spuren der althochdeutschen Liebeslyrik', in: W. Haubrichs *et al.* (eds.), *Theodisca. Beiträge zur althochdeutschen und altniederdeutschen Sprache und Literatur in der Kultur des frühen Mittelalters*, Berlin 2000, pp. 189–206

Eggers, H., 'Non cognovi litteraturam (zu "Parzival" 115, 27)', in H. Rupp (ed.), *Wolfram von Eschenbach*, Darmstadt 1966, pp. 533–48

Ehrenschwendtner, M.-L., 'Das Bildungswesen in Frauenklöstern des Spätmittelalters. Beispiel: Dominikanerinnen', in M. Liedtke (ed.), *Handbuch der Geschichte des bayerischen Bildungswesens I*, Bad Heilbronn 1991, pp. 332–48

'A library collected by and for the use of nuns: St Catherine's convent, Nuremberg', in L. Smith and J. H. M. Taylor (eds.), *Women and the book. Assessing the visual evidence*, London 1996, pp. 123–32

'*Puellae litteratae*: the use of the vernacular in the Dominican convents of southern Germany', in D. Watt (ed.), *Medieval women in their communities*, Cardiff 1997, pp. 49–71

Die Bildung der Dominikanerinnen in Süddeutschland vom 13. bis 15. Jahrhundert, Stuttgart 2004

Ehrismann, G., *Geschichte der deutschen Literatur bis zum Ausgang des Mittelalters. Zweiter Teil, I: Frühmittelhochdeutsche Zeit*, Munich 1922

Elliott, D., 'Alternative intimacies. Men, women and spiritual direction in the twelfth century', in S. Fanous and H. Leyser (eds.), *Christina of Markyate. A twelfth-century holy woman*, London 2005, pp. 160–83

Elm, K., 'Die Stellung der Frau in Ordenswesen, Semireligiosentum und Häresie zur Zeit der heiligen Elisabeth', in *Sankt Elisabeth. Fürstin – Dienerin – Heilige*, Sigmaringen 1981, pp. 7–28

Ennen, E., *Frauen im Mittelalter*, Munich 1987

Erler, M. C., *Women, reading, and piety in late medieval England*, Cambridge 2002

Ernst, U., 'Formen der Schriftlichkeit im höfischen Roman des hohen und späten Mittelalters', *FMS* 31 (1997), 252–369

Everett, N., *Literacy in Lombard Italy, c.568–774*, Cambridge 2003

Fanous, S., 'Christina of Markyate and the double crown', in S. Fanous and H. Leyser (eds.), *Christina of Markyate. A twelfth-century holy woman*, London 2005, pp. 53–78

Fanous, S. and Leyser, H. (eds.), *Christina of Markyate. A twelfth-century holy woman*, London 2005

Feld, H., *Frauen des Mittelalters. Zwanzig geistige Profile*, Cologne 2000

Ferrante, J. M., *Woman as image in medieval literature from the twelfth century to Dante*, New York 1975

'The education of women in the Middle Ages in theory, fact, and fantasy', in P. H. Labalme (ed.), *Beyond their sex. Learned women of the European past*, New York 1980, pp. 9–42

'Public postures and private maneuvers: roles medieval women play', in M. Erler and M. Kowaleski (eds.), *Women and power in the Middle Ages*, Athens GA 1988, pp. 213–29

'Whose voice? The influence of women patrons on courtly romance', in D. Maddox and S. Sturm-Maddox (eds.), *Literary aspects of courtly culture*, Cambridge 1994, pp. 3–18

'Women's role in Latin letters from the fourth to the early twelfth century', in J. H. McCash (ed.), *The cultural patronage of medieval women*, Atlanta GA 1996, pp. 73–104

To the glory of her sex. Women's roles in the composition of medieval texts, Bloomington 1997

'*Scribe quae vides et audis*. Hildegard, her language, her secretaries', in D. Townsend and A. Taylor (eds.), *The tongue of the fathers. Gender and ideology in twelfth-century Latin*, Philadelphia 1998, pp. 102–35

Fichtenau, H., 'Monastisches und scholastisches Lesen', in G. Jenal (ed.), *Herrschaft, Kirche, Kultur. Beiträge zur Geschichte des Mittelalters*, Stuttgart 1993, pp. 317–37

Finnegan, R., *Oral poetry. Its nature, significance and social context*, Cambridge 1977

Fischer, S. R., *A history of reading*, London 2003

Fleckenstein, J., 'Miles und clericus am Königs- und Fürstenhof', in J. Fleckenstein (ed.), *Curialitas. Studien zu Grundfragen der höfisch-ritterlichen Kultur*, Göttingen 1990, pp. 302–25

Fouquet, D., *Wort und Bild in der mittelalterlichen Tristantradition. Der älteste Tristanteppich von Kloster Wienhausen und die textile Tristanüberlieferung des Mittelalters*, Berlin 1971

Galloway, P., '"Discreet and devout maidens": women's involvement in beguine communities in northern France, 1200–1500', in D. Watt (ed.), *Medieval women in their communities*, Cardiff 1997, pp. 92–115

Gameson, R., 'The Gospels of Margaret of Scotland and the literacy of an eleventh-century queen', in L. Smith and J. H. M. Taylor (eds.), *Women and the book. Assessing the visual evidence*, London 1996, pp. 149–71

Gaunt, S., *Gender and genre in medieval French literature*, Cambridge 1995

Geddes, J., 'The St Albans Psalter: the abbot and the anchoress', in S. Fanous and H. Leyser (eds.), *Christina of Markyate. A twelfth-century holy woman*, London 2005, pp. 197–216

Geith, K.-E., 'Albertus von Augsburg', *VfL* 1, 114–16

Gillespie, V., '*Lukynge in haly bukes: Lectio* in some late medieval spiritual miscellanies', in J. Hogg (ed.), *Spätmittelalterliche geistliche Literatur in der Nationalsprache*, Salzburg 1984, pp. 1–27

'Strange images of death: The Passion in later medieval English devotional and mystical writing', in J. Hogg (ed.), *Zeit, Tod und Ewigkeit in der Renaissance Literatur*, Salzburg 1987, pp. 111–59

Gleba, G., '"Ock grote Arbeyt myt Schryven vor dyt convent gedån". Die spätmittelalterlichen Klosterreformen Westfalens in ihrem liturgischen und pragmatischen Schriftgut', in G. Signori (ed.), *Lesen, Schreiben, Sticken und Erinnern. Beiträge zur Kultur- und Sozialgeschichte mittelalterlicher Frauenklöster*, Bielefeld 2000, pp. 109–122

Gold, P. S., 'Male/female cooperation: the example of Fontevrault', in J. A. Nichols and L. T. Shank (eds.), *Medieval religious women. I: Distant Echoes*, Kalamazoo 1984, pp. 151–68

The lady and the Virgin. Image, Attitude, and experience in twelfth-century France, Chicago 1985

Graf, K., *Bildnisse schreibender Frauen im Mittelalter. 9. bis Anfang 13. Jahrhundert*, Basel 2002

Gravdal, K., *Ravishing maidens. Writing rape in medieval French literature and law*, Philadelphia 1991

Green, D. H., *Irony in the medieval romance*, Cambridge 1979

'Advice and narrative action. Parzival, Herzeloyde and Gurnemanz', in D. H. Green *et al.* (eds.), *From Wolfram and Petrarch to Goethe and Grass*, Baden-Baden 1982, pp. 33–81

The art of recognition in Wolfram's Parzival, Cambridge 1982

'Zur primären Rezeption von Wolframs "Parzival"', in K. Gärtner and J. Heinzle (eds.), *Studien zu Wolfram von Eschenbach*, Tübingen 1989, pp. 271–88

'Hören und Lesen. Zur Geschichte einer mittelalterlichen Formel', in W. Raible (ed.), *Erscheinungsformen kultureller Prozesse*, Tübingen 1990, pp. 23–44

Medieval listening and reading. The primary reception of German literature 800–1300, Cambridge 1994

'*Vrume rîtr und guote vrouwen /und wîse phaffen*. Court literature and its audience', in V. Honemann *et al.* (eds.), *German narrative literature of the twelfth and thirteenth centuries*, Tübingen 1994, pp. 7–26

'Zum Erkennen und Verkennen von Ironie- und Fiktionssignalen in der höfischen Literatur', in D. Peil *et al.* (eds.), *Erkennen und Erinnern in Kunst und Literatur*, Tübingen 1998, pp. 35–56

'Das Mittelalter – eine orale Gesellschaft?', in H.-W. Goetz and J. Jarnut (eds.), *Mediävistik im 21. Jahrhundert. Stand und Perspektiven der internationalen und interdisziplinären Mittelalterforschung*, Munich 2003, pp. 333–37

The beginnings of medieval romance. Fact and fiction, 1150–1220, Cambridge 2002

Green, M. and Schleissner, M., 'Trotula', *VfL* 9, 1083–88

Green, R. *et al.*, *Herrad of Hohenburg: 'Hortus decliciarum'*, London 1979

Greenspan, K., 'Autohagiography and medieval women's spiritual autobiography', in J. Chance (ed.), *Gender and texts in the later Middle Ages*, Gainesville FL 1996, pp. 216–36

Grubmüller, K., 'Die Viten der Schwestern von Töss und Elsbeth Stagel (Überlieferung und literarische Einheit)', *ZfdA* 98 (1969), 171–204

Grundmann, H., 'Die Frauen und die Literatur im Mittelalter. Ein Beitrag zur Frage nach der Entstehung des Schrifttums in der Volkssprache', *AfK* 26 (1936), 129–61

'Litteratus-illitteratus. Der Wandel einer Bildungsnorm vom Altertum zum Mittelalter', *AfK* 40 (1958), 1–65

Religiöse Bewegungen im Mittelalter, Darmstadt 1961

Gutfleisch-Ziche, B., *Volkssprachliches und bildliches Erzählen biblischer Stoffe. Die illustrierten Handschriften der Altdeutschen Genesis und des Leben Jesu der Frau Ava*, Frankfurt 1997

Haas, A. M., 'Deutsche Mystik', in I. Glier (ed.), *Die deutsche Literatur im späten Mittelalter 1250–1370*, Munich 1987, pp. 234–305

Hamburger, J. F., *The Rothschild Canticles. Art and mysticism in Flanders and the Rhineland circa 1300*, New Haven 1990

'Art enclosure and the *cura monialium*. Prolegomena in the guise of a postscript', *Gesta* 31, 2 (1992), 108–34

The visual and the visionary. Art and female spirituality in late medieval Germany, New York 1998

Hamesse, J., 'Le vocabulaire de la transmission orale des textes', in O. Weijers (ed.), *Vocabulaire du livre et de l'écriture au moyen âge*, Turnhout 1989, pp. 168–94

'Le modèle scolastique de la lecture', in G. Cavallo and R. Chartier (eds.), *Histoire de la lecture dans le monde occidental*, Paris 1997, pp. 125–45

Hamilton, B., 'Wisdom from the East: the reception by the Cathars of Eastern dualist texts', in P. Biller and A. Hudson (eds.), *Heresy and literacy, 1000–1530*, Cambridge 1994, pp. 38–60

Hanna, R., 'The difficulty of Ricardian prose translation", *MLQ* 51 (1990), 319–40

Hartham, J., *Books of hours and their owners*, London 1977

Hasebrink, B., 'Tischlesung und Bildungskultur im Nürnberger Katharinenkloster. Ein Beitrag zu ihrer Rekonstruktion', in M. Kintzinger *et al.* (eds.), *Schule und Schüler im Mittelalter. Beiträge zur europäischen Bildungsgeschichte des 9. bis 15. Jahrhunderts*, Cologne 1996, pp. 187–216

Haubrichs, W., *Die Anfänge: Versuche volkssprachiger Schriftlichkeit im frühen Mittelalter (ca. 700–1050/60)*, Tübingen 1995

Haug, W., 'Artussage und Heilsgeschichte. Zum Programm des Fußbodenmosaiks von Otranto', in W. Haug, *Strukturen als Schlüssel zur Welt. Kleine Schriften zur Erzählliteratur des Mittelalters*, Tübingen 1989, pp. 409–46

Head, T., 'The marriages of Christina of Markyate', in S. Fanous and H. Leyser (eds.), *Christina of Markyate. A twelfth-century holy woman*, London 2005, pp. 116–37

Heimbach, M., *'Der ungelehrte Mund' als Autorität. Mystische Erfahrung als Quelle kirchlich-prophetischer Rede im Werk Mechthilds von Magdeburg*, Stuttgart 1989

Heinzle, J., *Wandlungen and Neuansätze im 13. Jahrhundert*, Tübingen 1994

(ed.), *Geschichte der deutschen Literatur von den Anfängen bis zum Beginn der Neuzeit*, Tübingen 1994ff.

Hellgardt, E., 'Seckauer Handschriften als Träger frühmittelhochdeutscher Texte', in A. Ebenbauer *et al.* (eds.), *Die mittelalterliche Literatur in der Steiermark*, Bern 1988, pp. 103–30

'Deutsche Gebetsanweisungen zum Psalter in lateinischen und deutschen Handschriften und Drucken des 12.–16. Jahrhunderts', in H. Reinitzer (ed.), *Deutsche Bibelübersetzungen des Mittelalters*, Bern 1991, pp. 400–13

'Lateinisch-deutsche Textensembles', in N. Henkel and N. Palmer (eds.), *Latein und Volkssprache im deutschen Mittelalter 1100–1500*, Tübingen 1992, pp. 19–31

Hen, Y., 'Gender and the patronage of culture in Merovingian Gaul', in L. Brubaker and J. M. H. Smith (eds.), *Gender in the early medieval world. East and West, 300–900*, Cambridge 2004, pp. 217–33

Hendrickson, G. L., 'Ancient Reading', *CJ* 25 (1929/30), 182–96

Henkel, N., 'Bildtexte. Die Spruchbänder in der Berliner Handschrift von Heinrichs von Veldeke Eneasroman', in FS for D. Wuttke, Baden-Baden 1989, pp. 1–47

'Religiöses Erzählen um 1200 im Kontext höfischer Literatur. Priester Wernher, Konrad von Fußesbrunnen, Konrad von Heimesfurt', in T. R. Jackson *et al.* (eds.), *Die Vermittlung geistlicher Inhalte im deutschen Mittelalter*, Tübingen 1996, pp. 1–21

Hill, J., 'Learning Latin in Anglo-Saxon England: traditions, texts and techniques', in S. Rees Jones (ed.), *Learning and literacy in medieval England and abroad*, Turnhout 2003, pp. 7–29

Hindman, S., *Sealed in Parchment. Rereadings of knighthood in the illuminated manuscripts of Chrétien de Troyes*, Chicago 1994

'Æsop's cock and Marie's hen: gendered authorship in text and image in manuscripts of Marie de France's *Fables*', in L. Smith and J. H. M. Taylor (eds.), *Women and the book. Assessing the visual evidence*, London 1996, pp. 45–56

Hollis, S., *Anglo-Saxon women and the Church*, Woodbridge 1992

Hollis, S. and Wogan-Browne, J., 'St Albans and women's monasticism: lives and foundations in Christina's world', in S. Fanous and H. Leyser (eds.), *Christina of Markyate. A twelfth-century holy woman*, London 2005, pp. 25–52

Hubrath, M., *Schreiben und Erinnern. Zur 'memoria' im Liber Specialis Gratiae Mechthilds von Hakeborn*, Paderborn 1996

'Monastische Memoria als Denkform in der Viten- und Offenbarungsliteratur aus süddeutschen Frauenklöstern des Spätmittelalters', *LiLi* 27, Heft 105 (1997), 22–38

Hudson, A., '*Laicus litteratus*: the paradox of Lollardy', in P. Biller and A. Hudson (eds.), *Heresy and literacy, 1100–1530*, Cambridge 1984, pp. 222–36

Huneycutt, L. L., '"Proclaiming her dignity abroad": The literary and artistic network of Matilda of Scotland, queen of England 1110–1118', in J. H. McCash (ed.), *The cultural patronage of medieval women*, Atlanta GA 1996, pp. 155–74

Hunt, T., 'The significance of Thomas's *Tristan*', *RMS* 7 (1981), 41–61

'The life of St Alexis, 475–1125', in S. Fanous and H. Leyser (eds.), *Christina of Markyate. A twelfth-century holy woman*, London 2005, pp. 217–28

Huot, S., *From song to book. The poetics of writing in Old French lyric and lyrical narrative poetry*, Ithaca 1987

'Polytextual reading: the meditative reading of real and metaphorical books', in M. Chinca and C. Young (eds.), *Orality and literacy in the Middle Ages*, Turnhout 2005, pp. 203–22

Hutchison, A. M., 'Devotional reading in the monastery and in the late medieval household', in M. G. Sargent (ed.), *De Cella in Seculum. Religious and secular life and devotion in late medieval England*, Cambridge 1989, pp. 215–27

'What the nuns read: literary evidence from the English Bridgettine house, Syon Abbey', *MS* 57 (1995), 205–22

Illich, I., *In the vineyard of the text. A commentary on Hugh's 'Didascalicon'*, Chicago 1993

Jaeger, C. S., *The origins of courtliness. Civilizing trends and the formation of courtly ideals 939–1210*, Philadelphia 1985

Ennobling love. In search of a lost sensibility, Philadelphia 1999

'*Epistolae duorum amantium* and the ascription to Heloise and Abelard', in L. Olson and K. Kerby-Fulton (eds.), *Voices in dialogue. Reading women in the Middle Ages*, Notre Dame 2005, pp. 125–66

Jambeck, K. K., 'Reclaiming the woman in the book: Marie de France and the *Fables*', in L. Smith and J. H. M. Taylor (eds.), *Women, the book and the worldly*, Cambridge 1995, pp. 119–37

'Patterns of women's literary patronage: England, 1200–ca. 1475', in J. H. McCash (ed.), *The cultural patronage of medieval women*, Atlanta GA 1996, pp. 228–65

Janota, J., *Orientierung durch volkssprachige Schriftlichkeit (1280/90–1380/90)*, Tübingen 2004

Johnson, L. S., 'The trope of the scribe and the question of literary authority in the works of Julian of Norwich and Margery Kemp', *Speculum* 66 (1991), 820–38

Jong, M. de, 'Bride shows revisited: praise, slander and exegesis in the reign of the empress Judith', in L. Brubaker and J. M. H. Smith (eds.), *Gender in the early medieval world. East and West, 300–900*, Cambridge 2004, pp. 257–77

Kartschoke, D., *Geschichte der deutschen Literatur im frühen Mittelalter*, Munich 1990

Keck, A., *Die Liebeskonzeption der mittelalterlichen Tristanromane. Zur Erzähllogik der Werke Bérouls, Eilharts, Thomas und Gottfrieds*, Munich 1998

Keller, H. E., *My secret is mine. Studies on religion and eros in the German Middle Ages*, Louvain 2000

Kerby-Fulton, K., 'When women preached. An introduction to female homiletic, sacramental and liturgical roles in the later Middle Ages', in L. Olson and K. Kerby-Fulton (eds.), *Voices in dialogue. Reading women in the Middle Ages*, Notre Dame 2005, pp. 31–55

Keynes, S. and Lapidge, M., *Alfred the Great. Asser's Life of King Alfred and other contemporary sources*, London 1983

Klaes, M., *Vita sanctae Hildegardis*, Turnhout 1993

Klapisch-Zuber, C. (ed.), *A history of women in the West. II. Silences of the Middle Ages*, Cambridge MA 1998

Knapp, F. P., *Die Literatur des Früh- und Hochmittelalters in den Bistümern Passau, Salzburg, Brixen und Trient von den Anfängen bis zum Jahre 1273*, Graz 1994

Knox, B. M. W., 'Silent reading in antiquity', *GRBS* 9 (1968), 421–35

Köbele, S., *Bilder der unbegriffenen Wahrheit. Zur Struktur mystischer Rede im Spannungsfeld von Latein und Volkssprache*, Tübingen 1993

Köhn, R., 'Monastisches Bildungsideal und weltgeistliches Wissenschaftsdenken. Zur Vorgeschichte des Mendikantenstreites an der Universität Paris', *MM* 10 (1976), 1–37

'Latein und Volkssprache, Schriftlichkeit und Mündlichkeit in der Korrespondenz des lateinischen Mittelalters', in J. O. Fichte *et al.* (eds.), *Zusammenhänge, Einflüsse, Wirkungen*, Berlin 1986, pp. 340–56

Kolve, V. A., 'The annunciation to Christine: authorial empowerment in *The Book of the City of Ladies*', in B. Cassidy (ed.), *Iconography at the crossroads*, Princeton 1993, pp. 171–91

Köpf, U., 'Bernhard von Clairvaux in der Frauenmystik', in P. Dinzelbacher and D. R. Bauer (eds.), *Frauenmystik im Mittelalter*, Ostfildern 1985, pp. 48–77

Kraus, C. von, *Des Minnesangs Frühling. Untersuchungen*, Stuttgart 1981

Krone und Schleier. Kunst aus mittelalterlichen Frauenklöstern. (Catalogue of the exhibition held in 2005 in Essen and Bonn)

Krueger, R. L., 'Misogyny, manipulation, and the female reader in Hue de Rotelande's *Ipomedon*', in K. Busby and E. Kooper (eds.), *Courtly literature. Culture and context*, Amsterdam 1990, pp. 395–409

Women readers and the ideology of gender in Old French verse romance, Cambridge 1993

'Questions of gender in Old French courtly romance', in R. L. Krueger (ed.), *The Cambridge Companion to medieval romance*, Cambridge 2000, pp. 132–49

'Female voices in convents, courts and households: the French Middle Ages', in S. Stephens (ed.), *A history of women's writing in France*, Cambridge 2000, pp. 10–40

'Marie de France', in C. Dinshaw and D. Wallace (eds.), *The Cambridge Companion to medieval women's writing*, Cambridge 2003, pp. 172–83

Krug, R., *Reading families. Women's literate practice in late medieval England*, Ithaca 2002

Krüger, S., '"Verhöflichter Krieger" und miles illitteratus', in J. Fleckenstein (ed.), *Curialitas, Studien zu Grundfragen der höfisch-ritterlichen Kultur*, Göttingen 1990, pp. 326–49

Küsters, U. *Der verschlossene Garten. Volkssprachliche Hohelied-Auslegung und monastische Lebensform im 12. Jahrhundert*, Düsseldorf 1985

Labarge, M. W., *Women in medieval life*, London 2001

Langer, O., 'Enteignete Existenz und mystische Erfahrung. Zu Meister Eckharts Auseinandersetzung mit der Frauenmystik seiner Zeit', in K. O. Seidel (ed.), *Sô predigent etelîche. Beiträge zur deutschen und niederländischen Predigt im Mittelalter*, Göppingen 1982, pp. 49–96

Christliche Mystik im Mittelalter, Mystik und Rationalisierung – Stationen eines Konflikts, Darmstadt 2004

Latzke, T., 'Robert von Arbrissel, Ermengard und Eva', *MlJb* 19 (1984), 116–54

Leclercq, J., 'Recherches sur les sermons sur les Cantiques de saint Bernard', *RB* 64 (1954), 208–23

The love of learning and the desire for God. A study of monastic culture, New York 1962

Legge, M. D., *Anglo-Norman literature and its background*, Oxford 1963

Lejeune, R., 'Rôle littéraire d'Aliénor d'Aquitaine et de sa famille', *CN* 14 (1954), 5–57

'Rôle littéraire de la famille d'Aliénor d'Aquitaine', *CCM* 1 (1958), 319–37

Lewis, G. J., *By women, for women, about women. Sister-books of fourteenth-century Germany*, Toronto 1996

Leyser, H., *Hermits and the new monasticism. A study of religious communities in Western Europe 1000–1150*, London 1984

Medieval women. A social history of women in England 450–1500, London 1996

Leyser, K. J., *Rule and conflict in an early medieval society. Ottonian Saxony*, London 1979

LoPrete, K. A., 'Adela of Blois: familial alliances and female lordship', in T. Evergates (ed.), *Aristocratic women in medieval France*, Philadelphia 1999, pp. 7–43

Lucas, A. M., *Women in the Middle Ages. Religion, marriage and letters*, Brighton 1983

Lundt, B., 'Zur Entstehung der Universität als Männerwelt', in E. Kleinau and C. Opitz (eds.), *Geschichte der Mädchen- und Frauenerziehung*, Frankfurt 1996, pp. 103–18

Lutz, E. C., 'Überlegungen zu lese- und erkenntnistheoretischen Implikationen von Gottfrieds Schreiben', in C. Huber and V. Millet (eds.), *Der Tristan Gottfrieds von Straßburg*, Tübingen 2002, pp. 295–315

Mann, J., *Feminizing Chaucer*, Cambridge 2002

Martin, R., *Chaucer's women. Nuns, Wives and Amazons*, Basingstoke 1996

McCash, J. H., 'The cultural patronage of medieval women: an overview', in J. H. McCash (ed.), *The cultural patronage of medieval women*, Atlanta GA 1996, pp. 1–49

McKitterick, R., *The Carolingians and the written word*, Cambridge 1989

'Frauen und Schriftlichkeit im Frühmittelalter', in H.-W. Goetz (ed.), *Weibliche Lebensgestaltung im frühen Mittelalter*, Cologne 1991, pp. 65–118

'Nuns' scriptoria in England and Francia in the eighth century', *Francia* 19/1 (1992), 1–35

'Ottonian intellectual culture in the tenth century and the role of Theophanu', *EME* 2 (1993), 53–74

McNamer, S., 'Lyrics and romances', in C. Dinshaw and D. Wallace (eds.), *The Cambridge Companion to medieval women's writing*, Cambridge 2003, pp. 195–209

McSheffrey, S., 'Literacy and the gender gap in the late Middle Ages. Women and reading in Lollard communities', in L. Smith and J. H. M. Taylor (eds.), *Women, the book and the godly*, Cambridge 1995, pp. 157–70

Gender and heresy. Women and men in Lollard communities, 1420–1530, Philadelphia 1995

Meale, C. M., 'Legends of good women in the Middle Ages', *ASNSL* 144 (1992), 55–70

'". . . alle the bokes that I haue of latyn, englisch, and frensch": laywomen and their books in late medieval England', in C. M. Meale (ed.), *Women and literature in Britain, 1150–1500*, Cambridge 1996, pp. 128–58

(ed.), *Women and literature in Britain 1150–1500*, Cambridge 1996

Meier, C., 'Eriugena im Nonnenkloster? Überlegungen zum Verhältnis von Prophetentum und Werkgestalt in den *figmenta prophetica* Hildegards von Bingen', *FMS* 19 (1985), 466–97

'Scientia divinorum operum. Zu Hildegards von Bingen visionär-künstlerischer Rezeption Eriugenas', in W. Beierwaltes (ed.), *Eriugena redivivus. Zur Wirkungsgeschichte seines Denkens im Mittelalter und im Übergang zur Neuzeit*, Heidelberg 1987, pp. 89–141

'*Ecce auctor*. Beiträge zur Ikonographie literarischer Urheberschaft im Mittelalter', *FMS* 34 (2000), 338–92

Mertens, V., 'Deutsche Literatur am Welfenhof', in J. Luckhardt and F. Niehoff (eds.), *Heinrich der Löwe und seine Zeit. Herrschaft und Repräsentation der Welfen 1125–1235*, Munich 1995, II 204–12

Merveldt, N. von, *Translatio und Memoria. Zur Poetik der Memoria des Prosa Lancelot*, Frankfurt 2004

Meyer, P., 'Versions en prose des *Vies des Pères*', *HLF* 33 (1906), 254–328

Michalove, S. D., 'The education of aristocratic women in fifteenth-century England', in S. D. Michalove and A. Compton Reeves (eds.), *Estrangement, enterprise and education in fifteenth-century England*, Stroud 1998, pp. 117–39

Miethke, J., *Die mittelalterlichen Universitäten und das gesprochene Wort*, Munich 1990

Millett, B., 'Women in No Man's Land: English recluses and the development of vernacular literature in the twelfth and thirteenth centuries', in C. M. Meale (ed.), *Women and literature in Britain, 1150–1500*, Cambridge 1996, pp. 86–103

Ancrene Wisse and the Book of Hours', in D. Renevey and C. Whitehead (eds.), *Writing religious women. Female spiritual and textual practice in late medieval England*, Cardiff 2000, pp. 21–40

Millett, B. and Wogan-Browne, J. (eds.), *Medieval English prose for women. Selections from the Katherine Group and Ancrene Wisse*, Oxford 1992

Minnis, A. J., *Medieval theory of authorship. Scholastic literary attitudes in the later Middle Ages*, Aldershot 1988

Magister amoris. The Roman de la Rose and vernacular hermeneutics, Oxford 2001

Mohr, W., 'Wolframs Kyot und Guiot de Provins', in W. Mohr, *Wolfram von Eschenbach. Aufsätze*, Göppingen 1979, pp. 152–69

Mölk, U., *Französische Literarästhetik des 12. und 13. Jahrhunderts. Prologe – Exkurse – Epiloge*, Tübingen 1969

Nagel, B., *Hrotsvit von Gandersheim*, Stuttgart 1965

Nelson, J. L., 'Queens as Jezebels: the careers of Brunhild and Balthild in Merovingian history', in D. Baker (ed.), *Medieval women*, Oxford 1978, pp. 31–77

Neumann, H., 'Beiträge zur Textgeschichte des "Fließenden Lichts der Gottheit" und zur Lebensgeschichte Mechthilds von Magdeburg', in K. Ruh (ed.), *Altdeutsche und altniederländische Mystik*, Darmstadt 1964, pp. 175–239

Newman, B., *Sister of wisdom. St. Hildegard's theology of the feminine*, Aldershot 1987

'Authority, authenticity, and the repression of Heloise', *JMRS* 22 (1992), 121–57

From virile woman to WomanChrist. Studies in medieval religion and literature, Philadelphia 1995

'Hildegard and her hagiographers. The remaking of female sainthood', in C. M. Mooney (ed.), *Gendered voices. Medieval saints and their interpreters*, Philadelphia 1999, pp. 16–34

God and the goddesses. Vision, poetry, and belief in the Middle Ages, Philadelphia 2003

'More thoughts on medieval women's intelligence. Denied, projected, embodied', in L. Olson and K. Kerby-Fulton (eds.), *Voices in dialogue. Reading women in the Middle Ages*, Notre Dame 2005, pp. 231–43

Nolan, K., 'The queen's choice. Eleanor of Aquitaine and the tombs at Fontevraud', in B. Wheeler and J. C. Parsons (eds.), *Eleanor of Aquitaine. Lord and Lady*, New York 2003, pp. 377–405

Noonan, J. T., 'Power to choose', *Viator* 4 (1973), 419–34

Nordenfalk, C., 'Der inspirierte Evangelist', *WJbK* 36 (1983), 175–90

O'Brien O'Keeffe, K., 'Listening to the scenes of reading: King Alfred's talking prefaces', in M. Chinca and C. Young (eds.), *Orality and literacy in the Middle Ages*, Turnhout 2005, pp. 17–36

Ochsenbein, P., 'Deutschsprachige Privatgebetbücher vor 1400', in V. Honemann and N. F. Palmer (eds.), *Deutsche Handschriften 1100–1400*, Tübingen 1988, pp. 379–98

'Das Gebetbuch von Muri als frühes Zeugnis privater Frömmigkeit einer Frau um 1200', in R. Schnell (ed.), *Gotes unde der werlde hulde. Literatur in Mittelalter und Neuzeit*, Bern 1989, pp. 175–99

'Latein und Deutsch im Alltag oberrheinischer Dominikanerinnenklöster des Spätmittelalters', in N. Henkel and N. F. Palmer (eds.), *Latein und Volkssprache im deutschen Mittelalter 1100–1500*, Tübingen 1992, pp. 42–51

Oexle, O. G., 'Memoria in der Gesellschaft und Kultur des Mittelalters', in J. Heinzle (ed.), *Modernes Mittelalter: neue Bilder einer populären Epoche*, Frankfurt 1994, pp. 297–323

Offergeld, T., *Hugo von Sankt Viktor. Didascalicon de studio legendi. Studienbuch*, Freiburg 1997

Ohly, F., 'Ein Admonter Liebesgruß', *ZfdA* 87 (1956/1957), 13–23

Hohelied-Studien. Grundzüge einer Geschichte der Hoheliedauslegung des Abendlandes bis um 1200, Wiesbaden 1958

'Wolframs Gebet an den Heiligen Geist im Eingang des "Willehalm"', *ZfdA* 91 (1961/62), 1–37

Das St. Trudperter Hohelied. Eine Lehre der liebenden Gotteserkenntnis, Frankfurt 1998

Oliver, J. H., *Gothic manuscript illumination in the diocese of Liège (c.1250–c.1330)*, Louvain 1988

'Worship of the word: some Gothic *Nonnenbücher* in their devotional context', in L. Smith and J. H. M. Taylor (eds.), *Women and the book. Assessing the visual evidence*, London 1996, pp. 106–122

Oliver, J. H. and Simons, W., 'Reflections on beguines and psalters', *OGE* 66 (1992), 249–59

Olson, L., 'Did medieval English women read Augustine's *Confessiones*? Constructing feminine interiority and literacy in the eleventh and twelfth centuries', in S. Rees Jones (ed.), *Learning and literacy in medieval England and abroad*, Turnhout 2003, pp. 69–96

'Reading, writing, and relationships in dialogue', in L. Olson and K. Kerby-Fulton (eds.), *Voices in dialogue. Reading women in the Middle Ages*, Notre Dame 2005, pp. 1–30

Orme, N., *From childhood to chivalry. The education of the English kings and aristocracy 1066–1530*, London 1984

Ortmann, C., 'Das Buch der Minne. Methodologischer Versuch zur deutschlateinischen Gegebenheit des "Fließenden Lichts der Gottheit" Mechtilds von Magdeburg', in G. Hahn and H. Ragotzky (eds.), *Grundlagen des Verstehens mittelalterlicher Literatur. Literarische Texte und ihr historischer Erkenntniswert*, Stuttgart 1992, pp. 158–86

Ott, N. H., 'Texte und Bilder. Beziehungen zwischen den Medien Kunst und Literatur in Mittelalter und früher Neuzeit', in H. Wenzel *et al.* (eds.), *Die Verschriftlichung der Welt. Bild, Text und Zahl in der Kultur des Mittelalters und der frühen Neuzeit*, Vienna 2000, pp. 105–43

Pächt, O. *et al.*, *The St Albans Psalter (Albani Psalter)*, London 1960

Pagels, E. H., 'What became of God the mother? Conflicting images of God in early Christianity', *Signs* 2 (1976/77), 293–303

Palmer, N. F., 'Kapitel und Buch. Zu den Gliederungsprinzipien mittelalterlicher Bücher', *FMS* 23 (1989), 43–88

'Das Buch als Bedeutungsträger bei Mechthild von Magdeburg', in W. Harms and K. Speckenbach (eds.), *Bildhafte Rede in Mittelalter und früher Neuzeit. Probleme ihrer Legitimation und ihrer Funktion*, Tübingen 1992, pp. 217–35

Paolini, L., 'Italian Catharism and written culture', in P. Biller and A. Hudson (eds.), *Heresy and literacy, 1000–1530*, Cambridge 1994, pp. 83–103

Parkes, M. B., 'The influence of the concepts of *ordinatio* and *compilatio* on the development of the book', in J. J. G. Alexander and M. T. Gibson (eds.), *Medieval learning and literature*, Oxford 1971, pp. 115–38

'Lire, écrire, interpréter le texte. Pratiques monastiques dans le haut moyen âge', in G. Cavallo and R. Chartier (eds.), *Histoire de la lecture dans le monde occidental*, Paris 1997, pp. 109–23

'Lectio (OE *rædan*)', *ASE* 26 (1997), 2–20

Paterson, L. M., *The world of the troubadours. Medieval Occitan society, c.1100–c.1300*, Cambridge 1993

Patschkovsky, A., 'The literacy of Waldensianism from Valdes to c.1400', in P. Biller and A. Hudson (eds.), *Heresy and literacy, 1000–1530*, Cambridge 1984, pp. 112–36

Penketh, S., 'Women and Books of Hours', in L. Smith and J. H. M. Taylor (eds.), *Women and the book. Assessing the visual evidence*, London 1996, pp. 266–81

Percival, P., *Chaucer's legendary good women*, Cambridge 1998

Peters, U., 'Das "Leben" der Christine Ebner: Textanalyse und kulturhistorischer Kommentar', in K. Ruh (ed.), *Abendländische Mystik im Mittelalter*, Stuttgart 1986, pp. 402–22

'Frauenliteratur im Mittelalter? Überlegungen zur Trobairitzpoesie, zur Frauen-mystik und zur feministischen Literaturbetrachtung', *GRM* 38 (1988), 35–56

Religiöse Erfahrung als literarisches Faktum. Zur Vorgeschichte und Genese frauen-mystischer Texte des 13. und 14. Jahrhunderts, Tübingen 1988

Pevsner, N., *Cambridgeshire*, Harmondsworth 1954

Pohl, W., 'Gender and ethnicity in the early Middle Ages', in L. Brubaker and J. M. H. Smith (eds.), *Gender in the early medieval world. East and West, 300–900*, Cambridge 2004, pp. 23–43

Poor, S. S., 'Cloaking the body in text: the question of female authorship in the writings of Mechthild von Magdeburg', *Exemplaria* 12 (2000), 417–53

'Mechthild von Magdeburg. Gender and the "unlearned tongue"', *JMEMS* 31 (2001), 213–50

Mechthild of Magdeburg and her book. Gender and the making of textual authority, Philadelphia 2004

Poorter, A. de, *Catalogue des mss. de la Bibliothèque publique de la ville de Bruges*, Gembloux 1934

Power, E., *Medieval women*, Cambridge 2000

Pratt, K., 'The strains of defense: the many voices in Jean LeFèvre's Livre de Leesce', in T. S. Fenster and C. A. Lees (eds.), *Gender in debate from the early Middle Ages to the Renaissance*, New York 2002, pp. 113–33

Rashdall, H., *The universities of Europe in the Middle Ages*, Oxford 1895

Reuvekamp-Felber, T., *Volkssprache zwischen Stift und Hof. Hofgeistliche in Literatur und Gesellschaft des 12. und 13. Jahrhunderts*, Cologne 2003

Reynolds, S., *Medieval reading. Grammar, rhetoric and the classical text*, Cambridge 1996

Riché, P., 'Le Psautier, livre de lecture élémentaire d'après les vies des saints mérovingiens', in *Études mérovingiennes. Actes des journées de Poitiers 1–3 Mai 1952*, Paris 1953, pp. 253–6

'L'instruction des laïcs au XIIᵉ siècle', in *Mélanges Saint Bernard. XXIVᵉ Congrès de l'Association Bourguignonne des Sociétés Savantes, Dijon 1953*, Dijon 1954, pp. 212–17

'Recherches sur l'instruction des laïcs du IXᵉ au XIIᵉ siècle', *CCM* 5 (1962), 175–82

Education and culture in the barbarian West, Columbia SC 1976

Ecoles et enseignement dans l'occident chrétien de la fin du Vᵉ siècle au milieu du XIᵉ siècle, Paris 1979

'L'éducation religieuse par les femmes dans le haut moyen âge: le "Manuel" de Dhuoda', in J. Delumeau (ed.), *La religion de ma mère. Les femmes et la transmission de la foi*, Paris 1992, pp. 37–49

Ridder, K., 'Parzivals schmerzliche Erinnerung', *LiLi* 114 (1999), 21–41

Riddy, F., '"Women talking about the things of God": a late medieval sub-culture', in C. M. Meale (ed.), *Women and literature in Britain, 1150–1500*, Cambridge 1996, pp. 104–27

Riedlinger, H., *Die Makellosigkeit der Kirche in den lateinischen Hoheliedkommentaren des Mittelalters*, Münster 1958

Robertson, E., '"The living hand": thirteenth-century female literacy, materialist immanence, and the reader of the *Ancrene Wisse*', *Speculum* 78 (2003), 1–36

Robinson, P. R., 'A twelfth-century *scriptrix* from Nunnaminster', in P. R. Robinson and R. Zim (eds.), *Of the making of books. Medieval manuscripts, their scribes and readers*, Aldershot 1997, pp. 73–93

Rösener, W., 'Die höfische Frau im Hochmittelalter', in J. Fleckenstein (ed.), *Curialitas, Studien zu Grundfragen der höfisch-ritterlichen Kultur*, Göttingen 1990, pp. 171–230

Rosenfeld, H.-F., 'Alexius', *VfL* 1, 226–35

Rouse, M. A. and R. H., '*Statim invenire*: schools, preachers, and new attitudes to the page', in R. L. Benson and G. Constable (eds.), *Renaissance and renewal in the twelfth century*, Oxford 1982, pp. 201–25

'La naissance des index', in H.-J. Martin *et al.* (eds.), *Histoire de l'édition française, I: Le livre conquérant du moyen âge*, Paris 1983, pp. 77–86

'The vocabulary of wax tablets', in O. Weijers (ed.), *Vocabulaire du livre et de l'écriture au moyen âge*, Turnhout 1989, pp. 220–37

Illiterati et uxorati. Manuscripts and their makers. Commercial book producers in medieval Paris 1200–1500, Turnhout 2000

Roy, G., '"Sharpen your mind with the whetstone of books". The female recluse as reader in Goscelin's *Liber confortatorius*, Aelred of Rievaulx's *De institutione inclusarum* and the *Ancrene Wisse*', in L. Smith and J. H. M. Taylor (eds.), *Women, the book and the godly*, Cambridge 1995, pp. 113–35

Rubin, M., *Corpus Christi. The eucharist in late medieval culture*, Cambridge 1991

Ruh, K., 'Beginenmystik. Hadewijch, Mechthild von Magdeburg, Marguerite Porete', *ZfdA* 106 (1977), 265–77

Meister Eckhart. Theologe – Prediger – Mystiker, Munich 1985

Geschichte der abendländischen Mystik, Munich 1990–6

(ed.), *Die deutsche Literatur des Mittelalters. Verfasserlexikon*, Berlin 1978ff.

Ruiz-Calvez, E., 'Religion de la mère, religion des mères. Sainte Anne éducatrice: les images de la mère selon l'iconographie de sainte Anne, XVᵉ–XVIIᵉ siècle', in J. Delumeau (ed.), *La religion de ma mère. Les femmes et la transmission de la foi*, Paris 1992, pp. 123–55

Rushing, J. A., *Images of adventure. Yvain in the visual arts*, Philadelphia 1995

Saenger, P., 'Silent reading: its impact on late medieval script and society', *Viator* 13 (1982), 367–414

'Books of hours and the reading habits of the later Middle Ages', in R. Chartier (ed.), *The culture of print. Power and the uses of print in early modern Europe*, Cambridge 1989, pp. 141–73

'Lire aux derniers siècles du moyen âge', in R. Chartier and G. Cavallo (eds.), *Histoire de la lecture dans le monde occidental*, Paris 1997, pp. 147–74

Space between words. The origins of silent reading, Stanford 1997

Sauerländer, W., 'Die Naumburger Stifterfiguren. Rückblick und Fragen', in R. Haussherr and C. Väterlein (eds.), *Die Zeit der Staufer. Geschichte – Kunst – Kultur. Katalog der Ausstellung Stuttgart 1977*, Stuttgart 1979, V 169–245

Scase, W., 'St Anne and the education of the virgin: literary and artistic traditions and their implications', in N. Rogers (ed.), *England in the fourteenth century*, Stanford 1993, pp. 81–96

Scattergood, J., 'The jongleur, the copyist, and the printer: the tradition of Chaucer's Wordes unto Adam, his own scriveyn', in K. Busby and E. Kooper (eds.), *Courtly literature. Culture and Context*, Amsterdam 1990, pp. 499–508

Schaller, D., 'Probleme der Überlieferung und Verfasserschaft lateinischer Liebesbriefe des hohen Mittelalters', *MlJb* 3 (1966), 25–36

Schibanoff, S., 'Taking the gold out of Egypt: the art of reading as a woman', in E. A. Flynn and P. P. Schweickart (eds.), *Gender and reading. Essays on readers, texts, and contexts*, Baltimore 1986, pp. 83–106

Schiewer, H.-J., 'Möglichkeiten und Grenzen schreibender Ordensfrauen im Spätmittelalter', in B. Helbling *et al.* (eds.), *Bettelorden, Bruderschaften und*

Beginen in Zürich. Stadtkultur und Seelenheil im Mittelalter, Zürich 2002, pp. 179–87

'Literarisches Leben in dominikanischen Frauenklöstern des 14. Jahrhunderts: das Modell St. Katharinental bei Diessenhofen', in F. Eisermann *et al.* (eds.), *Studien und Texte zur literarischen und materiellen Kultur der Frauenklöster im Spätmittelalter*, Leiden 2004, pp. 285–309

Schirmer, E., 'Reading lessons at Syon Abbey. *The Miroure of Oure Ladye* and the mandates of vernacular theology', in L. Olson and K. Kerby-Fulton (eds.), *Voices in dialogue. Reading women in the Middle Ages*, Notre Dame 2005, pp. 345–76

Schirmer, W. F., 'Die kulturelle Rolle des englischen Hofes im 12. Jahrhundert', in J. Bumke (ed.), *Literarisches Mäzenatentum. Ausgewählte Forschungen zur Rolle des Gönners und Auftraggebers in der mittelalterlichen Literatur*, Darmstadt 1982, pp. 232–47

Schirmer, W. F. and Broich, U., *Studien zum literarischen Patronat im England des 12. Jahrhunderts*, Cologne 1962

Schmolke-Hasselmann, B., *Der arthurische Versroman von Chrestien bis Froissart. Zur Geschichte einer Gattung*, Tübingen 1980

Schneider, K., *Gotische Schriften in deutscher Sprache. I. Vom späten 12. Jahrhundert bis um 1300*, Wiesbaden 1987

Schneidmüller, B. (ed.), *Die Welfen und ihr Braunschweiger Hof im hohen Mittelalter*, Wiesbaden 1995

Schnell, R., *Causa amoris. Liebeskonzeption und Liebesdarstellung in der mittelalterlichen Literatur*, Bern 1985

Frauendiskurs, Männerdiskurs, Ehediskurs. Textsorten und Geschlechterkonzepte in Mittelalter und früher Neuzeit, Frankfurt 1998

Scholz, M. G., *Hören und Lesen. Studien zur primären Rezeption der Literatur im 12. und 13. Jahrhundert*, Wiesbaden 1980

Schreiner, K., '"... wie Maria geleicht einem puch". Beiträge zur Buchmetaphorik des hohen und späten Mittelalters', *AGB* 11 (1970), 1437–64

'Laienbildung als Herausforderung für Kirche und Gesellschaft. Religiöse Vorbehalte und soziale Widerstände gegen die Verbreitung von Wissen im späten Mittelalter und in der Reformation', *ZHF* 11 (1984), 257–354

'Konnte Maria lesen? Von der Magd des Herrn zur Symbolgestalt mittelalterlicher Frauenbildung', *Merkur* 44, 1 (1990), 82–8

'Marienverehrung, Lesekultur, Schriftlichkeit. Bildungs- und frömmigkeitsgeschichtliche Studien zur Auslegung und Darstellung von "Mariä Verkündigung"', *FMS* 24 (1990), 314–68

'Verschriftlichung als Faktor monastischer Reform. Funktionen von Schriftlichkeit im Ordenswesen des hohen und späten Mittelalters', in H. Keller *et al.* (eds.), *Pragmatische Schriftlichkeit im Mittelalter. Erscheinungsformen und Entwicklungsstufen*, Munich 1992, pp. 37–75

Maria. Jungfrau, Mutter, Herrscherin, Munich 1994

'Buchstabensymbolik, Bibelorakel, Schriftmagie, Religiöse Bedeutung und lebensweltliche Funktion heiliger Schriften im Mittelalter und in der frühen

Neuzeit', in H. Wenzel *et al.* (eds.), *Die Verschriftlichung der Welt. Bild, Text und Zahl in der Kultur des Mittelalters und der frühen Neuzeit*, Vienna 2000, pp. 59–103

Schröder, W., 'Die von Tristande hant gelesen. Quellenhinweise und Quellenkritik im Tristan Gottfrieds von Straßburg', *ZfdA* 104 (1975), 307–38

Schulenburg, A. T., *Forgetful of their sex. Female sanctity and society ca. 500–1100*, Chicago 1998

Schupp, V. and Szklenar, H., *Ywain auf Schloß Rodenegg. Eine Bildergeschichte nach dem 'Iwein' Hartmanns von Aue*, Sigmaringen 1996

Schützeichel, R., *Codex Pal. lat. 52. Studien zur Heidelberger Otfridhandschrift, zum Kicila-Vers und zum Georgslied* (Abhandlungen der Akademie der Wissenschaften in Göttingen, Philologisch-historische Klasse, Dritte Folge, 130), Göttingen 1982

Seeberg, S., *Die Illustrationen im Admonter Nonnenbrevier von 1180. Marienkrönung und Nonnenfrömmigkeit – Die Rolle der Brevierillustration in der Entwicklung von Bildthemen im 12. Jahrhundert*, Wiesbaden 2002

Semple, B., 'The consolation of a woman writer: Christine de Pizan's use of Boethius in *La vision Christine*', in L. Smith and J. H. M. Taylor (eds.), *Women, the book and the worldly*, Cambridge 1995, pp. 39–48

Shahar, S., *The fourth estate. A history of women in the Middle Ages*, London 2003

Sheingorn, P., 'The Holy Kinship: the ascendency of matriliny in sacred genealogy of the fifteenth century', *Thought* 64 (1989), 268–86

'"The wise mother". The image of St. Anne teaching the Virgin Mary', *Gesta* 32 (1993), 69–80

Simons, W., 'Beguines and Psalter', *OGE* 65 (1991), 23–30

'Reading a saint's body: rapture and bodily movement in the *vitae* of thirteenth-century beguines', in S. Kay and M. Rubin (eds.), *Framing medieval bodies*, Manchester 1994, pp. 10–23

Cities of ladies. Beguine communities in the medieval Low Countries 1200–1565, Philadelphia 2001

Smith, J., 'Robert of Arbrissel's relations with women', in D. Baker (ed.), *Medieval women*, Oxford 1978, pp. 175–84

Smith, L., '*Scriba, femina*: medieval depictions of women writing', in L. Smith and J. H. M. Taylor (eds.), *Women and the book. Assessing the visual evidence*, London 1996, pp. 21–44

Somerset, F., '*Eciam mulier*. Women in Lollardy and the problem of sources', in L. Olson and K. Kerby-Fulton (eds.), *Voices in dialogue. Reading women in the Middle Ages*, Notre Dame 2005, pp. 245–60

Southern, R. W., *Western society and the Church in the Middle Ages*, London 1990

Spearing, E. and A. C., *Julian of Norwich. Revelations of divine love*, London 1998. ST denotes the Short Text, LT the Long Text

Spitz, H.-J., 'Zur Lokalisierung des St. Trudperter Hohenliedes', *ZfdA* 121 (1992), 174–77

Stadler, H., 'Die Sünderin Eva aus frauenmystischer Sicht: zur Genesis-Auslegung Mechthilds von Magdeburg', in A. M. Haas and I. Kasten (eds.), *Schwierige*

Frauen – schwierige Männer in der Literatur des Mittelalters, Bern 1999, pp. 201–20

Stafford, P., *Queens, concubines and dowagers. The king's wife in the early Middle Ages*, London 1998

Stanton, A. R., 'From Eve to Bathsheba and beyond: motherhood in the Queen Mary Psalter', in L. Smith and J. H. M. Tayor (eds.), *Women and the book. Assessing the visual evidence*, London 1996, pp. 172–89

Staples, K. K. and Karras, R. M., 'Christina's tempting: sexual desire and women's sanctity', in S. Fanous and H. Leyser (eds.), *Christina of Markyate. A twelfth-century holy woman*, London 2005, pp. 184–196

Steer, G., 'Der Laie als Anreger und Adressat deutscher Prosaliteratur im 14. Jahrhundert', in W. Haug *et al.* (eds.), *Zur deutschen Literatur und Sprache des 14. Jahrhunderts*, Heidelberg 1983, pp. 354–67

Steinhoff, H.-H., 'Eleonore von Österreich', *VfL* 2, 470–3

'Elisabeth von Nassau-Saarbrücken', *VfL* 2, 482–8

Stevens, A., 'Memory, reading and the renewal of love: on the poetics of invention in Gottfried's *Tristan*', in V. Honemann *et al.* (eds.) *German narrative literature of the twelfth and thirteenth centuries*, Tübingen 1994, pp. 319–35

Stierle, K., 'Die Unverfügbarkeit der Erinnerung und das Gedächtnis der Schrift', in A. Haverkamp and R. Lachmann (eds.), *Memoria. Vergessen und Erinnern*, Munich 1993, pp. 117–59

Stock, B., *The implications of literacy. Written language and models of interpretation in the eleventh and twelfth centuries*, Princeton 1983

Augustine the reader. Meditation, self-knowledge, and the ethics of interpretation, Cambridge MA 1996

Strauch, P., *Margaretha Ebner und Heinrich von Nördlingen*, Freiburg i. Br. 1882

Summit, J., 'William Caxton, Margaret Beaufort and the romance of female patronage', in L. Smith and J. H. M. Taylor (eds.), *Women, the book and the worldly*, Cambridge 1995, pp. 151–65

Talbot, C. H., 'Die Entstehung der Predigten über Cantica Canticorum', in J. Lortz (ed.), *Bernhard von Clairvaux. Mönch und Mystiker*, Wiesbaden 1955, pp. 202–14

Thali, J., *Beten – Schreiben – Lesen. Literarisches Leben und Marienspiritualität im Kloster Engelthal*, Tübingen 2003

Thiébaux, M. (ed.), *Dhuoda, Handbook for her warrior son. Liber manualis*, Cambridge 1998

Thompson, J. W., *The literacy of the laity in the Middle Ages*, New York 1960

Triller, A., 'Marienwerder, Johannes', *VfL* 6, 56–61

Turner, R. V., 'The *miles literatus* in twelfth- and thirteenth-century England: how rare a phenomenon?', *AHR* 83 (1978), 928–45

Tyson, D. B., 'Patronage of French vernacular history writers in the twelfth and thirteenth centuries', *Romania* 100 (1979), 180–222

Uhlman, D. R., 'The comfort of voice, the solace of script: orality and literacy in *The Book of Margery Kempe*', *StPh* 91 (1994), 50–69

Vàrvaro, A., 'Scuola e cultura in Francia nel XII secolo', *SMV* 10 (1962), 199–330

Vassilevitch, D., '"Schrei der Seele" oder didaktische Stilisierung? Schwesternbücher aus Dominikanerinnenklöstern', in G. Signori (ed.), *Lesen, Schreiben, Sticken und Erinnern. Beiträge zur Kultur- und Sozialgeschichte mittelalterlicher Frauenklöster*, Bielefeld 2000, pp. 213–29

Vitz, E. B., *Orality and performance in early French romance*, Cambridge 1999

Voaden, R., 'God's almighty hand: women co-writing the book', in L. Smith and J. H. M. Taylor (eds.), *Women, the book and the godly*, Cambridge 1995, pp. 55–65

'All girls together: community, gender and vision at Helfta', in D. Watt (ed.), *Medieval women in their communities*, Cardiff 1997, pp. 72–91

God's words, women's voices. The discernment of spirits in the writing of latemedieval women visionaries, York 1999

(ed.), *Prophets abroad. The reception of continental holy women in late medieval England*, Cambridge 1996

Vollmann-Profe, G., *Kommentar zu Otfrids Evangelienbuch. Teil I: Widmungen. Buch I, I–II*, Bonn 1976

Wiederbeginn volkssprachiger Schriftlichkeit im hohen Mittelalter (1050/60–1160/70), Tübingen 1994

(ed.), *Mechthild von Magdeburg. Das fließende Licht der Gottheit*, Frankfurt 2003

Vollrath, H., 'Das Mittelalter in der Typik oraler Gesellschaften', *HZ* 233 (1981), 571–94

Walther, I. F. (ed.), *Codex Manesse. Die Miniaturen der Großen Heidelberger Liederhandschrift*, Frankfurt 1988

Wandhoff, K., 'Gemalte Erinnerung. Vergils *Aeneis* und die Troja-Bilddenkmäler in der deutschen Artusepik', *Poetica* 28 (1996), 66–96

Wand-Wittkowski, C., *Briefe im Mittelalter. Der deutschsprachige Brief als weltliche und religiöse Literatur*, Herne 2000

Ward, S. L., 'Fables for the court: illustrations for Marie de France's *Fables* in Paris, BN, MS Arsenal 3142', in L. Smith and J. H. M. Taylor (eds.), *Women and the book. Assessing the visual evidence*, London 1996, pp. 190–203

Warner, G., *Queen Mary's Psalter: miniatures and drawings by an English artist of the fourteenth century*, London 1912

Warren, A. R., 'The nun as anchoress: England 1100–1500', in J. A. Nichols and L. T. Shank (eds.), *Distant echoes: medieval religious women*, Kalamazoo 1984, pp. 197–212

Watson, N., 'Censorship and cultural change in late-medieval England: vernacular theology, the Oxford translation debate, and Arundel's Constitutions of 1409', *Speculum* 70 (1995), 822–64

'Conceptions of the word: the mother tongue and the incarnation of God', *NML* 1 (1997), 85–124

'Visions of inclusion: universal salvation and vernacular theology in pre-Reformation England', *JMEMS* 27, 2 (1997), 145–87

'The making of the Book of Margery Kempe', in L. Olson and K. Kerby-Fulton (eds.), *Voices in dialogue. Reading women in the Middle Ages*, Notre Dame 2005, pp. 395–434

Watt, D., *Secretaries of God. Women prophets in late medieval and early modern England*, Cambridge 1997

Weigand, H. J., *Wolfram's Parzival. Five Essays with an introduction*, Ithaca 1969

Weitlauff, M., '"dein got redender munt machet mich redenlosz . . ." Margareta Ebner und Heinrich von Nördlingen', in P. Dinzelbacher and D. R. Bauer (eds.), *Religiöse Frauenbewegung und mystische Frömmigkeit im Mittelalter*, Cologne 1988, pp. 303–52

Wenzel, H., *Hören und Sehen. Schrift und Bild. Kultur und Gedächtnis im Mittelalter*, Munich 1995

Wessley, S., 'The thirteenth-century Guglielmites: salvation through women', in D. Baker (ed.), *Medieval women*, Oxford 1978, pp. 289–303

Wiberg Pedersen, E. M., 'The in-carnation of Beatrice of Nazareth's theology', in J. Dor et al. (eds.), *New trends in feminine spirituality. The holy women of Liège and their impact*, Turnhout 1999, pp. 61–79

Williams-Krapp, W., 'Ordensreform und Literatur im 15. Jahrhundert', *Jahrbuch der Oswald von Wolkenstein Gesellschaft* 4 (1986/87), 41–51

'Frauenmystik und Ordensreform im 15. Jahrhundert', in J. Heinzle (ed.), *Interessenbildung im Mittelalter*, Stuttgart 1993, pp. 301–13

'Observantenbewegungen, monastische Spiritualität und geistliche Literatur im 15. Jahrhundert', *IASL* 20, 1 (1995), 1–15

Wilson, K. M., *Hrotsvit of Gandersheim: the ethics of authorial stance*, Leiden 1988

Windeatt, B. A., *The Book of Margery Kempe*, London 1994

Winny, J., *The Wife of Bath's Prologue and Tale*, Cambridge 1965

Wogan-Browne, J., '"Clerc u lai, muine u dame": women and Anglo-Norman hagiography in the twelfth and thirteenth centuries', in C. M. Meale (ed.), *Women and literature in Britain, 1150–1500*, Cambridge 1996, pp. 61–85

Saints' lives and women's literary culture c.1150–1300. Virginity and its authorization, Oxford 2001

Wolf, J., 'Psalter und Gebetbuch am Hof: Bindeglieder zwischen klerikal-literater und laikal-mündlicher Welt', in M. Chinca and C. Young (eds.), *Orality and literacy in the Middle Ages*, Turnhout 2005, pp. 139–179

'*vrowen phlegene zu lesene*. Beobachtungen zur Typik "weiblicher Bücher" und weiblicher Texte', to appear in *Wolfram-Studien* 19 (2006)

Buch und Text. Literatur- und kulturgeschichtliche Untersuchungen zur volkssprachlichen Schriftlichkeit im 12. und 13. Jahrhundert, forthcoming.

Wolter-von dem Knesebeck, H., *Der Elisabethpsalter in Cividale del Friuli. Buchmalerei für den Thüringer Landgrafenhof zu Beginn des 13. Jahrhunderts*, Berlin 2001

'La nascita del salterio di S. Elisabetta: il concorso tra lo *scriptorium*, l'*atelier* dei miniatori e la committenza', in C. Barberi (ed.), *Salterio di santa Elisabetta*, Trieste 2003, pp. 49–118

Woods, M. C., 'Shared books. Primers, psalters and the adult acquisition of literacy among devout laywomen and women in orders in late medieval England', in J. Dor *et al.* (eds.), *New trends in feminine spirituality. The holy women of Liège and their impact*, Turnhout 1999, pp. 177–93

Yates, F. A., *The art of memory*, London 1966

Zieman, K., 'Reading, singing and understanding: constructions of the literacy of women religious in late medieval England', in S. Rees Jones (ed.), *Learning and literacy in medieval England and abroad*, Turnhout 2003, pp. 97–120

Index

In this index special attention is paid to naming women, historical or fictional, who were engaged in literacy as well as to other persons, places or communities with which they were associated in that context.

CAMBRIDGE STUDIES IN MEDIEVAL LITERATURE